WHY WILSON MATTERS

PRINCETON STUDIES IN INTERNATIONAL HISTORY AND POLITICS
SERIES EDITORS
G. JOHN IKENBERRY, MARC TRACHTENBERG, AND WILLIAM C. WOHLFORTH

Recent Titles

WHY WILSON MATTERS

The Origin of American Liberal Internationalism
and Its Crisis Today

TONY SMITH

PRINCETON UNIVERSITY PRESS
PRINCETON AND OXFORD

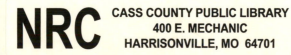

For JDO

It is character and good principle, after all, which are to save us, if we are to escape disaster. . . . It is for this that we love democracy: for the emphasis it puts on character; for its tendency to exalt the purposes of the average man to some high level of endeavor; for its just principle of common assent in matters to which we are all concerned; for its ideals of duty and its sense of brotherhood. Its forms and institutions are meant to be subservient to these things.

—*Woodrow Wilson, "Democracy and Efficiency," 1900*

Contents

Preface

When friends or colleagues have been kind enough over the last three years to ask me what I'm working on, I have always answered, "On Woodrow Wilson." Eyes usually glazed over—except in the few cases when hostile comments were made: from the left, "He was a racist," and from the right, "He introduced state controls of the economy we have to abolish." Could the lack of interest have been related to ignorance? *Newsweek* reported in 2011 that 80 percent of the American public did not know who was president during World War I and thus presumably had no idea whatsoever of the impact Wilson's thinking has had over the last century on world affairs.[1] My own guess is that the reaction reflected judgments by prominent historians and political scientists who from the late 1930s through the early 1950s dismissed our twenty-eighth president altogether as "idealistic" and "moralistic" and hence as a bad guide for policies to consider by those in power in Washington.[2] As a result, even when Wilsonian policies were being adopted (in changed form, to be sure) on a massive scale as the basis of American foreign policy after 1939, recognition of his legacy was not widely expressed.

Certainly today, awareness of Woodrow Wilson is growing. April 2017 will mark the centennial of the American entry into the Great War. By 1918 discussions were beginning in earnest for the creation of the League of Nations, whose Covenant was voted by the victors in Paris in the spring of 1919. The centennial of the creation of the League is sure to be accompanied by international conferences reviewing not only the decisions reached in 1918–1919, but also the lessons American policy-makers drew as only a generation later they confronted the question of how to win the peace that would follow winning the war over the Axis powers in 1945. How can the spirit of Wilson not preside at these gatherings?

More recently, with the rise of the consciousness-raising campaign Black Lives Matter in 2015, sensibility to racial injustice in the United States has in due course turned to Woodrow Wilson, whose racism during his presidency in Washington is undeniable.[3] The question then naturally turns to the extent to which his commitment to "the color line" in the United States related to such matters as Wilson's rejection of the Japanese proposal in February 1919 that a "racial equality clause" be entered into the Covenant of the League of Nations.[4]

A greater familiarity with Wilson's name should not imply the existence of a deeper understanding of his policies and their repercussions on world affairs over the near-century since he left office, however. Hence, the title of this book: *Why Wilson Matters: The Origin of American Liberal Internationalism and Its Crisis Today*. Such a study is called for because the American liberal internationalist tradition—"Wilsonianism"—has been a basic element of American foreign policy over the last seventy-five years, contributing decisively to the greatest achievements in the Republic's history in world affairs, yet contributing just as decisively to its greatest setbacks.

Today the tradition is in deep trouble, and this in good measure because our ability to grasp Wilsonianism's basic identity is so limited, and hence liberals' ability to be self-critical, and thus rise to the challenges facing them, is so wanting. Liberal internationalism's capacity to live up to its commitment to promote human rights and democracy worldwide, to champion open, integrated world markets that effectively increase social prosperity and so the strength of our egalitarian institutions, and to provide for the collective defense of the free market democratic world is in serious doubt. For this approach to world affairs to save itself, if indeed it can, it needs better to understand the original premises on which it was built. My ambition is to end the glazed—or sternly negative—reaction I so often got to the mention of Woodrow Wilson's name and to replace it with an understanding of the importance today, as in years past, of the way of thinking we call Wilsonianism, a term whose definition, tellingly, admits of no easy consensus that might foster debates, and agreements on how to proceed, within the liberal community.

At the moment this book is being written, there is much debate about the "legacies of World War I"—that is, the way the terrible conflagration between 1914 and 1918 decisively shaped the rest of the twentieth century and remains with us still today. Three momentous developments are commonly asserted to have arisen from the conflict. First, we can attribute to the war the success of Lenin's daring act of seizing power through the Russian Revolution of 1917, and his sponsorship of the international spread of communism to every corner of the world in an astonishingly short period thereafter. Second, in reaction to the expansion of communism as well as to the Treaty of

Versailles of June 28, 1919, with Germany (and to the treaties that followed with Austria-Hungary, Bulgaria, and the Ottoman Empire), we can attribute a major impetus to the rise of fascism, a form of political organization also international in scope, but whose most deadly consequences came with the rise of Nazism in Germany and the horrors of World War II that followed. Third, the moral and physical weakness of the European powers, evident by 1918, combined with the two factors already mentioned to give critical stimulation over time to the growth of nationalist movements not only of colonized peoples under the direct rule of London and Paris but also of ancient civilizations in the Middle East and most of Asia (especially in China). Here was a prelude to the rise of these peoples after World War II completed the destruction of Europe's global power that World War I had initiated.

Yet there was a fourth legacy of enormous importance that arose from World War I, a consequence that is too seldom analyzed in any depth: the birth of American liberal internationalism as a concept of dynamic importance worldwide thanks in good measure to the legacy of Woodrow Wilson, president of the United States from 1913 to 1921. From the White House, Wilson dealt first with the American response to the Mexican Revolution and the question of how to assure a stable Western Hemisphere with the opening of the Panama Canal in 1914 and the advent of war in Europe. Far more critically, once conflict began in earnest in Europe and the United States joined the war in April 1917, Wilson tried to promote a concept of world order that would take this nation permanently out of isolationism, founding its leadership role in the name of promoting democratic governments, open markets, and a mutual defense pact that came to be called collective security. The result was an argument for American "exceptionalism" that has persisted until today, a claim not simply that the United States was the "indispensable nation" because its relative power position made it a party to all major international issues, but rather that its primary reason to expect deference from other states was that it did not seek to pursue its own narrow self-interest so much as to insure an international order that at a minimum could (in Wilson's most famous and debated phrase) deliver on his conviction that "the world must be made safe for democracy."

Given the role liberal internationalism played in the success of the United States in the cold war with the Soviet Union, and the part that it has continued to play with even more self-assurance over the past three decades, certainly Wilsonianism deserves the kind of attention, as a legacy of World War I, that communism, fascism, and the rise of nationalism in Asia, Latin America, and Africa have received. Here were three ideologies fighting for world dominion—fascism collapsing in 1945, communism losing its international appeal in 1989, and liberal internationalism still very much alive but under threat today. The task of this book, then, is to make the identity and character of this tradition more apparent so that its ability to act with effective purpose may be enhanced.

Since 1990, I have been writing on the logic and practice of the history of American human rights and democracy promotion abroad. My first book on the subject appeared in 1994, and then again in 2012 in an expanded edition published by Princeton University Press, under the title *America's Mission: The United States and the Worldwide Struggle for Democracy*. Given its list of leading works on Woodrow Wilson, the American president most closely associated with democracy promotion, Princeton was the natural home for this volume as well as other related books, including one that I collaborated on with G. John Ikenberry, Anne-Marie Slaughter, and Thomas Knock in 2009: *The Crisis of American Foreign Policy: Wilsonianism in the Twenty-first Century*. My part in this latter volume involved defending the terms of another book of mine on American democracy promotion that Routledge/Taylor & Francis had brought out in 2007: *A Pact with the Devil: Washington's Bid for World Supremacy and the Betrayal of the American Promise*.

In these various works, I traced the origin and development of attempts by the United States to foster democracy abroad over the century stretching from the days of the presidency of Woodrow Wilson (1913–1921) through the first administration of Barack Obama (2009–2013). What I noted was the extraordinary success of this ambition during the cold war and in the years that immediately followed. High points are obvious: from the creation of the Bretton Woods system to open and integrate the world's capitalist markets in 1944 to the creation of the North Atlantic Treaty Organization in 1949, passing by the most critical of all—innovations introduced during the American occupations of Japan and Germany. Here Washington laid the basis for the victories of the United States in 1989 and 1991 in the epic contest with the Soviet Union. With the fall of the Berlin Wall in November 1989 and the implosion of the Soviet Union at the end of 1991, democracy movements that had been gathering strength in Central Europe, Latin America, and East Asia since the 1970s redoubled their efforts to take power politically. Critical to these developments was Washington's determination to create a world order typified not only by human rights and democratic government but also by its leadership of efforts to establish the terms of an open and integrated world economy, and by the development of a complex set of multilateral institutions to coordinate the policies of like-minded peoples.

However, as I had warned as early as 1994, by exaggerating the appeal of liberal values, practices, and institutions, as well as the ease of putting them in place, liberals could fail to anticipate the strength of the resistance that cultures as powerful as those in the Muslim world, Russia, and China would likely throw up to oppose these foreign ways.[5] More, democracy activists might well underestimate the ability of anarchic forces, typical of societies based on weak social contracts and the absence of democratizing political traditions and institutions, to foil the efforts of outsiders to bring them new ways quite foreign to established patterns of social, economic, and political interaction. The birth of what I call "neo-Wilsonianism" in the 1990s, with its extraordinary self-confidence and self-righteousness, which soon translated into military action in the Muslim world, confirmed my fears.

As a result, my work that appeared prior to 2001 was quite different in tone from the publications which appeared in the aftermath of the American invasion of Iraq in March 2003. In my earlier publications, whatever my warnings that liberalism should not overplay its hand, I could laud American policies both in practical and moral terms. The scale of success in Washington's liberal ambitions in Germany and Japan was irrefutable, as was the appeal of democracy in many lands with the collapse of Soviet communism after 1989—even if one could lament the unwarranted brutality of the containment doctrine in Latin America, the Middle East, and Southeast Asia. By contrast, in publications after 2003, I pointed out how the triumphalism in elite American policy-making and university circles had laid the groundwork for self-defeating policies adopted by official Washington, which instead of spreading freedom, prosperity, and peace were sponsoring endless wars and the tragedies associated with them as well as endangering democracy at home—and all this, ironically or tragically enough—in the name of founding a perpetual peace based on freedom.

In these circumstances, what future was there for liberal internationalism as a compass for policy-making for the United States in world affairs? If democracy promotion and economic openness had been the source first of American strength, yet then, when pushed too uncritically, of this country's weakness, could a cure be found that did not involve a return to Realism and a caustic dismissal of liberalism's appeal but instead that might refurbish the confidence of those who sought to see human rights and democracy promotion as conducive to American interests and to world peace in the twenty-first century?

Here were the questions that prompted the writing of this book. My answer was found by going back to the source of this thinking in the writings and policy-making of Woodrow Wilson. I was convinced that in addition to the two books (and numerous articles) I had published between 1994 and 2014 on American liberal internationalism, one more volume was called for: on the historical origins of the idea that by promoting democracy worldwide American national security would be enhanced because world peace would be more likely secured. It was not enough to have demonstrated in the expanded edition of *America's Mission* in 2012 how the package of concepts that constituted Wilson's worldview had metamorphosed in the generations since his death into "Wilsonianism" and then, in the 1990s, into neo-Wilsonianism in its neoliberal and neoconservative embodiments. The task was to see if neo-Wilsonianism could be combated by a return to the more realistic—that is, more cautious—thinking of Woodrow Wilson himself as he confronted revolutionary upheavals in lands as different as Mexico, the Soviet Union, and Germany.

As a political scientist, Wilson had been a "comparativist." That is, he studied countries in terms of their unique, individual evolutions as cultures and as political centers of action. These studies were to give him a solid footing as president in deciding where the United States might stop short of pushing its hopes for democracy worldwide. As it happens, I was in my early professional years a comparativist myself in political science before moving more deeply into international relations theory and the interdisciplinary link between the forces of world and domestic events. From 1970 through the 1980s, I was a continual participant in the conferences centered at Harvard University and the Massachusetts Institute of Technology (which brought together leading political comparativists from universities around the country) that on many occasions debated the character of democratic government and the likelihood that this form of the state could be sponsored where its roots were shallow so as to oppose the appeal of international communism. At one point or another during this period, I met virtually every well-known senior political comparativist in the country, was the student of and then did collaborative work with Samuel Huntington, Barrington Moore, and Stanley Hoffmann, presented several papers at these universities' long-lived Joint

Seminar on Political Development (chaired by Samuel Huntington, Lucian Pye, and Myron Weiner), and published in leading journals in this field.[6]

It was thus perfectly apparent to me that Wilson's deliberations on the likely future of democracy worldwide could be brought into harmony with debates within the field of international relations and so explain the basis of his convictions as an academic that were to stimulate his thinking about collective security after he became president. This personal experience also allows me to speak with the authority of "oral history" on the deliberations over containment and liberal internationalism covering a period of two decades. During these sessions, senior comparativists with influence on policymakers in Washington debated the ill-fated Alliance for Progress, the lessons of the Vietnam debacle, the character of U.S. support for military coups in Latin America, and the fall of the shah in Iran. These experiences laid basic groundwork for my later studies of Wilson's commitment to advance democracy worldwide.

The object of this book, accordingly, is to lay out how Woodrow Wilson saw America's mission in world affairs in the years before and after he became president of the United States. To do this means to attempt to find a working definition of the term "Wilsonianism" and to see the way it has evolved over the last century. The introduction and first four chapters of the book are devoted to Wilson himself, building on initiatives of a number of historians to bring the full range of his academic work into a comprehensive understanding of his policies as president. I consider this the most important section of the study, one that can provide today's liberal internationalists with a clear definition of their field of endeavor as it was originally conceived while exposing the intellectual mistakes that have led to policy-making errors of the first order since 2003 with respect to the heart of the Muslim world (quite broadly defined as reaching from North Africa to Southwest Asia, including not only the Arab world but Turkey, Iran, and Pakistan as well as Afghanistan).

In the following three chapters (part II of this book), based on research I have published over the last twenty-five years, I attempt to show how these elemental ideas that may be called "classical" Wilsonianism became the substance of "hegemonic" Wilsonianism from the half-century that stretches from 1940 to 1990. What follows is an anomaly to be regretted: the tradition's evolution into an "imperialist" neo-Wilsonianism thereafter that remains with us today. The conclusion is that a return is called for to the earlier prudence of Wilson's own time as well as to the Realism (call it "liberal realism" or "realistic liberalism") of the successive generations that managed the cold war.

Finally, I should note that I have tried to convey the political world the way Wilson saw it. My concern throughout has been to explain, not to glorify, Wilson, although I certainly believe that those whom I call in this book neo-Wilsonians have much to learn from the measured approach he took to what America might accomplish in global matters. My hope has above all been to reinvigorate a tradition in United States foreign policy that has been impoverished by those who would turn it to purposes for which it originally was neither even dimly intended nor at all appropriate.

INTRODUCTION

Know Thyself: What Is "Wilsonianism"?

The world must be made safe for democracy. Its peace must be
planted upon the tested foundations of political liberty. . . . A steadfast concert for peace can never be maintained except by a partnership of democratic nations. No autocratic government could be
trusted to keep faith within it or observe its covenants. It must be a
league of honor, a partnership of opinion. . . . Only free peoples can
hold their purpose and their honor steady to a common end and
prefer the interests of mankind to any narrow interest of their own.
—*Woodrow Wilson, April 2, 1917, asking Congress for a declaration*
of war against Germany

American liberal internationalism is in crisis. Its dedication to the promotion of human rights and democratic government abroad, its trust in
the general prosperity that an open, integrated international economic system could bring the world, its commitment to multilateral institutions to
promote international peace, its claims that America is "exceptional" because
its power serves our country's national security and democratic institutions
by promoting global peace—this enormous agenda is today endangered by a
foreign policy unable to restrain itself from excesses built on the success of
these very endeavors during the cold war.

For the purposes of this book, the most notable problem has been a suc-
cession of American imperialist wars based on a self-confident and self-
righteous claim that democracy has a "universal appeal," and that since "our
interests and values are one" we have a right to invade at will countries that
fail to live up to their "responsibility to protect" and to set them right. Where
did such a set of assumptions come from? How could ancient civilizations, or

societies proud of their histories yet riven by deep cleavages, respond positively to these vainglorious assaults, combining as they do calls to rework not
only political and economic relations but social, cultural, and family relations
as well? Can we doubt that since 2002 the West, led by the United States, has
unleashed a "clash of civilizations" freighted with enormous negative consequences? Combine this with America's manifest inability to put its financial
house in order in a period of slow growth combined with arguably the most
sustained period of unequal wealth distribution in the country's history—a
condition that threatens not only our international standing but also our
democracy at home. On the economic inequality front, no solution is in evidence, with the toll this must take on our political institutions. More, we
appear to have lost the war on drugs while our health-care system lags far
behind other rich countries in terms of coverage and expense. As the economic and social evidence accumulates after 2007, how could this country
continue to fancy itself, as John Winthrop foresaw nearly four centuries ago,
a "shining city on the hill"?

We risk exaggerating the negatives when in fact the tenets of liberal internationalism (a term synonymous with "Wilsonianism" because of Woodrow
Wilson's formulation of this framework for American involvement in world
affairs) underlay the greatest achievements in the Republic's history with the
democratization of Japan and Germany and the subsequent victory in the
cold war over proletarian internationalism sponsored by Moscow. But with
victory in the cold war, Washington pushed its achievements promoting the
liberal agenda too far. Republicans following President Ronald Reagan
(1981–1989), their first unabashedly liberal internationalist (much as he disliked the "L" word), took the lead both in greatly deregulating the economy
at home and abroad and later by laying the groundwork intellectually and
emotionally for an aggressive agenda abroad, touting the contribution to
world peace of what since the days of President Bill Clinton has been called
"free market democracy." In both instances, the Republicans were strongly
seconded by most Democrats, members of the party historically most closely
identified with liberal internationalism. In the 1980s, a bipartisan team began
an unprecedented market opening of corporate capitalism, and this with disastrous results two decades later that remain with us years afterward in the
form of an income inequality that reflects the domination of banks and business that in his calls for a "New Freedom" Woodrow Wilson had explicitly
warned could undermine democracy. On the international political front, in
the 1990s the expansion of the European Union and the North Atlantic

Treaty Organization raised concerns of overextension that were quickly eclipsed by forms of progressive imperialism justified as attempts to promote democracy in the Muslim world that had virtually no chance of bearing fruit.

Machiavelli's admonitions from nearly half a millennium ago (1531) in his *Discourses on Livy* (2:27) should be recalled: "Men always commit the error of not knowing where to limit their hopes, and by trusting to these rather than to a just measure of their resources, they are generally ruined." After triumphs over international fascism and communism for which the nation can justly be proud, America's worst enemy over the past quarter century—and one could make much the same case for the European Union—has ironically (or better, tragically) turned out to be none other than itself.

At the origin of both the triumph of the fifty years that stretch roughly from 1941 to 1991, and the tragedy since 2001, was a variety of forces, the most evident of which was a set of ideas called American liberal international- ism. (We need to insist on the "American" designation both because of its association with President Woodrow Wilson, who first put together the pack- age of concepts that then came to bear the name "Wilsonianism," as well as because of the claim of "exceptionalism" for the United States that they con- tained, which was not necessarily shared by liberal internationalists in other parts of the world.) When concepts are systematically organized in such a way that they give individuals and peoples a sense of their common history, their place in world events, and the purposes they should pursue, ideas have con- sequences, especially when they have a religious cast (even if secular, national- ist, and patriotic) that inspires their followers to aggressive behavior, often of global, and thus historical, importance.

It is often debated whether America is "in decline." Perhaps the emer- gence of an imperial presidency, working with a Congress dominated by cor- porate influence and using its power in foreign adventures, will not add up to decline in this country's international position. It might instead herald to some a continued era of "greatness." What is nonetheless evident is the obvi- ous decline of American liberal internationalism as a progressive force even if Washington itself continues to dominate global affairs.

To make such an assertion rather obviously requires having a defensible definition of liberal internationalism's agenda, a matter admittedly challeng- ing to confront. For concepts as complex as those possessed by Wilsonianism not only necessarily change over time in terms of the conditions they con- front, but in any case inevitably have blind spots, often turn out to contradict rather than to complement one another, or may run in separate directions

however much they may at times synergistically interact. Change and incoherence may be as real as continuity and congruity. Nor do intellectual concepts themselves necessarily serve as a primary motive for action. Instead,
material interests or powerful emotions may manipulate ideas for their own
purposes, so that ideas may be thought of as the agents of more dynamic
forces than they possess in and of themselves. Hence, to say that today Wilsonianism is in decline—that it appears liable to meet the same fate and to
disappear as did its rival ideological competitors, communism and fascism—
requires a definition of the subject.

The problem of capturing liberalism's identity was best expressed by the
great Protestant theologian Reinhold Niebuhr, who put his finger on liberalism's "fortunate vagueness," which applied to Wilson as well as to his cold
war followers. As Niebuhr wrote in 1952, "In the liberal version of the dream
of managing history, the problem of power is never fully elaborated." Here
was the happy fact that distinguished us from the communists, who assumed,
thanks to their ideology that posited "iron laws of history," that they could
master events such that world revolution under their auspices would bring
about universal justice, freedom, and that most precious of all promises,
peace. In contrast, Niebuhr declared:

> On the whole, we have as a nation learned the lesson of history tolera-
> bly well. We have heeded the warning "let not the wise man glory in his
> wisdom, let not the mighty man glory in his strength." Though we are
> not without vainglorious delusions in regard to our power, we are saved
> by a certain grace inherent in common sense rather than in abstract
> theories from attempting to cut through the vast ambiguities of our
> historic situation and thereby bringing our destiny to a tragic conclu-
> sion by seeking to bring it to a neat and logical one.[1]

Yet despite Niebuhr's salute to the "fortunate vagueness" of liberal internationalism, "saved by a certain grace inherent in common sense rather than
in abstract theories," with victory in the cold war American Wilsonianism in
the 1990s became something of a "hard" ideology—more certain than it had
ever been before that it indeed had the key to progress in world affairs and
that, given Washington's status as the capital of the only global superpower,
American policy-makers could use this key to good effect. With its new conceptions of "democratic peace theory" (that democracies do not fight each
other), "democratic transition theory" (that with the cold war over, democracy was the only game in town and would be widely appreciated as such by

peoples under authoritarian rule), and a "Just War" doctrine eventually labeled "The Responsibility to Protect" (that allowed liberal states to attack authoritarian states for their domestic policies with the aim of democratizing them), "fortunate vagueness" was fast becoming a thing of the past.

The result of moving beyond fortunate vagueness was the birth of "neo-Wilsonianism," a combination of neoliberalism (whose theorists had established to their satisfaction the major concepts of the new world order Washington should preside over and who were mostly Democrats) and the neoconservatives (who could militarize and popularize such ideas and were mostly Republicans). Here was exactly the development that Niebuhr most feared for his country:

> If we should perish, the ruthlessness of the foe would be only the secondary cause of the disaster. The primary cause would be that the strength of a great nation was directed by eyes too blind to see all the hazards of the struggle, and the blindness would be induced not by some accident of nature or history but by hatred and vainglory.[2]

Some are tempted by the failures of the past quarter century to reject liberal internationalism in its entirety. They would replace it with a Realist agenda stressing narrow American self-interests based on military prowess and diplomatic retrenchment. "National interest," not "world order," should be our ambition.[3] Sage as this advice most surely may be in some respects, the temptation to jettison liberal internationalism altogether should be avoided. We must not forget the historic accomplishments of the Wilsonian tradition from the mid-1940s to the early 1990s.

What this book would encourage is the conviction that we need to work as best we can for the continued survival (in reformed ways) of the European Union and the North Atlantic Treaty Organization; engage in domestic economic reform that revitalizes the economy while ending the dramatically growing income and wealth inequality that has few parallels in our history and that threatens both our relative national strength and the social basis of our democracy; and pursue an agenda of promoting human rights and democratic reform abroad where our influence may count. The ambition of this book is exactly this: to establish a more secure footing for the American variant of liberal internationalism by reminding it of its origins in the thinking and policies of Woodrow Wilson and to maintain that it may find there the prudence and insight that today his intellectual great-grandchildren so often forget to our peril.

WILSONIANISM, THE AMERICAN VARIANT
OF LIBERAL INTERNATIONALISM

How can the liberal internationalist project be salvaged as a framework contributing positively to American foreign policy? A good part of the current
crisis is due to the simple but important fact that American liberal internationalism has only a vague sense of its identity (much as Niebuhr affirmed).
A review of what American and British historians have had to say over the
past decade in defining the tradition makes the point. No one I have read has
tried with any seriousness to define what "Wilsonianism" means in a way that
commands general assent; several historians have suggested that while some
usages may be more fortunate than others, none is terribly persuasive.

So we must ask a delicate question: Is there in fact a Wilsonian tradition,
or is the existence of "Wilsonianism" a figment of the collective imagination?
Thus, historian John A. Thompson subtitles an essay on Wilsonianism "the
dynamics of a conflicted concept" and includes a section devoted to the topic
of "a creed at war with itself." For his part, historian Stephen Wertheim caus-
tically points out, in an essay entitled provocatively "The Wilson Chimera,"
that "'Wilsonianism' is at once ubiquitous in usage and deeply contested in
substance: "everyone affirms that it matters but few agree what it means." In
an extended commentary on the matter, historian Thomas Knock concludes,
after reviewing a string of articles and books by noted authors who he finds
most certainly "have had something worthwhile to say," that the term nevertheless has a "protean nature . . . in danger of becoming what literary critics
call a 'free-floating signifier'—that is, one constantly deployed, yet stripped of
any consistent meaning or historical context."[4] As Knock suggests, the term
"Wilsonianism" has as many definitions as it has writers who employ the
word. Perhaps here is the reason that the Realist school of analysis of international relations is often referred to with a capital R, signifying that it is a coherent body of discourse whose theorists debate its concepts within the pa-
rameters of a consensus on what this approach to world affairs assumes in
common, whereas liberal internationalism is usually left lower-case, an indication that the field is too fluid to have an internal discourse based on any serious unity to its assumptions.

A personal example illustrates the problem. In 2007, Princeton political
science professor John Ikenberry invited Anne-Marie Slaughter, Thomas
Knock, and me to write essays for a volume to which he would also contribute, asking simply that everyone answer his question: "Was George W. Bush

the heir of Woodrow Wilson?" The resulting debate appeared as a book in 2009 entitled *The Crisis of American Foreign Policy: Wilsonianism in the Twenty-first Century*.[5] Our four-sided debate centered over whether to privilege democracy promotion or multilateralism as the defining characteristic of Wilsonianism, but we came to no convincing conclusion on the question.

Worse, we most certainly had not exhausted the range of possible answers to Ikenberry's question. Had someone of a Marxist bent been invited to the discussion, that person would surely have emphasized instead the open door international economic policy promoted by Wilson as the distinguishing characteristic of American liberal internationalism, and related it to the question of the Bush administration's concern with Middle East energy reserves. At the same time, a Realist would presumably have insisted that the entire package Wilson proposed was either a thin disguise for the exercise of American leadership (or domination) of world affairs under the self-righteous claim of this country's exceptionalism or an exercise in political naïveté of the first water. Realists were, in fact, the primary—and therefore best—critics of the invasion of Iraq before it actually occurred, and many did not hesitate to relate Bush's policy to Wilson's allegedly noxious influence.

The problem that remains is evident. More than a century after Wilson became president of the United States, his country is still not certain how to understand the important legacy for this country's foreign policy of the tradition that bears his name.

But why does it matter? Are there not many other "isms" whose identities are the object of sharp debate? What is to be gained by acquiring a better grasp on an approach to world politics that by its very nature may best be left "fortunately vague"? The answer is that Wilsonianism remains (unlike communism and fascism) a living ideology whose interpretation continues either to motivate, or to serve as a cover for, a broad range of American foreign-policy decisions. However, if there is no consensus on what the tradition stands for, or, worse, if there is a consensus but its claims to be part of the tradition are not borne out by the history of Wilsonianism from his day until the late 1980s, then clearly a debate is in order to provide clarity and purpose to American thinking about world affairs today.

If liberal internationalism in its "classic" form was articulated by Woodrow Wilson, then used to good effect from the half century that stretches from Pearl Harbor to the implosion of the Soviet Union, why have we failed to study our past to gain insights for today? One point is clear: Wilson himself would surely have wished such an investigation.

A RETURN TO THE SOURCE OF AMERICAN LIBERAL INTERNATIONALISM

To engage in an exercise in self-understanding, I suggest that we go back to the presidency of Woodrow Wilson (1913–1921), generally recognized as the father of the American variant of liberal internationalism, and to the thinking that informed his view of world affairs for more than three decades before he took high office. We should not attribute too much originality to Wilson, to be sure. Aspects of his thinking were already readily apparent at the time of the American Revolution. Nor has liberal internationalism ever been a monopoly of the United States alone. Indeed, Great Britain may lay claim to being its original homeland (and Britons its most articulate supporters after 1900). So, too, as names such as Vaclav Havel, Nelson Mandela, Oscar Arias, Kim Dae Jung, and Pope John Paul II vividly attest, individuals from around the globe have thought of themselves as political liberals without for a moment thinking that they thereby were following in the footsteps of the man who was the twenty-eighth president of the United States, or that they were necessarily reflecting in their convictions the sentiments of the Revolution of 1776.

Indeed, Mikhail Gorbachev's name should perhaps be at the head of the list of notable liberal internationalists. In May 1992, in Fulton, Missouri, on the anniversary of Winston Churchill's famous address in 1946 in that very place warning that an Iron Curtain was falling across Europe, Gorbachev declared that the end of the cold war was "a victory for common sense, reason, democracy. [The United Nations] should create structures . . . which are authorized to impose sanctions, to make use of other means of compulsion when rights of minority groups especially are being violated." Gorbachev then went on to underscore "the universality of human rights . . . the acceptability of international interference wherever human rights are violated. . . . Today democracy must prove that it can exist not only as the antithesis of totalitarianism. This means it must move from the national to the international arena. On today's agenda is not just a union of democratic states, but also a democratically organized world community."[6]

If Gorbachev, Havel, Kim, Arias, and other world leaders of the 1990s were undeniably liberal, in its American context the term "liberal internationalist" is interchangeable with "Wilsonian." For it was Woodrow Wilson who was the first president to articulate such an agenda, and the force of his ideas and policies created the tradition of Wilsonianism (the only "ism" to be attached to a president's name in the history of our foreign policy). More, he made one claim that only the United States would assert: that without American leadership the liberal agenda of securing a stable global peace of benefit to all would be impossible to achieve, a claim that can be said to lie at the basis of the American claim to a special privilege of action in world affairs, one that other countries should defer to for the sake of the greater good.[7] To read any of the Inaugural Addresses of those becoming president of the United States since World War II (to which could be added their State of the Union speeches) is to be struck by the way American nationalism finds expression in a confident internationalism resting on the conviction that whatever the issue, the buck stops in Washington, and this for the common good of all humanity.

If we think of liberal internationalist ideas as existing in what might be called "pre-classical" form before Wilson—the vaunting of democratic government, the opposition to mercantilism and imperialism, the conviction, in Abraham Lincoln's oft-quoted words that the United States was "the last, best hope of earth"—it was nevertheless Wilson who linked these notions together into a coherent framework for American foreign policy. His achievement was to usher America out of its isolationist fear of what Thomas Jefferson in his Inaugural Address of 1801 had warned could be "entangling alliances" (an argument that was basic to George Washington's Farewell Address of 1796) and so to give to American nationalism an internationalist vocation. Wilson's tenure as president thus constitutes the "classical stage" of liberal internationalism.

During the half century that stretched from Pearl Harbor in December 1941 to the final implosion of the Soviet Union in December 1991, American liberal internationalism became possessed of such vision and purpose that historians and social scientists since have spoken with confidence about "Wilsonianism" as a relatively coherent approach to the role this country should take in world affairs (even if defining the word has proved difficult). We might label this period the "hegemonic stage" of liberalism, for its terms were willingly shared by leaders and populations of many other countries, and they became embedded in multilateral institutions covering the full spectrum of international concerns from military security to economic relations.

By the early 1990s, however, an "imperialist stage" that should be called neo-Wilsonianism (combining neoliberalism and neoconservatism) had emerged, a phase that remains with us today even if in somewhat less aggressive fashion under President Barack Obama than had been the case with his immediate predecessor in office. The resiliency of this tradition over generations of American leaders thus deserves close attention. Following Niebuhr, it is at once our glory and our vainglory.

THE WILSONIAN VISION IN THEORY

Let us start by delimiting the question of identifying a coherent logic to liberal internationalism by setting out what it is *not*. A first point of agreement may be located in the distinctiveness of the liberal approach to the understanding of world affairs in comparison with other approaches to the study of international relations, such as Realism, Marxism, or Constructivism (which includes feminism). All of these perspectives are similar in their hope of grasping the logic for war in world affairs, but their ways of understanding the causes of conflict and its solution are quite different. The result is that although liberal internationalists may differ among themselves on how we define the several concepts that guide our studies, we nevertheless feel a commonality of identity when confronted with rival paradigms of explanation.

Thus, unlike Realism, which posits the relative power position of states within the international system as the primary explanatory variable of their behavior, liberalism focuses instead on what is today called "regime type," or on the character of governments as the best predictor of conduct in world affairs. To the liberal mind, democratic peoples and states are different in fundamental ways from authoritarian political cultures and institutions: democracies are relatively well equipped to work out their differences among one another in a way that makes war unlikely, whereas authoritarian peoples and governments are inherently possessed of militaristic dispositions both domestically and internationally (although allowance may be made for moderation among some of them). With the advent of democracy in domestic and international history, the possibility is open for a dramatic shift in the conduct of political life from one that is frankly Hobbesian to one that is proudly Kantian.

As a result, for liberals, the relative power positions of democratic peoples are of no serious importance. "Balance of power" considerations, the hallmark of Realist thinking, belong to a historical era that needs to be superseded. Mutual respect expressed through institutions that allow negotiation, compromise, and mutual understanding should be counted on to work out an amicable settlement. The failure of Realists to appreciate how the special character dispositions of democratic regimes and popular cultures predispose people to act in world affairs means that their models of war proceed from narrow national self-interest that cannot grasp the character of democratic ways. Until its Hobbesian attitude toward the world is replaced by a Kantian appreciation of the virtues of international liberalism, Realism constitutes something of a self-fulfilling prophecy: there will never be an end to war because Realist theory anticipates distrust and balance-of-power calculations in such a fashion that its thinking leads to the very behavior it seeks to control.[8]

Or unlike Marxism, which insists that economic interests as defined by the needs of the ruling class drive a country's foreign policy and this more often than not into armed conflict, liberals instead focus on different types of political order as acting on the global stage as a consequence of their inherent character. More, where Marxists find capitalism to be a source of struggle both on the domestic and international fronts, liberals argue that, if properly regulated, capitalism may be a force for democracy and peace. For capitalism contains the promise of prosperity, which underlies the strength of the middle class (the historic bearer of democratic interests and values), while the integration it can give to peoples may create trust and mutual understanding. Liberals maintain as well that Leninism (which is not necessarily allied with Marxism but nonetheless has shown itself to be quite compatible) is inherently opposed to social freedom and so to the ennoblement of thought and purpose that makes democracies able to live in peace with one another.

Finally, unlike Constructivism, which sees ideas as molding history, liberals maintain that as important as ideas and values surely are, they must be grounded in democratically functioning institutions both domestically and internationally. A homogeneity of values and ideas alone (which Constructivism centers on), even if achievable (which is unlikely), is far from adequate for keeping the world from war. Liberals insist that values, interests, and ideas must be embedded in political organizations, and they underscore the difficulty of establishing and maintaining democratic ways. Constructivists may appreciate the way social institutions are the necessary forums in which ideas emerge as social constructs, such that of all the theories that may be contrasted to liberalism it is the most similar. Still, to liberals, the lack of a sustained focus on the creation of a complex of social and political institutions that operate both domestically and internationally makes Constructivism appear, theoretically speaking, to be rather lightweight.[9]

If we can establish what liberalism is *not*, it nonetheless remains our task to see what holds liberal internationalism together internally as an approach

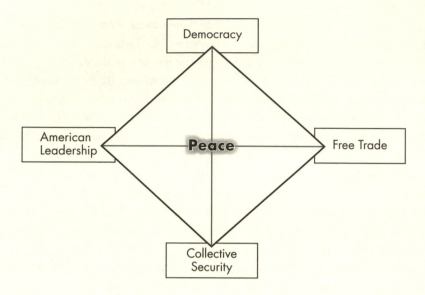

to defining America's place in the world. In hopes of working toward a consensus, I propose that four separate, but interrelated, elements constitute its essence: (1) cooperation among democratic governments, (2) linked through economic openness, (3) negotiating differences and common interests through well-structured multilateral institutions that foster a robust sense of the importance of economic integration, international law, and a commitment to mutual defense, and (4) dependent on an America that willingly assumes the responsibilities of leadership of a community of nations pledged to peace through collective security, even if this means going to war to preserve it.

To envision the integration of the concepts that typify liberalism more graphically, imagine a four-sided diamond, each point of which represents one of the elemental features of liberal internationalism (see figure).

Each facet of the diamond has its own distinctive quality, yet each relates to the other three in ways that are not only mutually reinforcing but that also actually work to mix the characteristic features of each element into compounds that are equally distinctive. More, the synthesis created by the integration of the four elements yields an effective unity greater than the mere sum of its parts. *For the promise of this unity is mutual defense and peace,* which no aspect alone can be expected convincingly to deliver, but whose possible establishment, thanks to the interaction of these various developments, is the prime tenet of liberalism's secular faith.

Hence, when the admixture of these forces is achieved in practice—when theory is embodied in values, interests, institutions, and policies that endure over time—the result is what came by the 1990s to be called a "pacific union," a "zone of democratic peace." Today the European Union is the leading historical example of the freedom, prosperity, and peace that liberal practices may bring—although others have looked at American-Canadian relations or at the cooperation apparent in Mercosur, founded in 1991 in the southern cone of Latin America. The brilliance given by the facets of the diamond of synergistically related forces arises from the radiance of its promise—Immanuel Kant's "perpetual peace," a conviction shared by a variety of American presidents from Woodrow Wilson's time on, including most especially Franklin D. Roosevelt, Ronald Reagan (who made the approach firmly bipartisan), George W. Bush, and Barack Obama.[10]

If this definition is fortunate enough to pass muster with most students of the question of how to lay out a workable definition of the constituent elements of Wilsonianism, differences are nonetheless sure to surface in efforts to explain how these elemental forces interact with one another to create an identity in theoretical terms that is convincingly unified. Some may favor a leading position for economic openness and integration; others may prefer multilateralism; still others will opt for American leadership; while others (including this author) emphasize a confederation of democratic peoples and states. Let us look at each of these elements in turn, then see why the argument that favors giving pride of place to the phrases "a pacific union" and "a zone of democratic peace" deserves special commendation.

WILSONIANISM AND ECONOMIC OPENNESS

Let us begin with the character of the role of economic openness and integration in the liberal paradigm, which some authors consider the principal force behind the liberal diamond. One may either condemn or salute this process of world economic integration. Many on the political left who are hostile to liberalism see in its embrace of "the Open Door" the dynamic power of corporate global capitalism driving all else before it. They interpret liberal appeals to the fostering of human rights and democracy as camouflaging a self-interested, predatory global economic system that enriches the few, keeps weak "democratic" states that are beholden to corporate influence, and manipulates multilateralism to augment American power—a process that in due course will feed conflict domestically, regionally, and globally in a manner that may well sap the strength of the United States as well as democratic government itself.

By contrast, liberals who endorse a leading role for international economic integration stress the pacifying interdependence such arrangements encourage. They can point to the experience of the European Union (born in important measure as a result of the Marshall Plan and the changes imposed on West Germany under American occupation) as a demonstration of the proposition that prosperity gives strength to the middle class (perhaps the most potent social force favoring democratic culture and government), while interdependence increases the harmonization and sharing of sovereignty that over time can reduce, possibly even eradicate, the differences in interest and perception that give rise to armed conflict. Following in the steps of Presidents Franklin Roosevelt (and the Bretton Woods agreements of 1944) and Harry Truman (with the Marshall Plan especially), the administrations of Presidents George H. W. Bush and Bill Clinton might be cited as promoting the expansion of what the latter first called "free market democracies" (a term picked up by subsequent presidents), so making economic issues the dominant aspect of their liberal internationalist agendas.[11]

There should be no doubt but that the importance of economic openness to world peace was a definite concern of Wilson's.[12] In his juxtaposition of democratic with authoritarian states and people, Wilson described the latter as inherently protectionists and, as a result, militaristic imperialists, while the former were not. To end balance-of-power competition and the threat of war, an open, integrated international economic system was of fundamental importance. His important proviso, however, was that democratic states needed to regulate not only the domestic but also the international economy, failing which globalization could become a danger to freedom and stability worldwide.

WILSONIANISM AND MULTILATERALISM

Arguments may also be heard for the dominant position of multilateralism in the liberal agenda. In a politically plural world supposed by the character of sovereign democratic nations linked through pacts of mutual defense and ties of economic interdependence, rules-based international regimes capable of authoritative determination as to the rights and obligations of member countries are an imperative need. Multilateralism (to the point of what is sometimes called a "pooling of sovereignties") is thus both cause and effect of political pluralism and market integration—especially in the domain of international law, which some liberals see as a form of world constitution-building.[13]

Hence, while multilateralism maintains its independent identity as a distinct aspect of liberalism for analytical purposes, in practice its character melds into hybrid features with other forces. Indeed, for some liberal theorists, the result is to make multilateralism the dominant variable of the liberal internationalist framework, and so they insist on the centrality of the League of Nations as Woodrow Wilson's greatest contribution to world peace.[14] Woodrow Wilson's notions with respect to "collective security" were clearly the high point of his multilateral ambitions. But as we shall see in chapter three, while the League's basic premise was the need for a mutual defense pact to unite its members against the threat of war, this organization itself was designed to be a seedbed of democracy under American leadership. There is good reason, then, to consider Washington's appeals for multilateralism as a disguised way of asserting American unilateralism, given the control it would wield over the member states. Hence to credit its identity as existing apart from other features of the Wilsonian peace is not theoretically tenable, however fundamental international institutions and laws are to its existence. More, to ignore multilateralism's dependence on, and contribution to, democratic statecraft is to miss the essence of the Wilsonian message.

WILSONIANISM AND AMERICAN LEADERSHIP

A third aspect of the liberal agenda is American leadership. For those given to talking of American exceptionalism, here is the key variable in the liberal project. By virtue of recognizing its dominant position in world affairs, the United States has assumed the role of representing not only its own self-interest but also the common interest of a region, if indeed not all the globe, in its foreign policy. American nationalism is thus transmuted from being parochially self-interested into being universal in its concerns. Washington's efforts to create a world order dominated by free-market democracies linked by multilateral organizations under its leadership are thus the essence of the liberal promise for peace. At its inception, Wilsonian schemes of multilateralism would necessarily be run under American auspices, in which case we should speak of a *Pax Americana* and not a *Pax Democratica*, even if the latter were its eventual goal.

America's ordained role hereby becomes the primary force in the pursuit of world peace because Washington, D.C., alone has the power, the character, and the interest to act in this manner. (Others may argue that with a universal mission, America becomes the primary imperialist actor on the world stage, unleashing a "clash of civilizations.")[15] Other aspects of the liberal agenda include the promotion of democracy abroad, the opening of the world's economic markets to commercial integration, and the growth of multilateral institutions to deal with an increasingly plural world politically concerned with economic harmonization and peace. But all this can be accomplished only through Washington's leadership, failing which crisis upon crisis is sure to occur. American patriotism thus becomes a form of internationalism, giving unity to the nation through its promise of a world mission.[16] Such a claim for a privileged role for Washington began with Woodrow Wilson and has been the refrain of presidents and secretaries of state for over three-quarters of a century now.

WILSONIANISM AND DEMOCRACY PROMOTION

Nevertheless, it is the fourth aspect of liberal theory, democracy promotion, that I maintain is the prime moving force of the Wilsonian agenda. From Wilson's day until ours, the chief argument in the liberal internationalism project for promoting world peace has been that democratic peoples and governments have the capacity to maintain an enduring mutual respect among themselves based on their character as individuals, groups, and political units. Other elements that are part of the liberal agenda—economic interdependence, multilateral institutions, and American leadership—each has its own identity, and together they synergistically complement democracy as constituent elements of the project. Of that there should be no doubt. Yet in theoretical terms their contribution is secondary to the key role played by the spirit and institutions of peoples living in constitutional democracies.

To make the case that democracy is the key element that guarantees world peace, let us look at the way the importance of democratic peoples dominates each of the other constituent aspects of liberal internationalism. Consider first the proposition that an indispensable aspect of the liberal agenda is the creation of an open, integrated world economic system. Yes, it is. But a critical element of such a process of integration is that it requires, multilaterally in the world arena, regulation under democratic governments working individually at the domestic level. Otherwise the economic integration might fail to contribute to be the common good and even be a force for imperialism and war.

Wilson left no doubt about it. He came to the presidency as a progressive, inveighing against the greed, cruelty, and anti-democratic characteristics of the monopoly capitalism of his era. He was critical of what he sometimes called "predatory capitalism" both at home and abroad. In his early writings—which he confirmed in later years—Wilson revealed a certain sympathy toward socialism, for it recognized that economic forces often betrayed the common interest for their own selfish gain and it promised to correct this situation by government controls. Although he believed that a free market was nonetheless the best way to assure general prosperity, the power of the middle class (an indispensable element of democratic life), and the common interest of the nation, Wilson never doubted but that this meant state regulation through administrative structures that would see democracy strengthened, not diminished, by corporate power.[17] Think Scandinavia, Canada, or Germany today.

As Wilson put it in 1910 in an address to the American Political Science Association, of which he had just become president:

> Business is no longer in any proper sense a private matter . . . it is pursued by great companies, great corporations, which exist only by express license of the law and for the convenience of society. . . . Suppose we define business as the economic service of society for private profit and we define politics as the accommodation of all social forces, the forces of business of course included, to the common interest. . . .
>
> Business must be looked upon, not as the exploitation of society, not as its use for private ends, but as its sober service; and private profit must be regarded as legitimate only when it is in fact a reward for what is veritably serviceable—serviceable to interests which are not single but common . . . and politics must be the discovery of this common interest in order that the service may be tested and exacted. In this conception, society is the senior partner in all business. . . .
>
> If private profits are to be legitimatized, private fortunes made honorable, these great forces which play upon the modern field must, both individually and collectively, be accommodated to a common purpose. . . .
>
> Business serves our material needs, but not often our spiritual. But business forces are nowadays the most powerful (perhaps they have always been the most powerful) with which politics has to deal. They are the hardest to correlate, tame, and harness.[18]

Addressing American business leaders in Mobile, Alabama, on October 27, 1913, President Wilson expressed similar concerns as he contemplated the great opportunities the opening of the Panama Canal would soon bring (a reduction of the sailing distance from New York to San Francisco of 7,900 miles with equally striking benefits for trade with East Asia and parts of Latin America from the eastern half of the United States):

> Interest does not tie nations together; it sometimes separates them. But sympathy and understanding does unite them. . . . It is a spiritual union which we seek. . . . *I mean the development of constitutional liberty in the world. Human rights, national integrity and opportunity as against material interests.* . . .
>
> What is at the heart of all our national problems? It is that we have seen the hand of material interest sometimes about to close upon our dearest rights and possessions. *We have seen material interests threaten constitutional freedom in the United States.* Therefore we will now know how to sympathize with those in the rest of America who have to contend with such powers, not only within their borders but from outside their borders also.[19]

In June 1914, in an interview with John Reed, President Wilson made it clear that he suspected that international economic forces were looking to turn the Mexican Revolution to their benefit—and not simply to protect the holdings they already had in that country. By Reed's account, "What [Wilson] meant is perfectly plain. The United States did not intend to lend its support, directly or indirectly, to the looting of the people of Central and South America."[20] In a similar manner, Wilson opposed loans by American banks to China under conditions that would in short order endanger the sovereignty of that country as bankers moved in (as they already had in parts of the Ottoman Empire, Africa, and Latin America) to reclaim politically the credits they had extended. As he put it on March 18, 1913, speaking of United States participation in a six-power loan to Beijing, which he canceled: "The conditions of this loan seem to us to touch very nearly the administrative independence of China itself, and this administration does not feel that it ought, even by implication, to be a party to those conditions."[21]

Indeed, as much as Wilson feared the Bolshevik Revolution, he recognized in its origins the hand of exploitive capitalist forces. As he put it toward the end of his life, commenting on the Russian Revolution:

Everyone who has an intelligent knowledge of social forces must know that the great and widespread reactions like that which is now unquestionably manifesting itself against capitalism do not occur without cause or provocation . . . we ought frankly to put to ourselves the question, Is the capitalistic system unimpeachable . . . have capitalists generally used their power for the benefit of the countries in which their capital is employed and for the benefit of their fellow men? Is it not, on the contrary, too true that capitalists have often seemed to regard the men whom they use as mere instruments of profit, whose physical and mental powers it was legitimate to exploit with as slight cost to themselves as possible, either of money or sympathy? . . .

And if these offenses against high morality and true citizenship have been frequently observable, are we to say that the blame for the present discontent and turbulence is wholly on the side of those who are in revolt against them? Ought we not, rather, to seek a way to remove such offenses and make life itself clean for those who will share honorably and cleanly in it? . . .

That supreme task, which is nothing less than the salvation of civilization, now faces democracy, insistent, imperative. There is no escaping it, unless everything we have built up is presently to fall in ruin about us; and the United States, as the greatest of democracies, must undertake it.[22]

In short, to Wilson's mind, capitalism as an economic system assuring prosperity and underpinning democratic ways needed the regulation of democratic governments to keep its energies in line with the common good. Left to its own machinations, open world markets alone were no guarantee of a better world, any more than capitalism left to its own devices would automatically be at the service of democracy in the United States. Indeed, left unsupervised, capitalism could bring on war, imperialist exploitation, and the undermining of democratic institutions—very much as its Marxist critics maintained. The antidote to this danger was a regulatory democratic state, or combination of democratic states, bending capitalism's strength to the well-being of society at large.

As a variable in the set of concepts that constitute liberal internationalism, democracy promotion thus obviously trumps economic openness. Those who allege that Wilsonianism is a form of American economic imperialism, detrimental to democracy domestically as well as elsewhere, may have points to score on the American practice at different times in our history; that is beyond doubt and never more true than over the past few decades. But to make this the intention, wittingly or otherwise, of Woodrow Wilson himself is to falsify his thinking beyond recognition.

Similarly, Wilson's support for multilateralism as critical to the creation of a stable world peace was qualified by his conviction that democratic countries needed to be the driving forces of such institutions. Only democratic peoples had the sense of honor and the conviction that international law and procedures should be respected for the sake of the general good. Hence the resistance Wilson put up at the Paris peace negotiations in the first months of 1919 to the idea that the League of Nations might admit governments not based on the consent of the governed (much as he originally hoped that mandates created by the League would be governed in such a way that the people under international control be introduced to democracy). Eventually he recognized the practical futility of maintaining this position. In any case, he realized that even authoritarian governments could benefit from cooperating among themselves in terms of mutual interests. Still, Wilson was unwavering in his recognition of the proclivity of authoritarian states and people for war and in his conviction that were the democracies in charge of world affairs, then peace would be far more likely.

In line with Enlightenment thinking, especially as embodied in the organizational practices of Reformed Protestantism in the United States (Wilson was a Presbyterian, the child and grandchild of Presbyterian ministers, as was his first wife), men and women of reason and conscience were capable of a degree of honesty, disinterestedness, trustworthiness, and honor that made government based on the consent of the governed not only possible, but also more effective than any other form of government known to history. In terms used today, governments that are transparent and accountable, based on an informed and engaged citizenry acting in terms of "covenanted" or constitutional agreements (and for Wilson these two terms were synonyms), were capable of rising above self-interested passions and entering into accord with other similarly constituted peoples for the sake of the general good—a common peace. The same virtues that made mutual understanding and cooperation domestically possible could be transferred to the world stage. The primary force basic to an enduring peace was thus not multilateralism unqualified by the character of its membership but rather the democratic citizen member of a democratic society working through a democratic state with like-minded peoples elsewhere.

As Wilson famously put it to Congress in asking for a declaration of war against Germany on April 2, 1917:

> The world must be made safe for democracy. Its peace must be planted upon the tested foundations of political liberty. . . . A steadfast concert for peace can never be maintained except by a partnership of democratic nations. No autocratic government could be trusted to keep faith within it or observe its covenants. It must be a league of honor, a partnership of opinion. . . .
>
> Only free peoples can hold their purpose and their honor steady to a common end and prefer the interests of mankind to any narrow interest of their own.

Since Wilson's time, American leaders have recognized the power of Wilson's vision. Thus, almost three-quarters of a century after his death, when Secretary of State Madeleine Albright called in 1998 for a "Community of Democracies" to add strength to American leadership in world affairs, her appeal was quintessentially Wilsonian in its hope. Authoritarian members of the United Nations Security Council seemed to be inherently hostile to American wishes for the world community, so that the democracies of the world should combine outside the confines of the UN to cooperate together for their collective good and the sake of world peace.

So too when the Princeton Project in 2006 proposed a "Concert of Democracies" to rectify the shortcomings of the United Nations in democracy promotion, and when Senator John McCain proposed a "League of Democracies" in his 2008 campaign for president as the Republican candidate, such innovations were very much in line with Wilson's thinking in 1919. In a word, it was not multilateral institutions in and of themselves that would establish world peace, but rather such organizations as were dominated by the world's democracies.[23]

In short, multilateralism, like economic openness (the Open Door), was basic to the liberal peace agenda. Nevertheless, in each case democratic government was critical to the overall functioning of these two subordinate forces and thus the more critical to the Wilsonian project.

Finally, let us turn to the leadership role of the United States in world affairs for the Wilsonian agenda. For Wilson, the raw power of the United States made it an obvious candidate for leadership. But the origin of this power lay in important measure in this country's democratic nature, whose robust individualism and vibrant, educated middle class had given rise to its preeminent position in world affairs. Nor was it just the efficiency of American ways that recommended it to world leadership, but rather its moral authority, which gave it the ability to act in a "disinterested" way (a term Wilson often used) not only for the sake of its own security but also for the common interest of world peace.

Hence, Washington's guidance could compensate for the League's deficiency in terms of the democratic credentials of some of its members, even some of those that were manifestly "democratic." The world would welcome this leadership because of what Wilson conceived to be a general recognition, both at the popular and the elite levels abroad, of the qualities of the United States in moral terms as a democracy, assuring it a fitness to lead. Here was the enduring aspect of America's singular character—and most certainly not its relative power alone.

To summarize: The liberal promise of world peace is composed of four elemental arguments that meld into one another to create a unity greater than any one alone could provide. Of these, the dominant, because indispensable, force posited for progress to be achieved was in Wilson's mind that democratic cultures, societies, and governments gain in strength the world around. America's mission was therefore to sponsor the expansion of democracy as best it could, using not only direct suasion to achieve this end but by sponsoring open economies and multilateral institutions as well.

But take note. The evident problem nevertheless had to do with the likelihood that democratic peoples could in fact dominate in global relations. What was desirable and what was feasible were thus two very different matters, as Wilson well recognized. When he declared that "the world must be made safe for democracy," he surely meant by this that he hoped to see democratic countries increase in number and in influence. Their dominance was indispensable for an enduring world peace. But by no means was he convinced that such a forward step would be quick or easy to take—if indeed it were likely to occur at all. The result was a decided dose of realism that mixed with Wilson's idealism, a recognition that the developments that would serve the interests of world peace might not be at hand, indeed might never be attained. To reduce Wilson to being "messianic," a "crusader," who believed in America's "redemptive" mission to cure the world of what ailed it is to caricature a man whose thinking was far more realistic in analysis and prudent in action than many believe him to have been.[24]

WHAT WOULD WOODROW WILSON SAY?

There is some reason to think that Woodrow Wilson himself might have disliked an attempt to see his legacy "Wilsonianism" systematized in the way I have presented it here. He might have criticized a coherence I have given to his thought, a logic that is too sharply articulated, that he would have distrusted as leading to ideologically dictated conclusions for action. Wilson disdained what he called "abstract theory" for an important reason: it can run roughshod over the details of a people and a period that must be grasped in their uniqueness to be appreciated for their capacity to act and to change. Given what we shall see was his "organic" view of peoples, states, and the movement of history, he would perhaps have preferred to see himself remembered for his "fortunate vagueness," as we saw Reinhold Niebuhr endorsing liberalism, rather than for having a system of thinking that could be depicted in the form of a diamond and laid out in terms of a set of four synergistic variables. That a set of blueprints of "Wilsonianism" might emerge to authoritatively direct decision-making in Washington would presumably not be to his liking. That he might be amused by the graphic of his concepts as the diamond I presented earlier in this chapter is the best we could hope for. As he put it in 1889:

> The captain of a Mississippi steamboat had made fast to the shore because of a thick fog lying upon the river. The fog lay low and dense upon the surface of the water, but overhead all was clear. A cloudless sky showed a thousand points of starry light. An impatient passenger inquired the cause of the delay. "We can't see to steer," said the captain. "But all is clear overhead," suggested the passenger, "you can see the North Star." "Yes," replied the officer, "but we are not going that way." Politics must follow the actual windings of the channel of the river; if it steers by the stars it will run aground again.[25]

But we must not be detained by these objections, even if they come from Woodrow Wilson himself. If we turn from the strictly theoretical logic of Wilsonianism to a study of the lessons to be learned from Wilson's own writings, speeches, and policies, we can imagine that the twenty-eighth president of the United States might be more receptive to our investigations. For Wilson's life ambition was to make democracy more vibrant by making it more self-conscious—better aware of its origins, its character, its need for constant monitoring, the challenges facing it, its need for patriotic commitment. Here is the reason that Wilson might salute the effort to see his thinking as having a coherence whose logic in his day might serve to instruct those who were to come later.

Given the scope and the speed of the domestic economic reforms Wilson made in his first two years as president, and given the enormity of the task he confronted in being the lead player at the Paris Peace Conference that ended World War I in 1919, it is unthinkable that Wilson would not have wanted to leave an intellectual legacy of the achievements and ambitions of his years in office. On the domestic front, he had succeeded in the greatest series of economic reforms in the history of our Republic up to his times. On the international stage, he presided over the peace settlement of the most important war the United States had ever engaged in—with clear-eyed foreboding that should he and his colleagues fail to win the peace that followed, an even greater war was certain to break out in Europe in the not too distant future.

How could such a man with such a record want to leave behind no intellectual legacy? That his efforts would ultimately give rise to a tradition labeled "Wilsonianism" surely would not have disappointed him, especially given the Senate's rejection of American membership in the League. He would presumably have wanted these decisions reversed, as eventually they were under the leadership of two Americans who had been close to him: Franklin D. Roosevelt and Cordell Hull. The present, he firmly held, must learn from the past—not only from its achievements but also from its failings—in order to safeguard its future. That we might learn from his thinking and actions should be expected.

Even as a young man, Wilson's hopes were to strengthen democracy in the United States by his work as a writer and teacher. As he wrote in his Confidential Journal on his thirty-third birthday, December 28, 1889:

> It was in keeping with my whole mental make-up, therefore, and in obedience to a true instinct, that I chose to put forth my chief strength in the history and interpretation of institutions, and chose as my chief ambition the historical explanation of the modern democratic state . . . an analysis of the thought in which our age stands, if it examine itself. . . . *Why may not the present age write, through me, its political autobiography?*[26]

Just as Wilson had learned how best to serve American democracy by closely studying its past, so others might learn from his experiences lessons equally suitable for the Republic's well-being. As he put it in "Princeton in the Nation's Service" in 1896:

> The world's memory must be kept alive, or we shall never see an end to its old mistakes. We are in danger to lose our identity and become infantile in every generation. . . .
>
> I need not tell you that I believe in full, explicit instruction in history and in politics, in the experiences of peoples and the fortunes of governments, in the whole story of what men have attempted and what they have accomplished through all the changes both of form and purpose in their organization of their common life. . . . It is plain that it is the duty of an institution of learning set in the midst of a free population and amidst signs of social change, not merely to implant a sense of duty, but to illuminate duty by every lesson that can be drawn from the past. . . .
>
> You do not know the world until you know the men who have possessed it and tried its ways before ever you were given your brief run upon it. And there is no sanity comparable with that which is schooled in the thoughts that will keep. . . .
>
> Do you wonder, then, that I ask for the old drill, the old memory of times gone by, the old schooling in precedent and tradition, the old keeping of faith with the past as a preparation for leadership in the days of social change?[27]

In keeping with this encouragement of the "old drill, the old memory of times gone by, the old schooling in precedent and tradition, the old keeping of faith with the past as a preparation for leadership in days of social change," we should turn to Wilson the academic and only then to Wilson the president.

As the great Wilson scholar Professor Arthur S. Link wrote of Wilson's 1885 essay "The Modern Democratic State": "it was the ideological framework from which Wilson never seriously deviated." Link adds that with the publication in 1889 of the first edition of *The State*, whose general chapters tell us a great deal about Wilson's thinking about history and politics (and which did not change markedly in its many revised editions through 1911), we have "ample evidence of what [his never written *magnum opus*] *The Philosophy of Politics* would have been had circumstances ever permitted Wilson to write it."[28]

However, Link (like other scholars deservedly of note), despite his superb accounts of aspects of Wilson's foreign and domestic policy, does little to reach back to the academic material to show us the continuity of Wilson the academic to Wilson the president. As a result, we are left with few professional guides to lead us through the maze that stretches from his first academic work of interest to us in 1879 to the final revised version of *The State*, published in 1911, the year before he was elected president.[29]

Surely Woodrow Wilson would be surprised that to understand his decisions as president so little had been done to understand the years when his ideas had been formulated as a professor. For he knew perfectly well that the time he had spent thinking about history and politics, and most particularly about the meaning of democracy, had to have an enormous influence on his policies as president. As he had said of Abraham Lincoln in 1893:

> Mr. Lincoln can be known only by a close and prolonged scrutiny of his life before he became president. The years of his presidency were not years to form but rather years to test character. The strain was too great to harden and perfect any sinew but that which was already tough and firmly knit.[30]

Let us turn, then, to the lessons to be derived from Woodrow Wilson's writings and speeches between the late 1870s and 1911 (when the last revised version of *The State* appeared), to be augmented, of course, by his speeches, written communications, and policies after he became president in 1913. What we will see is confirmation of the theoretical argument presented earlier in this chapter: that the guiding light of Wilson's ambitions was to safeguard American democracy, and that the surest way of doing this, aside from constant vigilance at home, was to work for world peace by defending and promoting democracy through the multilateralism of the League of Nations, guided by Washington's leadership.

Under these conditions, the world might be made safe for democracy. That this goal was his primary objective, Wilson never doubted. That it was actually obtainable was, however, an altogether different question, a matter on which he was altogether more restrained. Whatever the force of his rhetoric on occasion, his caution is equally evident. Recognizing the gap between what Wilson desired and what he reasonably expected is a key point to capture once he began to determine policy after becoming president of the United States in 1913. It explains that as much as he wished for human freedom based on the strength of democratic institutions and so saluted the uprising of oppressed peoples, whether in Mexico or Russia, in the lands dominated by the Ottomans or the Austro-Hungarians, he nonetheless realized from his earliest work on the French Revolution that not all cultures are capable of engendering a democratic political order. Nor was his initial reaction to the outbreak of war in 1914 to rush in to a conflict with Germany under the name of democracy combating autocracy (that would come later). Hence the tension between Wilson the idealist and Wilson the realist—one he finally resolved by his hopes for what the League of Nations might accomplish in ending war if only it could be led by the spirit of democracy.

THIS BOOK: WHY WILSON MATTERS

There are three principal reasons Woodrow Wilson's thought matters today. First, linking his presidential policies to his academic understanding has seldom been done meticulously yet has direct bearing on the policies he came to formulate as president. To take the cardinal example: Wilson's emphasis on the genesis, character, and importance internationally of democracy has to my knowledge never been systematically studied in its breadth or depth. While his definition of liberal democracy fell within the Enlightenment understanding of this form of society and government, the meaning Wilson ascribed to it was in many ways particular to him. The trust he placed in democracy morally, for domestic as well as international well-being, is thus typically underappreciated in the vast literature on Wilsonianism.

Second, the emergence in the 1990s of a "neo-Wilsonianism," which claimed a good part of its pedigree from the American liberal tradition founded by Wilson, rests on traditional liberal internationalism in part, but far from entirely. Here lies the explanation as to why a tradition that gave rise to the greatest successes of American foreign policy—of which the occupations of Japan and Germany have pride of place—gave way after the end of the cold war to arguments that surely Wilson himself would have disavowed. Neither the invasion of Iraq in 2003 nor the degree to which the domestic and international markets were deregulated beginning in the 1980s could conceivably be justified from the positions that he adopted and that had been followed by liberal internationalists during the cold war.

Third, American liberal internationalism may well meet the fate of communism and fascism and disappear in any meaningful way from the world political forum. A major purpose of this book is an effort to rescue the tradition in effect from itself, from the damage done to it since the 1990s by intellectuals and policy-makers who work in the name of a tradition they do not adequately understand if for no better reason than that the character of Wilson's thinking has not been adequately understood. The clarification of the liberal internationalist tradition is thus a primary purpose of this book.

Finally, this book is likely to be subject to two criticisms. First, that it is simplistic—that is, that I insist on a coherence to the Wilsonian worldview that forces concepts and policies together within a mold that does not do justice to the improvised and sometimes even contradictory character of Wilson's positions. My answer to this charge is that I can only agree that, as with any worldview, Wilson's too is replete with blind spots, tensions if not contradictions, and changes over time. Yet coherence there is as well, which is the reason that the term "Wilsonian" deserves to be seen as standing for an integrated, if multifaceted, approach to world affairs. I therefore privilege coherence over incoherence in looking at the complexity of Wilson's thinking not only because I genuinely think it is there but especially because pointing it out is basic to the task of establishing a definition of "Wilsonianism" and so contributing to the refurbishment of this tradition by strengthening its sense of identity.

The second criticism is likely to be that I put too much weight on human rights and democracy promotion as the aspect of liberal internationalism that most determines its spirit—in effect, that my argument is overly "monocausal." Certainly other studies have exaggerated out of due proportion isolated aspects of Wilson's liberal internationalism, so I am aware of the damage that can be done to a complex approach to thinking about world affairs by elevating one consideration above all others. Yet by insisting on the importance of American leadership, world market integration, and multilateralism as indispensable aspects of Wilsonianism, I hope I have to some extent met this criticism. I would also note how critical the League of Nations was to Wilson's hopes. He meant it to be both the protector and promoter of not only peace but also democratic government. Nevertheless, I must plead guilty to the charge that the driving force I see in the liberal tradition is one where morality and practicality come together in a conviction based on faith and reason (the two properties that Wilson himself always championed in combination) that of its various characteristics, the spirit of democracy as he envisioned it has indeed always been (and should remain) the principal motivating agent of the Wilsonian tradition.

PART I

THE ESSENTIAL WILSON:
WILSON'S WILSONIANISM

CHAPTER ONE

Woodrow Wilson on Democracy Promotion in America

The consent of the governed must at every turn check and determine the action of those who make and execute the laws. . . . That is "constitutional government." When we speak of a constitutional government we mean a government so constituted that those who govern and those who are governed are brought by some systematic and efficient means into concord and counsel; and in which law, accordingly, is made and enforced in conformity with principles and by methods agreed upon between them. The real problem of democracy, therefore, is how to devise and maintain in full efficiency the best means of intimate counsel between those who are to make and administer the laws and those who are to obey them . . . governments should retain their power as it is that [the citizenry] should be free . . . modern democracy . . . speaks always of the sovereignty of the people, and of rulers as the people's servants. . . . Modern democracy is government subject to systematic popular control.[1]
    —*Woodrow Wilson, "The Real Idea of Democracy," 1901*

The problem is to find a form of association which will defend and protect with the whole common force the person and goods of each associate, and in which each, while uniting himself with all, may still obey himself alone and remain as free as before.
    —*Jean-Jacques Rousseau, The Social Contract, 1762*

The introduction argued that in strictly theoretical terms the dominant theme of the Wilsonian tradition is demonstrably democracy promotion. The institutions and character that the spirit of democracy calls forth assure that the good functioning of the other aspects of liberal international-ism is reinforced—the virtues of open markets integrating the world's econo-mies and fostering the strength of the middle class; multilateral institutions that handle a host of issues among democratic nations, from national security to economic coordination; the responsible conduct of American foreign pol-icy as the world's foremost democracy—which together provide us the best hope we can reasonably argue for to establish the foundations of a world of enduring peace.

However, my argument rested basically on the logic of liberal theory, not so much on proof offered from Woodrow Wilson's own writings and speeches, which he gave in abundance and to which we now turn in more detail. Here we shall see that his guiding concern from a young age was not simply to understand the historical origins of democratic life as a scholar, but as an ac-tivist to promote the well-being of democratic society and institutions at home and (at a somewhat later point in his life) to do as best he could for the sake of world order to foster such ideals and practices elsewhere around the globe.

Here the comparison between Karl Marx and Woodrow Wilson is surpris-ingly illuminating. As Marx (1818–1883) was to an economic explanation of the dynamics of historical change and development, so Wilson (1856–1924) was to a political explanation. For both men, history moves in terms of what Marx would have called (and Wilson surely would have agreed) a "material-ist" fashion. That is, changes occur over time because of developments within the structure of economic relations (for Marx) or political relations (for Wil-son). Such changes are "unconscious" in the sense that as these developments take place, the men and women who bring them about are unaware of the larger, long-term consequences of their acts. More, prior to the nineteenth century, the mix of forces defied conceptualization because of their very com-plexity and apparently random nature. "It is now plain to everyone that [de-mocracy's] inspiration is of man and not of God," Wilson wrote in 1885. Marx would most decidedly have held the same to be true of international capitalism.[2]

Moreover, as both Marx and Wilson might agree, by the late eighteenth century, changes in the material base of society meant political "conscious-ness" was for the first time coming into its own as an active agent of history. In line with Enlightenment thinking, reasoned analysis could provide correct ways of perceiving the world and improving the human condition. People could control their lives and their destinies in a way never before imaginable.

Leaders of men might see this earlier than others, but in due course the working class (for Marx) or the middle class (for Wilson) would insist on taking charge of affairs directly. Marx awaited the beginning of political change leading to what he called "the dictatorship of the proletariat" in an advanced industrial country (Germany being the most likely, but perhaps Great Britain), whereas Wilson saw the United States as leading the world toward democracy.

The analytical focus of Marx's work was on the logic of capitalism. The industrial revolution and the rise of international capitalism—whatever the horrors they had brought forth—had created a new and more promising stage of history, the prelude to human freedom and peace. Marx knew himself to be a man of genius, yet ideas such as his had to await a certain level of material development for his thinking to appear. But once it did, he was confident of what he could contribute to the forward march of history: "Communism is the riddle of history solved and knows itself to be that solution," he wrote as he awaited the worsening contradictions of "the anarchy of capital" and the rise in working-class "consciousness."

For Wilson, in contrast, the analytical focus was on democracy. The rise of a democratic culture and institutions, starting most vividly with the American Revolution, opened a new stage in history that by the beginning of the twentieth century was moving this country into being what Marx might have called "the vanguard nation," one whose domestic freedom and stability, Wilson felt sure as early as 1885, would be of relevance to the greater forces of history moving abroad. As Marx would instruct the working class, so Wilson would instruct his fellow Americans and, in due course, those who sought a model for the construction of constitutional democracy elsewhere.

In something akin to a religious calling, Wilson's life's mission was to be among the first to explain democracy to those favored to live under its terms so that this form of government and society might gather its strength for the sake of a better world:

> When political institutions come to be viewed in their true historical proportions and perspective, it will be seen that it has not been without reason that Americans have regarded their system of government as standing at the front of the world's progress and politics. . . . Our best claims upon the world's attention will appear when . . . we penetrate further, to the analysis of our constitutional being and discover in full historical light the true genesis of our form of government and, by

consequence, *the general principles which lie at the foundation of all practicable government by the people.* The present trend of all political development the world over towards democracy is no mere episode in history. It is the natural resultant of now permanent forces which have long been gathering, which brought modern lights out of mediaeval shades, and which have made the life of the most advanced nations of our day the wide, various, vigorous, complex expanding thing that it is.[3]

Thus, for Marx and Wilson alike, this new stage of history should be welcomed as one of enormous promise. Marx could foresee the development of a new world order of freedom emerging from the anarchy of capitalist production and the maturity of the class consciousness of an increasingly numerous and immiserated working class. The result would be not bourgeois, but genuine, popular democracy and world peace. For his part, Wilson could foresee the eventual triumph of democratic government worldwide based on an increasingly educated, cosmopolitan, prosperous middle class: "it is a more serious matter for the individual to belong to a great democratic nation than to live under any other polity. He is put upon his honor; he is challenged to use his strength; he is thrown into the midst of solemn opportunities, and trusted to use them; he is given leave to create great occasions."[4] As a result of the emergence of these "new men," be they communists for Marx or constitutional democrats for Wilson, the promise would be an expansion of world freedom and peace.

But political action had to be taken. As a young man, Marx wrote, "the philosophers have only understood the world; the point is to change it." The young Wilson was much of the same mind. As early as 1885, he could write, "The object of all political thought should be action . . . it should always point out the way of progress. It ought to teach that wise sort of boldness which can afford to make mistakes because it knows what is essential and guards that from risk while it ventures all else for the sake of liberty. . . . It ought, in brief, to produce a philosophy of statesmanship."[5]

An important source of Wilson's commitment to the protection and expansion of democratic culture, institutions, and leadership came from the inspiration he found at Princeton University, the leading institution of higher learning for Presbyterians and one of the greatest centers of learning in the United States. After being a student at Princeton (1875–1879), he became a professor of politics there (1890–1902) before becoming president of the university (1902–1910). Calvinist beliefs were obviously of importance to Wilson, who read the Bible daily and who invoked his reliance on Providence with some regularity.

However, Christian teachings were not of as much importance so far as Wilson was concerned in his relations with others as much as the teachings of duty, honor, a sense of the communal interest, and a need to come to an organized, and so institutional, form of group solidarity that for Calvinists meant "covenanting," which to Wilson was a form of constitutionalism. The practice was of immense importance to Wilson, for it meant that other peoples who might not be Reformed Protestant Christians could nonetheless be constitutionalists. Thus, Reformed Judaism would appeal to his sense of proper group behavior (and presumably helps explain his willingness to appoint Jews for the first time to the Princeton faculty, then to high office in unprecedented numbers when he became president). By contrast, Catholics, with their dependence on a rigid clerical authority structure over a congregation, or evangelical Christians who followed the teachings of a self-appointed, charismatic "frontier preachers," as Wilson called them, were in organizational terms less suited to provide a social base to democratic government, although Wilson appeared confident that in due course persons of all religious confessions could become practiced in the spirit of self-government.

The secular mission of Princeton to advance the cause of democracy was thus bound up in its religious vocation both doctrinally and in terms of the organizational structure of Calvinist churches. In his famous address of October 1896, "Princeton in the Nation's Service," Wilson stressed that although the university had been founded primarily to train ministers of the faith, it was from the first "a school of duty," "a seminary of statesmen." He reminded his listeners of the great John Knox Witherspoon, president of Princeton from 1768 to 1794. This Scottish, Presbyterian minister who arrived in New Jersey having been acquainted with some of the most brilliant minds of the Enlightenment in his homeland (including both David Hume and Adam Smith), presided over a new class of some 100 young men every year. Witherspoon had himself signed the Declaration of Independence, been a leading member of the Continental Congress from 1776 to 1782, then saw nine former students during his years at Princeton sign the Constitution of 1787 (there were a total of thirty-nine signatures), twenty become senators and twenty-three representatives in the national Congress, thirteen be elected governors, three join the Supreme Court, one made vice president of the United States, and James Madison (a student at Princeton from 1769 to

1771, who stayed on to study Hebrew, in which he became fluent, and political philosophy with Witherspoon after his graduation) be elected president of the United States.

Amazingly, Witherspoon achieved all of this out of a combined student population during his tenure of some 2,600 students. Here was a man for Wilson truly to measure himself against, and he set himself to the task. Invoking Witherspoon's spirit, Wilson declared:

> Princeton is not likely to forget that sharp schooling of her youth, when she first learned the lesson of public service. . . . The quiet scholar has his proper breeding and truth must be searched out and held aloft for men to see for its own sake. . . . But not many pupils of [Princeton] are to be investigators: they are to be citizens and the world's servants in every field of practical endeavor. . . .
>
> The University in our day is no longer inclined to stand aloof from the practical world, and, surely, it ought never to have had the disposition to do so. It is the business of a University to impart to the rank and file of the men whom it trains the right thought of the world, the thought which it has tested and established, the principles which have stood through the seasons and become at length part of the immemorial wisdom of the race. . . . The business of the world is not individual success, but its own betterment, strengthening, and growth in spiritual insight.[6]

WILSON EXPLAINS DEMOCRACY TO ITSELF TO INCREASE ITS SELF-AWARENESS

Before becoming governor of New Jersey (1910–1912) and so a policymaker, Wilson's ambition was to explain democracy to itself through an impressive corpus of books and articles (augmented by a demanding round of public lectures) and thereby to strengthen the nation's fiber, both morally and efficiently. "Only history can explain modern democracy either to itself or to those who would imitate it," he wrote in 1885, and the efforts he deployed in this endeavor were prodigious. As he put it decades later, in 1919, "I have saturated myself in the traditions of our country; I have read all the great literature that interprets the spirit of our country; and when I read my own heart with regard to these great purposes, I feel confident that it is a sample American heart."[7]

Accordingly, Wilson wrote with authority on the "nature and form of government"; on "the functions and objects" of the state; on the character of law in the Western experience from ancient Greece and Rome to his day; on the structure of constitutional government in the United States; on the administrative adaptations that would make governmental bureaucracies function more perfectly with respect to improving state-society relations; on the character of social forces that would behave responsibly in such a political order (with special attention to the behavior of corporate capitalism, whose reform he urgently pushed forward for the sake of democratic life); on political parties (for here was the key to the success of representative democracy, modernity's great advance over ancient democracy, one that would keep it from degenerating as Aristotle had warned democracy always would); on the demanding role of political leadership in a democracy (both in general and in terms of great American personalities, selecting out especially Washington and Lincoln); and on the history of the American people (in five volumes, later reprinted as ten) from the founding of the colonies unto his day.[8]

With respect to domestic legislation as president, Wilson's greatest acccomplishments deriving from his work as a political scientist were surely the range of economic reforms he convinced the Congress to pass during his first term in office. His most outstanding successes in his drive for "The New Freedom" lay in his efforts to secure tariff, banking, and business reforms, which included the lowering of tariff rates (combined with an offsetting raise in the income tax) in the Revenue Act of October 1913; the Federal Reserve Act of December 1913; the Clayton Anti-Trust Act of October 1914; the Federal Farm Loan Act of July 1916; the Child Labor Act of 1916; the Workingmen's Compensation Act of September 1916; the Adamson Act of August 1916 (which established better working conditions for interstate railway employees); and the introduction of the inheritance tax.[9] Wilson's core argument with respect to all these reforms was not simply that they served the prosperity of the nation but rather, much more critically, that they undergirded the common interest and so strengthened democracy in America.

The striking aspect of Wilson's impact on world affairs after he became president is that in his academic writing there is little indeed on the subject of democracy worldwide. Instead, Wilson remained a student of what he calls "comparative politics" (a term still used in political science departments today), which focuses on individual peoples and states in ways that tend to emphasize their unique identities based on a combination of cultural, economic, political, and social forces considered historically. Historian John Milton Cooper, Jr. cites an offhand comment by Wilson shortly after he became president, "It would be an irony of fate if my administration has to deal chiefly with foreign problems; for all my preparation has been in domestic matters."[10]

Nevertheless, Wilson was able to use his insights into the way various societies evolve politically to make the transition to views on world affairs and the role of the United States within it as early as the Spanish-American War of 1898. As I shall explain in the following chapter, Wilson's understanding of democracy was critical to his foreign policies as president, for his prime effort was to work where he thought there was some possibility of success to push forward the process of democratization abroad, a subject on which he was surely the foremost expert of his day in the United States, if not globally. Although in his earlier years, Wilson believed that there was a natural, global force behind the worldwide spread of democracy, by the time he had reached his forties, he had linked the prospects for the expansion of democratic life increasingly to an engagement by the United States to make this promise a reality.

THE HISTORICAL ORIGINS OF DEMOCRACY

But we are running ahead of ourselves. For some quarter of a century before he embraced a forward role for the United States in global affairs that came with the victory of 1898 in the Spanish-American War, Wilson had reflected long and hard on the history of democracy as a form of government and on the specific characteristics of American democracy as a political order that could permit the United States to play a leading role in the eyes of the world. Given the circumstances in which modern democracy had appeared on the historical scene, Wilson might be understood through his thirties as reluctant to believe that its expansion as a form of government was likely outside Britain and the world of British colonial descent. Yet it was just this analysis of domestic political events, which long preceded his concern with world affairs, that prepared him for the American mission in the Western Hemisphere and Europe that he would eventually formulate. For by understanding both the origins and organization of this country's democracy, something of a blueprint might be established of benefit to all the world.

For democracy to understand itself and to organize a world according to its desires, it must first understand its origins. Here was a prime motivation for Wilson in 1889 to publish *The State: Elements of Historical and Practical*

Politics. In its various revised editions, the book charted a course of more than two thousand years, from the first political order based on kinship structures without formal institutional structure to the Greeks and Romans and thence to his own times.[11] If we conflate this book with Wilson's 1885 important, unpublished manuscript "The Modern Democratic State," the eventual emergence of democratic government is recounted in ways that make it unique to the circumstances of its birth yet nonetheless of relevance to other peoples of very different historical backgrounds.

At the risk of overly schematizing, we can see that the first stirrings that Wilson clearly identified as bearing the seeds of modern democracy were unself-consciously planted by a fortuitous process of a regionally specific development that combined Christian belief with Germanic individualism and feudal institutions with the enduring influence of Roman law—all of which he dated to the fifth century. Here history laid the groundwork for what, with further accretions, could later be recognized as modern democracy.

Wilson identified a second contribution to the eventual birth of democracy as the Renaissance from the fourteenth to the seventeenth centuries, and with it the rediscovery of Roman and Greek philosophy and the rise of secular humanism. Here was the fountainhead, in turn, of the Enlightenment of the seventeenth and eighteenth centuries. Reason now supplemented (but most certainly did not replace) faith in thinking about the world, and the age of modern science opened.

For many Christians of Wilson's time, the Enlightenment and religion were difficult, if not impossible, to reconcile. But religious faith of the sort that Wilson espoused had been changing for a full century before he came of age. Thus, by the time he was writing on the subject in the 1880s, Wilson was able to blend seamlessly the arguments of reason with those he found with the Protestant Reformation and the evolution of its Calvinist branch in the United States (thanks in good measure to its roots in Scotland, where Enlightenment thinking was especially vigorous). Here, Wilson was of the same mind as was John Witherspoon, who in the opening page of a book of his collected lectures, published by his students after his death under the title *Lectures on Moral Philosophy,* declared that there need be no clash between Enlightenment appeals to reason and Christian appeals to the Bible:

> Moral Philosophy is that branch of Science which treats of the principles and laws of Duty or Morals. It is called Philosophy, because it is an inquiry into the nature and grounds of moral obligation by reason, as

distinct from revelation. . . . If the Scripture is true, the discoveries of reason cannot be contrary to it; and therefore it has nothing to fear from that quarter. . . . There may be an illustration and confirmation of the inspired writings from reason and observation, which will greatly add to their beauty and force.[12]

The result by the second half of the eighteenth century among most mainstream American Protestants was a celebration of the marriage of reason with faith, a union that greatly appealed a century later to Woodrow Wilson, who found Charles Darwin's works to be especially to his liking when he considered the logic of political evolution.

However, the development to which Wilson gave the greatest attention in the history of the emergence of democratic government was the evolution of political power in England and the consequences this would have in due course on the American colonies. Here the feudal system grew in a fashion that limited the absolute power of the monarch, replacing it with a form of limited government that over the centuries laid the institutional grounds of modern democracy. Following Montesquieu (1689–1752), Wilson credited the checks on absolutist power eventually set up in England, stretching from the Magna Carta of 1215 (although seeds had been planted even earlier) to the Glorious Revolution of 1688, as a final piece putting in place what outside the United States was the congeries of forces that would eventually combine to become modern democracy.

Of this precious legacy, Americans needed to be reminded:

The people of the United States have never known anything but self-government since the colonies were founded. They have forgotten the discipline which preceded the founding of the colonies, the long drill in order and in obedience to law, the long subjection to kings and to parliaments which were not in fact of the people's choosing. They have forgotten how many generations were once in tutelage in order that the generations which discovered and settled the coasts of America might be mature and free. No thoughtful student of history or observer of public affairs needs to be told the necessary conditions precedent to self-government: the slow growth of the sense of law; the equally slow growth of the sense of community and of fellowship in every general interest; the habit of organization, the habit of discipline and obedience to those entrusted with authority, the self-restraint of give and take; the allegiance to ideas, the consciousness of mutual obligation; the patience and intelligence which are content with a slow and universal growth.[13]

Yet if English order prepared the way, it was nonetheless in the American colonies, then in the United States itself, according to Wilson, where the combination of circumstances ultimately converged to bring about the highest form of democratic life anywhere by the end of the nineteenth century. Here was neither the established church nor the royalty that held back the British advance; instead here were to be found the prosperity, learning, and religious convictions of a people who could bring democracy securely into the twentieth century. The result was that by the late nineteenth century it was America, not Britain, that was the world's foremost democracy. "It was her drilled classes that [England] sent to America: and that first blood has so far kept its advantage. We have many things to fear; but we have, nevertheless, a mighty fund of unsurpassed civil capacity: we can impart it to the best of those who come to us with other blood in their veins. Think what it is that you have in a democratic nation made as ours has been. You have an adult, disciplined, self-possessed nation—with a self-possession born of long experience."[14]

In short, Wilson's view of the historical appearance of modern democracy depended upon a fortuitous set of occurrences that were uniquely Western, better uniquely Teutonic, indeed ultimately English, leading in time to what seemed like a charmed circle of English-speaking peoples to whom alone (with reservations for the Swiss and the Scandinavians) democratic government had been vouchsafed. But could this achievement be duplicated elsewhere? Only with difficulty. However, the way would be made easier by the example of the American experience so that others could use the United States as a model for their own self-improvement to the level of also having self-government.

THE FOUNDATIONS OF AMERICAN DEMOCRACY—INDEED OF ANY DEMOCRACY

As Wilson well knew, history alone could not explain the genius of American democracy. In order to pursue his life's calling of explaining democracy to his fellow Americans so that its promise would be strengthened, Wilson turned himself to the complex and difficult task of laying out analytically the foundations of this way of life. What emerged was something of a blueprint that could increase the self-consciousness of Americans as to the logic of their success. Here too was an approach that might be of service to other peoples contemplating the creation of such a political order.

But where should one understand the beginning of a democratic polity? In Wilson's view—one continued still today among Americans with their seemingly endless internal debates since the 1950s over how to bring about democratic "nation- and state-building" abroad—the question is that of synchronizing elite institutions with the popular will in a way that provides not only stability but also freedom. How is it brought about? Which is the chicken, which the egg, or can a process of simultaneous genesis be formulated where each body—society and state—reinforces the other in a virtuous circle?

The debate has its proponents on every side. (Today, for example, there are those who would start with state-building, whose success would then lead to nation-building, while others would reverse the process, and still others would work on both together.) However, for Wilson the historical record was clear: democracy begins with elites who limit the power of central authority through institutions that have the force of law behind them, supported by a population increasingly conscious that its will is the necessary basis for legitimate government. In its early stage, the population knows it wants responsible government—that is, political institutions resting on the consent of the governed—but is unsure just what achieving this setup entails. To be sure, America's Revolution was based on society's demands for rights it considered the government in London to be repudiating. However, for Wilson a people's discontent alone was not enough to make democratic government possible. Only at a later stage is society expected to have the cohesion and the consciousness to become increasingly active in political life. At its origins, enlightened leadership is thus the primary vehicle of democratization; but in due course, the active consent of the governed comes into play, until finally, with society dominating government, we can speak of "democratic self-government."

Even when the highest stage of democracy is achieved—what he also labeled "popular self-government"—Wilson considered the independence of the political institutions from overly intrusive popular involvement basic to the rule of law. Indeed, in *Constitutional Government in the United States*, Wilson actually recommends as the characteristics of one who would become president "a man who understands his own day and the needs of the country, and who has the personality and initiative to enforce his views both upon the people and upon Congress."

He is the only national voice in affairs. Let him once win the admiration and confidence of the country and no other single force can withstand him, no combination of forces will easily overpower him. His position takes the imagination of the country. He is the representative of no constituency, but of the whole people. When he speaks in his true character, he speaks for no special interest. If he rightly interpret the national thought and boldly insist upon it, he is irresistible; and the country never feels the zest of action so much as when its president is of such insight and caliber. Its instinct is for unified action, and it craves a single leader.[15]

While this image of the president bears a disturbing resemblance to fascist leaders like Mussolini, who would appear on the scene only fourteen years later, any such comparison would be misleading. For Wilson balanced his view of the character of democratic leadership with a sense of its limitations given the character of the individual and the citizenry in a democracy: informed, involved, jealous of their liberties, aware of their rights and their strength, convinced that the government was legitimate only when it served the common interest as validated by the consent of the governed. "Such an attitude presupposes both intelligence and independence of spirit on the part of the individual; such a system elicits intelligence and creates independence of spirit . . . and the government set over such men must look to see that it has authority for every act it ventures upon." As a consequence, leaders are expected to be transparent in presenting the reasoning behind the decisions they reach and ultimately are to be held accountable to the electorate for their roles in office. In short, leaders and institutions give birth to democracy, but never without a healthy degree of socially felt need such that at its highest stage, that of "self-government," society would play a role greater than that of the elite in controlling the character of institutions.[16]

THE ROLE OF LAW, INSTITUTIONS, AND LEADERSHIP IN THE BIRTH OF FREEDOM

"The life of society is a struggle for law," Wilson declared in the opening line of his 1910 presidential address to the American Political Science Association.[17] So, too, is liberty premised on its protection through law articulated and enforced through political institutions.

Liberty is not identical with individual privilege. It is a thing of social organization. A man's freedom is lost the moment he is cut off from society and thrown upon his own resources, to do everything for himself. . . . His strength lies of course in cooperation, in combined and regulated social effort. It is not in being let alone by government that my liberty consists, but in being assisted by government to maintain my equal place among my fellows. Some power stronger than I am must define my rights; else they are measured by might and not by my right. . . . Liberty is like steam, effective only when confined. It is the order of society that makes me free. . . . Law is the external organism of human freedom. . . . In it, we are obedient to what? To standards of character. Our liberty is measured by our assent to the general virtue, our participation in the general steadfastness of spirit.[18]

Liberty thus depends on law; law in turn depends on institutions run by leaders of competence and integrity; such individuals are to be selected by the people, aware of the responsibilities of citizenship, and are accountable to them through elections organized on the basis of parties. The state thus is essential for freedom, for society left to its own devices would surely fall into being anarchic or becoming the possession of a limited sector of society that would control the citizenry for its own convenience. In contrast, to be democratic, the state must reflect popular consciousness, and the laws it decrees and enforces need the consent of the citizenry concerned that their common interest is engaged when the state speaks.

Historically speaking, the capacity for this sort of state and society arose out of the experience of people living under English monarchs constrained by institutions to permit limits to their power, followed by the appearance of a middle class capable of combining secular reason with spiritual faith, as America best demonstrated. However, once created, such a form of life could be imitated by others.

Yet imitation would not come easily. Wilson's preferred example, from as early as 1879 to as late as 1922, was that of France. The problem for the French in their demand for "liberty, equality, and fraternity" was that they had had no experience with any institutional form of the state but that of an absolute, centralized monarchy. Here was the lesson that Montesquieu had pointed out in texts that profoundly influenced the American Founders and that were carefully studied by Wilson as well; here was the critical difference between the fortunes of liberty in the two lands.

As Wilson often put it in another of his forms of thinking in stages about history, periods of individual maturation were useful analogies for entire peoples so that democracy "is possible for a nation only in the adult age of its political development."

> A people must have gone through a period of political tutelage which shall have prepared them by gradual steps of acquired privileges of self-direction for assuming the entire control of their affairs. Long and slowly widening experience in local self-direction must have prepared them for national self-direction. They must have acquired adult self-reliance, self-knowledge, and self-control, adult soberness and deliberateness of judgment and sagacity in self-government, adult vigilance of thought and quickness of insight. . . .

> It is the heritage of races purged alike of hasty barbaric passions and of patient servility to rulers, and schooled in temperate common counsel. It is an institution of political noon-day, not of the half-light of political morning. It can never be made to sit easily or safely on first generations, but strengthens through long heredity. It is poison to the infant, but tonic to the man. *Monarchies may be made but democracies must grow.*[19]

The American Revolution was successful, then, because it confirmed traditional rights, traditional terms of a social contract, traditional institutional forms and promises (even if they evolved over time, many unique to the context of the British administration of the American colonies). Through their Revolution, Americans confirmed their long-understood rights and liberties through institutions based on laws that set out a series of obligations at the same time. So, too, Australia, New Zealand, and Canada had evolved, as in due course India and South Africa might as well.

> Look into any constitutional document of the English-speaking race and you shall find the same spirit, the same way of action: its aim is always an arrangement, as if of business: no abstract setting forth of liberties, no pretense of grants of privilege or political rights, but always a formulation of limits and of methods, a regulation of the way governments shall act and individuals be dealt with . . . the whole of constitutional history is similarly concerned with definition, with method, with machinery. . . . The question of machinery of ways and means is manifestly of capital importance in a constitutional system.[20]

For such institutions to be created and to endure, statesmanship is necessary that has the moral fiber, intellectual acumen, and political courage to lead the citizenry to a consciousness of its common values, interests, and purpose. The critical importance of leadership was apparent in Wilson's writings as early as 1891:

> What we really mean when we say that the people govern is that they freely consent to be governed, on condition that *a certain part* of them *do* the governing—that part which shall, by one process or another, be selected out of the mass and elevated to places of rule: and that is the best democratic government in which the processes of this selection are the best. . . .
>
> A self-instructed, self-mastered, self-elevated man, *like Lincoln*, is no more a man of the people than Washington was. He has *come out* from the people; has separated himself from the indistinguishable mass of unknown men by reason of excellency and knowledge; has *raised himself above* the common level of others and constituted himself as a master-spirit among men. . . .
>
> The people do indeed govern. They govern just in proportion as they produce the stuff out of which governors and kings are made; just so far as they show the discrimination to choose such when they are made manifest. . . . There must be character on the part of the people to judge character on the part of the official. That is the condition precedent to democracy.[21]

For Wilson, the wisdom of the Founders had been of paramount importance to the creation of the United States. As things stood in the late eighteenth century:

> Virginia was much more unlike Massachusetts than Massachusetts was unlike England. The Carolinas, with their lumber forests and their rice fields, felt themselves utterly unlike Virginia. . . . [Happily] Men of first-rate capacity and high political ambition entered upon the service of their states readily enough. . . . Only the extraordinary foresight and sagacity of the men who framed and advocated the federal constitution—only the prevailing force of men such as Washington, and Hamilton, and Madison—could have secured so compact and strong a central government in the face of the jealousy of local interests.[22]

FINALLY, DEMOCRACY

But institutions with great leaders are alone not enough to call a people democratic. For what is finally necessary in Wilson's scheme of historical development (and what constitutes the best rebuttal to the charge that he was a proto-fascist) is that the people themselves come to rule, even if only indirectly through representatives they select to govern them, whose actions they closely monitor, and whom they may hold accountable most commonly through general elections but also by freedom of speech, assembly, and the press. The ability of such a citizenry to appear depends on its "organic" development.

Throughout his writings, Wilson employed the term "organic" to apply to the force of popular consciousness, sentiment, and habit. But the fact of its existence by no means meant that a people was capable of becoming democratic. It was thus *a particular form* of organic connectedness that distinguished a democratic people from those who existed at earlier stages of development, even if all of them might be possessed of an organic sense of social unity.[23]

First, the character of the people must be ready for self-government by dint of a coming to consciousness of their desire for a state whose legitimacy rests on the consent of the governed. More, such a people must share a fund of common values, interests, historical memories, and sense of purpose so that they can establish a social contract, open to change over time but securely anchored in sentiment and experience. What might be called, following Emile Durkheim, a "collective conscience" capable of formulating a common interest, as well as ways of reformulating such an agreement should change be warranted, must be possible. Where these preconditions combined, Wilson delineated such a community as "organic." Still, in *The State* he wrote that many peoples who were not democratic might also have a form of organic unity. By contrast, the organic nature of a democratic people was peculiar to their political organization. As he put it as early as 1885 in concepts that he would not deviate from for the rest of his life, "Nothing establishes the democratic state save trained capacity for self-government, practical aptitude for public affairs, habitual soberness and temperateness of united action." Hence:

> The successful operation of democratic institutions depends upon several
> all-important conditions: as [first] upon homogeneity of race and com-

munity of thought and purpose among the people. There is no amalgam in democracy which can harmoniously unite races of diverse habits and instincts or unequal acquirements in thought and action. . . . The second requisite is that the nation should not only feel itself an organic, homogeneous body, but should also be accustomed or at least prepared to *act* as an organic body. Democracy is the sovereignty of the people made real. Consequently its existence is dependent upon several all-important conditions: as 1) upon a sense of unity, of community of thought and purpose among the people . . . 2) upon a habit of concerted purpose and cooperate action. The nation which is to try democracy successfully must not only feel itself an organic body, but must be accustomed to *act* as an organic body. Not Parisian mobs, but national majorities must make and unmake governments. . . . *Not a habit of revolution, but a habit of resolution must constitute the political life of the nation.*[24]

A critical aspect of an organic community was the merging of the individual will with that of the general population. To repeat: a criticism of Wilson might well be that a general will combined with a decisive leader could begin to sound like proto-fascism, for in Wilson's mind patriotism was a sentiment of common currency that both expressed and enforced the organic unity of a people he called democratic. Yet as his Reformed Protestant background would dictate, individual conscience and reason—not conformity to group thinking—must always be championed. A problem that nonetheless would inevitably surface and urgently needed to be addressed was how to handle the divisions sure to arise among a free people. Wilson's answer was to stress as much as he could the creation of the sense of a common interest that superseded that which was individual, while maintaining that with further debate, and as circumstances changed, so too might the general will. Still, the sense of unity was critical:

Patriotism in its redeeming quality resembles Christianity. Christianity makes a man forget himself and square everything that he does with a great love and a great principle, and so does patriotism. It makes him forget himself and square every thought and action with something infinitely greater than himself. I believe, and you believe, that the interests of America are coincident with the interests of the world, and that, if we can make America lead the way of example along the paths of peace and regeneration for herself, we shall enable her to lead the whole world along those paths of promise and achievement.[25]

Wilson made this assertion in 1910. Two years earlier, in a more formal statement, he had been of the same mind.

> Evidently, if a constitutional government is a government conducted on the basis of a definite understanding between those who administer it and those who obey it, there can be no constitutional government unless there be a community to sustain and develop it—unless the nation, whose instrument it is, is conscious of common interests and can form common purposes. A people not conscious of any unity, inorganic, unthoughtful, without concert of action, can manifestly neither form nor sustain a constitutional system. The lethargy of an unawakened consciousness is upon them, the helplessness of unformed purpose. They can form no common judgment; they can conceive no common end; they can contrive no common measure. Nothing but a community can have a constitutional form of government, and if a nation has not become a community, it cannot have that sort of polity.[26]

The result of a mature organic consciousness is the ability of the citizens to control the state; it is the highest form of democracy, "self-government," "government based on the consent of the governed." Here we have democracy:

> The consent of the governed must at every turn check and determine the action of those who make and execute the laws. . . . That is "constitutional government." When we speak of a constitutional government we mean a government so constituted that those who govern and those who are governed are brought by some systematic and efficient means into concord and counsel; and in which law, accordingly, is made and enforced in conformity with principles and by methods agreed upon between them. The real problem of democracy, therefore, is how to devise and maintain in full efficiency the best means of intimate counsel between those who are to make and administer the laws and those who are to obey them . . . governments should retain their power as it is that [the citizenry] should be free . . . modern democracy . . . speaks always of the sovereignty of the people, and of rulers as the people's servants. . . . Modern democracy is government subject to systematic popular control.[27]

Accordingly, the problem of leadership in a democracy is that while it must have the wisdom and the institutional autonomy to be in charge of national affairs, it must at the same time listen to the voice of the people not only to be true to the democratic creed but also out of its own self-interest to survive and to be effective. So Wilson could warn in 1889, "no reform may succeed for which the major thought of the nation is not prepared. . . . The general sense of the community may wait to be aroused and the statesman must arouse it; may be inchoate and vague, and the statesman must formulate and make it explicit. But he cannot, and should not, do more."[28]

To be sure, Wilson was quick to recognize greatness in individuals and to see that systemic crises could be especially effective in bringing them to direct a people and to reshape its organic being. On Wilson's list of great leaders (in *The State* especially) appeared many Christian moralists, and like Elizabeth I of England and Frederick the Great of Prussia, Voltaire and Carlyle, and the greatest of American statesmen, he accords them their due. Yet he takes as an example of a man of exceptional wisdom whose ideas could not take hold when he uttered them Edmund Burke, the thinker whom Wilson himself declared to be the most important influence on his own thought:

> Everyone knows that Burke's life was spent in Parliament, and everyone knows that the eloquence he poured forth there is as deathless as our literature; and yet everyone is left to wonder that he was of so little consequence in the actual direction of affairs. How noble a figure in the history of English politics: how large a man, how commanding a mind; and yet how ineffectual in the work of bringing men . . . toward the high purposes he had ever in view. "Burke is a wise man," said Fox, "but he is wise too soon." He was wise also too much. He went on from the wisdom of today to the wisdom of tomorrow, to the wisdom which is for all time; and it was impossible he should be followed so far. . . . If you would be a leader of men, you must lead your own generation, not the next. . . . Burke's genius made conservative men uneasy. How could a man be safe who had so many ideas?

So Wilson could conclude, "No cause is born out of its time. Every successful reform movement has had as its efficient cry some principle of equity or morality already accepted well-nigh universally but not yet universally applied in the affairs of life. The ear of the leader must ring with the voices of the people. He cannot be of the school of prophets; he must be of those who studiously serve the slow-paced daily needs."[29]

Given the power that he credited to society relative to that of the state, Wilson must therefore have hoped that with the maturation of self-government, society would recognize for itself the need for change, presumably lessening the burden of leadership, as power devolved from the state to the society. While leaders still would have need of autonomy based on respect and power, the ultimate authority so far as the law itself is concerned centered more and more on society. "Political liberty is the right of those who are governed to adjust government to their own needs and interests," Wilson declared in his last deliberations on the matter. Thus, "the philosophy of constitutional government" must be that "liberty fixed in unalterable law would be no liberty at all. Government is a part of life and, with life, it must change, alike in its objects and in its practices."[30]

The result, as Wilson put it in 1900, is that "Democracy is unquestionably the most wholesome and livable kind of government the world has yet tried. It supplies as no other system could the frank and universal criticism, the free play of individual thought, the open conduct of public affairs, the spirit and pride of community and of cooperation which makes governments just and public spirited."[31]

Wilson located the distinctiveness of this highest stage of democracy in the Declaration of Independence, which "expressly leaves to each generation of men the determination of what they will do with their lives, what they will prefer as the form and object of their liberty, in what they will seek their happiness."[32] Nor is the American Constitution immune from alteration. Based on the organic character of American nationalism:

> [T]here is a national unity and purpose amongst us which rest upon unwritten laws higher than any constitutions. . . . The federal Constitution is, indeed, the formal basis of the Union and its provisions while they stand must be held inviolable. . . . But it can be changed; and there is a law greater than it which cannot be changed—a law which makes the Constitution possible, without which the Constitution would be but a dead letter. . . . This is that law written on our hearts which makes us conscious of our oneness as a single personality in the great company of nations; conscious of a common interest, a common vocation, and a common destiny: not only a "spirit of '76," but a spirit for all time.[33]

In this vein Wilson could write that the United States:

> is a country not merely constitutionally governed but also self-governed. Self-government is the last, the consummate stage of constitutional development. . . . Self-government is not a mere form of institution . . .

it is a form of character. . . . [Hence democracy falls] under the theory of organic life. It is accountable to Darwin, not to Newton. . . . There can be no successful government without leadership or without the intimate, almost instinctive, coordination of the organs of life and action. . . . Living political constitutions must be Darwinian in structure and in practice . . . modified by [their] environment, necessitated by their tasks, shaped to their functions by the sheer pressure of life.[34]

CALVINISM AND WILSON'S NOTION OF A DEMOCRATIC PEOPLE AND GOVERNMENT

Wilson's understanding of the critical importance to stable government of law embedded in institutions came largely from his reading of American and English history (augmented, to be sure, by study of other peoples, and especially of the Romans). But I have seen no discussion, in Wilson's own writings or of those concerned to explain his thinking, of the extent to which his concepts reflected importantly his participation in the institutional practices of the Calvinist community. Wilson's reticence may have been due to the fact that he had so completely imbibed the conduct of his church that he failed to see how it influenced his views toward political organization in general. More likely, however, he felt that Calvinism embodied a universal prescription for democracy in institutional but not doctrinal form, a kind of social contract and relationship between the state and the citizenry that he in no way wanted to reduce to the values of a particular religious denomination.

If this notion gives insight into the character of constitutional democracy that Wilson adhered to, then it was not so much the Presbyterian *Book of Worship* that is relevant, with its outline of the religious beliefs of this community of faith, but instead the *Book of Order*, the way in which Presbyterians have organized themselves politically over some two centuries now in terms of the relationships among the clergy and the congregation. Wilson's close familiarity with the organizational form and its justifications is beyond question.[35]

As an institution, the Presbyterian Church changed doctrinally over time, but for Wilson's purposes its formal structure must have mattered most when he thought of democratic organization. By the late eighteenth century, the Church involved an expansive set of organizations composed of divinity schools, assemblies of clergy (usually including elders selected from congregations), and the congregations themselves, empowered both to hire and to expel their ministers. The checks and balances within the formal structure of the Church and between congregants and clergy were by Wilson's time a model of democratic practice.

Yet the Presbyterians lacked one essential of a state: they had no means of enjoining compliance by force. Reason and prayer alone were the glue of its unity—a unity that did not preclude the secession of the Southern Presbyterians during the Civil War to side with the Confederacy, a process in which Wilson's own father figured prominently. Indeed, this reliance on reason and conscience alone is one of the reasons Calvinists so often found their unity fragmented, as different confessions formed convinced of sectarian arguments that set back their ecumenical spirit. We might say that they had a form of "states' rights" that contradicted Wilson's own commitment to the unity of the United States and that, in fact, concerned him given his dedication to the Union.

Aside from its formal political structure, what for our purpose is the single most critical contribution of these Calvinists to Wilson's thinking was surely their Covenant. Here was the equivalent of a constitution subscribed to by members of the Church as reflecting their beliefs but subject to alteration over time. At the time he was working on drafts of the Covenant for the League of Nations, his concern as a Presbyterian was certainly not to make the world Christian but rather to make it "constitutional" in the sense of having institutions capable of formulating rules that would be the basis of international law promoting the common peace and responding to the perceived need of humanity to keep the world from war.

For Presbyterians, the Covenant was (and is today) an expression of the "general will" in the sense that its terms were generated by, then binding upon, the members of the congregation. Yet at the same time, the congregation could change these terms; to represent it as a final statement of faith would have contradicted basic premises of these Calvinists. For by the late eighteenth century, American Calvinists were coming to believe that those who were certain they knew God's will were likely to be blasphemers—who else could proudly claim to possess such knowledge?—and hence the congregation became tolerant of those who questioned their beliefs and aware of the need for discussions of change in their own creed.

In this account, Wilson's appreciation of the dependence of a constitution on the spirit of the people is apparent. Constitution making and remaking were thus at the core of Presbyterian worship of God, but with one proviso:

only through reason and conscience could an individual or a group hope to know God's will, and this interpretation was open to error and so to correction.

In such circumstances, ordained ministers necessarily enjoyed a special role. They had the religious vocation and academic training to equip them to be community leaders. Still, a congregation needed to assent to a minister's role, and should it later come to disagree with him (and more recently *her*) the minister might well be discharged from their local functions. Power was thus democratically structured. Moreover, the individual was empowered to have his or her own interpretation of living a proper life, as Wilson frequently insisted. There is no reason that a Calvinist such as Wilson would do other than endorse Martin Luther's famous statement at the tribunal of the Diet of the Holy Roman Empire put in place to judge him for heresy at Worms in 1521: "Unless I am convinced by the testimony of the Scriptures or by clear reason (for I do not trust either in the pope or in councils alone, since it is well known that they have often erred and contradicted themselves), I am bound by the Scriptures I have quoted and my conscience is captive to the Word of God. I cannot and will not recant anything, since it is neither safe nor right to go against conscience. May God help me. Amen." (Luther is sometimes also quoted as saying: "Here I stand. I can do no other," which many authorities argue is a later interpolation.)

Yet reason combined with conscience was not enough for Wilson and the Presbyterians. An institutional form with a constitution needed to be elaborated, which takes us to that key aspect of social organization in Wilson's religious life, the Presbyterian practice of covenanting. The noted theologian Richard Niebuhr (brother of Reinhold) wrote:

> Covenant meant that political society was neither purely natural nor merely contractual, based on common interest. Covenant was the binding together in one body politic of persons who assumed through unlimited promise responsibility to and for each other and for the common laws, under God. It was government of the people, for the people and by the people but always under God, and it was not natural birth into natural society that made one a complete member of a people but always the moral act of taking upon oneself, through promise, the responsibilities of a citizenship that bound itself in the very act of exercising its freedom. For in the covenant conception the essence of freedom does not lie in the liberty of choice among goods, but in the ability to

commit oneself for the future to a cause . . . as moral man he was a being who could be trusted or ought to be trustworthy because he had given his word, pledged himself to be faithful to the cause and the fellow-servants of the cause.[36]

The transposition of the Presbyterian practice of covenanting to the creation in the United States of constitutional government is transparent. As we have already seen, Wilson put it clearly enough in *Constitutional Government*:

[P]olitical liberty is the right of those who are governed to adjust government to their own needs and interests. . . . Liberty fixed in unalterable law would be no liberty at all. Government is a part of life and, with life, it must change, alike in its objects and its practices. Only this principle must remain unaltered, this principle of liberty, that there must be the freest right and opportunity of adjustment. . . .

[Thus democracy is] a quick concert of thought, uttered by those who know how to guide both counsel and action . . . institutions are creatures of opinion. Their breath and vigor goes out of them when they cease to be sustained by the conscious or habitual preference of the people whose practice has created them; and new institutions take their place when once that practice is altered.

That is what gives dignity to citizenship among a free people. Every man's thought is part of the vital substance of his institutions. With the change of his thought, institutions themselves may change. That is what constitutes citizenship so responsible and solemn a thing. Every man in a free country is, as it were, put upon his honor to be the kind of man such a polity supposes its citizens to be: a man with his thought upon the general welfare, his interest consciously linked with the interests of his fellow-citizens, his sense of duty broadened to the scope of public affairs. . . .

"Eternal vigilance is the price of liberty." The threadbare phrase seems new stuff when we wear it on our understandings. . . . It is the essence of a constitutional system that its people should think straight, maintain a consistent purpose, look before and after, and make their lives the image of their thoughts.[37]

From the sphere of Calvinism to that of democratic government of a people religiously plural was a giant step. But Wilson took his approach even further, for the Covenant of the League of Nations rather clearly emerges exactly from this credo as well. As Wilson explained the League's spirit to the American public on his Western Tour in the fall of 1919:

> [T]he principle of public right must henceforth take precedence over the individual interests of particular nations, and that the nations of the world must in some way band themselves together to see that that right prevails as against any sort of selfish aggression . . . that there must be a common agreement for a common object, and that at the heart of that common object must lie the inviolable rights of peoples and of mankind. It is to their interest that they should understand each other. In order that they may understand each other, it is imperative that they should agree to cooperate in a common cause and that they should so act that the guiding principle of that common cause shall be even-handed and impartial justice . . . some common force will be brought into existence which shall safeguard right as the first and most fundamental interest of all peoples and all governments, when coercion shall be summoned not to the service of political ambition or selfish hostility, but to the service of a common order, a common justice and a common peace.[38]

Wilson thus had it exactly right when he emotionally declared to the public assembled in Kansas City on September 6, 1919: "I have come out to fight for a cause. That cause is greater than the Senate. It is greater than the government. It is as great as the cause of mankind, and I intend, in office or out, to fight that battle as long as I live. My ancestors were troublesome Scotchmen and many of them were some of that famous group that was known as the Covenanters. Very well, here is the Covenant of the League of Nations. I am a Covenanter!"[39]

THE AMERICAN REVOLUTION OF 1776 VERSUS THE FRENCH REVOLUTION OF 1789

A telling example of what Wilson meant by the preconditions for democratic life comes from his contrast of the American and French Revolutions. Throughout his life Wilson took special pains to privilege the success of the American Revolution over what he considered with undisguised disdain to be the failures of the French. As early as 1879 (when he was only twenty-two), Wilson had written a long essay entitled "Self-Government in France," wherein he set out the major differences between France and Great Britain in terms of their religious and political institutions.[40] Over time, he expressed his opinions more sharply. Thus, by 1885, Wilson was phrasing his argument in terms of an important comparative political question:

> Why has democracy been a cordial and a tonic to little Switzerland and big America, while it has been as yet only a quick intoxicant or a slow poison to France and Spain, a mere maddening draught to the South American states? Why has England approached democratic institutions by slow and steady stages of deliberate and peaceful development, while so many other states have panted toward democracy through constant revolution? Why has democracy existed in America and in Australia virtually from the first, while other states have utterly failed in their efforts to establish it? What is democracy that it should be possible to some, impossible as yet to others?[41]

The answer came easily to him. The French Revolution had been directed against both the state as a system and the Roman Catholic Church as an institution, but it had no traditional rights or institutions to substitute for that which it destroyed. By contrast, the American Revolution had been waged in the name of long-established English rights—more against a specific monarch (George III) than the idea of limited monarchy itself—and this with the backing of powerful religious organizations in the United States, surely none more determined than the Presbyterian Church, of which Wilson and his family had been prominent members for generations.

Put differently, Throne and Altar—the very foundations of political and cultural order—were under attack in France, without any consensus on what was to replace them. By contrast, American revolutionaries targeted only a particular king and only quite indirectly a particular church (the Anglican), while rebelling in the name of established English values, traditions, and institutions, and all of this with the blessing of leading American Protestant religious authorities. Hence Wilson's explanation in 1885:

> There is almost nothing in common between popular reactions such as took place in France at her great Revolution and the development of a government like that of the United States or Switzerland. Democracy in Europe . . . has acted always in rebellion, as a destructive force: it can scarcely be said to have had, even yet, any period of organic development. . . . Democracy in America, on the other hand, and in the En-

glish colonies, has had, almost from the first, a truly organic growth. There was nothing revolutionary in its movements: it had not to over-throw other politics, it had only to organize itself. It had not to create but only to expand self-government. . . . It was this democracy, the natural growth of transplanted English politics, that was to serve as the norm of social development for other races less habituated to orderly change than the English race.[42]

As he put it again in 1896:

The American Revolution wrought a radical work of change in the world: it created a new nation and a new polity. But it was a work of conservation after all, as fundamentally conservative as the revolution of 1688 or the extortion of Magna Carta. . . . Its object was the preservation of a body of liberties, to keep the natural course of English development in America clear of impediment. . . . If it brought change, it was the change of maturity, the fulfillment of destiny, the appropriate fruitage of wholesale and steady growth. It was part of English liberty that America should be free. . . . There is nothing so conservative of life as growth: when that stops, decay sets in and the end comes on apace. Progress is life, for the body politic as for the body natural. To stand still is to court death.[43]

And still more:

The English alone have approached popular institutions through habit. All other races have rushed prematurely into them through mere impatience with habit: have adopted democracy instead of cultivating it. A particular form of government may no more be adopted than a particular type of character may be adopted: both institutions and character must be developed by conscious effort and through transmitted aptitudes. . . . It is not the result of accident merely . . . that the English race has been the only race standing forward amidst the fierce contests of national rivalries—that has succeeded in establishing and maintaining the most liberal forms of popular government. It is, on the contrary, a perfectly natural outcome of organic development.[44]

By contrast, the French had revolted in the name of liberty, as had the peoples of Latin America, but without enjoying the precedents that could lead to the establishment of a set of shared values and institutions that could meet these new demands, to be embodied in a set of laws backed by forceful institutions and resting on a wide public consensus. For these people, stable democratic government was unlikely to appear. As he put it yet again in 1901:

> It is plain enough that the reason why the English in America got self-government and knew how to use it, and the French in America did not, was that the English had had a training under the kings of England and the French under the kings of France. In the one country men did all things at the bidding of officers of the crown; in the other, officers of the crown listened, were constrained to listen, to the counsels of lay-men drawn out of the general body of the nation. . . . No doubt a king did hold us together until we learned how to hold together of our-selves. No doubt our unity as a nation does come from the fact that we once obeyed a king.[45]

Hence, whereas liberty through law could be achieved in places of English heritage, elsewhere liberty more often than not meant chaos. The reason was obvious enough: "A people not conscious of any unity, inorganic, un-thoughtful, without concert of action, can manifestly neither form nor sus-tain a constitutional system. . . . They can form no common judgment; they can conceive no common end; they can contrive no common measures."[46]

As a result, Wilson could cite Edmund Burke with approval when he de-clared in 1790, "the French Revolution is the most astonishing event that has hitherto happened in the world," yet then went on to wonder where such an enthusiasm for liberty might lead if unrestrained by law embedded in institu-tions that created and enforced them:

> When I see the spirit of liberty in action, I see a strong principle at work; and this for a while is all I can possible know of it. . . . We ought to suspend our judgment . . . until we see something deeper than the agitation of a troubled and frothy surface. . . . I should therefore sus-pend my congratulations on the new liberty of France until I was in-formed how it had been combined with government, with public force, with the discipline and obedience of armies, with the collection of an effective and well-distributed revenue, with morality and religion, with solidity and property, with peace and order, with civil and social man-ners . . . without them, liberty is not a benefit whilst it lasts and not likely to continue long.[47]

Wilson's assault on the French never ended. It had started as early as 1879, and at the end of his life, he was still hammering away at their revolution. As he wrote at the end of his life in 1922, there was still no organic strength to that country. Instead, "France, caught in a luminous fog of political theory, was groping her way from revolution to revolution in bewildered search of a firm ground upon which to build a permanent government."[48]

COULD THE AMERICAN
EXPERIENCE BE EXPORTED?

We should recall at this point that in the introduction to this book, I argued not only that in theoretical terms democracy promotion was the central feature of American liberal internationalism, but that in historical terms as well, Woodrow Wilson had made the expansion of democratic government a centerpiece of the new world order he wanted America to put forward after he became president in 1913. Yet the evidence in this chapter would seem rather to suggest quite forcefully that such an undertaking would be a difficult, perhaps an impossible, undertaking. Where were the peoples whose historical experience had subjected them to anything like the combination of forces that had brought about modern democracy in the United States: the influence of Christianity (and especially, in more recent times, the Protestant Reformation), Germanic feudalism, the Renaissance and the Enlightenment, the experience of being brought up under the strictures of English law, customs, and institutions? And who were the peoples capable of producing the leaders, institutions, laws, and organic social contracts that could hope to measure up against what had been the experience of the English-speaking peoples (augmented by others of Teutonic origins, such as the Scandinavians and the Dutch, with special commendation for the Swiss)? Few indeed they surely were, and hence there was reason to doubt that an American policy of worldwide democracy promotion would bear fruit quickly, easily, or indeed at all.

In fact, none other than Woodrow Wilson could be cited to this effect. Consider his requirement for democratic self-government in 1885:

Democracy is wrongly conceived when treated as merely a body of doctrine. It is a stage of development. It is not created by aspirations or by a new faith; it is built up by slow habit. Its process is experiences, its basis old wont, its meaning national organic oneness and effectual life.

It comes, like manhood, as the fruit of youth . . . the maturity to which it is vouchsafed is the maturity of freedom and self-control, and no other. It is conduct, and its only stable foundation is character.[49]

Two decades later Wilson's mind had not changed in his last academic publication, *Constitutional Government*, published in 1908:

[N]o body of people could constitute a community in any true or practical sense who did not have a distinct consciousness of common ties and interests, a common manner and standard of life and conduct, and a practiced habit of union and concerted action in whatever affected it as a whole . . . only a community can have a constitutional government. No body of people which is not clearly conscious of common interests and of common standards of life and happiness can come to any satisfactory agreement with its government, and no people which has not a habit of union and concerted action in regard to its affairs could secure itself against the breach of such an agreement if it existed. . . .

[I]f constitutional government is a government conducted on the basis of a definite understanding between those who administer it and those who obey it, there can be no constitutional government unless there be a community to sustain and develop it—unless the nation, whose instrument it is, is conscious of common interests and can form common purposes.[50]

So, too, in various editions of *The State*, including both the first, dated 1889, and the last before he became president, dated 1911, Wilson writes in ways that make it seem that but for the peoples of the North Atlantic, and those further afield of British ancestry, democracy is an unlikely form of government to appear. As he described it:

Government is merely the executive organ of society, the organ through which its habit acts, through which its will becomes operative, through which it adapts itself to its environment and works out for itself a more effective life. There is clear reason, therefore, why . . . sudden or violent changes of government lead to equally violent and often fatal reactions and revolutions. It is only the exceptional individual who is not held fast to the common habit of social duty and comity. The despot's power, like the potter's, is limited by the characteristics of the materials in which he works, of the society which he manipulates. . . .

Society, like other organisms, can be changed only by evolution, and revolution is the antipode of evolution. The public order is preserved because order inheres in the character of society.[51]

We may well wonder, on the basis of the foregoing discussion, how the United States could possibly think it might work to promote democracy for other peoples. According to Wilson's scheme, a very particular kind of political history had produced a culture with values and practices that induced its citizenry first to create, then to sustain, a government of the people and for the people. There seemed in these writings up to the 1890s to be no reason to believe that other people not of English descent, or of an ancestry equivalent to that of the English-speaking people, could ever expect to develop such a form of state. Indeed, Wilson implied exactly this in the opening of a concluding chapter of *The State* in the 1911 edition:

Human choice has in all stages of the great world-processes of politics had its part in the shaping of institutions; but it has never been within its power to proceed by leaps and bounds: it has been confined to adaptation, altogether shut out from raw invention. Institutions, like morals, like all other forms of life and conduct, had to wait upon the slow, the almost imperceptible formation of habit. The most absolute monarchs have had to learn the moods, observe the traditions, and respect the prejudices of their subjects; the most ardent reformers have had to learn that too far to outrun the more sluggish masses was to render themselves powerless. . . . Political growth refuses to be forced; and institutions have grown with the slow growth of social relationship; have changed in response, not to new theories, but to new circumstances.[52]

Or, as he put it yet more forcefully with the last entry in *The State*:

In politics nothing radically novel may safely be attempted. No result of value can ever be reached in politics except through slow and gradual development, the careful adaptations and nice modifications of growth. Nothing may be done by leaps. More than that, each people, each nation, must live upon the lines of its own experience. Nations are no more capable of borrowing experience than individuals are. The histories of other peoples may furnish us with light, but they cannot furnish us with conditions of action. Every nation must constantly keep in touch with its past; it cannot run towards its ends around sharp corners.[53]

Given these convictions, how can we conclude that Wilson saw democracy sponsored globally thanks to American power as the meaning of Lincoln's statement that the United States was "the last, best hope of earth," that he intended that the Wilsonian tradition that bears his name should see democracy promotion as its central mission? Would we not better understand Wilson as believing democracy to be the best form of government on earth, yet unlikely to be universally appreciated, much less adopted?

The argument here is basic to our consideration of Wilson's foreign policy once he became president of the United States. That he hoped democracy would expand worldwide seems self-evident; that it would necessarily do so was not a position to which he could easily subscribe. His earliest assumption was that democracy would spread rather of itself, as part of global enlightenment and the model of American success. But in due course, despite a limited enthusiasm for what can be called "progressive imperialism," his answer would be to put his hopes in the League of Nations as basic to the defense of that part of the world that was democratic and the seedbed for what might be its later expansion.

As a result, efforts to describe him as a "liberal imperialist" in his later years as president badly miss the mark. Be it toward Mexico or the Soviet Union or Germany, his prudent refusal to let the force of arms attempt to make the governments of these people into democracies was abundantly on display. The decision to go to war with Germany was taken reluctantly, initially not to sponsor democracy so much as to end a series of outrages engaged in by Berlin, which made the very idea of a civilized world community an impossibility to conceive. Only when it came time to think about a postwar order did Wilson's thinking turn to democracy, and then not so much to expand it (although that was his hope) as to protect it. Liberty required institutions capable of formulating laws serving the public good and resting on popular support. In a word, it required time and changes of a basic sort in the culture of peoples having been subjected to authoritarian rule for centuries, without which the French example was there for all to behold, oscillating between anarchy and despotism with painfully little idea of how to anchor freedom in law.

Having seen sentiments such as these spelled out in some detail, how can we maintain that democracy promotion was the central focus of Wilson's efforts as president and that it should be seen as the dominant feature of the Wilsonian tradition, indeed the central aspect (when combined with human rights promotion) of what constitutes American "exceptionalism"?

It is to explaining this matter that we now must turn in the three following chapters.

The first discusses Wilson's relatively (for the period) modest efforts to promote democracy through what we might call "progressive imperialism," by which the United States took over foreign people militarily and politically and tried to democratize them. The second turns to Wilson as a multilateralist, to his hopes that, through the creation of international organizations dedicated to a common interest for peace and to the making of rules that would be the basis of international law, democracy might be fostered worldwide for the benefit of all, or at least protected for those people capable of its practice. The leading agency to promote this ambition was to be, obviously enough, the League of Nations. The third provides a synthesis of the development of Wilson's thinking from 1885 to 1919 to the point that we may finally speak of "Wilsonianism" as a coherent set of aims for American foreign policy that could be bequeathed to later generations of Americans, and this with democratic government as its defining feature.

CHAPTER TWO

Democracy Promotion through Progressive Imperialism

It is by the widening of vision that nations, as men, grow and are made great. We need not fear the expanding scene. It was plain destiny that we should come to this . . . the [twentieth] century that shall see us a great power in the world. Let us pray that vision may come with power; let us ponder our duties like men of conscience and temper our ambitions like men who seek to serve, not to subdue, the world; let us lift our thoughts to the level of the great tasks that await us, and bring a great age in with the coming of our day of strength.

—*Woodrow Wilson's closing words in "The Ideals of America,"*
saluting the American victory over Spain in 1898, delivered
December 26, 1901, the 125th anniversary of the Battle of Trenton

The previous chapter recounted Woodrow Wilson's reservations on the likelihood that democracy could be easily or quickly (if indeed at all) promoted by outsiders for peoples beyond the English-speaking world (exception made for the Swiss and Teutonic nations). He was confident that the process would spread beyond this area, but that of its own accord as history moved forward and made for a convergence between styles of government and society by the logic of trade, education, and the growth of a middle class. That one country could democratize another other than by giving birth to it—as England had to the American colonies—was not an idea that, before 1900, Woodrow Wilson would have for a moment entertained for the United States. Democratization (should it occur) would be an internal affair, based on an evolution of cultural forces combined with visionary political leadership.

Yet by reflecting on the Spanish-American War of 1898, Wilson was able to find a mission for the United States in world affairs: fostering democracy through what I would call "progressive imperialism." Later still, he would give birth to the idea that democracy might be promoted by way of multilateral organizations dominated by Washington. But the focus of this chapter is on Wilson's efforts, first as an academic, later as president of the United States, to promote democracy through the use of force to a degree that was imperialist.

A first step for Wilson was to embrace America's democratizing mission in the Philippines. Later, he would continue in this fashion after he became president and faced the challenge of providing stability in the Western Hemisphere during the Mexican Revolution and with the opening of the Panama Canal in 1914—the same year that war broke out in Europe. Wilson's driving concern now became focused: how to provide for a stable peace based on freedom. His answer: through protecting, indeed if possible expanding, democratic government the world around as the best way to end violence among states and provide freedom to peoples.

Let us wait until the next chapter to explore Wilson's ideas of fostering democracy through multilateralism in the League and Nations—the principles of which became the heart and soul of what was to become "Wilsonianism"—concentrating here instead on the American role through progressive imperialism of achieving this goal more directly. What we also shall see here, however, is Wilson's appreciation of the limits of American power in the Western Hemisphere, evident first and most importantly from his experience dealing with the Mexican Revolution, then in his hopes for a Pan-American Treaty in 1914–1916 whereby multilateralism might foster democratic values and practices abroad in a way that could serve as a template for bringing peace to Europe.

A major problem that would face Wilson's ambition to play an active role in the global expansion of democracy was the isolationist tradition in American foreign policy set in place by George Washington. Washington's warning, combined with a widespread domestic sentiment (which much of Wilson's own writings implicitly endorsed, as we saw in the preceding chapter) that only peoples of English descent or Teutonic ancestry were capable of being democratic, meant Wilson's task was no easy matter.

In promoting his ideas on progressive imperialism, Wilson was doubtless helped by the example of Theodore Roosevelt, who had been president from September 1901 to March 1909. As political science professor Adam

Quinn has pointed out, Roosevelt was the first president not only to make international greatness a national mission for the United States, but also to tie this ambition to a "civilizing mission" that was self-consciously imperialist. Nevertheless, there were two important differences between Roosevelt and Wilson: the former was unabashedly militaristic, whereas Wilson was not; and Wilson tied his objectives to a policy of democracy promotion, which it is not evident that Roosevelt's conception of "uplifting humanity" involved.[1]

Wilson's challenge was therefore twofold. On the one hand, he had to orient Americans toward a new sense of themselves, not so much as being Protestants of British descent but rather as being constitutional democrats. Here were steps toward what later would be called "the melting pot," the notion put on the Great Seal of the United States at the suggestion of Benjamin Franklin and others of *E pluribus unum*, one people out of many. But a way to foster this nationalist identity had yet to be found convincing in elite circles. Wilson's contribution was to give Americans a sense that their national identity as democrats implied a worldwide mission to support constitutional movements abroad, not simply for the sake of national security but with the goal of creating over time a region, perhaps a world, of stable states based on cooperation among people living in liberty. In the process, to champion freedom for others would enhance unity and freedom for the United States as well.[2] Wilson's success in this dual endeavor laid the foundation for what would later be called Wilsonianism. Constitutional democracy would become at once a feature of the American national identity and a characteristic of this country's considerations with respect to its national security.

Nevertheless, there was a distinct reservation in Wilson's initial conceptualization of the appeal of democracy worldwide. In his earliest statements on the global movement toward democracy, Woodrow Wilson found that what might be called "the winds of History" were pushing all peoples in this direction so that the United States need serve only as an example, by its success, of what others might achieve for its accomplishments to be imitated. Material progress, the spread of education, and cosmopolitan exchanges could well encourage other peoples to model themselves after the democracies, especially as these more modern countries would inevitably become more powerful in world affairs. Convergence would come of itself.

"We can nowadays discern a tendency, long operative but only of late days predominant, towards the adoption of the same general principles of government everywhere," Wilson wrote as early as 1885:

Governments are tending to become alike. Monarchies are being put into the straight-jackets of popular constitutions . . . [as a consequence, there might come into being an] equally great principle of confederation. There is to be wide union, with divisions of prerogative instead of universal centralization of power; cooperation with individual independence. There are tendencies towards a common governmental type, and that type the American.[3]

Four years later, in *The State*, he reiterated this conviction:

If Aristocracy seems about to disappear, Democracy seems about universally to prevail. Ever since the rise of popular education in the last century has assured a thinking weight of the masses of the people everywhere, the advance of democratic opinion and the spread of democratic institutions have been most marked and most significant. They have destroyed almost all pure forms of Monarchy and Aristocracy by introducing into them imperative forces of popular thought and the concrete institutions of popular representation; and they promise to reduce politics to a single form by excluding all other governing forces and institutions but those of a wide suffrage and a democratic representation—by reducing all forms of government to Democracy.[4]

It is evident from these quotations that in the 1890s, Wilson's view of the global spread of democracy did not involve a break in the American tradition of isolationism. Instead, democracy would spread by virtue of general conditions in the world gradually changing, a leading element of which would be the example the United States set for others to emulate. True, in 1891, Wilson was speaking "not of national so much as international and common forces," as the "Spirit of the Age," terms that nevertheless did not indicate the necessity of a forward policy on the part of the United States to advance the movement.[5]

The advent of a world dominated by democratic peoples nevertheless appealed to Wilson as the coming of a new age, one to be typified by freedom and prosperity and especially by peace:

If democracy fulfill the best and most characteristic of its promises, its coming will be the establishment of the most humane results of the world's peace and progress, the substitution of agreement for command, of common rights of purposing for exclusive rights of purposing—the supreme and peaceful rule of counsel. The goal of political development is identical with the goal of individual development. Both singly and collectively man's nature draws him away from that which is brutish towards that which is human—away from his kinship with beasts towards a fuller realization of his kinship with God. The rule of counsel, the catholic spirit of free debate, is an earnest of the ascendancy of reason over passion. Society has attained to its full manhood when it has put away crude hasty action and has come to guide itself by the slow resolutions of deliberate choice. This manhood of society is the promise of democracy.[6]

As we have seen in the previous chapter, the reasons for Wilson's confidence in democracy rested on his conviction that such a people, working together in such a polity, would combine reason with morality in a way that would ennoble the human condition. Such a community and their leaders could see the common interest predominate over special interests, the good of all emerging from reasoned argument based on a moral commitment to progress. As he put it in 1900:

Democracy is unquestionably the most wholesome and livable kind of government the world has yet tried. It supplies as no other system could the frank and universal criticism, the free play of individual thought, the open conduct of public affairs, the spirit and pride of community and of cooperation which make governments just and public-spirited.[7]

However, the obvious question was whether democracy would indeed spread globally. There was abundant reason for Wilson to conclude before 1898 that American foreign policy would have much to do with this prospect.

REFLECTIONS ON THE SPANISH-AMERICAN WAR OF 1898

Yet with the Spanish-American War, Wilson's tone changed dramatically—not with respect to his faith in democracy but in terms of how the United States should anticipate its expansion globally.[8] In October 1900, Wilson gave an important talk on the place of democracy in America's thinking about world affairs, declaring, "A new era has come upon us like a sudden vision of things unprophesied. . . . Our almost accidental possession of the Philippines has put us in the very presence of the forces which must make the politics of the twentieth century radically unlike the politics of the nine-teenth." Now he could foresee the United States playing an active role in democracy promotion, and this for its own sake as well as for the peoples to be brought into the democratic fold. "We have taught the world the princi-ple of the general welfare as the object and end of government, rather than the prosperity of any class or section of the nation, or the preferment of any private or petty interest." As a consequence, "Germany, Canada, Australia, Switzerland herself, have built and strengthened their constitutions in large part upon our model."

But Wilson also sounded a note of alarm. Where he had once seen a con-vergence of peoples on democratic order, now instead he warned that afoot in the world was the "peril of reactionary revolution" against the model the United States represented. Faced with this danger, Wilson appealed to his fellow Americans:

> We have made the law appear to all men an instrument wherewith to secure equality of rights and a protection which shall be without respect of persons. . . . [Yet we] are now put in such jeopardy amidst the con-test of nations, the future of mankind faces so great a peril of reaction-ary revolution . . . [that] we dare not stand neutral.
>
> All mankind deem us the representatives of the moderate and sensi-ble discipline which makes free men good citizens, of enlightened sys-tems of law and a temperate justice, of the best experience in the reason-able methods and principles of self-government, of public force made consistent with individual liberty; and we shall not realize these ideals at home if we suffer them to be hopelessly discredited amongst the peo-ples who have yet to see liberty and the peaceable days of order and comfortable progress.
>
> We should lose heart ourselves, did we suffer the world to lose faith in us as the champions of these things.

Nor did Wilson stop there. "We have, like provincials, too habitually con-fined our view to the range of our own experiences. . . . [But] our interests must march forward, altruists though we are; other nations must see to it that they stand off and do not seek to stay us." His words deserve to be cited at some length, for they mark a critical turn in Wilson's own thinking and to the Wilsonian tradition that would eventually carry his arguments forward. Speaking at length of "experiments in the universal validity of principle and method," he asked that "justice may be done to the lowly no less than to the great; that government may serve its people, not make itself their master . . . that authority may be for leadership, not for aggrandizement; that the people may be the state."

> [I]t is our present task to extend self-government to Puerto Rico and the Philippines. . . . [Before our conquest] the whole world had already become a single vicinage; each part had become neighbor to all the rest. . . . The East is to be opened and transformed, whether we will or no; the standards of the West are to be imposed upon it; nations and peoples which have stood still the centuries through are to be quickened and made part of the universal world of commerce and of ideas which has so steadily been a-making by the advance of European power from age to age. It is our peculiar duty, as it is also England's, to moderate the process in the interests of liberty; to impart to the peoples thus driven out upon the road of change . . . our own principles of self-help; teach them order and self-control in the midst of change; impart to them . . . the drill and habit of law and obedience . . . secure for them the free intercourse and natural development which shall make them at least equal members of the family of nations. In China, of course, our part will be indirect, but in the Philippines it will be direct. . . .
>
> This we shall do . . . by giving [the Filipinos], in the spirit of service, a government and rule which shall moralize them by being itself moral, elevate and steady them by being itself pure and steadfast, inducting them into the rudiments of justice and freedom . . . we shall ourselves recognize the fact . . . that the service of democracy has been the development of ideals. . . . We shall teach them order as a condition precedent to liberty, self-control as a condition precedent to self-government.[9]

We must take care to stress that in Wilson's mind, what we might today call "progressive imperialism" would benefit the United States itself not so much economically or geopolitically but above all *morally*. "Until 1890 the United States had always a frontier; looked always to a region beyond, unoccupied, unappropriated, an outlet for its energy, a new place of settlement and of achievement. . . . There was always space and adventure enough and to spare, to satisfy the feet of our young men." The question of how America would find purpose when its continental expansion had been completed could now be answered: "These new duties now thrust upon us will not break [our] unity. They will perpetuate it, rather, and make it complete." Indeed, taking self-government to others might teach America more about its own methods of self-government: "The reactions which such experiments in the universal validity of principle and method are likely to bring about in respect of our own domestic institutions cannot be calculated or forecast."[10] Nevertheless, the main beneficiaries of American benevolence would be others.

> We have sympathized with freedom everywhere; have deemed it niggardly to deny an equal degree of freedom to any race or community that desired it; have pressed handsome principles of equity in international dealings; have rejoiced to believe that our principles might someday make every government a servant, not a master, of its people. Ease and prosperity have made us wish the whole world to be as happy and well-to-do as ourselves; and we have supposed that institutions and principles like our own were the simple prescription for making them so.[11]

AMERICAN DEMOCRATIZATION
OF THE PHILIPPINES

The critical point to make with respect to America's quick victory over Spain in 1898 (the local repercussions within the Philippines were to continue on for years with heavy loss of life) was that Wilson could find that the United States had now entered its period of "manhood" among the nations. Had some other American leader been speaking of the American conquest of the Philippines, the subject of the speech might have focused on the archipelago's geostrategic position in the Pacific or its commercial promise to nearby China—each served by the magnificent harbor of Manila Bay. President William McKinley himself identified America's mission as bringing Christianity to the Filipinos, thereby betraying a Protestant disdain for Catholicism typical of his times. But for Wilson, the United States was not thinking in self-interested commercial terms about its own national security or a religious crusade. Instead, he anticipated the country using the Philippines as an example of what a "disinterested" friend the United States might be to the inhabitants of this former Spanish colony by making it into a democratic nation.

In the course of a year after he first laid out a new historical destiny for the United States in 1900, Wilson's tone grew still more insistent. In an address entitled "The Ideals of America," delivered in December 1901, in commemoration of the 125th anniversary of the Battle of Trenton—the first clear military victory of the colonists in the revolution against Britain—Wilson expressed again an unalloyed pride in what the American experience meant for the world. His spirit was far different from what we encountered in his writings prior to the Spanish-American War. No longer was his country simply to be emulated; it could take positive actions to promote democracy worldwide. In 1776, "in our stroke for independence, we struck a blow for all the world," he declared. By revolting in the name of traditional English values, "We had begun the work of freeing England when we completed the work of freeing ourselves."

If the idea here was that the British road to democracy was helped along its way simply by example, in the Philippines, by contrast, America would promote democracy by conquest. Two of his pronouncements were especially striking. As one of the country's leading historians, Wilson found that:

> No war ever transformed us quite as the war with Spain transformed us. No previous years ever ran with so swift a change as the years since 1898. We have witnessed a new revolution. We have seen the transformation of America complete. . . . The Battle of Trenton was not more significant than the Battle of Manila. The nation that was 125 years in the making has now stepped forth into the open arena of the world.

Then, calling Americans, thanks to the Spanish-American War, nothing less than "apostles of liberty and self-government," Wilson proclaimed: "We fought but the other day to give Cuba self-government. It is a point of conscience with us that the Philippines shall have it, too, when our work there is done and they are ready." In other words, America had now come of age, and its self-appointed mission was to make the world a better place, and this through democracy promotion. Confident in his judgment, Wilson closed his address asserting: "nations, as men, grow and are made great. We need not fear the expanding scene. It was plain destiny that we should come to this . . . let us ponder our duties like men of conscience and temper our ambitions like men who seek to serve, not to subdue, the world; let us lift our thoughts to the level of the great tasks that await us, and bring a great age in with the coming of our day of strength."[12]

Wilson's approach to progressive imperialism derived from his earlier writings on the origins of democracy in America. As English discipline had done for the future United States, so too, he maintained, American discipline would do for the Philippines. "Liberty is not itself government," the future president affirmed. "In the wrong hands—in hands unpracticed, undisciplined—it is incompatible with government. Discipline must precede it—if necessary the discipline of being under masters. Then will self-control make it a thing of life and not a thing of tumult, a tonic, not an insurgent madness in the blood." Hence for the Philippines: "We cannot give them any quittance of the debt than we ourselves have paid. They can have liberty no cheaper than we got it. They must first take the discipline of law, must first love order and instinctively yield to it. . . . We are old in this learning and must be their tutors."

Wilson took pains to be clear. The United States must "govern with a strong hand that will brook no resistance." He mocked those who would give the islands "independence" without solidly implanted institutions, else they have:

> . . . the independence of a rudderless boat adrift. But self-government? How is that "given"? Can it be given? Is it not gained, earned, graduated into from the hard school of life? . . . You cannot call a miscellaneous people, unknit, scattered, diverse of race and speech and habit, a nation, a community. That, at least, we got by serving under kings: we got the feeling and the organic structure of a community. No people can form a community or be wisely subjected to a common form of government who are as diverse and as heterogeneous as the people of the Philippines Islands. They are in no wise knit together. They are of many races, of many stages of development, economically, socially, politically disintegrate, without community of feeling because without community of life, contrasted alike in experience and in habit, having nothing in common except that they lived for hundreds of years together under a government which held them always where they were when it first arrested their development.[13]

To be sure, a secular notion of American exceptionalism divorced from explicit racial or religion notions but based instead on this country's governmental institutions and civic virtue—America as "the last, best hope of earth" (Lincoln), America as "the ark of the liberties of the world" (Melville)—goes back to the American Revolution, when such assurances were fervently advanced not only by Thomas Paine but by Washington, Franklin, Adams, and many others. In their eyes, as in Wilson's, one need not be Christian or of British descent to share with Americans a desire for constitutional democracy.

However, Wilson was now pushing his viewpoint in an increasingly multiethnic immigrant America, one that needed a unifying theme more than ever. His definition of American national identity differed sharply from the terms of Manifest Destiny, suggesting God had ordained American expansion, and so legitimizing this country's occupation of the continent from sea to shining sea in mid-century (taking a generous portion of Mexico in the process). His definition differed as well from Social Darwinism, with its arguments for racial inequality where the white race (especially from northern Europe) reigned supreme. The threat of these doctrines was not only to increase ethno-religious divisions within the United States but to reinforce as well American insularity from the major contests of world events. By redirecting American feelings about the world outside to one based on its democratic character—and away from one that was racial or religious—Americans might continue to feel superior, even exceptional, but nonetheless involved in developments outside their borders in a more expansive and positive fashion. Indeed, if more of the world came to be democratic—and from his early writings on, Wilson was convinced this might eventually be the case—then the American mission in global affairs would correspondingly gain in stature, building as it did so a patriotic unity at home bridging the multiple divisions of race, religion, ethnicity, class, and geographic allegiance that continued to trouble the United States. Accordingly, as he put it in 1910, "The manifest destiny of America is not to rule the world by physical force . . . but its leadership and destiny are that she shall do the thinking of the world."[14]

In reflecting on these matters, Wilson and his wife became fans of Rudyard Kipling, keeping a book of his poems with them and appreciating especially "The White Man's Burden," which Kipling published in 1899 in celebration of the American takeover of the Philippines.[15] Its first and last stanzas bear repeating:

Take up the White Man's burden-
Send forth the best ye breed-
Go bind your sons to exile
To serve your captives' need;
To wait in heavy harness,
On fluttered folk and wild-
your new-caught sullen peoples,
Half-devil and half-child. . . .

Take up the White Man's burden-
Have done with childish days-

The lightly proferred laurel,
The easy, ungrudged praise.
Comes now, to search your manhood
Through all the thankless years,
Cold-edged with dear-bought wisdom,
The judgment of your peers!

Here, then, is a foundation stone of Wilsonianism: the conviction that democratic culture and political institutions, combined with economic power and geostrategic advantage, gave the United States an exceptional role to play on the stage of history. By its very nature, democracy was anti-imperialist, for it permitted distinct peoples to follow their own destinies (what Wilson later called "self-determination") in hopes that their route would be democratic (what Wilson labeled "self-government"). Should this higher goal one day be reached, then the prospects for a world of freedom and peace would be substantially improved. But for this to happen, the American tradition of isolationism had to be overcome by a different view of America's national security, one that linked it firmly to the evolution of political events across the seas and where its most abiding hope was to foster constitutional orders of freedom for others.

That was in 1900 and 1901. However, Wilson's interest in the Philippines continued for another two decades. In 1908, he returned yet again to the matter in a manner that sums up his convictions as to the origins of democratic government, here or in other places that he might encounter thereafter, a distinctly conservative argument that privileged institution and character building above all else:

> We can give the Filipinos constitutional government, a government which they may count upon to be just, a government based on some clear and equitable understanding, intended for their good and not for our aggrandizement; but we must ourselves for the present supply that government. It would, it is true, be an unprecedented operation, reversing the process of Runnymede, but America has before this shown the world enlightened processes of politics that were without precedent. It would have been within the choice of John to summon his barons to Runnymede and of his own initiative enter into a constitutional understanding with them; and it is within our choice to do a similar thing, at once wise and generous, in the government of the Philippine Islands.

But we cannot give them self-government. Self-government is not a thing that can be "given" to any people, because it is a form of character and not a form of constitution. No people can be "given" the self-control of maturity. Only a long apprenticeship of obedience can secure them the precious possession, a thing no more to be bought than given. They cannot be presented with the character of a community, but it may confidently be hoped that they will become a community under the wholesome and salutary influences of just laws and a sympathetic administration; that they will after a while understand and master themselves, if in the meantime they are understood and served in good conscience by those set over them in authority. . . .

Having ourselves gained self-government by a definite process which can have no substitute, let us put the peoples dependent upon us in the right way to gain it also.[16]

Thereafter, as president, Wilson kept his eye on the Philippines, a constant example of what progressive imperialism might achieve. So, in his Annual Address to Congress in December 1913, he lauded the work he had done in the few months he had been in office by according the islands "a majority in both houses of their legislative body." This and other measures will mean that

Step by step we should extend and perfect the system of self-government in these islands, making test of them and modifying them as experience discloses their success and their failures; that we should more and more put under the control of the native citizens of the archipelago the essential instruments of their life, their local instrumentalities of government, their schools, all the common interests of their communities, and so by counsel and experience set up a government which all the world will see to be suitable to a people whose affairs are under their own control. . . . We must hold steadily in view their ultimate independence, and we must move toward the time of that independence as steadily as the way can be cleared and the foundations thoughtfully and permanently laid.[17]

Accordingly, in 1916 President Wilson endorsed the Philippine Autonomy Act, known as the Jones Act, which permitted the creation of the first fully elected national Philippine legislature by the fall of that year. In his last State of the Union Address, in December 1920, President Wilson was able to salute the creation of a stable government in the Philippines in line with American expectations. The United States had indeed effectively "reversed the process of Runnymede." So he could conclude triumphantly: "I respectfully submit that this condition precedent having been fulfilled, it is now our liberty and duty to keep our promise to the people of those Islands by granting them the independence which they so honorably covet."[18]

DEMOCRACY PROMOTION IN MEXICO DURING ITS GREAT REVOLUTION

If evidence is needed of Wilson's ability to act decisively on matters of world affairs upon becoming president, and this with respect to his understanding of the virtues of democratic government, his policy toward Mexico should lay any doubts to rest. This observation is especially true of the "nonrecognition doctrine" that Wilson issued only weeks after assuming the presidency in 1913. Here Wilson acted quickly and decisively, in terms of a policy that had little precedent in American (or indeed European) policy, for it was based on the presumption that Washington would do as best it could to encourage the Mexican Revolution in the direction of stable constitutional democracy.

In 1910, a great revolution began to sweep Mexico against the autocratic rule of Porfirio Diaz, who had monopolized power (except for a brief interlude in 1884) since he had seized it in 1877. In May 1911 Diaz resigned. Francisco Madero, a democratic reformer much of the stripe that Wilson wanted to encourage, became president. Though a fragile constitutional order was now being set in place, serious differences remained to plague the revolutionary forces. Finally, in February 1913, the forces of counterrevolution triumphed when General Victoriano Huerta murdered Madero and took power.[19] Ten days later Wilson was inaugurated as president.

As the State Department informed the new president, standard America procedure would be to recognize the Huerta government forthwith, for it seemed in effective control of the country. Prior to Wilson, the United States—like other world powers—had acted in accordance with Secretary of State James Buchanan's words in 1848: "We do not go behind the existing Government to involve ourselves in the question of legitimacy. It is sufficient for us to know that a government exists, capable of maintaining itself, and then its recognition on our part invariably follows."[20] The American ambassador to Mexico, who had conspired with Huerta in Madero's death, and a number of businessmen with large investments in Mexico argued as the State Department did. By the end of March 1913, Great Britain (whose preference had for some time been to recognize only constitutional regimes) and most other powers had extended recognition to the new government in Mexico City.[21]

Wilson would have none of it. As we might expect from his dedication to democracy promotion for the sake of other peoples but also for American security, by flouting respect for constitutional rule Huerta was setting a precedent for Mexico that Wilson believed could only perpetuate instability there, to the detriment of regional peace and so American interests, not to speak of the well-being of the Mexican people. As Wilson put it in a letter dated November 2, 1913, "I lie awake at night praying that the most terrible [outcome] may be averted. No man can tell what will happen while we deal with a desperate brute like that traitor, Huerta. God save us from the worst."[22]

In his draft of an address to Congress that Wilson had already written only two days prior to this letter, the president declared:

> We are bound by every obligation of honor and by compulsion of sacred interests which go to the very foundations of our national life to constitute ourselves the champions of constitutional government and of the integrity and independence of free states through America, North and South. It is our duty to study the conditions which make constitutional government possible for our neighbor states in this hemisphere, as for ourselves, and, knowing those conditions, to suffer neither our own people nor the citizens or governments of other countries . . . to violate them or to render them impossible of realization.[23]

Three weeks later, Wilson sent a circular note to the European powers, declaring:

> Usurpations like that of General Huerta menace the peace and development of America as nothing else could. They not only render the development of ordered self-government impossible; they also tend to set law entirely aside, to put the lives and fortunes of citizens and foreigners alike in constant jeopardy. . . . It is the purpose of the United States, therefore, to discredit and defeat such usurpations whenever they occur. . . . Its fixed resolve is that no such interruptions of civil order shall be tolerated so far as it is concerned. Each conspicuous instance in which usurpations of this kind are prevented will render their recurrence less likely, and in the end a state of affairs will be secured in Mexico and elsewhere upon this continent which will assure the peace

of America and the untrammeled development of its economic and social relations with the rest of the world.[24]

Wilson returned to the theme yet again in his Annual Message to Congress
on December 2, 1913, when he spoke of his "watchful waiting":

> There can be no certain prospect of peace in America until General
> Huerta has surrendered his usurped authority in Mexico; until it is un-
> derstood on all hands, indeed, that such pretended governments will
> not be countenanced or dealt with by the Government of the United
> States. We are the friends of constitutional government in America; we
> are more than its friends, we are its champions; because in no other way
> can our neighbors, to whom we would wish to make proof of our
> friendship, work out their own development in peace and liberty.[25]

Accordingly, Washington began to use every diplomatic means available to
evict Huerta from power. At first, Wilson offered to let the "usurper" (a term
adopted in Spanish as well) stand for office, should he agree to adopt a democratic constitution. Following Huerta's refusal, Wilson rescinded his offer and
increased pressure. Within six months, Wilson secured British agreement not
to aid the Mexican general with loans or munitions; sent American arms to
Huerta's opponents, the Constitutionalists; and, in April 1914, ordered the
occupation of the key port of Veracruz, so denying Huerta arms and critical
tax revenues. By July 1914, Huerta had fallen.

Given the power of domestic Mexican forces mobilized against Huerta, it
is doubtful that Wilson's actions made more than a marginal difference to the
dictator's ultimate downfall. And the Constitution of 1917, which finally
ended the revolutionary period in Mexico and provided the country with
remarkable stability after 1920, was a wholly Mexican document.[26] By setting
out social rights (provisions for land reform, free education, restrictions on
the Catholic Church, and nationalization of subsoil rights) as well as the
character of a strong constitutional government, the coming of a genuinely
democratic constitution to Mexico might understandably have convinced
Wilson that his policy had been vindicated: the United States had stood for
constitutional government in Latin America, had acted with a show of resolve
to see it strengthened there, and it appeared the end sought had finally been
gained by the Mexicans themselves. Here was the first occasion on which
Wilson's commitment to self-determination can be said to have been invoked
and this with success.[27] As Wilson put it in an interview published in the *Sat-*

urday Evening Post on May 23, 1914, "They say the Mexicans are not fitted for self-government; and to this I reply that, when properly directed, there is no people not fitted for self-government."

The president thereupon made an extraordinary statement:

> It is a curious thing that every demand for the establishment of order in Mexico takes into consideration not order for the benefit of the people of Mexico, the great mass of the population, but order for the benefit of the old-time regime, for the aristocrats, for the vested interests, for the men who are responsible for this very condition of disorder. No one asks for order because order will help the masses of the people to get a portion of their rights and their land; but all demand it so that the great owners of property, the overlords, the hidalgos, the men who have exploited that rich country for their own selfish purposes, shall be able to continue their processes undisturbed by the protests of the people from whom their wealth and power have been obtained. . . . They want order—the old order; but I say to you that the old order is dead.[28]

Yet Wilson quickly recognized a limit to what Washington could hope to achieve in a situation such as that presented by the Mexican Revolution. If American policy could make some difference in the struggle for constitutional government abroad, nonetheless the power of foreign nationalism would seldom fail to unite to fend off Washington's influence. No major Mexican movement or Latin American government approved of Wilson's attack on Veracruz. For his part, Pancho Villa may have gained more support than he lost when an American Punitive Expedition under John Pershing was launched against him into Mexico in the spring of 1916 after his forces had entered Columbus, New Mexico, murdering Americans and leaving the town in flames.

There can be debate over whether Wilson's nonrecognition doctrine, and later the landing at Veracruz, constituted intervention in the Mexican Revolution—a case of "progressive imperialism." The argument turns on what the term "intervention" actually means. The president repeatedly denied that such a term applied, maintaining the limited scope of his actions, whose scale was as nothing compared to the American presence in the Philippines or later in Haiti and the Dominican Republic. Moreover, he claimed that he was protecting the Revolution by shielding it from outside interests themselves bent on "intervention," chief of which were American and British oil companies and the Roman Catholic Church, as well as those in the press and the military clamoring for the United States to march upon Mexico City. What he decried were the Americans who wanted to get their hands on "the oil and metals of Mexico and were seeking intervention to get them." One thing was certain: Wilson would not allow his country to be party to a "predatory war."[29]

With only nudges from Washington, as Wilson saw it, domestic Mexican forces would work their own way to a solution to their differences. While there are documents that indicate some military planning had occurred, in August 1914, Wilson wrote to his secretary of war:

> We shall have no right at any time to intervene in Mexico to determine the way in which the Mexicans are to settle their own affairs. . . . I say very solemnly that this is no affair of ours. . . . There are in my judgment no conceivable circumstances which would make it right for us to direct by force or by threat of force the internal processes of what is a profound revolution, a revolution as profound as that which occurred in France. All the world has been shocked ever since the time of the revolution in France that Europe should have undertaken to nullify what was done there, no matter what the excesses then committed. I speak very solemnly but with clear judgment in the matter, which I hope God will give me strength to act upon.[30]

Already in a lengthy interview with the journalist John Reed in June 1914, President Wilson had expounded at length on the matter in Mexico. "There is nothing sacred about Democracy unless it expresses the will of the people," he had declared. Yet, "We boast still that the Revolution of 1775 gave impetus and encouragement to revolutionary democracy all over Europe. We are proud that this nation was dedicated as a refuge for the oppressed of the world; that American sympathy has always been on the side of a people in revolt—the Poles, the French, the Russians." Then Reed continued in his own words:

> The dominant note of the President's words—the point to which he returned again and again—was that as long as he was there the United States government would not give its support to tyrannies. That sounds harmless—as harmless as any platitude spoken by any statesman. But if a platitude is translated literally into terms of action, it becomes a startling thing.[31]

Reed nonetheless agreed with the president that American actions did not constitute "intervention," which presumably to both of them meant the use of force intended to seize political power. Yet both men recognized that the doctrine of nonrecognition, followed by the Europeans and combined with a limited occupation of the key port city of Veracruz, meant Washington's influence in Mexico was unquestionably considerable. Wilson believed, then, that he was in effect sheltering the civil war in Mexico from noxious influences from without that were basic to that country's eventual self-determination. As he put it in an interview with the *New York Times* in January 1915:

> I hold it as a fundamental principle, and so do you, that every people has the right to determine its own form of government. . . . It is none of my business and it is none of your business how long [the Mexicans] take in determining it. . . . The country is theirs. The Government is theirs. The liberty, if they can get it, and God speed them in getting it, is theirs. And so far as my influence goes, while I am President nobody shall interfere with them.[32]

On this question of what constitutes "intervention" we need not spend more time. Nevertheless, progressive Wilsonian imperialism for the sake of democracy promotion was, as we have seen, quite different in the Philippines and in Mexico. In the Philippines, American control was direct—involving an administrative control of the country based on armed force. In quick order after the Spanish defeat, Americans had introduced all the trappings of modern government, from parties and elections to centralized governing institutions with a division of powers. As early as 1899, the Americans were conducting municipal elections to form local councils with which they would deal on issues ranging from preserving the peace to introducing public health and universal primary education. By 1907, the United States supervised elections to the national legislature, the first time such an institution had existed in that country, and the party the Americans favored went down to defeat. Americans created an independent judiciary; reorganized the bureaucracy, allowing Filipinos to control most high positions; and disestablished the Roman Catholic Church, redistributing Church lands and ending religious control of education. Baseball, a love of John Philip Sousa marches, and a proliferation of lawyers—all were legacies of America rule. But equally enduring, and of far more importance, was the provision of a political framework for liberal democracy.[33]

By contrast, intervention in Mexico was a pale affair. Without doubting that nonrecognition of the Huerta government (combined with the insistence that the other powers follow suit) and the occupation of Veracruz for the sake of establishing in power a stable constitutional government in Mexico City were indeed exercises in imperialism, Wilson's policy was obviously far less directly interventionist than was the case of American involvement in Manila. The fate of political order was predominately in Mexican hands throughout the Revolution, which was not the case for Filipinos under direct American rule, even if in time they achieved self-government. Here would be Wilson's first experiment with self-determination, a prominent feature of his proposals for peace in Europe from 1916 through 1919.

In short, Wilson's policy toward Mexico was surely far more than "a minor part of a significant career," as historian Howard Cline put it in his survey of the president's approach to Revolution.[34] For it was here that Wilson came to terms with the power of nationalism and revolution (forces he already knew a great deal about as a result of growing up in the American South immediately after the Civil War and doing his first writing on the French Revolution); decided on what might well be called a policy of self-determination by leaving Mexicans to themselves to determine their destiny, seeing his restraint confirmed by the Mexican Constitution of 1917; and carried these lessons with him to Europe when considering demands for American intervention against the Bolshevik Revolution and encouragement for him to take Berlin. Wilson's involvement with the Mexican Revolution emerges as a fundamental factor informing the prudent restraint he was to show so often in other circumstances that confronted his presidency.

DEMOCRACY PROMOTION IN HAITI
AND THE DOMINICAN REPUBLIC

In Hispaniola, the island in the Caribbean that is composed of the Dominican Republic and Haiti, Wilson's approach reflected his attitude toward the Philippines, not his policies with respect to Mexico. In essential ways, however, Haiti and the Dominican Republic differed greatly from the Philippines. On the one hand, Hispaniola was far closer to vital geostrategic positions than the Philippines—the American Gulf coast and the Panama Canal—and Haiti especially had an important German colony in sympathy with Berlin. On the other hand, American influence in Hispaniola was more difficult to exercise by virtue of the fierce contention in both lands between rival caudillos, who nonetheless shared a dislike of Washington's efforts to intervene in domestic affairs. To this problem must be added the complications that arose out of racial divides that in the case of the Dominican Republic ran far deeper than anything the Americans had encountered in the Philippines.

With respect to the Dominican Republic, several figures sum up the intractability of the political situation in a striking manner. Between 1844 and 1916, the country had nineteen constitutions and twenty-three successful coups; only three of its forty-two president actually completed a term in office. Despite the fact that some 70 percent of the government's budget went for military spending, the country was effectively controlled by regional caudillos, usually called "generals," of whom four were contending for power when the United States finally intervened in force in 1916.[35]

Although it was for strategic reasons that Washington wanted stable, pro-American governments in Santo Domingo and Port-au-Prince, the means Wilson proposed to serve this end were the establishment in both countries of constitutional government. As early as September 1913, the Wilson administration had tried to create a stable political climate on the island by sending Minister James M. Sullivan there with written orders from Secretary of State William Jennings Bryan that he said came directly from the president. As Bryan put it, Wilson had made clear in March that controversies should be settled by constitutional means and that violence should not ever be seen as a way of bringing about reform.

> First, that we can have no sympathy with those who seek the power of government to advance their own personal interests or ambition; and second, that the test of a republican form of government is to be found in its responsiveness to the will of the people, its just powers being derived from the consent of the governed. . . . I am sure that when the disinterestedness of our Government is fully understood, its friendship will be appreciated and its advice sought.[36]

However, by the end of July 1914, Wilson and Bryan had determined that "the only solution" to the ongoing violence, as historian Arthur S. Link presents it, "was American intervention to end the fighting and to establish a new provisional government that a majority of the factions would support. This would be done peacefully if the Dominican leaders cooperated, by force if they resisted. But it would be done."[37] Unlike Mexico, where President Wilson had foresworn "intervention," here he was involved in it as fully as might be imagined.

By July 27, 1914, President Wilson had himself prepared in writing what came to be called "the Wilson Plan." Its terms specified in some detail how he proposed to go about implementing the stability the country needed. If hostilities could not be ended by the Dominicans themselves, then "the Government of the United States will itself name a Provisional President, sustain him in the assumption of office, and support him in the exercise of his temporary authority." Thereafter, a date would be set for congressional and presidential elections under the power of the Provisional President (himself not to be candidate for office). Once Washington

> is satisfied that these elections have been free and fair and carried out under conditions which enable the people of the republic to express their real choice, it will recognize the President and Congress thus chosen as the legitimate and constitutional Government of the Republic and will support them in the exercise of their functions and authority in every way it can. . . . A regular and constitutional government having thus been set up, the Government of the United States would feel at liberty thereafter to insist that revolutionary movements cease and that all subsequent changes in the Government of the Republic be effected by the peaceful processes provided in the Dominican Constitution.[38]

There is no reason here to cover in any detail the story of American policy as it now unfolded, but by May 1916, Wilson ordered the military occupation of the Dominican Republic and in November authorized the creation of an American military government. (Under analogous terms, Haiti's military occupation had commenced in July 1915.) Thereafter, the United States tried to complement its moves to assure political stability by surveying the land and registering ownership titles, demonstrating new farming techniques, and expanding road and port facilities.

But as it turned out, the single most important innovation introduced by the American occupation came with the creation of a national constabulary to provide a force of order to sustain the governments backed by Washington. As is well known, the eventual role of these national guards was to seize power for themselves, leading to the emergence of the Trujillo family in the Dominican Republic. Whatever the intentions of Washington, American intervention did assure stability, but one based on firepower, not on constitutional agreement.

The main point by now should be established: in order to end regional turmoil, the Wilson administration had established early on in its dealings with Mexico, Central America, and the Caribbean that it sought the promotion of constitutional democracy there so as to provide for an enduring peace deemed beneficial to the people of the area and essential to American national security. Seizing customs houses to control local affairs, as the United States had done in the recent past, was no longer enough. By the summer of 1914, as the Panama Canal was opened and war in Europe broke out, Washington needed political stability in what it increasingly saw as its own backyard. The creation of democratic governments under the auspices of American rule would, as in the Philippines, serve the interests at once of this country, the people directly affected, and the region in general.

To conclude, let us return to the pattern that emerges from these acts of progressive imperialism between 1913 and 1916 in Latin America. A vision Woodrow Wilson had first announced in 1900, as he reflected upon the impact on the place of the United States in the world with the taking of the Philippines in 1898, had now played out in parts of Latin America close to the American homeland as well. Here the United States was standing as the champion of a new form of internationalism, which if followed carried the promise of an enduring peace to regional if not world politics, and all this through the expansion of democratic government. Here was a defining mark of Wilsonianism and of a modern conception of American exceptionalism—that it had the ability to define its national security in terms of fostering a form of government beneficial to all peoples by its offer of peaceful coexistence.

THE MANDATES AS EFFORTS AT PROGRESSIVE IMPERIALISM

Wilson did not limit his support for progressive imperialism to the exercise of American power alone. The victors in the war against Germany, Austria-Hungary, Bulgaria, and the Ottoman Empire had to decide what to do with the peoples no longer under imperial rule (to which should be added the peoples lost to the Soviet Union by the Treaty of Brest-Litovsk in March 1918). Under Wilson's auspices, the great powers determined some of these people to be capable of self-determination at the war's conclusion: Poland, Czechoslovakia, Yugoslavia, and Romania. However, other peoples liberated from imperial rule but "not yet able to stand by themselves under the strenuous conditions of the modern world" would be "entrusted to advanced nations who by reason of their resources, their experience or their geographical position can best undertake this responsibility . . . as Mandatories on behalf of the League." Articles 22–26 of the final text of the Covenant as finally adopted and published on April 21, 1919, set out the intentions of the League of Nations with respect to these peoples.

Article 22 laid out a division of the mandates into three categories. A first category held that the peoples once under Turkish rule had "reached a stage of development where their existence as independent nations can be provisionally recognized, subject to the rendering of administrative advice and assistance by a mandatory until such time as they are able to stand alone." However, a second category, those mainly located in Central Africa, "are at such a stage that the mandatory must be responsible for the administration of the territory." Yet a third category—for example, Southwest Africa or the South Pacific islands—characterized by their small size or population or remoteness "can be best administered under the laws of the mandatory as integral portions of its territory."

Article 23, on the basic conditions of trusteeship, followed from the authority established in the terms outlined above. The mandatory was obliged to work for "secure fair and humane conditions of labor," to prohibit traffic in children, women, and drugs, to establish a judiciary to enforce such rights and obligations as the League laid out, and to ensure that all members of the League had equal standing in commercial relations in all of the mandates. Moreover, in Articles 24–26, the League reserved to itself the right to have access to all mandates through the "international bureaus" it would set up (as, for example, the International Red Cross) and laid out that its Council, working through "a permanent Commission," would maintain oversight of the mandatories' compliance with these rules.

President Wilson was obviously a party to this final text. Yet it represented a significant departure from the terms he had laid out for the mandates in early drafts he had formulated for the Covenant of the League. In what is generally called "the first Paris draft" of January 8, 1919 (sometimes dated as January 10), Wilson had laid out six "Supplementary Agreements" for the trusteeships to be set up by the League. The first of these went much further than what the final text provided for in the version of April 1919, stating principles that once again constituted democracy promotion through progressive imperialism:

> . . . that in the future government of these peoples and territories, the rule of self-determination, or the consent of the governed to their form

of government, shall be fairly and reasonably applied, and all policies of administration or economic development be based primarily upon the well-considered interest of the people themselves.

Wilson's second and third articles affirmed more clearly than the April text would do the superior supervisory role the League itself would play with respect to mandatory powers. The League would thus reserve to itself "complete power of supervision and of intimate control, and shall also reserve to the people of any such territory or governmental unit the right to appeal to the League for the redress or correction of any breach of the mandate . . . for the substitution of some other state or agency as mandatory." Article 5 called for "fair hours and humane conditions of labor for all those within their several jurisdictions who are engaged in manual labor." The sixth article provided yet another prompt for democracy as it required all mandates, prior to the recognition of their independence as sovereign states, to bind themselves "to accord to all racial or national minorities within their several jurisdictions exactly the same treatment and security, both in law and in fact, that is accorded the racial or national majority of their people."[39]

On January 20, 1919, Wilson completed his "second Paris draft," composed now of ten articles; it affirmed all the measures of the first draft but went even further in the direction of promoting constitutional governments for the mandates. Wilson added "religious persecution and intolerance" to practices that would be barred by the mandatory power and would be reviewed by the League with respect to any mandates applying for recognition as a sovereign people.

Yet when we arrive at the third Paris draft, dated February 2, allowances are made for eventual independence of the mandates, but no stipulation appears as to what form of government such freedom will take—reference to "self-determination" and "the consent of the governed" no longer are in the text. Instead, according to Article 3, "The object of all such tutelary oversight and administration . . . shall be to build up in as short a time as possible out of the people or territory under its guardianship a political unit which can take charge of its own affairs, determine its own connections, and choose its own policies."[40] Wilson did leave in place, however, matters that could help a democracy emerge by affirming once again the rights of labor, religious tolerance, and equality for minorities.[41]

What then occurred between late January and late April to cause the Covenant to abandon Wilson's provisions on eventual self-determination and self-government for the mandates, complete with equal treatment of all religious and ethnic minorities in such areas? Although the records of the meetings of the various commissions on the Covenant are extensive, I was unable to find precise answers to these questions. What can be noted, however, is that, later, in February meetings of the Commission (discussed in the next chapter), Wilson continued to insist on making "self-government," defined as constitutional democracy, a condition for admitting states. Presumably the opposition of other members drafting the statutes of the Covenant had made their influence known, so Wilson did as he usually did in such circumstances, giving in to demands he did not agree with for the sake of the League's ratification, in the hope that eventual American leadership of the League would restore the ends he sought.

Given the actual evolution of the mandates, it is obvious that the Covenant, as it was published late in April 1919, cannot be construed as a telling example of "progressive imperialism." Indeed, in short order its fate was to become an example of imperialism pure and simple. The story of the French and British machinations in the Arab world are evidence enough of that.[42] The point here, however, is that these final determinations did not represent the much more progressive elements of President Wilson's earlier drafts, which he must have felt obliged to surrender under pressure, but which he presumably hoped would be reinstated in due course as the League grew in maturity.

Despite these setbacks, Wilson nevertheless remained involved in the question of the trusteeship arrangements set up by the League. On May 24, 1920, he submitted to the Congress a proposal that would have made Armenia a mandate of the United States. Wilson's resolution pointed out the terrible hardships the Armenian people suffered under Turkish rule. Citing what he termed an "invitation of the Council at San Remo" to work out the details of a final peace settlement with the Central Powers, Wilson insisted upon the Christian conscience of the United States responding to the suffering of Christian Armenia. "Our recognition of the independence of Armenia will mean genuine liberty and assured happiness for her people, if we fearlessly undertake the duties of guidance and assistance involved in the functions of a mandatory." A week later, on June 1, 1920, the Senate rejected the president's proposition.[43]

Wilson's thinking with respect to the mandates of the League of Nations seemed a relatively minor matter in the first months of 1919. Yet it did demonstrate once again his attention to fostering democracy where he could—in this instance by what obviously amounted to a replay of his belief that the proper kind of rule over foreign peoples could lead to democratic government. If others persuaded Wilson to abandon his position, it is worth noting that, for a brief period in January 1919, he had given considerable thought and effort to this end. Nor is it far-fetched to think that at a later date he would have hoped that the United States might work to reassert the measures he had called for with respect to the mandates that winter once it gained leadership of the League.

DEMOCRACY PROMOTION THROUGH MULTILATERALISM: THE PAN-AMERICAN TREATY, 1915–1916 AS A PRELUDE TO THE LEAGUE OF NATIONS

What I have tried to establish in this chapter is that from the time of the Spanish-American War through his presidency, Woodrow Wilson followed a form of progressive imperialism under which direct American military intervention in the affairs of foreign peoples was intended to bring about a democratic form of government that would assure stable constitutional governments, while establishing the groundwork for regional peace conducive to the security interests of the United States.

Yet there are three reasons not to exaggerate these policies as leading hallmarks of the president's two administrations. First, with the possible exception of the Philippines, these policies failed—and that in countries far more open to American penetration than could be said for Germany and the Soviet Union in the wake of World War I.

Second, Wilson learned from his contact with Mexico the limits of American power over a country with a large population and a heightened sense of nationalist consciousness. Countries that had what might be called an "organic" political consciousness, even if one group was in contention with another, were quite different from those altogether lacking such a background, as in Haiti and the Dominican Republic and as had been the case earlier in the Philippines. The success of what can rightly be called Mexican self-determination in the creation of their widely respected Constitution of February 1917 (and whose government Wilson recognized de jure in August 1917) demonstrated that leaving peoples to their own devices might well have salutary outcomes.

Third, sensing the clear limits of progressive imperialism, Wilson was working as early as December 1914 on another track that might foster stability at the national and regional levels in the Western Hemisphere: a Pan-American Pact or Treaty designed to establish a regional institutional structure conducive to hemispheric peace through a system of collective security that would establish the conditions to reduce regional tensions and produce solidarity among peoples. It should come as no surprise that membership in such a pact would have as its first provision that the member governments be "republican" in form.

As early as October 1913, Wilson had expressed his concern that with the coming of the Panama Canal the following year, hemispheric solidarity could be aided if increased integration fostered democratic ways. The following April, with the Treaty of Bogota, the Wilson administration expressed its "sincere regrets" for damages Theodore Roosevelt had caused in 1903 as he seized the province of Panama, making it into a separate country to facilitate American control over the eventual canal. Again, in the Pan-American Financial Conference of May 1915, the president pushed for a more open and integrated hemispheric economic system in the name of regional peace and to give an example to the world of how a collection of countries could improve their relations by forging multilateral bonds with a sense of their common interests. Throughout these affairs, Wilson's paramount concern appeared to have been the gains for constitutional democracy in Latin America that could be encouraged by these arrangements.[44]

However, Wilson's single most important initiative came toward the end of 1914, when, while considering the terms of an eventual negotiated settlement of the Great War, he had hit on the idea of a collective security pact for the Western Hemisphere that might also serve as a template for ending the fighting in Europe. In doing so, the president set forth, with the Pan-American Treaty, a self-conscious prelude to the League of Nations, a proposal floated in 1915–1916 so as to improve the prospects for the tranquillity and solidarity of the Americas.[45]

In October 1915, Secretary of State Robert Lansing transmitted to President Wilson the first draft of his proposed Pan-American Treaty, which he had previously given to the Argentine ambassador. The American proposal included articles covering a cooling-off period and arbitration details. But its Article 1 in all the drafts for the Treaty pledged "that the high contracting parties to this solemn covenant and agreement hereby join one another in a common and mutual guarantee of territorial integrity and of political independence under republican forms of government." Subsequent articles specified cooling-off and arbitration provisions before any signatory would resort to war with any other signatory. While the draft treaty did not provide the explicit terms for collective security that the Covenant of the League of Nations would set up in 1919, one can see clearly the embryo of such thinking in the texts of 1915.[46]

Some two weeks later, Lansing sent to the president a revised draft of the Pan-American Treaty to which two articles had been added. Article 1 nonetheless remained the same in November 1915 as it had been a month earlier. At this point, Brazil and Chile were included in the exchanges. The result, in June 1916, was a final version of the Treaty in which yet again Article 1 provided that all signatories to the Treaty pledged to live in "political independence under republican forms of government."[47]

Ultimately, the Latin Americans failed to ratify the Treaty. Their concern over settling territorial disputes was an element of their eventual opposition, along with what they construed as illegitimate American interventions by force on Wilson's watch elsewhere in the Americas. What they never voiced to Washington were presumably their reservations over Article 1 in a region where religious and military authorities had at times been heads of state (and this in some cases by explicit constitutional measures). We may speculate on what "republican forms of government" called for in Article 1 meant to the Latin signatories of the Treaty and conclude it did not mean constitutional democracies. But to Woodrow Wilson and Secretaries of State Bryan and Lansing, it meant nothing less than representative democracy.

Surely this was a condition that would have concerned Latin American heads of states, even if they were evasive on the matter. To be sure, Wilson issued his customary reassurances that "the trend of the world [was] toward the idea of popular government" and that the proposed Pact was "an arrangement by which you would be protected from us." But how convincing was this likely to be to Latin leaders?[48] Given the political influence of military forces in the region, which were sometimes given the constitutional right to take over the government should domestic disorders prove menacing, the question was what Washington might do in the event of the breakdown of republican institutions in the hemisphere. In the event of a military establishment coming to power, or of monarchical ambitions, as might occur in Brazil, or of clerical influence on the state, might the United States not take the pledge to maintain republican government as a license for intervention? Whatever Wilson's protestations that the United States saw such an agreement as a guarantee against intervention on its part, precisely the opposite would conceivably be the case. Under the terms of the proposed treaty, serious and prolonged civil strife could serve as justification for American military occupation in the name of defending and promoting constitutional rule. Wilson had made his position on this matter clear in 1913, and he had acted on it repeatedly from 1914 to 1916 in Mexico, Haiti, Nicaragua, and the Dominican Republic. Previously, Washington had sought to bring stability to restive areas in the hemisphere by taking over custom house revenues and so controlling some 90 percent of the revenues of governments there. With the United States having pledged itself to "republican government," might not American intervention now be legitimized on the basis of removing autocrats from power in the region, to be replaced by constitutionalists?

The obvious question is whether American leadership of the League of Nations would have led to more acts of progressive imperialism of the kind we saw Wilson engaging in, with weak states ruling over oppressed populations subject to endemic civil wars. Do we find here the seeds of what would become after the year 2000 the terms of what is called "the Responsibility to Protect"? It is to matters such as these that the final chapters of this book will turn. The next task is to turn to the character of the League of Nations, the embodiment of Wilson's hopes for a world order able to stop war.

CHAPTER THREE

Democracy Promotion through Multilateralism

The question upon which the whole future peace and policy of the world depends is this: Is the present war a struggle for a just and secure peace, or only for a new balance of power? If it be only a struggle for a new balance of power, who will guarantee, who can guarantee, the stable equilibrium of the new arrangement? Only a tranquil Europe can be a stable Europe. There must be, not a balance of power, but a community of power; not organized rivalries, but an organized common peace.

—*Woodrow Wilson addressing the Congress, January 22, 1917*

With the outbreak of a generalized war in Europe in the summer of 1914, Wilson was faced with the greatest question of his presidency: how the United States might work for an enduring world peace once the military struggle was won. "The world must be made safe for democracy," he declared in asking for a declaration of war in April 1917, using a phrase whose meaning has since been subject to endless debate. The phrase was electric, but what did it mean?

Wilson's initial posture toward the conflict in Europe was not to cast it as a struggle between autocracy and democracy, as his Secretary of State Robert Lansing was framing it.[1] Indeed, it should be emphasized that the promotion of democracy against an authoritarian regime such as existed in Berlin was not what persuaded Wilson and the United States to declare war on Germany. Rather he felt the need to confront Germany's uncivilized war tactics—its U-boat attacks on commercial shipping and the passenger vessel the *Lusitania* in 1915, Germany's assault on international law with respect to neutrality, and the Zimmermann telegram in early 1917, which promised to award large parts of the United States to Mexico, should that country support Berlin in the event of American entry into the European war. What Wilson at first had hoped for was an end to the fighting and a return to conditions as they were before the war. It had been on this basis he had campaigned in 1916 on the slogan that he was the man "who kept us out of war" (a phrase that surely related to the possibility of war with Mexico and not only to that in Europe). But faced with German challenges to world order and American national security, the president finally decided to ask for a declaration of war.[2] Yet if democracy promotion were thus not the cause that Wilson had championed before 1917, as he considered whether the nation should enter the war, the president moved it to center stage as he contemplated how the peace that followed military struggle might be kept.

Prior to America's entry into the war, Wilson had deliberated, as had many others, on the formulation of an international institution whose purpose would be to keep the peace, and his thinking turned naturally enough to the privileged position democratic countries would play in this respect.[3] By the time he reached Paris in December 1918, his public declarations—combined with the deployment of a massive amount of equipment and well over 1 million American troops in Europe, at the cost of more than 53,000 combat fatalities—had decisively turned the war against Germany, meaning that his leadership of the victorious powers was beyond question. The battle won, how would Wilson win the peace that the world hoped to see follow?

Enter the League of Nations. Although many different proposals were to appear to provide for what came to be called a system of collective security to protect the world from war, Wilson's role in shaping the League was decisive in many respects. Here was the international institution that the president trusted might provide for regional if not world peace through a system of mutual defense that involved rules and organizational mechanisms to encourage disarmament, provide for the arbitration of disputes among governments, and coordinate its members to act against warlike peoples and states through a series of measures ranging from embargos to the eventual use of force. In addition to its formal structure, which included an Executive Council, a General Assembly, and a Permanent Secretariat, collateral organizations would serve a variety of functions, including a Mandates Commission, a Disarmament Commission, the Health Organization, the International Labor Organization (ILO), and the Permanent Court of International Justice (the last three of which were continued under slightly changed names through the United Nations after its creation in 1945).

The League had the implicit capacity as well to extend its activities. On his

Western Tour in September 1919, Wilson repeatedly pointed out that the ILO and the mandate system were among methods to promote international commerce in a way that favored business interests far more than if world affairs remained a dog-eat-dog affair as a balance-of-power/imperialist scramble for economic interests would have it. The president took pains to insist that the mission of the League would expand with time: "the simplicity of the document seems to me to be one of its chief virtues . . . it is not a straitjacket but a vehicle of life. A living thing is born and we must see to it what clothes we can put on it."[4]

According to Wilson's vision of political responsibility, democratic people would presumably be the best members of the League, for a commitment to the common good as decided by reasoned discussion and compromise was the essence of their character nationally and so could be counted on to carry over into international institutions as well. Nevertheless, it was evident from the start that some countries that were not democratic could be League members. Among others, Guatemala, Siam, and Japan were automatically signatories of the Covenant by virtue of having joined the struggle against the Central Powers—Germany, Austria-Hungary, the Ottoman Empire, and Bulgaria. The League also gave India a seat after British insistence that this country's participation in the war needed to be recognized.[5] Moreover, there was little guarantee in 1919 that an institution dominated by democracies would serve the purpose liberal internationalists intended. As Wilson quickly learned at the Peace Conference in Paris, there was no reason to think that just because states were democratic they would easily agree on how to handle essential issues.[6] Nevertheless, the Covenant affirmed in its Article 1 that only "self-governing" peoples pledged to the conditions laid out for membership might apply to join the association.

But what did the term "self-government" mean, and just how important was it that the League be based largely on their participation?

AUTOCRACY VERSUS DEMOCRACY: THE BALANCE OF POWER VERSUS COLLECTIVE SECURITY

Whether for good or for ill, Woodrow Wilson was not easily given to abstract theorizing about the logic of world history. Nor would his ambition to write a major work he would entitle *The Philosophy of Politics* come to fruition, given his precarious health and the pressing events that crowded his life as president, and never more so than when the United States entered the war in

Europe in the spring of 1917. Yet from his writing and speeches it is possible
to tease out a coherent viewpoint that he developed as he looked at the
sources of the Great War and used the ideas he had already developed as an
academic to provide a solution for future generations anxious to avoid repeating the butchery of 1914–1918.

What needed to be achieved, in Wilson's formulation, was the replacement
of an international system in which states predicated their behavior in terms
of the concerns of self-interested balance-of-power calculations by "a community of power; not organized rivalries, but an organized common peace."
Even if the Calvinist origins of such an inspiration should be evident in the
terms that surrounded Presbyterian "covenanting," I can only repeat that to
subscribe to this hope was not in the slightest conditional on being Christian,
even less so Calvinist. Instead, in terms of traditional Western political
thought, balance-of-power thinking reflected a logic to world affairs that was
largely the anarchic state of nature as Hobbes had described. It was necessary
to tame its brutal existence by a social contract in which the interests of all
would be served by the rule of law subscribed to through institutions meeting
with the consent of its members. While there is only scant evidence that Wilson was familiar with the writings of Immanuel Kant, the liberal faith he put
forward was highly reminiscent of the late eighteenth-century German philosopher.[7] In Wilson's words:

> The old order of things was . . . to base policies upon international
> power. . . . [This balance of power was] not the balance that you try to
> maintain in a court of justice, not the scales of justice, but the scale of
> force—one great force balanced against another force. . . . It was either
> the advantage of Germany or the advantage of Great Britain or the
> advantage of Italy or the advantage of Japan. I am glad to say that I am
> not justified in adding that the policy of the world was ever conceived
> by us upon the basis of the advantage of America. We wished always to
> be the mediators of justice and of right, but we thought that the cool
> spaces of the ocean to the east and the west of us would keep us from
> the infection that came, arising like miasmatic mists out of that arrange-
> ment of power and of suspicion and of dread. . . .
>
> Now the catastrophe has come. Blood has been spilt in rivers, the
> flower of the European nations has been destroyed . . . the old order is
> gone.[8]

If it were "justice," not "force," that should decide international relations, what would be the character of the peoples capable of maintaining a League of Nations dedicated to ending war? At the heart of the old order driving the spirit of the balance of power was a political order that Wilson habitually referred to as "autocracy" (although on occasion he spoke of "tyranny"). Autocracy could be linked not only to militarism and repression at home but also to imperialism abroad in favor of securing economic interests or to perceived geostrategic advantages that served strictly national ends. Here was the syndrome of characteristics that made war among the powerful states an ever-present possibility. Accordingly, the task of the world community was to replace the state of nature that typified the world community with a peaceful international order based on a covenant of rights and responsibilities that had the assent of its members to its terms—a system of collective security. What democracy had achieved at home it now had to establish in regional, if not world, affairs. A body of international law dedicated to establishing a just peace, created and enforced by world institutions, and resting on the approval of public opinion, needed to be called into existence.

While democracies were the most likely source of such effective moral action, authoritarian states that thought of themselves as committed to constitutional order might be admitted to such an organization. Wilson was easily able to see gradations of difference among autocratic states. Just as he could recognize that Austria-Hungary was not the predatory power that Germany was, so too he could refer to czarist Russia as "an old and distinguished and skillful autocracy" far more benign than that of Lenin and his followers, "a little handful of men exercising without the slightest compunction of mercy or pity the bloody terror that characterized the worst days of the Czar."[9] Nevertheless, the concurrence of attributes that made autocracy as a regime type so dangerous was the problem that Wilson chose to diagnose.

By contrast, "democracies" were by their very character much less likely to be either repressive at home or imperialist abroad. They could foster open economies and were anti-militarist. In concert with other democracies, they could do in world affairs as they did domestically: negotiate compromises among different groups with the idea of serving the common interest without recourse to violence, except in mutual defense. Once again, of course, Wilson could nonetheless see gradations among them. Given its monarchical, religious, and imperialist habits and institutions, for example, Great Britain was obviously more likely to think in balance-of-power terms than the United

States could, whose isolationism and relative purity of character—no monarchy, no established church, and little to show in the way of imperialism beyond North America—had spared it from making such calculations a central part of its perspective on world affairs.

These nuances aside, the contrast between the two forms of political order—the one autocratic, the other democratic—was the heart of the matter of war and peace so far as Wilson was concerned. If we think in theoretical terms, the old order and the new were each typified by a series of interlocking characteristics. Thus, the balance of power found expression in autocracy, but it characteristically included as well (especially in its most malignant forms, as with Germany) militarism, imperialist expansion, economic protectionism, and ruthless oppression of foreign populations under a nation's dominion combined with strict discipline of its own domestic citizenry. By contrast, what came to be called collective security needed to be anchored among democracies, which characteristically (especially in its most benign forms, as with the United States) were antimilitaristic; economically open; uninterested in the subjugation of foreign peoples, who were to enjoy self-determination; and built upon societies based on freedom so that their political legitimacy stemmed from the consent of the governed, which presupposed an engaged citizenry. In a word, autocracies anticipated war, and this was what they got; democracies worked for peace, and the hope for the future lay with them.

Clear as this may seem, there is nonetheless an ambiguity about what Wilson meant in terms of collective security provided by the League. Because it would be dominated by democratic countries, the League could be seen as a form of balance-of-power organization, much as Wilson failed to state the point. For the League was meant not only to dampen disagreements that could lead to war among the peoples who were its members, but it was also pledged, by Article 17 of its Covenant, to act in unison against states outside its ranks who threatened a League member. In this respect, a primary task of the League of Nations would be to serve as a coordinator of its members against hostile powers in general, a responsibility that by its very nature could be construed as associating democracies together against autocracies. In short, to draw too sharp a distinction between balance-of-power states acting only in terms of their self-interest and League peoples concerned to keep the common peace is to miss an essential element of the League's identity.[10]

Given Wilson's approach to history, which emphasized politics as the dominant force in historical development and democracy as the watchword of that which could be true to the promise of freedom and peace, the ultimate existential contest of his time was therefore between autocracy and democracy. The choice was stark. As Wilson declared on the first anniversary of America's entry into war for the sake of the common good (sounding a bit like Theodore Roosevelt):

> German purpose is a dominion . . . an empire of force upon which they fancy they can then erect an empire of gain and commercial supremacy—an empire as hostile to the Americas as to the Europe which it will overawe—an empire which will ultimately master Persia, India and the peoples of the Far East.
>
> [Should Berlin triumph] everything that America has lived for and loved and grown great to vindicate and bring to a glorious realization will have fallen in utter ruin and the gates of mercy once more pitilessly shut upon mankind!
>
> . . . There is, therefore, but one response possible from us: Force, Force to the utmost, Force without stint or limit, the righteous and triumphant Force which shall make Right the law of the world, and cast every selfish dominion down in the dust.[11]

As the president presented the matter on his Western Tour popularizing the League to the American public in September 1919, "You have either got to have the old system, of which Germany was the perfect flower, or you have got to have a new system. . . . Your choice is between the League of Nations and Germanism."[12] There could be no doubt about the matter. At stake in Europe was something existential: "The Past and the Present are in deadly grapple and the peoples of the world are being done to death between them. . . . The settlement must be final. There can be no compromise." Peace therefore required:

> The destruction of every arbitrary power anywhere that can separately, secretly, and of its single choice disturb the peace of the world . . . [as well as] the establishment of an organization of peace which shall make it certain that the combined power of free nations will check every invasion of right and serve to make peace and justice the more secure by affording a definite tribunal of opinion to which all must submit. . . . *These great objects can be put into a single sentence. What we seek is the reign of law, based upon the consent of the governed and sustained by the organized opinion of mankind.*[13]

Indeed, should the United States not succeed in serving as the midwife to a new world order, this country itself might indeed slip into "Germanism" as it pulled back from a liberal order to balance-of-power calculations. Because President Wilson habitually cited Germany as his prime example of the embodiment of such machinations, let us consider in more detail its attributes.

Germany was autocratic. As Wilson put it in February 1919, "no one would have looked at the German government before the war and said that the nation was self-governing . . . the Reichstag was controlled by the Chancellor and it was an absolute monarchy."[14] That September he was more explicit: "The object of the war was to destroy autocratic power; that is to say to make it impossible that there should be anywhere, as there was on Wilhelmstrasse, in Berlin, a little group of military men who could . . . say, 'We have perfected a machine with which we can conquer the world. Now stand out of the way, we are going to conquer the world.'"[15]

Germany was also militaristic. In the president's words in Sioux Falls on September 8, 1919, *Machtpolitik* was a fundamental element of that country's thinking on world affairs:

> Germany had been preparing for [war] for generations. Germany had been preparing every resource and perfecting every skill, developing every invention, which would enable her to master the European world and to dominate the rest of the world. . . . The assassination of the Austrian Crown Prince in Serbia was not what started the war. [The Germans] were ready to start it and merely made that an occasion and an excuse.[16]

But just as militarism had been a product of autocracy, so Wilson warned Americans that militarism could give birth to autocracy—even in the United States, were it forced to think in balance-of-power terms itself.

> We may say what we please of the German government that has been destroyed . . . but it was the only sort of government that can handle an armed nation. . . . You can't have an armed nation if it is democratic because democracies don't go to war that way. You have got to have a concentrated, militaristic organization of government to run a nation of that sort . . . you can't do that under free debate. . . . You know how impossible it is to effect social reform if everybody must be under orders from the government. You know how impossible it is, in short, to have a free nation if it is a military nation and under military orders.[17]

So, too, German autocracy was imperialistic and oppressive. Wilson underscored:

> . . . the tragedy of this war, but the tragedy that lay back of it was greater than the war itself, because back of it lay long ages in which the legitimate freedom of men was suppressed. Back of it lay long ages of recurrent war in which little groups of men, closeted in capitals, determined whether the sons of the land over which they ruled should go out upon the field and shed their blood. For what? For liberty? No, not for liberty, but for the aggrandizement of those who ruled them.[18]

The problem of peace in central Europe was that these empires "had lived in open violation of many of the rights for which the war had been fought, dominating alien peoples over whom they had no natural right to rule, enforcing not obedience but veritable bondage, exploiting those who were weak for the benefit of those who were masters and overlords only by force of arms. There could be no peace until the whole order of central Europe was set right."[19]

Or again, in San Diego two months later: "Other autocratic powers may spring up, but there is only one soil in which they can spring up—that is the wrongs done to free peoples of the world. And the heart and center of this treaty is that it sets at liberty people all over Europe and in Asia who have hitherto been enslaved by powers which were not their rightful sovereigns and masters. So long as wrongs like that exist, you cannot bring permanent peace to the world." As he forcefully concluded, "I will not take any part in composing difficulties that ought not to be composed, and a difficulty between an enslaved people and its autocratic rulers ought not to be composed."[20]

Wilson's remedy for this condition was what he labeled "self-determination." Establishing political units based essentially on ethno-religious identity divisions—a reaffirmation of the Westphalian system of government for the region that had reigned since 1648 as an essential element of peace—might be at once a seedbed for democratic government while at the same time serving as a barrier to the imperial ambitions of autocratic countries always thinking in terms of the balance of power:

> The trouble was at the heart of Europe. At the heart of Europe there were suffering peoples, inarticulate but with hearts on fire against the iniquities practiced against them; held in grip of military power, sub-

mitting to nothing but force; their spirits insurgent. And so long as that condition existed, there could not be the expectation of continued peace. . . . [But the League as now created] considered the cry of the people and did not listen to the pleas of governments. It did not listen to dynastic claims . . . but it said: "The door is closed on that. These lands belong to the stocks, the ancient stocks of people that live upon them. We are going to give them to those people. The land always should have been yours; it is now yours, and you can govern it as you please."[21]

Finally, Germany was protectionist. Wilson was adamant on this matter. As he put it in November 1917:

There is no important industry in Germany upon which the Government has not laid its hands to direct it and when necessity arose, to control it. . . . You will find that they were the same sort of competition that we have tried to prevent by law within our own borders. If they could not sell their goods cheaper than we could sell ours at a profit to themselves they could get a subsidy for the Government which made it possible to sell them cheaper anyhow, and the conditions of the competition were thus controlled in large measure by the German Government itself. But that did not satisfy [them]. All the while, there was lying behind its thoughts and in its dreams of the future a political control which would enable it in the long run to dominate the labor and industry of the world. They were not content with success by superior achievement; they wanted success by authority. . . . [Thus] the Berlin-Baghdad Railway was constructed. . . .

I saw a map, in which the whole thing was printed in appropriate black the other day, and the black stretched from Hamburg to Baghdad—the bulk of German power inserted into the heart of the world.[22]

In short, to attack the system dominating world politics in 1914 was to attack balance-of-power politics, at the heart of which was autocratic government, based on militarism, domestic oppression, imperialism (with the brutal denial of ethno-religious identity that conquest entailed), and economic protectionism—all parts of a greater whole. The remedy that was apparent was also of a whole: the struggle for collective security and against the balance of power was in fact the struggle of democracy. For only here was there a character of people and government capable of collective action at a domestic level that could translate into a sense of common interest with respect to world affair—interests that expressed themselves in open, integrated economies, cooperative multilateral institutions, and mutual respect and mutual support, including the willingness to fight on behalf of one another. Here were the essential ingredients that a later generation would call "Wilsonianism."

WINNING THE PEACE

Wilson was throwing down the gauntlet, then, against a host of ills—past, present, and future—that were plaguing the world when he asked the Senate in January 1917: "Is the present war a struggle for a just and secure peace or only for a new balance of power?" His answer was unequivocal and worth repeating: "There must be not a balance of power, but a community of power; not organized rivalries, but an organized common peace." How might this be attained? His answer again was clear-cut: such a stable, peaceful order needed to depend on what later political scientists would call "regime type": "No peace can last, or ought to last, which does not recognize and accept the principle that governments derive all their just powers from the consent of the governed."[23]

Indeed, within weeks of war breaking out in Europe in August 1914, prominent Americans had begun to discuss ways in which war might be thwarted by concerted international action. In their efforts they were assisted by the former British ambassador to the United States, James Bryce, who was active in the League of Nations Society in the United Kingdom, founded in 1915. The same year, the League to Enforce Peace (LEP) came into existence in the United States, with former president William Howard Taft as its leader. Hundreds of prominent Americans joined in calling for a collective security organization to bring peace-loving people into agreements and for institutions to stop war. In 1919, the LEP gave its support to Senate approval of the League of Nations, only to dissolve in 1923 after Senate rejection and public opinion closed debate.

In May 1916, President Wilson gave an important address to the LEP in which he laid out his own hopes for the peace that would follow the fighting in Europe. What we witness here is the transposition of his thinking about democracy in America, with its roots in the structure of Presbyterianism as it had existed since the late eighteenth century, to what might be achieved on the world stage. Of course, one did not need to be a Calvinist to subscribe to such a plan, for the argument was secular, not religious, and so corresponded to the transformation Wilson had achieved at the turn of the century by making the spirit of democracy one of global concern, no longer the project of the Protestant English-speaking world alone. Such an organization would be possessed of a power structure that was democratic, whose purpose was the common interest, and whose method of action was law-making through an institution based on a covenant that over time could be changed in order to maintain the consent of those in a self-governed community. The parallel was nonetheless rather exact—running from the organization of Calvinist organizations by the 1770s, to the structure of democracy in America as it formulated its Constitution in the 1780s, and now transposed in 1916 to the world stage.

> Only when the great nations of the world have reached some sort of agreement as to what they hold to be fundamental to their common interest, and as to some feasible method of acting in concert when any nation or group of nations seeks to disturb those fundamental things, can we feel that civilization is at last in a way of justifying its existence and claiming to be finally established. . . .
>
> [T]he principle of public right must henceforth take precedence over the individual interests of particular nations, and that the nations of the world must in some way band themselves together to see that that right prevails as against any sort of selfish aggression . . . that there must be a common agreement for a common object, and that at the heart of that common object must lie the inviolable rights of peoples and of mankind. It is to their interest that they should understand each other. In order that they may understand each other, it is imperative that they should agree to cooperate in a common cause and that they should so act that the guiding principle of that common cause shall be even-handed and impartial justice . . . some common force will be brought into existence which shall safeguard right as the first and most fundamental interest of all peoples and all governments, when coercion shall be summoned not to the service of political ambition or selfish hostility, but to the service of a common order, a common justice and a common peace.[24]

Wilson's description in May 1916 therefore necessarily implied that democracies would be the cornerstones of any institution dedicated to maintaining world peace, even if autocracies might be present. Only such peoples were to be trusted to commit themselves to the pursuit of a general interest in a stable structure of orderly change, which in its initial stages meant having a character of duty and honor so that they could pledge themselves reliably to a common purpose, formulated in laws that over time might form a "covenanted" or constitutional form.

So it was in keeping with his thinking, developed over the decades since 1885, that in April 1917, in his request to the Congress for a declaration of war against Germany, Wilson had left no doubt about the primacy of seeing peace confirmed by the cooperation of democratic peoples. If, as he put it in his famous phrase, "the world must be made safe for democracy," then following the defeat of the Central Powers, only one way was possible:

> Its peace must be planted upon the tested foundations of political liberty. . . . A steadfast concert for peace can never be maintained except by a partnership of democratic nations. No autocratic government could be trusted to keep faith within it or observe its covenants. It must be a league of honor, a partnership of opinion. . . . Only free peoples can hold their purpose and their honor steady to a common end and prefer the interests of mankind to any narrow interest of their own.[25]

DEMOCRACY AND THE LEAGUE OF NATIONS

From President Wilson's perspective, then, a multilateral defense pact depended for its success not simply on the structure of its institutions but more fundamentally on the character of its members. Accordingly, throughout the deliberations of the leading powers over the eventual structure of the League, the question of who had a right to join it came up repeatedly. In the final declaration of the Covenant published on April 21, 1919, Article 1 defined as eligible for membership:

> Any fully self-governing state, dominion or colony . . . if its admission is agreed to by two-thirds of the Assembly, provided that it shall give effective guarantees of its sincere intention to observe its international obligations.

The question here turned, obviously enough, on what it meant to be "self-governing." In his academic writings, Wilson had made it clear enough that this meant a democracy, one that had passed the stage at which its creation was in the hands of an elite to a stage in which an informed, engaged, and empowered citizenry would check governmental power. Whatever the ambiguities that might appear in Wilson's academic writing, by 1913, in the process of redefining legitimate government as one based on constitutional order in Mexico and by the terms he set up in 1915 for a Pan-American Treaty and what he expected in Hispaniola as well as the Pan-American Treaty, the meaning had been set.

By 1919, then, Wilson meant by self-government modern representative, constitutional democracy.[26] Accordingly, in Article 12 of his "first Paris draft" of the Covenant of January 8, 1919 (sometimes dated two days later), Wilson proposed more concretely than in the final statement of the Covenant to limit membership in the League to "government based upon the principle of popular self-government."[27] In the "second Paris draft," dated January 18, Wilson used exactly the same language.[28] In both drafts, Wilson was obviously using clearer, stronger, language than that employed in the document as it was finally adopted in February and published in April 1919. Fortunately, however, we can see from these earlier statements rather exactly what the president meant by "self-government" during his stay in Paris.

On February 5, an important exchange occurred during the meeting of the Commission writing the Covenant. The occasion was the submission of the Anglo-American Hurst-Miller proposal for membership that omitted entirely any requirement concerning regime type for those applying to enter the League (a question that at this point was Article 6 of the draft). President Wilson immediately intervened, proposing that the following words be inserted: "Only self-governing states shall be admitted to membership in the League; colonies enjoying full powers of self-government may be admitted." The British thereupon brought up the question of membership for India, which they strongly endorsed, and asked whether Wilson intended to include or exclude Germany, the Philippines, and Japan.

As the minutes for the meeting indicate, "no one was able to define 'self-government'" with complete accuracy. Even President Wilson admitted, "I have spent twenty years of my life lecturing on self-governing states, and trying all the time to define one. Now, whereas I haven't been able to arrive at a definition, I have come to the point where I recognize one when I see it." The French then came to the rescue. One of their delegates drew attention to his country's draft, which made it quite clear that only democracies could be considered as self-governing: "*nations . . . pourvues d'institutions représentatives permettant de les considérer comme responsables elles-mêmes des actes de leur propre gouvernement*" (nations endowed with representative institutions allowing them to be considered as themselves responsible for the acts of their government).

A British delegate again objected: "'Self-government' is a word which is hard to define and it is hard to judge a country by this standard. Thus, Germany might fit the description and what about Turkey and Bulgaria? The bare use of the world 'self-governing' is therefore unfortunate." Moreover, India had mobilized a million men for the Allied effort in the war. "Part of India is autocratically governed—yet that part is willingly so governed, and incontestably the great part is democratically administered. . . . If the League of Nations were to employ words which would arbitrarily exclude India, it would be taken by those people as a bitter insult. . . . The British Government is trying just as rapidly as possible to advance India into a self-governing colony; and for anything to happen which would exclude India would be unfortunate indeed."[29]

President Wilson took the floor to disagree with the British:

The impression of the whole world is that [India] is not self-governed, that the greater part is governed by the laws of Westminster, and the lesser part is governed by princes whose power is recognized and supported by the British government . . . even though it may be hard to exclude India, still we ought to recognize that all governments derive their just powers from the consent of the governed.

Based on these considerations, Wilson agreed with the French definition and by its terms said that therefore it was inconceivable to him that the Philippines be invited for membership in the League. The president concluded:

We have said that this war was carried on for a vindication of democracy. The statement did not create the impulse but it brought it to consciousness. So soon as it was stated that the war was being waged to make the world safe for democracy, a new spirit came into the world. People began to look at the substance rather than at the form. They knew that governments derive their just powers from consent of the governed. I should like to point out that nowhere else in the draft is there any recognition of the principle of democracy. If we are ready to fight for this, we should be ready to write it into the document.[30]

The French delegate, Léon Bourgeois, this time speaking in English, sounded his agreement. His definition of self-government, with which Wilson agreed, was that it must mean "the government is responsible to the nation. Whether the form of the government is republican or monarchical makes no difference. The question ought to be, is this government responsible to the people? *We are establishing a League of Nations, not a League of States.*"[31]

With the Americans and the French in agreement, Article 6 (which would eventually be Article 1 in the Covenant's final form) was adopted by the Commission with President Wilson's wording. Self-government was by common agreement defined as a state resting on the consent of the governed.

On February 13, the matter was brought forth yet again. President Wilson thereupon read what was now Article 7 (formerly Article 6, later to become Article 1), and discussion then turned to what the words *pays libres* meant in what would be the French version of the Covenant. A French delegate said in English, much as his colleague had a week earlier, that in constitutional law this meant a regime whose institutions "were democratic or liberal." He then proposed that self-government be understood to mean "countries whose institutions are founded on political liberty." With this, the Italian delegate expressed his support. The French version would now read *pays de self-government total.* At this point the British delegate said his country would accept such wording provided it be understood that India would be admitted to the League as a signatory to the Covenant—to which Wilson readily agreed.[32]

What we see in these discussions is that the men responsible for drafting the Covenant had come to agree that the term "self-government" as contained in Article 1 of the final document meant as Wilson (along with the French and Italian delegates, but not necessarily the British) had hoped: government based on the consent of the governed. The result would be, as the French delegate had so well expressed it, "a League of Nations, not a League of States."[33]

This language allowed Wilson, in turn, to say in Minneapolis on September 9, 1919, during his extraordinary western railway trip in a daunting effort to convince the public of the League's merits:

[T]he object of the war was to destroy autocratic powers. . . . Hence the Treaty that ended the recent war provides for the destruction of autocratic power as an instrument of international control, admitting only self-governing nations to the League of Nations. . . . No nation is admitted to the League of Nations whose people do not control its government . . . we are saying: "It depends upon your attitude. If you take charge of your own affairs, then come into the game and welcome." The League of Nations sends autocratic governments to Coventry.[34]

Later on the same day, speaking in St. Paul, Wilson repeated the point, saying it sufficed to read the Covenant of the League, where:

[Y]ou will find that no nation is admitted to the League of Nations that cannot show that it has the institutions which we call free. Nobody is admitted except the self-governing nations, because it was the instinctive judgment of every man who sat around that board that only a nation whose government was its servant and not its master could be trusted to preserve the peace of the world. There are not going to be many other kinds of nations long, my fellow citizens. The people of this world—not merely the people of America, for they did the job long ago—have determined that there shall be no more autocratic governments.[35]

THE LEAGUE SPONSORS DEMOCRATIC PRACTICES, PRINCIPLES, AND PEOPLES

If the restrictions that Wilson insisted were in place making the League strictly a club of democracies were something of a fiction, there were other ways in which the organization might nonetheless foster democracy worldwide. If we recall Wilson's explanation of the emergence of democracy, it depended on two basic factors: first, on the growth of a popular consensus on the interests, values, and habits of a people whose principal spokespersons would emerge from an increasingly large, prosperous, and cosmopolitan middle class; and, second, on an elite body of leaders of vision and trustworthiness whose professional experience would equip them to create institutions, which in turn would formulate and implement policies in the forms of law that would serve the common good and command general assent. Wilson believed that each of these dimensions of political life worked on the other like a tuning fork. Society would eventually come to dominate political institutions as it matured; nevertheless, at an initial stage, representatives of the people endowed with greater experience and vision would create the institutions and formulate the laws that would give the identity to social forces and thereby allow them to grow in insight and strength. Such would presumably also be the evolution of the League.

Yet even if leaders had a commanding role to play in the first stages of the creation of a democratic order, social forces had to be appropriate to such innovations. In this respect, the impact of the war seemed decisive. People wanted their leaders to create a world in which peace would endure. In this deeply felt wish was their "organic" unity, inchoate as it might be on the terms of how to achieve this purpose. One of Wilson's expectations, therefore, was that the great outburst of enthusiasm for him when he first arrived in Europe in December 1918—an outpouring that virtually every observer of the moment remarked on with a degree of wonder—would become the basis of an increasingly "organic" sentiment that would favor world peace. British writers such as H. G. Wells and John Maynard Keynes recalled that Wilson had then been regarded by millions as "a Messiah" or "a prophet." "When President Wilson left Washington," Keynes wrote, "he enjoyed a prestige and a moral influence throughout the world unequalled in history."[36] A consequence was that at one point, Wilson declared "if necessary I can reach the peoples of Europe over the head of their rulers."[37]

So on January 22, 1917, the president had addressed the Senate calling for a general worldwide movement toward "government by the consent of the governed," insisting "I hope and believe that I am in effect speaking for liberals and friends of humanity in every nation and of every program of liberty."

> These are American principles, American policies. We could stand for no other. And they are also the principles and policies of forward-looking men and women everywhere, of every modern nation, of every enlightened community. They are the principles of mankind and must prevail.[38]

Some two years later, as he presented the final version of the Covenant of the League to representatives of the signatory nations represented at Versailles, President Wilson returned to the theme of the anticipated popular reception of the mission of this multilateral institution. He spoke of "a universal feeling" that rested on the "practically universal opinion of plain men everywhere" that the powers pledging to join in the Covenant did so with "the deepest of all meanings, the union of wills in a common purpose, a union of wills which cannot be resisted, and which, I dare say, no nation will run the risk of attempting to resist." In his closing words:

> Wrong has been defeated, but the rest of the world has been more conscious than it ever was before of the majesty of right. People that were

suspicious of one another can now live as friends and comrades in a single family, and desire to do so. The miasma of distrust, of intrigue, is cleared away. Men are looking eye to eye and saying: "we are brothers and have a common purpose. We did not realize it before, now we do realize it, and this is our covenant of fraternity and of friendship."[39]

Yet any such development was presumably sure to be very long term. Wilson might have hoped that the experience of living together under the terms of the League would eventually lead to a union of peoples such as the United States itself had itself come to enjoy after many generations and the terrible suffering of its Civil War. Nonetheless, despite his trust in the ability of international law to create a sense of unity based on justice in Geneva, the president most surely did not anticipate the League in any foreseeable future to be a "world government." Differences were far too great for an "organic unity" to develop such as he had used the term as an academic. Still, through international law formulated by committed liberals, through institutions backed by popular will, a start would be found to protect the democratic world from war.[40] As he had put it in his Second Inaugural Address in March 1917, only weeks before the United States entered the war:

> [Ours] are not the principles of a province or of a single continent. We have known and boasted all along that they were the principles of a liberated mankind. These, therefore, are the things we shall stand for, whether in war or in peace. . . . That governments derive all their just powers from the consent of the governed and that no other powers should be supported by the common thought, purpose, or power of the family of nations.[41]

Here, then, we find an explanation for Wilson's repeated call for the self-determination of people as protected by the League. To some interpreters of the term, Wilson's invocations of the term were little more than an empty response to Lenin's call in November 1917 for the "self-determination of peoples," rather cynically intended to protect the Bolshevik Revolution by creating troubles for the powers elsewhere. To others, the term remains frankly opaque and certainly naïve. Yet in its defense, surely it reflects Wilson's belief that only a homogenous community can be the home of an organic consciousness, the prelude to a democratic society, one that cohered through a consensus of values, interests, and habits, which in turn can give rise to appropriate institutions for self-government. Moreover, in Wilson's eye autocracy was dedicated by its nature to imperialist ventures that denied self-determination for weaker peoples, which in turn fed competitive annexations by the powerful and uprisings by the oppressed. Thus, for the League to promote self-determination might at one and the same time both thwart imperialist designs on weaker peoples and so stifle balance-of-power maneuvering, as well as protect an eventual seedbed of democracy. Whatever its problems in application, it was no empty or cryptic phrase that he used. It reasserted the legitimacy of a Westphalian system of states that at its core was anti-imperialist.

That said, there should be no doubting that the concept of self-determination was flawed conceptually and that in many ways it was proved dysfunctional by subsequent historical events. In theoretical terms, Wilson vastly overrated the ability of peoples at a populist level of political consciousness to develop in a stable constitutional democratic direction. Perhaps he had his forebodings. Both the Mexican and, more especially, the Bolshevik Revolutions occurred on his watch, and he certainly sensed in the turmoil of what was happening in Russia a political awakening that was profoundly hostile to what the communists labeled "bourgeois democracy," exactly the form of political organization that Wilson most desired. A right- or left-wing populism that could move in a totalitarian direction—one thinks of the Spanish Civil War of 1936–1939, for example, or perhaps better the consolidation of totalitarianism in the Soviet Union by Lenin at the Third Party Congress in 1921 and Mussolini's March on Rome in 1922—hence appeared to be more likely in the 1920s and 1930s than the emergence of a constitutional democracy such as the Czechoslovaks came to enjoy. Sandwiched as most of these new countries were between the Soviet Union and Germany, neither of which had been invited to join the League but instead were cast into at least momentary isolation, how bright could the prospects be?

More, cutting up the map of Europe into nations with some degree of ethnic homogeneity, as he had to do with his team called the Inquiry, proved to be not simply difficult, but indeed impossible, to accomplish. The kind of ethno-religious homogeneity Wilson sought to make the basis of new state power was in many areas unattainable. Recognizing this problem, the president insisted that, to be acceptable to Washington, new states recognize minority rights. He proved concerned especially by the claims of the new Poland and the new Romania—asserting their right to self-determination to an extent that left that internal affairs beyond foreign jurisdiction—that they need not accord their Jewish populations the same rights as the majority population.[42] More, when the Germans were denied the self-determination they desired with kinfolk elsewhere (not only in the Sudetenland but especially in Austria) while no plebiscite was held to ratify the attachment of Alsace and Lorraine to France or the loss of territory with German majorities in part of Poland (or Austrians to Italy), we can appreciate that the phrase created more problems than it solved.

The single exception were the Czechoslovakians, the only people of all those who enjoyed "self-determination" after 1918 who demonstrated the abilities that Wilson thought would be general after the disintegration of empires if only the people were empowered. Accordingly, when Czechoslovakia's President Vaclav Havel addressed an emotional joint meeting of Congress on February 21, 1990, the first American he mentioned was Woodrow Wilson, whose "great support" in 1918 for Czech and Slovak nationalists had meant that they "could found our modern independent state." Havel acknowledged the spirit of Wilsonianism as well: that small nations deserve to be free; that their sovereignty should be based on national self-determination, which in turned implied the establishment of constitutional democratic government; that the intercourse of nations should be based on nondiscriminatory, liberal economic arrangements; and that democratic states should defend their common interest against the threat of self-interested aggrandizement and war. Finally, Havel declared very much in Wilson's spirit:

> Without a global revolution in the sphere of human consciousness, nothing will change for the better in the sphere of our being. . . . We are still incapable of understanding that the only genuine backbone of all our actions, if they are to be moral, is responsibility—responsibility to something higher than my family, my country, my company, my success.[43]

Time would tell. If the League could give popular consciousness the opportunity to mature in a way that favored democratic government, so too could participation in its institutions give rise to a body of international law that over time could constitute something of a rule book for international behavior. Through participating in the institutions making these laws and regulations, a world elite might emerge that was increasingly democratic in its habits, values, and interests, a corps of leaders capable of taking these practices home to populations increasingly open to social contracts and political institutions in line with democratic ways. As the United States had developed under enlightened leadership—and as it was continuing to unify thanks to the new patriotism Wilson was trying to encourage—so too a hub of democracies, located in Geneva (the home of Calvinism) might in due course expand to become an integrated, dynamic whole.

DEMOCRACY IN GERMANY AND RUSSIA

But let us face the fact, as Wilson must have done: self-determination for the peoples of Central Europe was small beer. Far more important for the fate of peace in Europe were the political futures of Germany and Russia. Here were the countries whose dynamism, if turned against peace, could lead to a war even more terrible than the one the world had just passed through, as Wilson clearly preceived.

So far as the Soviet Union was concerned, scholarship for some decades now has had a settled consensus that Wilson was not going to follow Winston Churchill's counsel when, as British War Secretary as of January 1919, he sent troops into Russia and declared that "Bolshevism must be strangled in its cradle." The United States did intervene with several thousand troops to rescue Czechoslovak troops and limit Japanese incursions in the Far East; and the president was concerned, in the European theater, about German advantages that might be secured in territories surrendered by Moscow at Brest-Litovsk in March 1918 (a vast region that contained 90 percent of Soviet coal and 50 percent of the country's industry). But Wilson was not sure that the Soviet Union would remain under communist control after the war ended. More, if it did not, he was nonetheless distrustful of the most powerful anti-Bolshevik White general, Alexander Kolchak, whom he doubted would institute either democratic practices or land reform if he came to power, and whom might one day conclude a security pact with a revanchist Germany.[44] Surprisingly, Lawrence Gelfand's authoritative survey of Wilson's advisory team concluded that "all the Inquiry's plans assumed the imminent establishment of a democratic constitutional government in Russia."[45] The Civil War did not end until October 1922, and even in the event of a communist victory, what that meant for a Soviet Union reduced in power by the loss of territories at Brest-Litovsk was quite unclear. Moreover, the president realized the means at his disposition were limited, given the enormous expenditure in troops and treasure that had already been required to defeat Germany and its allies.

In any case, as we have seen in Wilson's reasoning from his early days reflecting on the French Revolution, then confirmed by his experiences with Mexico between early 1913 and early 1917, large countries with ancient civi-

lizations and a politically aroused citizenry decided their future by themselves. Foreign incursions were unlikely to come to any constructive end. Not
surprisingly, then, when asked by British liaison Sir William Wiseman (with
whom the president enjoyed a close relationship) about joining political conferences with the Allies regarding action to be taken in Russia, Wilson replied:
"My policy regarding Russia is very similar to my Mexican policy. I believe in
letting them work out their own salvation, even though they wallow in anarchy for a while. I visualize it like this: A lot of impossible folk fighting among
themselves. You cannot do business with them, so you shut them all up in a
room and lock the door and tell them that when they have settled matters
among themselves you will unlock the door and do business."[46]

In fact, of course, Wilson had intervened in Mexican affairs. His nonrecognition doctrine of March 1913 and his use of American units to occupy
Veracruz in April 1914 were widely interpreted by Latin Americans as interference in the Mexican Revolution. Yet had Wilson so desired, he might have
done as James Polk did in 1846 and ordered the American armed forces to
proceed to Mexico City (seized by General Winfield Scott in September
1847). Instead, once Huerta was deposed, Wilson left Mexico to its own
devices, a first example of self-determination. The result was the Constitution
of 1917, an extraordinary document of progressive political and social rights
that could only have satisfied Wilson that Mexico was moving well along in
the process of achieving self-government. Not by intervention so much as by
encouragement, Washington had succeeded in circumstances where more
forceful American action might well have undermined the outcome that Wilson sought.

This is not to say that President Wilson was unconcerned by positions the
Kremlin took on the world stage or, more immediately, by the threat posed
by Bolshevik parties maneuvering to take power in postwar Europe, acting
the way Lenin had operated in Russia, taking advantage of the suffering
caused by the war and the vacuum of state power to seize the government for
themselves along lines laid out in Moscow. Both the president and Secretary
of State Robert Lansing were well aware of the danger that communism
posed with its universal message of revolution leading to "the dictatorship of
the proletariat" and its complete contempt for what it referred to as "bourgeois democracy."

Nonetheless, in a statement he drafted on November 21, 1918, regarding
the Russian situation, Wilson's position on Lenin and his party followers was
clear. He denounced them for repressing their own people who "desire to

safeguard the principles of democratic freedom won by their Revolution [whom] the United States thus purposes to assist by all the means in its power." Stating that the Bolshevik regime was "as much opposed to democracy as was the autocratic militarism of Germany," Wilson concluded that the United States opposed a state that rules "by mass terror and murder" until such time as "the authorities at Moscow and Petrograd . . . restore order and the due process of law and set up a government based on the freely expressed will of the whole people."[47] But he made no move to intervene to stifle the baby in its crib. Despite the arguments advanced by Arno Mayer in the 1960s that thwarting Bolshevism was the lead topic of debate in Paris in 1919, few experts on the question today agree with his analysis.[48] As for Wilson, as he put it at a Council of Four meeting in May 1919, what he had learned by studying the French Revolution and attempting to shape the Mexican Revolution could be neatly stated: "trying to stop a revolutionary movement by troops is like using a broom to hold back a great ocean."[49]

Wilson would make his policy toward the Soviet Union, in short, something like how he had acted toward Mexico between 1913 and 1916: what he had called "watchful waiting." As his early insights into the French Revolution had taught him, and as his instincts as a political comparativist made him well aware, a bad situation could be made worse by meddling when nationalist consciousness was at a boiling point.

More important by far in terms of what Wilson might do, and what the long-term consequences for peace would be, was the German Question. Despite its defeat (disguised as an armistice to be followed by a peace treaty) and its substantial losses in terms of population and territory, Germany remained in virtually everyone's thinking the most powerful country in Europe. Its territory had not been directly touched by the war (despite as many as 2 million young men left dead), and Wilson resisted calls to invade Germany, arguing this would result in a "humiliated" and "vengeful" people. As the president remarked to Wiseman, "If we humiliate the German people and drive them too far, we shall destroy all form of government and Bolshevism will take its place. We ought not to ground them to powder or there will be nothing to build up from."[50]

Five months later, Wilson reiterated his concern not to humiliate Berlin. At one point he had called for German participation at Paris in formulating the peace settlement. He remained consistent as well in his refusal to endorse an embargo on postwar Germany, while he left open the door for its eventual membership in the League of Nations once its democratic credentials were in order.[51] Thus, on March 27, 1919, he sided with British Prime Minister Lloyd George, and against French Prime Minister Georges Clemenceau, by invoking "the moderation which must be shown towards Germany. We don't wish to destroy Germany, nor could we do so; our greatest error would be to give her powerful reasons for wishing one day to take revenge. Excessive demands would most certainly sow the seed of war."[52] Most certainly what the president would not do was to march on Berlin as former President Theodore Roosevelt and other prominent Americans were urging him to do.

Indeed, why should he think so aggressively, given the assist he had already given to the end of autocracy in Germany? At the top of Wilson's agenda was the end of German autocracy in the person of the kaiser and the throne. If there were a point when the president might have contemplated a constitutional monarchy for the country along the British model, that moment quickly passed.

In October 1917, Secretary of State Lansing could reply to Pope Benedict XV's suggestion of a cease-fire among the belligerents and "a return to the status quo ante bellum" that Germany possessed:

> [A] vast military establishment controlled by an irresponsible government which, having secretly planned to dominate the world, proceeded to carry the plan out without regard either to the sacred obligations of treaty or the long-established practices and long-cherished principles of international action and honor. . . . This power is not the German people. It is the ruthless master of the German people. . . .
>
> The American people . . . believe that peace should rest upon the rights of people, not the rights of governments. . . . The test, therefore, of every plan of peace is this: is it based upon the faith of all the peoples involved or merely upon the word of an ambitious and intriguing government. . . .
>
> We cannot take the word of the present rulers of Germany as a guarantee of anything that is to endure, unless explicitly supported by such conclusive evidence of the will and purpose of the German people themselves.[53]

The message was soon repeated. In his State of the Union address of December 4, 1917, Wilson was clear that he would not deal with the kaiser and the military establishment; peace with Germany could be concluded only "when the German people have spokesmen whose word we can believe and when these spokesmen are ready in the name of their people to accept the common judgment of nations as to what shall henceforth be the bases of law and of covenant for the life of the world."[54] Again, on July 4, 1918, in an address at Mount Vernon, which he later reasserted to be a serious expression of his attitudes toward the kaiser and the military high command, the president declared that for peace to come "the power which has hitherto controlled the German nation" must be altered, and this will "depend upon the definiteness and the satisfactory character of the guarantees which can be given in this fundamental matter."[55]

By the fall, as his patience with the German regime completely ran out, President Wilson left no doubt about the matter. As he put it in a carefully considered note to the German government on October 23, 1918:

> [T]he United States cannot deal with any but veritable representatives of the German people, who have been assured of a genuine constitutional standing, the real rulers of Germany. If it must deal with the military masters and the monarchical autocrats of Germany now, or if it is likely to have to deal with them later in regard to the international obligations of the German empire, it must demand not peace negotiations but surrender. Nothing can be gained by leaving this essential thing unsaid.[56]

Only a week later, on October 30, 1918, President Wilson received a message from the head of the German parliament that the country's constitution had been amended in basic ways that were surely to his liking. Several days earlier the Reichstag had legislated a number of constitutional reforms that clearly appeared to pave the way for democratic government. The October Constitution (*Oktoberverfassung*) asserted the power of the Reichstag over the executive, modeled on the British constitutional monarchy. As the Reichstag leader put it in his communiqué to the White House:

> The position of the chancellor is completely changed. Whilst hitherto the chancellor (*Reichskanzler*) was merely a minister appointed by the confidence of the Emperor, henceforward, according to a new and explicit clause of the constitution, he can assume office only with the confidence of the Reichstag and hold office as long as the confidence of this body is assured. . . .
>   The position of the Emperor as the supreme war lord of the German army and navy has been completely abolished. No longer can military acts of political consequence be performed without the consent of the

chancellor. The subordination of the military under civil power goes so far that even the commission to appoint and the dismissal of all officers of the army and navy, done thus far by advice of constitutionally responsible chiefs of the military and naval cabinets, now require the countersignature of the Minister of War . . . who thereby assume responsibility to the Reichstag.[57]

In addition, constitutional changes determined that the chancellor's cabinet positions needed parliamentary approval, the kaiser was explicitly subordinate to the chancellor on all political questions, and decisions by the minister of war had to be submitted to the Reichstag for its approval. The constitutional changes ordered as well the democratization of the Prussian Landtag, thus liberalizing regional as well as national politics.[58]

Nor did change stop there. In late October and early November 1918, the so-called "German Revolution" began as sailors refused to obey orders to continue the naval war against Great Britain. The insurgency triggered popular uprisings elsewhere that were not to end until the Weimar Republic's constitution was finally adopted in August 1919. Meanwhile, on November 9, 1918, Chancellor Prince Max von Baden announced Kaiser Wilhelm II's abdication. In his official proclamation two weeks later renouncing the thrones of both Prussia and Germany, Wilhelm declared, "I release all the officials of the German Empire and of Prussia, as well as all officers, noncommissioned officers and men of the navy and of the Prussian army, as well as the troops of federated states of Germany, from the oath of fidelity which they tendered to me as their Emperor, King, and Commander-in-Chief." Against the objections of those leaders who wanted the kaiser tried and hanged, President Wilson saw the deposed monarch sent to end his days in Holland.[59]

Much as Wilson might have hoped, the Social Democratic Party, the largest popular political formation in the country at the time, showed itself to be resolutely anti-Bolshevik and committed to constitutional democracy. In the Constituent National Assembly of January 1919, it had some 37 percent of the deputies and was the strongest party in the Reichstag. The Socialists thus had the ability to form a center coalition in alliance with three other major parties, the so-called Weimar Coalition, which by that summer was able to produce a constitution, the basis of the Weimar Republic. In his Inaugural Address of March 5, 1917, Wilson had reaffirmed that the United States stood for the principle "that governments derive all their just powers from the consent of the governed and that no other powers should be supported by the common thought, purpose, or power of the family of nations." Why should he not be satisfied with changes as were now occurring in Germany? "The Wilsonian peace," as the historian Klaus Schwabe calls it, would now be construed as effectively achieved and this on terms conceivably favorable to the eventual consolidation of democracy in Germany.[60]

Of course, the future might prove that constitutional democracy in Germany lacked staying power. The imponderables were enormous. But as with Mexico and the Soviet Union, Wilson knew the perfect could be the enemy of the good—that a difficult situation could be made more difficult yet if outsiders attempted to submit a country with the cultural and political history of Germany to forced political reconstruction from without.

While there were, then, important signs that German democracy might win out as he hoped, Wilson was under no illusion that it would necessarily be able to consolidate itself institutionally. As he put it in April 1918, to a group of foreign correspondents gathered in Washington:

> The amazing thing to my mind is that a lot of German people that I know like the government they have been living under. It took me a long time to believe it; I thought they were bluffing. But I found some Germans whom I had to believe who really liked it and thought all nations ought to live under that kind of government. Now, there isn't any one kind of government under which all nations ought to live. There isn't any one kind of government which we have the right to impose upon any nation. So that I am not fighting for democracy, except for the peoples that want democracy. If they want it, then I am ready to fight until they get it. If they don't want it, that is none of my business. That was the principle that I acted on in dealing with Mexico. I said that Mexico was entitled, so far as we were concerned, if she did not interfere with us, to have any kind of order or any kind of disorder that she pleased—that it was none of our business. . . . A peace is not going to be permanent until this principle is accepted by everybody, that, given a political unit, it has the right to determine its own life.[61]

Here in Wilson's words is a sentiment he had expressed repeatedly when confronted with domestic turmoil in countries engaged in revolutionary change domestically. Always he would recall the mistakes of foreigners intervening in the French Revolution of 1789, and congratulate himself once again on the restraint he had shown toward Mexico between 1913 and 1916.

More, the Mexican experience could be said to have rewarded his restraint. The Constitution that the Mexican Congress ratified in February 1917, and which the United States recognized de jure that August, was a model of constitutional social democratic principles of a kind that could only have corresponded to what Wilson hoped for that country to adopt.

We must recall as well his repeated observations as an academic before 1900 that democracy was not a form of culture or politics that many people were suited to adopt easily if at all. Thus, it was exactly in line with his thinking both on the Soviet Union and Germany that, in December 1915, President Wilson had given a talk to the Democratic National Committee in which he declared much the same sentiments with respect to Mexico, that he had always been:

> [a] man who really believed down in his heart, that a people had the right to do anything with their government that they damned pleased to do, and that it was nobody else's business what they did with it. That is what I believe. If the Mexicans want to raise hell, let them raise hell. We have got nothing to do with it. It is their government, it is their hell. And after they have raised enough of it, it will sit so badly on their stomachs that they will want something else . . . and make a government that will stay put, but unless you let them have it out, they won't have a government that will stay put.[62]

The comparison between Mexico and Germany should not be pushed too far, of course. The German Question was of far greater moment for world peace than events in Mexico. Nevertheless, with respect to Germany, Wilson might believe he had accomplished a great deal that could direct this critical country in a way that would keep the peace. He had secured the abdication of the kaiser; seen a constitutional reorganization that made the country, on paper at least, a liberal democracy; witnessed popular uprisings that suggested a movement toward democratic government could succeed; and noted the beginnings of political reforms that by the summer of 1919 led to the creation of what was called the Weimar Republic—a young and burdened government, to be sure, yet one with indisputable democratic credentials.

Notwithstanding the positive trends domestically, the Peace Treaty forced on the Germans in the spring of 1919 boded ill for the future. The War Guilt clause (Article 231), with its demands for reparations, was especially onerous for the Germans to accept.[63] So too was the loss of some 10 percent of its territory and population. The British feared the consequences of such a "punitive peace," as did many of Wilson's closest advisers. Indeed, Wilson himself was reported to have said to his confidant Ray Stannard Baker, "If I were a German, I think I should never sign [the treaty.]"[64]

Yet much had been accomplished toward moving Germany in a liberal direction. Given these achievements, suggestions that Germany be divided into separate pieces (returned to something of its character before its unification in 1871 under Prussia) or that the United States should take over the government in Berlin, seemed not simply uncalled for but highly provocative of just the kind of reaction in that country that Wilson hoped to avoid. In due course, German prosperity might return (so blunting the appeal of Bolshevism), constitutional government might consolidate itself, and the country would be admitted to the League as a democratic people (as occurred in 1926).

Admittedly, the discussions of self-determination and the future conduct of Russia and Germany leave us with a huge array of hypothetical speculations and imponderables as forecasts. So Wilson had given in to Japanese demands for control over Shandung, to the enormous displeasure of the Chinese government and people, and indeed against his own better instincts.

How could Wilson have rested easy in such circumstances? The answer was that all these unsettled matters could in due course be sent to the League of Nations, to be run largely under American auspices. Problems hanging fire could be referred to this body, Wilson's *deus ex machina*, for eventual solution—provided it were run under Washington's auspices. Or so the president must have prayed. Political writer John B. Judis cites a comment by the president to his close colleague Colonel House, after a political setback at Paris, that sums up comments he had several times made in passing: "At least, House, we are saving the Covenant, and that instrument will work wonders, bring the blessing of peace, and then when the war psychosis has abated, it will not be difficult to settle all the disputes that baffle us now."[65]

THE LEAGUE AND AMERICAN EXCEPTIONALISM

The obstacles facing the League were tremendous. Neither the Soviet Union nor Germany was a member. Bolshevik parties were everywhere on the rise. The significant advances toward democracy in Berlin were nonetheless plagued with internal challenges. Self-determination obviously was a weak reed to lean on for stability in the new countries of Central Europe. France,

Britain, and Italy had demonstrated by their behavior at Paris that even the democracies could be deeply at odds with one another and continue to hew to balance-of-power thinking rather than appreciate the virtues of collective security. Were all this not enough, Wilson had to face opposition at home to American membership in the League. That the League might eventually foster democracy was surely on Wilson's agenda. Nevertheless, to make the world safe for democracy his first reactions were understandably defensive, not offensive.

Still, the instrument that Wilson had created with the League of Nations had its promising features so far as democracy promotion was concerned. As we saw earlier, such a multilateral organization could be at once the home to the formation of an elite membership of international leaders working in a club of democracies and an international bureaucracy dedicated to formulating and enforcing a nascent rule of law, as well as to the autonomous growth of an organic consciousness among the peoples of the world. But by far the most likely reason it might be successful in defending the integrity of world democracy lay in the role that the United States would play in leading the League and in so doing forming a new consciousness of international unity based on following the legal findings of institutions dedicated to peace that were seen as legitimate by a major part of the world community.

As Wilson saw it, we might say that the success of *multilateralism* rested, in its initial stages, on a good degree of American *unilateralism*, without which the various agencies needed for the world to act in concert would lack the strength and vision for purposeful action. It would be far-fetched to say that America would play for world affairs the role the Founders had managed successfully when they brought together in one people the United States of America, even if the thought surely crossed his mind. He was, as he put it in explaining his hopes, "playing for a hundred years hence."[66]

Accordingly, in Wilson's words as he addressed the Senate on July 10, 1919, to explain the necessity of American leadership of the League of Nations, "America may be said to have just reached her majority as a world power. It was almost exactly twenty-one years ago that the results of the war with Spain put us unexpectedly in possession of rich islands on the other side of the world and brought us into association with other governments in control of the West Indies. . . . Our isolation was ended twenty years ago. . . . There can be no question of our ceasing to be a world power. The only question is whether we can refuse the moral leadership that is offered us, whether we shall accept or reject the confidence of the world." Wilson then challenged the Senate in phrases often repeated:

[At the Paris Peace Conference] it was universally recognized that America had entered the war to promote no private or peculiar interest of her own but only as the champion of rights which she was glad to share with free men and lovers of justice everywhere. We had formulated the principles upon which the settlement was to be made. . . .

We were welcomed as disinterested friends. . . . The united power of free nations must put a stop to aggression, and the world must be given peace. . . . The League of Nations was . . . the only hope for mankind. . . . Shall we or any other people hesitate to accept this great duty? Dare we reject it and break the heart of the world?[67]

In a similar vein, Wilson told his audience in St. Louis, on September 5, 1919, "We have come to redeem the world by giving it liberty and justice. Now we are called up before the tribunal of mankind to redeem that immortal pledge."[68] Again, in Sioux Falls three days later: "If America goes back upon mankind, mankind has no other place to turn. It is the hope of nations all over the world that America will do this great thing. . . . I want to call you to witness that the peace of the world cannot be established without America. America is necessary to the peace of the world. And reverse the proposition: the peace and good will of the world are necessary to America."[69]

The ground was thus prepared for the president to declare to a rousing ovation in St. Paul the next day:

Our fathers of the Revolutionary age had a vision, my fellow citizens. There were only 3 million Americans then in a little strip of settlements on the Atlantic coast. Now the great body of American citizens extends from ocean to ocean, more than a hundred millions strong. These are the people of whom the Founders of the Republic were dreaming— these great hosts of free men and women who should come in the future and who should say to all the world: "Here are the testaments of liberty. Here are the principles of freedom. Here are the things which we must do in order that mankind may be released from the intolerable things of the past." And there came a day at Paris when representatives of all the great governments of the world accepted the American specifications upon which the terms of the treaty of peace were drawn. . . . *Shall we keep the primacy of the world, or shall we abandon it?*[70]

As he put it most resoundingly of all, at the Hotel Portland, in Portland, Oregon, on September 15, 1919, "At last the world knows America as savior of the world."[71]

Establishing a new sort of world order would take time—that is why American leadership was indispensable. What we find in 1919 was transposed from the spirit that in 1900 would give democracy to the Philippines:

> Liberty is a thing of slow construction. Liberty is a thing of universal cooperation. Liberty is a thing which you must build up by habit. Liberty is a thing which is rooted and grounded in character. And the reason I am so certain that the leadership of the world, in respect of order and progress, belongs to America is that I know that these principles are rooted and grounded in the American character.[72]

What choice was there other than determination and patience? In his impassioned last Annual Message on the State of the Union in 1920, President Wilson reminded his listeners of Lincoln's "immortal sentence. . . . Let us have faith that right makes might, and in that faith let us dare to do our duty as we understand it. . . . This was the faith which won the war. . . . This is the time of all others when democracy should prove its purity and its spiritual power to prevail. It is surely the manifest destiny of the United States to lead in the attempt to make this spirit prevail."[73]

Yet whatever America's importance, Wilson was nonetheless acutely aware of the limits on the country's power. Speaking in St. Louis on September 5, 1919, Wilson mocked those who thought the United States could return to isolationism:

> They believe that the United States is so strong, so financially strong, so industrially strong, if necessary so physically strong that it can impose its will upon the world . . . they believe that the processes of peace can be processes of domination and antagonism, instead of processes of cooperation and good feeling. I therefore want to point out to you that only those who are ignorant of the world can believe that any nation, even so great a nation as the United States, can stand alone and play a signal part in the history of mankind.[74]

Here Wilson gave birth to a particular notion of American exceptionalism. It was not simply that the power of the United States made it the "indispensable country," as Secretary of State Madeleine Albright would call it in 1998, although that it surely was. Rather, its exceptionalism came from the conviction that its national security could not be narrowly defined but depended on a certain form of world order.

To achieve this order called implicitly, in turn, for a grand strategy—in fact, what might finally emerge as the grandest that the United States has ever enjoyed either before or since. Yet Wilson left only sketches—what, in the introduction, we saw Reinhold Niebuhr refer to as "fortunate vagueness." Although never explicitly expressed, his approach was based on the notion that democracies must be preserved from the danger of autocratic (or later totalitarian) threat by a mutual defense pact; that, if feasible, democratic government should be expanded where possible so as to enlarge the perimeter of defense; that both the unity of this zone of peace and its enlargement would be enhanced by the spread of an open international economic system (the Open Door writ large); that multilateralism was the indispensable corollary of a community of democracies with integrated economies; and that the leadership of such an order fell without the slightest question on the United States of America, the only country with the power and the purpose for the foreseeable future to make the common interest its own special interest.

To be sure, Wilson never spelled out his complex strategy in a fully coherent manner, and tensions, blind spots, changes, and contradictions beset it, as indeed they do any comprehensive vision of a policy to create world order. Nevertheless, here were assembled the ingredients of what came to be called "Wilsonianism," an integrated approach to world affairs that would be resurrected by President Franklin Delano Roosevelt when war broke out again in 1939. Here was the development of the thinking that would lead eventually to triumph in the cold war with the Soviet Union (a far greater threat to liberal internationalism than Prussian aggression ever had been). And here was the reigning ideology we have still today in the United States, one expressed in far more assertive form first by President George W. Bush and then continued by President Barack Obama.

Here, in short, remains the last of the universal ideologies of the twentieth century born of World War I. Fascism died in 1945, communism in 1989, and the question, we shall see, is whether liberal internationalism will make it even to the second quarter of the twenty-first century in any way other than as empty rhetoric. If not, then will the age of ideologies with their grand strategies finally be over, to be replaced in all likelihood (as Wilson himself presumably would have predicted) by a return to the old game of states in the contest known as the balance of power?

The League of Nations was therefore Wilson's bid for the creation of a new world order. But it was built of fragile material—a Germany and a Soviet Union whose future international conduct was highly uncertain, a democratic world plunged into confusion and suffering by the damage wrought of war, the rise of peoples in Asia especially who witnessed what they now understood clearly as the weakness of Europe in international relations, and most of all by a United States of America reluctant to take on the leadership position that alone could ensure a modicum of stable order to world affairs.

CHAPTER FOUR

Wilson's Wilsonianism

Unlike the government of every other state, ancient or modern, the government of the United States was set up for the benefit of mankind as well as for the benefit of its own people . . . undertaken with high purpose, with clear vision, and with thoughtful and deliberate unselfishness, and undertaken by men who were no amateurs but acquainted with the world they lived in, practiced in the conduct of affairs, who set up a new government with an orderliness and a self-possession which marked them as men who were proud to serve liberty with the dignity and restraint of true devotees of a great ideal . . . everywhere established government looked with deep concern upon this new thing in the West, heard with unconcealed alarm this new and confident voice of liberty. . . .

[My purpose in this book is to] show that America knows how to lead the world in the solution of modern political and industrial problems, and thus vindicate democracy.[1]

—*Woodrow Wilson in a draft for a book never completed*

The weight of this book's argument is that the heart of the Wilsonian project—the keystone of American liberal internationalism—is the promotion of democracy worldwide for the sake of a peaceful international system and thus for American national security. Here is the essential building block of the system of Wilson's notion of "collective security," itself the best guarantee of world peace his generation could hope to provide. Through the League of Nations, Wilson proposed that a community dominated by democracies pledge itself to a combined military effort to preserve the international system from the threat of a devastating war, or at least to preserve the security of the democratic world. Failing the maturity of democratic peoples to recognize how their values and interests could be preserved by united action, American leadership was called for through a multilateral system dedicated to keeping the peace. This leadership itself was morally sanctioned by the role of the United States as the world's paramount democracy, one whose exceptional vocation was to identify its national security not with narrow self-interests but instead with a world-order agenda assuming the protection of the democratic way of life wherever that seemed directly menaced. Whatever the differences between Wilson's "classical" Wilsonianism, "hegemonic" Wilsonianism of the cold war years, and "imperialist" neo-Wilsonianism born of the triumph of the United States over the Soviet Union between 1989 and 1991, they are in agreement on the primacy of democracy and the need for Washington's leadership in the liberal equation for world peace.

I argued in the introduction to this book that there is a theoretical logic to liberal internationalism that confirmed the necessary centrality of democracy promotion to the Wilsonian agenda should a just and lasting global peace be achieved. Collective security, economic openness, and American leadership— the other conceptual elements of Wilsonianism—all depend on the guiding hand of the spirit of democracy, one based on a sense of honor and duty combined with transparency and accountability, expressed in the rule of law emanating from institutions dedicated to the common interest and based on the consent of the governed. From the Wilsonian perspective, the expansion of what by the 1990s was sometimes called "the pacific union" or "the zone of democratic peace" constituted the world's best hope for diminishing, if not ending, the scourge of war. But this effort, argued on the logic of theory alone, was unlikely to persuade a field long predisposed to debate the meaning of "Wilsonianism" to end its doubts that a consensus could be reached on a working definition that was at all compelling.

Chapters one through three therefore moved to a more protracted analysis of Woodrow Wilson's writings and policies from 1885 to 1920. The point was to establish an argument for the character of Wilsonianism based on the president's own thinking; the investigation of the logic of liberal theory alone might be unpersuasive if his writings and speeches could not be presented in defense of this formulation of the concepts that, working together, constituted the fundamentals of American liberal internationalism.

Each of these three chapters reviewed a building block of Wilson's thinking as it evolved over time. In the first chapter, corresponding to an initial stage in Wilson's thought, essentially from 1885 to 1900, I demonstrated the

importance of democratic government to him as an event of decisive importance in world history even if for the time being it was limited to certain
peoples. Allegiance to constitutional democracy allowed an immigrant nation
a form of patriotic unity superior to one based on religious or racial identity
while giving the United States a personality to be envied by peoples around
the globe. However, at this stage of his thinking, Wilson did not call for a
forward American foreign policy, nor did he think that the country had a
mission to pursue abroad that involved imperialism for the sake of democracy
promotion; much less did he envision for the United States a role of world
leadership informed by a democratizing vocation.

In chapter two, I reviewed a second stage in Wilson's thinking that began
in 1900, as he reflected on the fruits of the American victory in its war with
Spain in 1898. His new concepts, which built on those of the first stage in his
historical analysis, showed Wilson's conversion to what might be labeled
"progressive imperialism," as he called for the United States to move out of
isolationism under the flag of democracy promotion. A direct action program
of the sort Rudyard Kipling praised in "The White Man's Burden" marked a
new phase in the maturation of Wilson's thinking and served as the underpinning for his policies as president. The second stage concerned most importantly the Philippines, but also was quite in evidence with respect to Mexico,
Haiti, and the Dominican Republic between 1913 and 1917 (where Wilson
expanded his thinking by focusing on hemispheric stability as well as the political development of individual states) and also to his thinking about the
mandates created by the League of Nations in 1919.

In the third chapter, corresponding again to a new set of concepts born of
Wilson's analysis of world affairs during his presidency, I showed his more
forthright embrace of multilateralism and international economic openness as
factors contributing initially to the protection of democratic peoples, in the
expectation that in due course democracy might spread to others. Although
such thinking was first expressed in Wilson's efforts to create a Pan-American
Treaty and so create on the basis of republican governments stable relations
in the Western Hemisphere, by far his greatest achievement lay in his ambitious hopes for a League of Nations to keep the world's peace. What came to
be called "collective security"—a form of multilateral military defense pact
based on preserving and promoting democracy so as to provide for an enduring peace by overcoming what he diagnosed as the dangers of balance-of-
power thinking and policies—now moved forward as the defining statement

of Wilson's ambitions, the ultimate basis of what later generations would refer to as "Wilsonianism," the American variant of liberal internationalism.

Such a fine-grained study showed a gradual metamorphosis in Wilson's thinking as it expanded earlier categories of understanding in new directions. What we saw was that while each stage did not necessarily anticipate the next, each nonetheless had elements that played into later arguments so that what later came to be called Wilsonianism should be understood as an integrated cluster of arguments that evolved in sequence, and so in force, over time.

THE FIRST STAGE: THE IMPORTANCE OF DEMOCRACY TO WORLD HISTORY

The first stage opens with Wilson's early writings on democratic government in 1885 and takes us to 1900, when a new way of thinking becomes apparent to him as a result of his reflections on the Spanish-American War of 1898, ideas that he was able to tie into his earlier positions. In this first stage, Wilson extolled democratic government as the highest form of social contract and state organization that humanity had yet achieved. The historical evolution (and Wilson was a confirmed Darwinist) began, as he saw it, in the fifth century as the character of Teutonic feudalism mixed with Christian beliefs and practices and the spread of Roman law. The pedigree of democracy was further strengthened from the fifteenth to the eighteenth centuries, thanks to the Renaissance, the Reformation, and the Enlightenment. Throughout this later period, due to the addition of English political thought and practice from the thirteenth through the eighteenth centuries, the groundwork was laid by the mid-eighteenth century for the American colonies, and then for the United States, to become the leading representative of this new form of state (in league with the continued evolution of Great Britain). Wilson's purpose during these three decades of writing and speaking on democratic government was not so much to speculate on world history or America's place in it, but instead to heighten the self-understanding of his fellow citizens as to the course of their historical development so as to make democracy in America a more vital force for the nation's well-being.

During this formative period, Wilson saw democracy as history's most advanced form of government and anticipated that, with time, the American example would be imitated by others, combined, as it was sure to be, with the growth of a middle class in the more prosperous (and so more powerful) countries around the world. He thus had some ideas on international change. Yet working in the comparative manner as a political scientist (using categories that are still used today, well over a century later), he was careful to restrict his analyses to discrete countries. Accordingly, he warned explicitly in *The State* that because of the decisive importance of the "organic" social base of every governmental form, each country would change in terms of its own internal dynamic; outside forces could be of only very secondary importance.

Nevertheless, it was during this first period that Wilson did have what we might call an "intellectual breakthrough," a conceptual argument important in its own right but one that was capable in due course of engendering other ideas and so to meld in basically important ways into his later position. For as early as the mid-1880s, when he was only in his late twenties, Wilson would mark his distance from contemporary efforts to see the United States as best defined by its ethno-racial descent from Great Britain and its dominant Protestant Christian practices. To be sure, he recognized that in historical terms these aspects of American life had made decisive contributions to the country's development as the world's most advanced democracy. It had mattered critically to be of English and Protestant heritage. However, Wilson could maintain that now that this form of government had been achieved, it could be seen as detachable from its historical origins. One need not necessarily be either of a British or Protestant lineage to be a democrat and so a patriot.

The definition of what it meant to be an American correspondingly grew far wider, to encompass all those who subscribed to the form of social contract and governing institutions that people of British and Protestant extraction had given the country in the eighteenth century. Jewish or Catholic, Slav or Latin, all (except, unfortunately, East Asians and, more particularly, African Americans—even if he were not specific on their exclusion) could be first-class Americans without fear of bias, based on their allegiance to constitutional democracy. (Women's rights were to come with some lag time. Wilson's wife and daughters were of importance in the evolution of his thinking on this question, which eventually led him to support a constitutional amendment guaranteeing women equal voting rights with men in 1920.)

Wilson's belief in the uniqueness of the American character and its ability to be a united people owes something to his association with Frederick Jackson Turner and the idea they both had (although Turner's version was more fully developed) that the cultural character of the United States had been decisively influenced by the frontier experience in the continental expansion. Wilson was of the same judgment, which, along with his conviction that America had an increasingly important role to play in world affairs, allowed him to see here the basis not only of the nation's unity but also of its uniqueness. As he put it in 1902:

> Of course the present separateness and distinctive character of the United States among the nations is due in part to the mixture of races in the make-up of their people. Men out of every European race, men out of Asia, men out of Africa have crowded in. . . . An infinite crossing of strains has made a new race. . . . The fact should a little daunt those who make much of physical heredity and speak of the persistence of race characteristics as a thing fixed and inevitable. . . . Nations grow by spirit, not by blood. . . . There has been no break in our constitutional development. Nothing has been done of which we can confidently say, "This would not have been done had we kept the pure Saxon strain." All peoples have come to dwell among us, but they have merged their individuality in a national character already formed; have been dominated, changed, absorbed.[2]

Wilson may not have been the first or the only person to argue in terms that suggested the later notion of America as a "melting pot," but his stand was taken early and clearly. Moreover, given his emerging stature as a leading figure in the American intellectual community and the role he would later play in the nation's domestic and international life, we must underscore the importance of his position. By bridging divisions among the country's population based on ethno-racial, class, religious, and geographic distinctions, Wilson was effectively redefining American patriotism, basing the nation's identity on a more extensive and inclusive definition of unity and of what it meant to be a citizen.

But how do we get from this intellectual breakthrough to a more activist foreign policy? New concepts did not come about immediately, but the scene was now set intellectually for the development of two additional arguments to appear later in Wilson's thinking. The first perception to grow out of Wilson's perspective was that because democracy was the highest form of government the world had yet seen, its freedoms could hypothetically benefit other peoples should they acquire it. More importantly still, a community of democracies might form, irrespective of inherited cultural or historical differences, capable of preserving not only domestic but also regional, and perhaps international, peace within its own ranks. The second possible extrapolation from Wilson's basic concept as to the character of democracy was that the "exceptional" vocation of the United States was to define its national security not in traditional terms of narrow self-interest but as creating a world order dedicated to freedom and so to peace.

THE SECOND STAGE: THE POSSIBILITY OF PROGRESSIVE IMPERIALISM

The American conquest of the Philippines in 1898 would become an important case in point as America's democratic vocation expanded in scope the seedbed of Wilson's second stage of thinking explored in the second chapter of this book. Yet control of the Philippines concerned only a single foreign people. Later, as the stand Wilson adopted on the Mexican Revolution and the idea of a Pan-American Treaty took shape, he came to envision democracy as providing regional stability in a way that promised increased American national security by way of promoting constitutional liberty for others. Hemispheric solidarity based on multilateralism among the region's democracies could ultimately metamorphose into the arguments that underpinned his more global hopes for the League of Nations. In its fullness, the idea was that the cooperation within such an institution might serve both as the training ground and as the forum for an increasing number of democracies, each with its life based on its own history but united in their sense of a common set of values and purposes, the most important of which was to preserve their form of social contract and government through a peace maintained by unity bestowed by formal institutions based on the rule of law and the consent of the governed. The first stage of Wilson's thinking had thus laid the foundation stone on which a greater edifice of political argument could in due course be built.

It is worth taking a moment to consider how ideas change over time. Wilson's thinking changed in 1900—that is evident—but it did not contradict itself. Instead he built on analytical concepts established in stage one, the opportunity to create new possibilities for America. Implicitly, that is, Wilson's conception of the value of democratic government was pregnant with the possibility of thinking that should this form of government spread worldwide, its benefits for universal peace could be enormous. Practices at home of political transparency and accountability, habits at home of civic honor and duty, values at home that tolerated difference and negotiated disputes nonviolently through institutions that could make and enforce the rule of law—why could these virtues not be extended to the world stage with positive results to a community of people of the same mind in such basic and important ways?

Yet, to repeat: at its first stage, Wilson's position on world politics was implicit, not explicit. We can see that the ability of his convictions on the transformative power of democracy had the capacity at a later point to engender the idea that the spread of this form of government could bring the benefit of freedom to those who adopted it and peace to those who joined together in a community of democracies. Multilateral institutions among democracies were therefore of a different sort than any others ever before undertaken, and the role of the United States would be to occupy a leadership position. The Concert of Europe among monarchies that followed the Napoleonic Wars with their conservative, not to say reactionary, opposition to populism and liberalism, for example, could not hope to match up to a Concert of Democracies such as Wilson might imagine it and such as his intellectual grandchildren and great-grandchildren would argue when what came to be called "democracy peace theory" made its appearance in the 1980s and 1990s.

More, the exceptional vocation of the United States was to have as its national ambition an international calling. Without a monarchy dominating its politics, as well as without an established church whose interests would be to promote conformity, not freedom of thought; crowned instead by the prosperity and dominion of a burgeoning middle class whose access to information and cosmopolitanism gave rise to demands for a responsible state; and blessed by its expansion across a vast continent rich in resources and protected by mighty oceans that gave it access to the Pacific as well as the Atlantic—all this taken in combination meant that the United States had acquired the capacity to become a world center, John Winthrop's "shining city on a hill."

What could have been an argument for insularity instead became in Wilson's hands an appeal for involvement abroad. The banner under which such a forward policy was to march would obviously enough be fostering democracy for others. Still, it took Wilson's reflections on the Spanish-American War for Wilson to give birth to the idea of America's mission to promote democracy abroad. Although Wilson's focus had been on strengthening democracy in the United States prior to 1900, scarcely a year after the victory of 1898 a new set of concepts was born of his past thinking and this in remarkably clear fashion.

At its inception, this step forward betrayed little urgency to push America to the forefront of world affairs. Washington was not being urged to join the "scrambles" for territories in Asia and Africa that obsessed the Europeans in the late nineteenth century. Instead, Wilson settled on the more modest course of maintaining a limited scope for the exercise of American power and character. It was quite enough in 1900 and 1901 to make the argument that the United States must leave the isolationist tradition bequeathed by George Washington to the country in his famous Farewell Address of 1796, by using the country's rule over the Philippines and Puerto Rico, and its dominating position with respect to Cuba (and therefore the Caribbean, Mexico, and Central America), as the basis for consolidating certain positions basic to his later thinking.

However, at this point, Wilson's thinking was necessarily prudential. He had spilled much ink prior to 1900 arguing that the spread of democratic government beyond the confines of countries predisposed to it by centuries of development would necessarily be slow, difficult, if indeed it should occur at all. It should not come as a surprise, then, that in later years when he was president, he never considered marching on Mexico City, Moscow, or Berlin, even if he was deeply concerned by events in these capitals and was urged by others to take aggressive action.

Wilson's initial steps in the second stage were to take on the democratization of countries that were small, whose societies were "organically" incoherent because of their deep internal divisions and inchoate sense of political legitimacy, and where one could begin with the creation of an elite trained in the importance of institutions giving rise to the rule of law that in due course would have the support of the governed to give them legitimacy. So he saw America's mission in the Philippines, so after he became president he treated Haiti and the Dominican Republic, and so he saw the role of the "civilized nations" that took over the mandates after World War I in the Middle East, Africa, and the Pacific. "The White Man's Burden" was their eventual democratization, which would give liberty to their populations, add to the security of the United States, and contribute to regional, perhaps even world, peace.

Faced with the Mexican Revolution and then with the coming of war to Europe, Wilson made impressive additions to the concepts he had already engendered. With respect to Mexico, the president did what he could to promote constitutional order there but realized quickly enough that his efforts could matter only marginally. Latin Americans in general, as well as Mexicans of virtually all stripes, firmly rejected outside intervention in their

internal affairs. Moreover, the Mexican Constitution of 1917 could only reward his restraint, for it represented a consensus among the major actors in
the Mexican Revolution and was a model of progressive legislation for its
time (and indeed since).

Wilson did not give up on progressive imperialism, to be sure—his military
interventions and the American-led economic and political reordering of
Haiti and the Dominican Republic are evidence enough of this. But in the
face of events in Mexico, where the organic basis of political thought was
in ferment, Mexicans themselves were best suited to determine the political
order they would live under. It should come as no surprise, then, that in 1918
and 1919, Wilson repeatedly cited his feelings about Mexico to explain why
he would not intervene militarily to shape political decisions made in Berlin
or Moscow any more than he had ever contemplated sending armed forces to
Mexico City. What he presumably recalled were his repeated warnings in the
various editions of *The State* between 1889 and 1911 against any such foolhardy ventures if democracy promotion in any of these countries was the aim
he sought. And he had been rewarded by the Mexican Constitution of 1917,
which demonstrated to Wilson that if left to their own devices—that is, allowed to "self-determine"—other peoples were capable of presiding over
what might well be construed as their own democratization.

Confronted as well with the reality of the limits of American power in the
vast realms of Latin America farther to the south, Wilson had recourse to a
new effort to produce peace: a Pan-American Treaty—that is, to multilateralism of a kind that could be considered an embryonic form of collective security. When the multilateral treaty was combined with an appeal to a kind of
economic openness that would come with the Panama Canal, Wilson insisted
that the new links of interdependence should not compromise the sovereignty of the various peoples of the hemisphere, but instead, as with his proposed Treaty, contribute to their gradual democratization.

Given that the first article of the various drafts of the Pan-American Treaty
that Wilson tried to negotiate with the ABC powers (Argentina, Brazil, and
Chile) called for all signatories to be "republican governments" (which by
this time Wilson had identified as resting on the consent of the governed),
here was reason enough for the treaty to fail. In Wilson's categories, the organic base of these countries—the consensus of their most powerful social
sectors—simply could not accept conditions of this sort (which were not
the only ones to which they objected). Still, what the exercise allowed—
and Wilson was clear on the matter—was to stimulate thinking on how the

United States might contribute to a stable peace in Europe after war there ended.

THE THIRD STAGE: COLLECTIVE SECURITY THROUGH THE LEAGUE OF NATIONS

Enter the League of Nations. Almost to a person, historians salute this initiative as the high-water mark of what it meant to be a Wilsonian or an American liberal internationalist, even if the effort went down to defeat by the Senate in March 1920 and could be construed as repudiated by the American people in the presidential election of that year. Between 1913 and 1919, Wilson pulled together all his earlier concepts and out of them engendered new ones. In this final stage of his thinking, for the sake of an enduring peace, President Wilson could identify democracy as the fulcrum of change that at first he hoped only to defend but that at a later point might have the ability to spread; call more clearly than before for an open world economic system; detail the functions of a multilateral organization dedicated to the peaceful resolution of conflicts among peoples and states but prepared to go to war should unwarranted aggression that might disturb world affairs persist; and insist on American global hegemony as the guarantee that this ambitious program might succeed.

To appreciate the boldness of the League as a concept is to understand the promise of "collective security" in Wilson's mind. Overcoming balance-of-power thinking was for him the locus of the problem of the logic dictating war or peace. As he put it, the "perfect flower" of such thinking was Germany by 1914, a society and government that typified the inevitable consequence of the congeries of concepts that melded together *authoritarianism, economic protectionism, militarism,* and *imperialism.* America itself could tend toward this type of social and political order if it were to act on the world stage imitating the German model. By contrast, the eventual success of collective security would call for *free societies depending on democratic governments, international economic openness, and international institutions affording collaboration among such peoples in a way that would address all manner of conflict but especially those that raised the threat of war.*

In a word, it was not so much Germany as it was tyranny that was at issue, with not so much America as it was democracy being the solution. Wilson rejected the dog-eat-dog world of Hobbes, his answer being to replace it with a set of values, habits, interests, and institutions that could foster global peace, somewhat as the German Enlightenment philosopher Emmanuel Kant had suggested in the late eighteenth century (as had Hugo Grotius, writing on international law, over a century before him). Although the end was peace, Wilson was no pacifist. The first obligation of the League of Nations was to function as a defense pact to stop aggression short of war if possible, but to be prepared to fight collectively to preserve democratic government should that prove necessary. If the order Wilson proposed was initially a *Pax Americana*, its vocation was to become as quickly as possible a *Pax Democratica*.

As we can see from this account, collective security did not emerge overnight from Wilson's mind when the United States joined the war in April 1917, as if by some kind of divine inspiration. Such ideas were current around him, especially in circles active in Great Britain. But however much liberal internationalism was a "spirit of the age" such that we should not attribute more originality to Wilson than he should have, his ideas nonetheless proceeded almost of themselves from his more than thirty years of analysis of democracy in America, and then to the fortunes of democracy worldwide, an intellectual journey that takes us back to 1885. A failure though his hopes for the League were in his lifetime, the legacy he left to his country was in modified form resurrected as war broke out again in Europe in 1939, in short order drawing the United States into its fiery embrace, then leaving Washington with the task of designing the peace that would follow military victory in 1945.

With Wilson's design for the League of Nations and his appreciation of the tenets of collective security, Wilsonianism as a set of integrated concepts that would serve as a framework for American foreign policy was ready to be incorporated into thinking about a new international order in the 1940s. Yet to speak of a master plan, much less a grand strategy, in Wilson's final years would be to exaggerate what he left for his successors. A key reason is that there was no particular ground to think that Wilson's ideas would bear fruit in his time. America's fellow democracies had not shown themselves at the governmental level to be especially cooperative with Wilson's leadership in Paris in 1919. Their very royal and imperial pasts, and their long experience with balance-of-power politics, suggested a certain "contamination" of their democratic credentials.

Moreover, much as Wilson must have feared for reasons he had set out in his academic publications prior to 1900, most peoples liberated from the empires fallen after 1918 were altogether incapable of translating their desire for "liberty" into institutions capable of giving rise to the rule of law based on the consent of the governed, while the rise of extremist populist agendas on the right and the left made it highly unlikely democracy would be the wave of the future politically. Nor was the future conduct of the Soviet Union and Germany at all assured. Most seriously of all, despite the brilliance of his rhetoric, whether due to the terrible shape of his health after October 1919 or to his decided aversion to anything that smacked of "abstract theory," Wilson was unable to lay out his ambitious hopes in a way that persuaded Americans that the sovereign independence of their country might not be compromised by entangling itself in the League. In 1920, first the Senate and then, with the victory in the presidential election that year of the Republican Party under Warren Harding, the American public rejected participation in the League. Lack of interest in the League continued thereafter under the Republican presidents Calvin Coolidge and Herbert Hoover. Wilson had postponed problem after problem for the League's deliberation, taking it as a sort of *deus ex machina*, but he found it difficult to maintain that it would necessarily be the panacea to the Pandora's Box of problems unleashed by the horrors of the Great War. Wilson's Wilsonianism was therefore a promising sketch more than a detailed blueprint that can properly be called a grand strategy.

We need to give credit where credit is due, however. In a lecture of 1889 entitled "Leaders of Men," Wilson distinguished between leaders and prophets, concluding that it was seldom that the vision of the latter succeeded, for, like Edmund Burke, they "were wise too soon." Yet at the same time he had expressed his admiration for prophets for their vision and their courage, sentiments that in retrospect seem to suit the man himself quite well:

> Great reformers do not, indeed, observe time and circumstance. Theirs is not a service of opportunity. They have no thought for occasion, no capacity for compromise. They are the early vehicles of the Spirit of the Age. They are born of the very times that oppose them. . . . Theirs to hear the inarticulate voices that stir the night-watches, apprising the lonely sentinel of what the day will bring.[3]

The question, then, was how Wilson's Wilsonianism would mature in the hands of his successors, especially those of Franklin Delano Roosevelt; interact with containment during the cold war; and engender what should be called neo-Wilsonianism in the 1990s in the aftermath of the disintegration of the Soviet empire in 1989 and the implosion of the Soviet Union itself only two years later.

It was this enduring impact of Woodrow Wilson's thought on American policy-makers during this three-quarters of a century that makes him the most important president the United States has ever had with respect to its conduct in world affairs. Getting Wilson right in his own terms is thus basic to our understanding of American foreign policy ever since his times.

It is to this story that we now turn.

PART II

WILSONIANISM AFTER WILSON

CHAPTER FIVE

Wilsonianism: The Construction of
an American Vernacular

Woodrow Wilson's ultimate greatness must be measured by the degree to which he rallied the tradition of American Exceptionalism . . . a prophet toward whose vision America has judged itself obliged to aspire. . . . Whenever America has been tested by crisis or conflict—in World War II, the Cold War, and our own era's upheavals in the Islamic world—it has returned in one way or another to Woodrow Wilson's vision of a world order that secures peace through democracy, open diplomacy, and the cultivation of shared rules and standards.

The genius of this vision has been its ability to harness American idealism in the service of great foreign policy undertakings in peacemaking, human rights, and cooperative problem-solving, and to imbue the exercise of American power with the hope for a better and more peaceful world. Its influence has been in no small way responsible for the spread of participatory governance throughout the world in the past century and for the extraordinary conviction and optimism that America has brought to its engagement with world affairs.

—*Henry Kissinger, World Order, 2014*

American democracy promotion in the hands of committed liberal internationalists has never been disinterested. At times it has effectively camouflaged nationalist, geostrategic, economic, or ethno-religious concerns deemed important to the country but made more palatable by a veneer of high moralism. Nonetheless, its most fundamental ambition has always been to remain true to its own statement of purpose: to defend the national security of the United States by promoting a type of government for others that, while extending the blessings of liberty abroad, would also redound to the benefit of this country by establishing a new basis for international order. Under American auspices, the threat of war based on dangers arising from the anarchy of world affairs and from predatory authoritarian movements and governments would be replaced by a community of peace anchored in the character of democratic peoples and their ability to work together through channels of economic openness and multilateral organizations. Think of it as a secular religion if you will (and you surely should), but as first articulated in self-conscious form with practical consequences by Woodrow Wilson, what came to be called "liberal internationalism" (or in its American context, "Wilsonianism") was a set of ideas with powerful consequences for foreign peoples, for international order, and for American power. Here was the basis of a distinctive claim to American exceptionalism: that this nation was indeed, as Lincoln had put it, "the last, best hope of earth" because in its power and in its character it carried the seeds of a new and better world.

Taken on its face, the liberal internationalist agenda could be thought of as grand strategy at as high a level as it has ever been laid out in the United States. The problem with giving it too much credit as a clearly guiding framework for American foreign policy, however, was that Woodrow Wilson had never spelled out the details with anything like enough care to call it a blueprint for action.[1] For example, the League of Nations had been his key conception. Although he had repeatedly juxtaposed balance-of-power thinking in world affairs to the logic of collective security, Wilson had never linked all the aspects of each system to one another in a manner that made their differences readily apparent. Or again, even if it is not overly difficult to surmise why self-determination of peoples was an important goal for him, he had never explicitly explained it in terms of his greater blueprint for world order, nor frankly recognized its ambiguities. Most important of all, he had understood the promise of democracy to create a new kind of individual, society, and state, but he never clearly linked his domestic appreciation of this form of political life to an argument for promoting democracy worldwide for the sake of national security and global peace in a way that was either clear or convincing.

Still, I must insist on the coherence of Wilson's thinking so as to place the notion of "Wilsonianism" on firmer ground than it now enjoys. For example, to call Wilson's ambitions "idealistic," "moralistic," "utopian," and the basis of a "messianic imperialism" badly overstates, indeed most usually seriously *mistakes*, the confidence he could place in his hopes. As he well demonstrated in terms he published in his academic years and policies he pursued as president, Wilson recognized that authoritarian regimes had staying power based on the character of the popular cultures they represented; that revolutionary movements involving mass political mobilization would unite nationalistically to defy foreign efforts to control their destinies; and that anarchy and despotism could succeed one another like the night the day if there were no popular consensus on the institutions to give a nation unity based on law—as the saga of the French Revolution had revealed to Wilson in an analysis he had written in his early twenties. Indeed, seemingly established democracies themselves might fall out with one another, as most certainly had been the case at the Paris Peace Conference in 1919. Indeed, democracy might be threatened even in the United States for any of a variety of reasons, the most likely reason for Wilson being what he was not reluctant to call the "predatory" behavior of capitalist interests at home and abroad. To label liberalism inherently imperialist, and to track, as a number of influential intellectuals have done, a "utopian, messianic liberalism" to Wilson shows nothing less than a thoroughgoing misunderstanding of his thought and policies, a misunderstanding that has blinded generations of students of American foreign policy to the lessons implied in his academic work and his policies as president.[2]

The job here is to remedy these misunderstandings. A first point is to find the coherence in Wilson's own thinking while nonetheless insisting on its complexity, its internal tensions, its recurrent lack of explication, and its blind spots—the shortcomings of anything we might call a Wilsonianism grand strategy issuing from Wilson's own hands. Nevertheless, implicitly the constituent concepts of his vision added up to something extraordinary: that the best way to enhance American security was through a plan for world peace whose primary means was the eventual spread of democratic government. Ultimately this promise of a transformation in the life of individuals, societies, and peoples depended on the creation of a new kind of citizen, domestic order, governmental structure, and international community—a change in psychology, economics, sociology, and politics both domestic and foreign based on what it meant to be democratic. The plan would be aided by global economic openness, by the spread of multilateral institutions to dampen conflict in this politically plural but economically integrated world order, and by American leadership for the foreseeable future of world affairs. Yet, far-fetched as such liberal internationalist "idealism" appeared to many during Wilson's time and still today (and indeed, on closer inspection, even at times to the president himself), these interconnected goals were to become a basic element of American foreign policy with the start of World War II and were to last a full half century thereafter, before recombining themselves in ways that sapped their strength, to play a leading role in thinking about American foreign policy since the end of the cold war.

A quick list makes the point. The Bretton Woods system that integrated the world's market economies; the occupations of Japan and Germany that democratized them; the Marshall Plan that proved basic to the economic foundation of what we today call the European Union (EU); the North Atlantic Treaty Organization (NATO) that established the world's longest-lasting voluntary system of collective security—here were the greatest initiatives in the realization of the Wilsonian vision, indeed the greatest moments in the entire history of American foreign policy.

More was to follow: the Alliance for Progress that called for land reform and democracy in Latin America under President John Kennedy; President Jimmy Carter's "human rights crusade"; President Ronald Reagan's "freedom crusade," which contributed to the end of the cold war as Mikhail Gorbachev himself saluted the growth of world freedom through democratic government; Presidents George H. W. Bush's and Bill Clinton's successes in promoting the expansion of both the EU and NATO, as well as the World Trade Organization and the North American Free Trade Association, for the sake of enlarging the scope of "free market democracies"; President George W. Bush's invasion of Iraq, premised on the determination to transform "the Broader Middle East" into a democratic region ("The establishment of a free Iraq at the heart of the Middle East will be a watershed event in the global democratic revolution"); President Barack Obama's assertion as he accepted the Nobel Peace Prize that he embraced a "just war" doctrine for the sake of human rights worldwide. All of these initiatives had their roots in a liberal international conviction, and became, thanks to Wilson, a part of the vernacular of American power. At its roots was the conviction that the spread of democracy could change the character of world politics in the direction of a lasting peace. It was thus America's mission to assume the role of leading history in a progressive direction.

One need *not* agree with the assumptions of this argument (Henry Kissinger and Zbigniew Brzezinski, prominent Republican and Democratic foreign policy advisers, respectively, did not when in office and still today do not, for example) to recognize the power of this framework for policy, both ideologically and in practice. Yes, it was ambitious; yes, it was self-righteous; yes, at points it was vague. But yes: during the cold war, whatever the excesses of containment in Latin America, Iran, and Indochina (and I would attribute to Realist thinking far more of the murderous mistakes of the cold war than to liberal internationalism, for we dare not minimize the needless suffering created by Washington as it sent troops in their hundreds of thousands to Southeast Asia or used the Central Intelligence Agency to assist the overthrow of constitutional regimes in Latin America), liberal internationalism proved its worth as it triumphed over proletarian internationalism with the fall of the Berlin Wall on November 9, 1989.

These Wilsonian achievements notwithstanding, there should be no exaggeration of the explicit (as opposed to implicit) coherence of the worldview that Wilson's successors found as they debated their hopes for what would one day be a lasting peace as World War II broke upon them in 1939. On the one hand, his reputation had been dimmed by the criticism he received during the debates over the League, with its eventual rejection by the Senate in March 1920. Then the election of November 1920 selected the Republican candidate Warren Harding as president, with the largest percentage of the vote in a full century, so confirming popular opposition to the League. Successor Republican presidents Calvin Coolidge and Herbert Hoover shared Harding's position. The woes that followed were without number: in the 1920s, hyperinflation in Germany, American hesitancy over a forward, regulated, international economic policy, and, as Wall Street crashed, the worldwide Depression, which began late in 1929; in the 1930s, the increasing strength of fascist and communist movements in Europe and Asia, then the eventual outbreak of World War II at the end of the decade. In the three-way struggle among fascism, communism, and liberal democracy—on display for all to see in the Spanish Civil War from 1936 to 1939—for a time it appeared as if those championing democratic constitutionalism were the weakest of the lot.

However, as historian Robert Divine has documented, the setbacks that Wilson's commitment to internationalism suffered in the years following his departure from office in 1921 were not enough to snuff out the appeal of his thinking. Indeed, these shocking developments may well have served to keep his arguments alive as liberals reflected on his proposals throughout the 1920s and 1930s. With the outbreak of World War II in 1939, Wilson's message returned in force. Now his warnings appeared to an increasingly large circle to have been prescient of the troubles that the American failure to head the League would bring. Without American leadership of an institution devoted to keeping the peace (by going to war if necessary), Wilson's warning time and again in 1918 and 1919 that another, more terrible war would take place, came back to haunt his successors. In the planning for the peace that would follow victory in 1945, how could his reiterated messages that a new world order was urgently needed not carry weight?[3]

Fortunately, the men who took leadership of the United States during the twenty years of control the Democrats had of the White House after Franklin Delano Roosevelt (FDR) became president in 1933, had in many cases known Wilson firsthand. They did not need to rely on an explicitly formulated legacy of his worldview; it was enough to select parts of it that appealed to the problems of the moment and move forward from there. Reviving pieces of his approach to international affairs in updated form (thanks to the experience of the New Deal as well as of a renewed conflict in Europe and Asia) thus could be brought about systematically without a great deal of ideological posturing.

Let us look briefly at some obvious examples. The story of Wilsonianism's eventual resurgence could be conveyed through the thinking of FDR, who had been Wilson's assistant secretary of the navy and as such had accompanied him to Paris (although he was not involved in actual peace negotiations there). In 1920, Roosevelt was the Democratic Party's nominee for vice president, campaigning in support of American entry into the League of Nations. Although he introduced the Good Neighbor Policy toward Latin America in 1933 as a deliberate reversal of Wilson's interventions there, FDR nonetheless identified his thinking both domestically and internationally with Wilson. Moreover, his positions on the relationship between regulating business interests in the common interest for the sake of preserving American democracy—forcefully articulated in every one of his Inaugural Addresses—were virtually identical in tone to those taken by Wilson when he had assumed the presidency a generation earlier.

Or we might review the career of Roosevelt's secretary of state from 1933 to 1944, Cordell Hull, who in the House of Representatives from Tennessee between 1907 and 1921 (and again from 1923 to 1931) had worked closely with Wilson on economic reforms designed to open markets and regulate corporations. Decades later, Hull worked under FDR as the longest-serving secretary of state in American history (1933–1944) and contributed to the creation of the Bretton Woods system as well as of the United Nations (for which in 1945, he was awarded the Nobel Prize for Peace), both of which would surely have won Wilson's endorsement.[4]

Hull was thus party to the deliberations on the future transformation of Germany and Japan, which were not only to be democratized but restructured so as to become members of an open international market. Both Wilson and Roosevelt would surely have agreed with him when, as Hull put it in his memoirs, stressing the political advantages of an open door international economic system:

> Economic warfare . . . offers constant temptation to use force, or threat of force, to obtain what could have been got through normal processes of trade. . . . The basic approach to the problem of peace is the ordering of the world's economic life so that the masses of people can work and live in reasonable comfort.
>
> The principles underlying the trade agreements program are therefore an indispensable cornerstone for the edifice of peace. . . . It is a fact that war did not break out between the United States and any country with which we had been able to negotiate a trade agreement. It is also a fact that with very few exceptions, the countries with which we signed trade agreements joined together in resisting the Axis. The political line-up followed the economic line-up.[5]

The list could be extended to much of the foreign-policy-making elite in Washington after 1940—both Harry Truman and George C. Marshall had seen combat in France during World War I, for example. We might also include Republicans, such as Secretary of State John Foster Dulles (serving under President Dwight Eisenhower from 1953 to 1959), whose father, like Wilson's, had been a Presbyterian minister, who was a student at Princeton when Wilson was president there, and whose uncle was Wilson's secretary of state, Robert Lansing (1915–1920), who took Dulles with him (at Wilson's suggestion) to the Paris Peace Conference in 1919.

The review of Wilson's influence on American leaders a generation after he left office could be extended, but the point has been made. Former Secretary of State Henry Kissinger sums it up well: "Wilson's principles were so pervasive, so deeply related to the American perception of itself, that when two decades later the issue of world order came up again, the failure of the interwar period did not obstruct their triumphal return. Amidst another world war, America turned once more to the challenge of building a new world order essentially on Wilsonian principles."[6]

IMPLEMENTING THE WILSONIAN AGENDA, 1941–1951

Wilson's legacy could thus be invoked in a variety of ways, all of which Washington undertook in myriad forms to do. With the Bretton Woods system agreed to in 1944, his liberal internationalist concern with world economic integration took a giant step forward. The International Bank for Reconstruction and Development (later the World Bank) and the International Monetary Fund, complemented in 1947 by the General Agreement on Tariffs and Trade (today the World Trade Organization), laid the basis over the decades to come for the greatest surge in international trade and investment in world history, and this overwhelmingly among democratic capitalist countries.

Or again, with the United Nations (UN) Charter, signed in San Francisco in 1945, a good bit of the spirit and organizational structure of the League was revived, or so those Americans who contributed to its creation hoped. For them, the UN, as President Truman affirmed, invoked the spirit of the League in the Preamble to its Charter, dated June 26, 1945:

WE THE PEOPLES OF THE UNITED NATIONS DETERMINED:
to save succeeding generations from the scourge of war, which twice in our lifetime has brought untold sorrow to mankind, and to reaffirm faith in fundamental human rights, in the dignity and worth of the human person, in the equal rights of men and women and of nations large and small, and to establish conditions under which justice and respect for the obligations arising from treaties and other sources of international law can be maintained, and to promote social progress and better standards of life in larger freedom,

AND FOR THESE ENDS:
to practice tolerance and live together in peace with one another as good neighbors, and to unite our strength to maintain international peace and security, and to ensure, by the acceptance of principles and the institution of methods, that armed force shall not be used, save in

the common interest, and to employ international machinery for the promotion of the economic and social advancement of all peoples,

HAVE RESOLVED TO COMBINE OUR EFFORTS
TO ACCOMPLISH THESE AIMS.[7]

A different example would be the North Atlantic Treaty Organization (NATO) founded on April 4, 1949, seen as an embodiment of Wilson's notion of collective security. NATO was clearly a club of capitalist democracies (such was the character of all twelve founding members) and so corresponded more closely to the ideal type of multilateral institution Wilson hoped to see than did the UN, even if its mission was more limited geographically and in terms of substance than the League had ever been. The Treaty opened by declaring:

> The parties to this Treaty reaffirm their faith in the purposes and principles of the Charter of the United Nations and their desire to live in peace with all peoples and governments. They are determined to safeguard the freedom, common heritage, and civilization of their peoples, founded on the principles of democracy, individual liberty, and the rule of law. They seek to promote stability and well-being in the North Atlantic area. They are resolved to unite their efforts for collective defense and the preservation of peace and security. They therefore agree to this North Atlantic Treaty.[8]

NATO was obviously a balance-of-power organization directed against the Soviet Union. But it is too often overlooked that it was designed in important measure to keep Germany under control and so had an internal collective-security dimension. Nor should we forget that the Covenant of the League had itself had a balance-of-power character following from Article 17, which applied to any "dispute between a member of the League and a state which is not a member of the League." Under its terms, a nonmember belligerent could be subject to the same terms of action that a member state would be, including not only embargoes but also the use of force to preserve the peace. Not surprisingly, annual reports from the NATO parliamentary assembly through 2016 have regularly confirmed the liberal inspiration of the alliance, another legacy of the Wilsonian tradition.

In Washington's deliberations from the outset of the war, the importance of promoting a democratic form of government was self-evident to winning the peace that would follow the conflict. From the Atlantic Charter of August

1941 to the Declaration of Liberated Europe in 1945, the United States had insisted on world recognition of the right of peoples to self-determination and self-government. Brief as it was, the Charter, agreed to by Churchill and Roosevelt, resounded with clear Wilsonian notes. Three of its eight "common principles" assisted the opening of the world's economic borders, three assured the integrity of territorial boundaries, one called nations to "respect the right of all peoples to choose the form of government under which they live," with the final (and longest) calling for measures to ensure the future peace through "the establishment of a wider and permanent system of general security."[9]

The Declaration of Liberated Europe (proposed by President Roosevelt and signed as well by Prime Minister Churchill and Premier Joseph Stalin at Yalta in February 1945) was even more politically pointed. In its opening paragraph, the signatories asserted "their mutual agreement" to assist "the peoples liberated from the domination of Nazi Germany and the peoples of the former Axis satellite states of Europe to solve by democratic means their pressing political and economic problems." Its second paragraph called for the right of liberated peoples "to create democratic institutions of their own choice. This is a principle of the Atlantic Charter—the right of all people to choose the form of government under which they will live." Of the four ways these ends should be pursued, the third called for "the earliest possible establishment through free elections of governments responsive to the will of the people," while the fourth underscored the necessity "to facilitate where necessary the holding of such elections."[10]

THE WILSONIAN HIGHPOINT: TRANSFORMING JAPAN AND GERMANY

Yet surely the most important impact of the Wilsonian legacy (excluding the New Deal, which could be seen as following upon Wilson's Progressive Era domestic economic reforms) concerned occupation policy in Germany and Japan. The democratization of these two militaristic, protectionist, and authoritarian countries should be taken as the gold standard by which Wilsonianism expressed itself. In these extraordinary undertakings—efforts whose success was doubted by many leading experts at the time—Washington joined all of the policies favored by Wilson into a single coherent whole. Washington would insist that economies be opened internationally while being restructured internally to reduce state-sponsored protectionism; democratic institutions were to be built at the local, regional, and national levels (in Germany with respect to the Western sectors only); multilateral institutions appeared to coordinate domestic and regional reforms; and American power was widely understood to be the essential ingredient in bringing these changes about, if for no other reason than that the threat of communism to both countries was readily apparent to the citizenry at large.

American High Commissioner in Germany John McCloy was therefore right to congratulate the United States for the occupation's success in Germany: "We made unthinkable another European civil war. We ended one of history's longest threats to peace." General Douglas MacArthur, supreme allied commander in Japan, put his objectives more concretely:

> Japan had become the world's great laboratory for an experiment in the liberation of a people from totalitarian military rule and for the liberalization of government from within. . . . From the moment of my appointment as supreme commander, I had formulated the policies I intended to follow. First, destroy the military power. Punish war criminals. Build the structure of representative government. Modernize the constitution. Hold free elections. Enfranchise the women. Release the political prisoners. Liberate the farmers. Establish a free labor movement. Encourage a free economy. Abolish police oppression. Develop a free and responsible press. Liberalize education. Decentralize the political power. Separate church from state.[11]

How was this prodigious feat accomplished? American postwar planners recognized that they needed to consider how to rework regional and international order so as to facilitate the changes in Germany and Japan. Japan's situation was especially difficult as its relations with both Korea and China were very tense. But the United States was the dominant power in Southeast Asia (a growing trade partner of Japan), and it could cooperate directly with Japan and so compensate for the missing regional partners needed by Tokyo (a relationship made all the more important for the Japanese economy with the outbreak of war in Korea in the summer of 1950). The problem for West Germany was to rebuild itself regionally in a way that would integrate the country into a new European order based on a liberally inspired federation of democratic states.[12]

The treatment of the Federal Republic of Germany (so named as the three Western occupation zones were merged in 1949) shows how the American liberal plan was formulated. At the Potsdam Conference of July-August 1945,

America confirmed in a Declaration on Germany that the Allies should "prepare for the eventual reconstruction of German political life on a democratic basis and for eventual peaceful cooperation in international life by Germany." Among the reforms called for were changes in the educational system "to make possible the successful development of democratic ideas," and an alteration in the judicial system "in accordance with the principles of democracy, of justice under law, and of equal rights for all citizens without distinction of race, nationality, or religion." Two years later these plans were reasserted in a way that expanded their clarity.[13]

A critical element in American thinking was the economic reconstitution of a war-stricken Europe on the basis of open market integration. The Marshall Plan (or European Recovery Program), announced in 1947 and passed by the Congress and signed by President Truman in early 1948, saw the need to integrate the democratic capitalist parts of Western Europe so as to provide the prosperity and confidence necessary to establish a permanent peace. As Truman put it in his December 19, 1947, "Special Message to Congress" asking for the enactment of the Marshall Plan:

> Our deepest concern with European recovery is that it is essential to the maintenance of the civilization in which the American way of life is rooted. It is the only assurance of the continued independence and integrity of a group of nations who constitute a bulwark for the principles of freedom, justice and the dignity of the individual. The economic plight in which Europe now finds itself has intensified a political struggle between those who wish to remain free men living under the rule of law and those who would use economic distress as a pretext for the establishment of a totalitarian state. . . . It is for these reasons that the United States has so vital an interest in strengthening the belief of the people of Europe that freedom from fear and want will be achieved under free and democratic governments.[14]

By the following spring, the Organization for European Economic Cooperation (OEEC) began to operate in Paris to administer American and Canadian aid as provided for by the Marshall Plan. In 1961, the OEEC was replaced by the Organization for Economic Cooperation and Development (OECD), which in due course invited other capitalist democracies—Japan, Australia, and New Zealand—to join, and that also created additional institutions such as the International Energy Agency (IEA).

Parallel efforts proceeded apace. By 1951, the European Coal and Steel

Community was established, which, thanks to the Treaty of Rome in 1957, led to the creation of the European Economic Community, which itself was superseded by the Maastricht Treaty (1992), whose ratification a year later created what today is called the European Union (EU). This list could be extended almost indefinitely to include not only the organizations that run the EU but also those that link these countries, in turn, to multilateral groups such as the Organization of Security and Cooperation in Europe (OSCE), founded in the early 1970s, whose membership is much wider than that of the EU.

There is no reason to rehearse in more detail the great number of institutional ties that link Europe together, even more of which have been established since the collapse of the Soviet empire and the Soviet Union itself between 1989 and 1991. The point instead is to stress how in the immediate aftermath of World War II, America's leaders resurrected the essentials of Wilson's ambitions and refashioned them to good effect.

Nevertheless, as Wilson's writings on the importance of understanding the character of foreign peoples would remind us, it is critical not to overstate the American role in the transition of Japan and Germany as they became what later were called "free market democracies." The Japanese and Germans themselves played leading roles such that the process could not have been a success without the presence of cultural and historical traditions that could be built on by popular leaders and movements in both countries. To be sure, American power and the force of American convictions most surely mattered when it came to changing authoritarian cultures and political systems. It is inconceivable that Germany and Japan would have been changed as deeply as they were had the United States not been present with a rather clear design for what it wanted. However, on closer inspection, the democratization of Germany after 1945, for example, was arguably as much the work of the Germans themselves and their concerned neighbors (like Jean Monnet and Robert Schuman in France, Paul-Henri Spaak in Belgium, Alcide De Gasperi in Italy, and Johan Willem Beyen in the Netherlands—indeed of Christian Democrats and Social Democrats across Europe) as it was the Americans acting alone. It is telling that lists today of the Founding Fathers of a united Europe scarcely ever make reference to anyone American.

In the case of both Germany and Japan, democratic institutions resembled Great Britain far more than the United States, reflecting their own governmental pasts. Political parties had fixed programmatic concerns and substantial power to ensure internal discipline (for example, they could appoint mem-

bers to run in specific electoral districts and expel them when they broke
ranks in parliamentary voting). Similarly, Washington did not insist on a presidential system for either country but instead endorsed an executive selected
by parliamentary procedures, which corresponded more to prewar practices
for both Japan and Germany. Or again, it was for the Germans themselves to
write their constitutions—at the local level as well as later for West Germany
itself. For their part, Americans did suggest a more federal structure for Germany, in large measure so as to weaken Prussia, and the creation of Supreme
Judicial Courts as an additional check on the power of the central government. By May 1949, the three Western zones were politically merged under
the terms of a new constitution (called the Basic Law). That August, Bunde-
stag elections were held, and on September 20, 1949—less than five years
after Germany's surrender—Christian Democratic leader Konrad Adenauer
became the first chancellor of the Federal Republic of Germany, with its capital in Bonn.

In economic matters as well, important American demands and support
aimed to open the European economies so as to link them together. Still, the
European Coal and Steel Community was in major part the work of French
foreign minister Robert Schuman and as a result bore his name, the Schuman
Plan. Ludwig Erhard was minister of the economy under Adenauer and the
leader of the reform movement—which stressed economic openness—called
the "economic miracle" (*Wirtshaftswunder*), credited for the tremendous
benefits it brought to the Federal Republic.

Whatever the limits of this description of Germany (and the fact that for
the sake of brevity I have made only passing mention of Japan, whose story is
of equal interest), here is the sort of analysis that Woodrow Wilson had been
trained by his academic experience in the study of comparative politics to
make of various peoples when it came to understanding their political systems
and the logic of their transformation. As a comparativist political scientist,
Wilson understood the emergence of a democratic polity to be the product
of the convergence of a number of factors from the social (an engaged citizenry with the desire for a government based on their wishes and led in most
respects by members of the middle class) to the political (institutions headed
by leaders of character who could make and enforce laws that corresponded
to the common interest and general will of the society). That Germany and
Japan were possessed of these capacities by virtue of their domestic histories
is what ultimately made their transition from authoritarianism to democracy
successful.

The point is worth emphasizing because beginning in the 1990s, a later generation of American liberals forgot rather completely the enormous obstacles that can make democracy promotion impossible. Operation Iraqi Freedom, launched in 2003 with the invasion of Iraq under the auspices of President George W. Bush, backed by his neoconservative advisers, is one telling example: their expectation that somehow democracy would flower of itself in the Arab world in 2003 was a delusion (to be continued into the Arab Spring) based on a complete failure to understand the local circumstances that had permitted American success more than half a century earlier in Japan and Germany. The final chapter of this book returns to this matter.

In short, Japan and Germany (especially the latter) possessed attributes to make the transition to stable democratic government that many other people might altogether lack. For these reasons, American occupation policy should be counted the high-water mark of Wilsonianism, the fulfillment of his ambitions not only in Germany but also in the European Economic Community (later the European Union) along with their associated multilateral institutions that both domestically and regionally had created by the 1990s the most vibrant liberal transnational union that had ever existed in modern history.

Still, the character of those subject to American occupation should not for a minute be left out of the equation for success. If Germany was, as Wilson had said in 1919, the "perfect flower" of what the balance of power could lead to, then we might say that the European Union eighty years later, with a reunited Germany at its head, had become the "perfect flower" of what collective security founded on liberal internationalist convictions could produce.

THE COLD WAR AND CONTAINMENT

But we have been looking only at the success stories of American liberal internationalism. Some may object that the cold war was won thanks to "containment," and that this was a Realist, not a liberal, doctrine, depending as it did on military resolve and diplomatic management of the contest with Moscow. Accordingly, liberal internationalism is too often depicted as being a "second track" during this period, important to be sure, but of lesser significance. Thus, National Security Council Paper 68 (NSC-68, April 1950), generally considered the defining document of containment, thought principally of in balance-of-power terms, with an emphasis on military preparedness, in the contest between the United States and the Soviet Union, even if it contained many references to the "free world" as having "free individuals" in "free countries" and devoted a lengthy section to "The Underlying Conflict in the Realm of Ideas and Values." What containment implicitly called for was working, where necessary, with authoritarian governments abroad for the sake of blocking communist advances (or even with communists if they were on bad terms with Moscow, as was the case with Josip Tito's Yugoslavia). What did working with authoritarians have to do with the liberal agenda?[15]

The answer should be apparent from Wilson's pattern of thinking. He did not expect the spread of democracy around the world to be a quick or easy process, or indeed that it was even inevitable. He might well (and correctly) have argued that the success of converting Germany and Japan to liberal democratic ways depended in critical measure on the character of German and Japanese political culture—their strong sense of national unity, the presence of a powerful middle class, an elite with entrenched traditions of civic honor and duty, the existence of some traditional constraints on the power of a strong central government (in the German case especially), and the courage of leaders wanting to lead their countries in a new direction toward democracy and economic openness (in the Federal Republic, credit goes to both Konrad Adenauer and Kurt Schumacher, leaders of the democratic right and left, respectively, while in Japan attention is due to the striking story of Yoshida Shigeru). When other countries lacked these prerequisites, they might be unable to make a democratic transition, try as Washington might. To work with them as they were—as authoritarian, that is—should not be thought of as necessarily contradicting liberal internationalism. Washington's responsibility was to defend what was increasingly referred to as the "free world" from communism. And as both Churchill and FDR agreed, in such circumstances one might have to sup with the devil—provided he was an anti-communist.

The problem for the postwar world, as indeed the problem remains today for Wilsonians, was to know when boldly to push ahead with the ambition to expand the perimeter of the liberal world and when to act with restraint. Put differently, when was liberalism possible, failing which, what did containment require? That both of the two approaches to world affairs were dedicated, even if for their own reasons and in their own ways, to stopping the expansion of communism meant that a "grand coalition" between containment and liberalism was possible, even if sometimes difficult to achieve.

Hence, as American policy spread under the impetus of the cold war with the Truman Doctrine to the eastern Mediterranean; then with the Korean

War to Northeast Asia; in short order thereafter to Vietnam and all of Southeast Asia; and finally, with the advent of the Cuban Revolution, to Latin America (and thence, with astonishing Cuban daring, to parts of Africa), the question became what relevance to these conditions did the example of American liberal successes in Japan and Western Europe (and especially Germany) have?

Here is where containment trumped liberal internationalism, for the answer, quite simply, was: in most instances, not much, if indeed any.[16]

THE PROBLEM OF STATE- AND NATION-BUILDING IN THE TWENTIETH AND TWENTY-FIRST CENTURIES

The problem general to political change in the twentieth and twenty-first centuries takes us back to the late eighteenth century, to the American and French Revolutions, which were popular uprisings in the name of a new political order that would connect the citizenry to the state in new and powerful ways. These internal demands were linked internationally to the growth of nationalism, depending on the mobilization of popular forces, as a potent force in world politics. In both instances, new forms of political organization were called for, but the question was what would eventually materialize institutionally so as to provide stability. The most clear-cut example of the problems that could arise, so far as Woodrow Wilson was concerned, came from the contrasts he drew throughout his life between the French and American Revolutions, as we saw in chapter one. As a consequence, he was well aware of the staying power of some authoritarian regimes, of the difficulty of creating a democratic society and state, and of the necessity of working on occasion with authoritarian states that, unlike Germany, were not militaristic and imperialist but were perhaps enlightened despotisms with a progressive agenda for their peoples.

In Woodrow Wilson's academic writings and speeches on democracy, we can find a series of preconditions to the emergence of democratic government, prerequisites that typified the birth of American democracy but that might be found among other peoples expressed in very different forms (the German and Japanese sense of civic duty and personal honor, so basic to democracy, had very different origins in these cultures and the American, to give but one example). Compared to a later generation of social scientists, Wilson's presumed markers for a likely democratic future were admittedly rather thin, lacking in both historic depth and analytical scope, for the simple reason that his main concern was the advent of democracy in America and its development thereafter. But his work deserves respect when we become aware of his prudent reserve as to the course political development would take, combined with his recognition of diversity and the powers of adaptation of different societies.

First, for democracy to take root, there needs to be, in the classic Wilsonian schema, some tradition of accountable political institutions, even if they be contained within a governmental system that is largely authoritarian, as London, even after 1688, most certainly remained. Prussia and the later German Empire were authoritarian as well, but possessed a *Rechtsstaat*, or constitutional state, explicitly granting rights to the population and a way of defending them. Popular as well as elite culture thus comes to feel the entitlement of some degree of the rule of law binding on the state as well as on the citizenry. The existence of bureaucratic procedures of a regulated kind, the emergence of divisions between the legislative and the executive branches of government—all of these may serve as preludes to democracy even if the state remains essentially authoritarian, with political power concentrated in an executive of substantial authority.

Second, there needs to be an elite leadership that understands that freedom depends on the rule of law and that the use of such an institutional base as was already in place to build a democratic order necessarily calls for the guidance of this elite, one capable of eliciting the consent by the public to the laws created, which would alone make government legitimate. The notion that every day there should be a plebiscite on the rules to govern collective behavior was not for a moment an idea that Wilson would have endorsed (including today's call for "term limits"). Great men can make history (given the opportunities of the moment), as the modern examples of Germany, the Czech Republic, and South Korea demonstrate—or indeed their remarkable influence after the end of the cold war, throughout the 1990s.

Third, there needs to be a citizenry with a sense of collective values, interests, history, and purpose that is concerned and capable—following reasoned dialogue and, for Wilson, spiritual reflection—of monitoring and holding accountable state officials. For Wilson, this set of characteristics in the American context involved an educated and informed middle class, a public with a sense of civic honor and duty (most apparent historically in mainstream Protestantism), and an "organic" sense of unity that required a broadly shared social contract informed by patriotism. Other peoples may draw such citizenry from different sources.

Whatever particular form it took, therefore (and these three conditions are only the surface manifestations of far more complex social and political orders), they constitute in outline the institutional, popular, and elite components of what in time might become a democratic society and government. However, just as surely, these same preconditions would help us understand that there would be communities unable to make a successful transition to democracy in any fast or sure manner.

After World War I, three forms of mass organization competed in politics bidding for popular support: liberal democracy, communism, and fascism. Each ideology of power made a bid for nationalist as well as international support, and each found in the major world powers a state to promote its ambitions. Thus, the three-sided struggle was not simply among leading states (the United States, the Soviet Union, and Germany) but also among rival nationalisms, alliance systems, and ideologies. In this contest, fascism was the first to be marginalized (it has never disappeared), undone by its own authoritarian militarism. By contrast, despite its terrible losses in both world wars, the Soviet Union after 1945 had become a world power based not only on its formidable military strength, geopolitical depth, natural resources, and the energies of its people, but also—indeed especially—on Marxist-Leninist ideology, which allowed it to coordinate the activities of communist parties worldwide through Moscow's control of the Comintern (or Third International). Here was the challenge that Washington, and liberal internationalism in general, had to confront after 1945: how to sponsor nation- and state-building in Asia and Latin America that served liberal internationalism's interests and not those of world communism.

The communist solution to the rise of populism in politics was to organize a revolution based on the exploited sectors of the population and led by a disciplined, secret, hierarchical Leninist party, which had a blueprint for "fraternal parties" the world around, the entire body of which was supposed to be led by Moscow. The genius of the party was its ability to harness nationalism and the class demands of what was often a substantial majority of the population into a movement at once local and international, through a blueprint that provided for the tactics of "united front" popular mobilization and the organization of the state in terms of a "dictatorship of the proletariat," which entailed party control of every sector of social life in the country in a bid to move forward toward a communist future. "Proletarian international-ism" would then bring together like-minded peoples through the intersec-tion of parties expected to submit to the control of Moscow (or later of Beijing or Havana).[17]

Wilson's long-standing concern about the grievances of large populations suffering under imperialist-authoritarian rule combined with his grasp of the power of issues of nationalist identity and the ability of tyrannies to maintain their power through militarism to alert him intuitively to the danger of Bol-shevism. However, prior to the Russian Revolution it had not occurred to him that this kind of populism was possible—a mass mobilization that the fascists were as capable of organizing for their own militaristic and authoritar-ian ends as were the Marxist-Leninists. If one looks at *Constitutional Govern-ment in the United States* (1908), Wilson's "third stage" of historical political development altogether misses any such development, instead seeing the rise of populism solely as related to demands for constitutional democracy.[18] Once Bolshevism appeared, however, Wilson immediately (and correctly) recog-nized the threat it posed to the liberal international order he was working to secure.

In the confrontation with communism outside the advanced industrial world, democratic forces were at an obvious disadvantage. The appeal of liberal internationalism was best suited to middle-class forces, to those pro-gressive elements among the traditional elite that understood the need to gamble on reform in order to preserve their socioeconomic privileges, and to marginalized ethno-religious minorities who saw in the rise of majoritarian nationalism typical of communism a threat to their security.

The problems of democratic state- and nation-building during the cold war were multiplied by the kinds of political obstacles set in place by tradi-tional authoritarian orders. Whatever the strengths of democracy once it was in place, the problems of democratization in an authoritarian context where communist forces were gaining strength were considerable. Traditional elites resisted the diminution of their power; excluded sectors of the population rose up in long-repressed indignation at the established order; and foreign influences were targeted for nationalist attack so as to rouse populist passions. The process that introduces democracy and incorporates the mass of the population in representative institutions whose decisions are validated by the consent of the governed is not an easy affair, as Woodrow Wilson recognized as early as 1885 and repeated in his academic texts through 1911, the year before he was elected president.

In fact, democratization in many circumstances may be totally impractical. In its formative phase, democracy is particularly weak. Unlike its totalitarian rivals, democracy cannot organize its strength through a single-party structure, but instead invites rival parties to appear. It cannot provide its supporters the euphoria of a particularly militant ideology, but instead will preach tolerance, compromise, and negotiation. Neither can the democratic promise guarantee traditional elites the preservation of their privileges, assure the mass of the population justice for the terrible wrongs they have long endured, nor reassure the middle class that their interests and values will become the basis of the rule of law. As a way of respecting (indeed encouraging) diversity; as a procedure for securing compromise (not hard decisions); as an ethic of toleration (which discourages militancy); as a limited (rather than absolute) state, its appeal is naturally limited almost solely to the middle class and some marginalized minorities—in short, to those with something to lose from revolution but with something to gain from the reform of authoritarian ways. Wilson would surely be among the first to recognize the justice of these obstacles to the expansion of democracy.

To put it bluntly, in the contest with communism, liberal democracy was not a match in most lands outside those that, like Germany and Japan, were already socially, culturally, economically, and politically "advanced." Part of the reason communism could be successful in many parts of the world was that its form of party organization, ideology, and governing structures were able to sink roots rather quickly (even if sometimes only temporarily) and, as China and Vietnam demonstrate still today, meld themselves into traditional cultural and political practices. In contrast, democratization involved two things simultaneously: the empowerment of civil society and limits on the power of the government.

Here could obviously be a recipe for disaster. For if civil society were deeply divided internally at just the point when a new political order was being inaugurated that was expected to rule with the consent of the governed, then anarchy might well be the outcome, to be followed by authoritarian restoration or communism. Again and again, with the history of France always in mind, Wilson had warned precisely of this: the appeal of "liberty," in a situation where institutions capable of generating and enforcing the rule of law in a way based on the consent of the government could not be created, was nothing more than a will-o'-the-wisp.

The question, then, was whether to analyze, on the basis of close study, the prospects of each people. Poland, for example, was a country that might well have made a transition to democracy after the defeat of Germany in 1945 had Moscow not blocked this outcome. Or consider the case of Czechoslovakia after 1918, where democracy succeeded on the basis of its own internal dynamic with only marginal help from the United States.[19]

We can learn as much from the failure of constitutional democracy to flower as from its successes. Thus, as the Greek Civil War was the first to reveal to Washington, the search for a "third way" solution in which democratic government emerges, rather than a state controlled by communists or fascists, might well be an untenable hope.

Such was the situation in Greece. In October 1944, when the Germans withdrew from Greece, the communist party (KKE) alone had the capacity to rule the country, controlling as it did the National Liberation Movement (EAM) and its armed wing (ELAS), not to speak of its appeal to Greek patriotism as the most effective domestic force fighting against the Nazis. It was only the arrival of a British occupation force that was capable of moving effectively against the KKE.

The problem for the British in 1946 when they were militarily supreme in Greece was how to govern when a fascistic monarchy, the military, and those who had collaborated with the Germans were best able to confront communists determined to use force. Unfortunately, the liberal Republican forces were too divided to offer a credible alternative. American ambassador to Greece Lincoln MacVeagh tried manfully to foster such a "third force" among liberal Greeks, warning Washington, just as liberals would in case after case over the following years, that should the right take power in that country, it would eventually be toppled by the communists. But MacVeagh's attempts to find a credible constitutional liberal movement in Greece came to nothing. In the fall of 1946, when the communists launched a bitter civil war that lasted until late 1949, the question was whether to let Greece join the communist world or to work with the Greek right for an authoritarian outcome. In short, Americans hoped that Greece would become a democracy, but when that alternative appeared closed, it would work with authoritarians against communists.

Containment, with its association of military force and authoritarian government, thus trumped liberalism. In fact, of course, this antagonism between the realism of containment and the hopes of liberals was only in part real, for in many respects the two arguments were complementary. Both focused on stopping communism; the question was one of means, not of ends. In a case like that of Greece in the late 1940s, the move to work with the fascistic right against the communist left was one that many Wilsonians could endorse, painful though it might be. For if the question were to preserve constitutional democracy worldwide, containment might serve greater liberal ends, while trusting to liberal means might be to court disaster.

Although Wilson may have been as ignorant of the threat of totalitarianism in his time, he most certainly was aware that something dangerously different was afoot in the Soviet Union, something that was not simply "autocracy" as he had defined democracy's enemy in the form of Prussia and Germany. Indeed, as early as October 1918, his secretary of state Robert Lansing had put the matter in no uncertain terms:

> There are at work in Europe two implacable enemies of the individual and its guardians, political equality and justice. These enemies are absolutism and Bolshevism. The former is waning; the latter is increasing. We have seen absolutism as the evil genius which plunged the world into the present war. We have fought against it and see its complete defeat drawing very near. . . .
>
> Meanwhile in Russia, disorganized and weakened by revolution, appeared Bolshevism, the doctrine of proletariat despotism. . . . Bolshevism is the most hideous and monstrous thing that the human mind has ever conceived . . . this monster which seeks to devour civilized society and reduce mankind to the state of beasts is certainly spreading westward. Emissaries of the Bolshevists, well supplied with funds, are in Germany and Austria-Hungary preaching their abominable doctrine to the starving, desperate and ignorant people who have suffered almost beyond endurance. . . .
>
> The question is as to what will be the result if the proletariat should overthrow orderly governments in Central Europe. A Bolshevik Germany or Austria is too horrible to contemplate. It is worse, far worse, than a Prussianized Germany and would mean an even greater menace to human liberty. We must not go too far in making Germany and Austria impotent or we may give life to a being more atrocious than the malignant thing created by the science of Frankenstein.[20]

Wilson was not slow to follow suit. Whatever his declamations against German autocracy, he was even more concerned after 1917 by a new kind of dictatorship and mass organization that called itself Bolshevik. Although he had sympathized with the Russian Revolution of March 1917, the Bolshevik Revolution that October was something altogether different.

The men who are now largely in control of the affairs of Russia represent nobody but themselves. They have again and again been challenged to call a constitutional convention . . . and they dare not attempt it. They have no mandate from anybody. There are only thirty-four of them. . . . There is a closer monopoly of power in Petrograd and Moscow than there ever was in Berlin, and the thing that is intolerable is not that the Russian people are having their way, but that another group of men more cruel than the Czar himself is controlling the destinies of that great people.[21]

Or again:

I wish we could learn the lesson of Russia so that it would be burned into the consciousness of every man and woman in America. And that lesson is that nobody can be free where there is not public order and authority. What has happened in Russia is that an old and distinguished and skillful autocracy has put in its place an amateur autocracy—a little handful of men exercising without the slightest compunction of mercy or pity the bloody terror that characterized the worst days of the Czar. That is what must happen if you knock things to pieces.[22]

Wilson's conclusions about what a later generation called totalitarianism were never clearly formulated by him for the obvious reason that the ability to see at all clearly the future development of communism and fascism was not possible during his lifetime. Yet like his secretary of state Robert Lansing, Wilson was persuaded that a new form of political organization was emerging whose threat to world peace was deeply disturbing. For with the birth of communism came a challenge of a fundamental sort to liberal internationalism. Now the Soviet Union could present itself as the United States did, as being "exceptional," its national security bound to a certain form of world order centered in Moscow, but called by its destiny to create through revolution an enduring form of world peace, one in direct competition with the future Wilson envisaged.

German power in 1914 had been that of a nation-state; Soviet power by 1921 was decidedly global in its pretensions, working through fraternal parties grouped in an allegiance to Moscow. More, unlike the Americans, who declined to occupy Berlin, the German Bolsheviks were for the most part ready to repeat in a war-exhausted Germany what their comrades had already accomplished in a Russia bled dry by combat: to take power with a state- and nation-building scheme, combined with talk of a world revolution, that made Wilson's ambitions seem modest by comparison. That these considerations weighed heavily on the deliberations in Paris in the first months of 1919 is beyond doubt, even if some sources give them more importance than they actually possessed.[23]

In short, much as Washington would have preferred peoples to be like the Japanese and the Germans, who could be brought with relative ease into the charmed circle of liberal democratic life, in most instances it found itself between the proverbial rock and a hard place. Other peoples did not possess the historical set of preconditions for a democratic transition that these two defeated great powers had had. Faced with a choice realistically limited to a standoff between a determined right and an equally determined left, Washington moved to back the authoritarians against the communists. On what grounds could liberals disagree?

In theory, there were two solid reasons for dropping liberal ambitions for the time being and moving instead to be counter-revolutionary—that is, to favor containment over liberalism as a framework for action, both of which might well have appealed to Wilson the academic. First, the communists were avowed enemies of what they called "bourgeois democracy" and the capitalist system it worked with. By contrast, authoritarians were much more likely to agree to work with Washington (or London or Paris), in good part because they too were the object of communist revolutionary ambitions. From the point of view of safe-guarding the democratic world, then, authoritarians made far better bed partners than liberal forces of no apparent political strength.

A second reason to prefer authoritarian states to communist movements was that autocrats in many instances had at least a hypothetical capacity, from their place atop a society politically, to begin a process of democratization if sufficiently encouraged by the United States. The transition could begin if authoritarian regimes progressively allowed popular forces to enter into political life in a way that moved them toward democracy—for example, by permitting institutions independent of the state to act as a check on the unrestrained power of the government (as President Jimmy Carter tried to encourage with his "human rights campaign"). Or, by coaxing the state itself to reform (as President Ronald Reagan did through his policy of "constructive engagement" and by his call for economic "privatization," or an end to state ownership of the means of production), authoritarianism might give way to pluralism. In many cases, the United States favored military elites, hoping that they would eventually retire to their barracks, their mission accomplished, or, even better, entrust to outstanding civic leaders (Nelson Mandela, Vaclav Havel, Kim Dae Jung, for instance, or to leaders like King Juan Carlos of Spain or Pope John Paul II) the success of democratic state- and nation-building. In short, some form of enlightened authoritarianism might prepare the way in time for the outcome of democracy that liberal internationalists hoped to see flower.

Wilson himself could make distinctions among authoritarian governments. The tyrants he opposed had Germany at the top of the list. But he had not viewed Austria-Hungary in the same baleful light. Indeed, in his academic publication of 1908, Wilson had shown an appreciation for the historical role played by certain authoritarians in nation- and state-building, including, ironically enough, the Prussian leader Frederick the Great, whose military reforms laid the basis for German unification. In his ruminations on history, Wilson did not limit himself to the progenitors of American democracy when it came to leaders who gave rise to a popular political consciousness. Queen Elizabeth I was a leader he enormously admired, as he did Frederick:

> He first made [Prussia] a compact and potentially powerful kingdom and then himself called it into consciousness . . . he saw her and understood her as a whole. She was in a sense of his own making. . . . He was a leader as well as a master, and his rule gave Prussia such prestige as England had had in the times of the great Elizabeth. He led a new nation out on to the stage of Europe and made it ready for at any rate the initial stages of self-government by giving it the self-consciousness and regard for its own interests which come of enterprise. A living people needs not a master but a leader.[24]

Could something of this leadership now dedicated to liberal constitutionalism help push forward world politics in a way favorable to freedom? So many liberals during the cold war hoped. We might call this perspective the outgrowth of a Wilsonian vision that was realistic every bit as much as it was liberal. That is, while Woodrow Wilson championed the expansion of democratic government around the globe for the sake of the people involved, the national security of the United States, and regional or world peace, he most certainly understood the limits set by culture, history, and nationalist pride to such a process. He was a "realistic liberal," we might say: liberal when he could be, realistic when he had to be.

Here were the reasons, as we have already noted, that Wilson limited the pressure he brought to bear on Mexico, Russia, and Germany between 1913 and 1919 to conform to some ideal hope that could never be realized by foreign intervention. Large established civilizations with a politically aroused citizenry—in these three instances, as more than a century earlier with France—needed to be left to their own devices, evolving toward constitutional democracy if possible, but not interfered with, especially when nationalist forces would have reacted violently against outside pressures in a way that served no constructive end.

Containment and liberal internationalism could, then, be points of view that complemented each other. A striking example of realistic liberalism is the role of General George C. Marshall in authoring both the Truman Doctrine, issued in 1947—a famous statement of the need to contain communism in the eastern Mediterranean and, by implication, elsewhere as well—and the European Recovery Program (which bears his name), a tremendous boost to democracy in Europe that was announced in 1947 and began in earnest in 1948. One can also see the difference in administrations. Presidents Carter and Reagan were much more dedicated to direct efforts to move democracy forward worldwide than were Presidents George H. W. Bush (who famously declared he did not have "the vision thing") and Bill Clinton, both of whom were more selective in the matters they pushed directly and modest in their claims.

Yet it must be emphasized that there were most certainly strains in the "grand anti-communist coalition" as well. Liberal internationalists remained true to the hope of seeing democracy spread, bringing with it the benefit of regional or even world peace, as indicated by the example of the John F. Kennedy's liberal Alliance for Progress or Jimmy Carter and his "human rights crusade." Proponents of containment were far more likely to be skeptical about how far democratic ways could reach or to see in such a form of government a panacea for the world's ills.

In the case of Iran in 1953, Guatemala in 1954, or Chile in 1993, for example, Washington would take no chance on communists coming to power and, reflecting the dictates of containment thinking, moved to topple leaders and their governments. Liberals for the most part sharply disagreed. They argued instead that Iran and Guatemala were on the right track, building constitutions that had some promise of liberal outcomes while engaging in needed social reforms, and that therefore the Central Intelligence Agency should not have interfered by coups to install authoritarian governments. For its part, Chile had a polity deeply enough entrenched in democratic ways for generations that the political system itself should have been counted on to solve threats to freedom; military intervention of the sort that President Richard Nixon and Secretary of State Henry Kissinger approved for the Chilean armed forces should not have been condoned by Washington. Or again, the reasoning underlying Operation Condor, a counter-communist effort that provided military support to right-wing elements in Latin America, which the United States supported with technical and military aid at least from 1975 to 1978, reactivated under President Ronald Reagan with his "contras" in 1981, were examples of what most liberals believed to be unnecessary, indeed counterproductive (not to say murderous) instances of containment run amok. In short, for good reason, liberals and Realists could be deeply at odds with one another.

If Realist thinking and the dictates of containment could be rightly criticized by liberals, there were nonetheless other occasions when liberals did indeed seem naïve in their optimism about progressive change. That is, if supporters of containment could overreact to what to liberals seemed a vastly inflated sense of danger from communism (as in the aforementioned cases), liberals could try to support democracy in places where it made no sense at all. Consider, for example, the preachy lectures President Carter gave the Shah on human rights in 1977 and 1978, when it was much too late in the day to be offering such vacuous advice to save the Peacock Throne.

Some instances of liberal failure are more difficult to fault, however. Let us consider a particularly difficult, concrete case, that of President John F. Kennedy, who in 1961 launched the Alliance for Progress, with its call to combine land reform in Latin America with the strengthening of democratic institutions there. His intention was to counter the appeal of the Cuban Revolution throughout Latin America, formulating his outlook as "those who make peaceful evolution impossible, make violent revolution inevitable." Moreover, what made his hope seem practically possible was that the Alliance was responding to calls for Washington to come to the aid of reform from many established Latin leaders, including Brazil's Juscelino Kubitschek, Venezuela's Romulo Betancourt, Chile's Eduardo Frei, and Costa Rica's José Figueres, not to mention Christian Democratic parties in many sectors of the region.

The question, then, was whether Latin America was ready to undertake a democratic transition in the 1960s, not simply to stave off the threat of communism but also to introduce its people into a better way of life. Were the internal conditions such that such an effort might succeed? One certainly may criticize the administration of President Lyndon Johnson (and later the team of Secretary of State Henry Kissinger and President Richard Nixon) for giving green lights to military interventions in Brazil, Argentina, the Dominican Republic, and Chile. But an essential problem remained the inability of Latin American liberals to constitute enough of a domestic political force in most countries to hold the middle ground against the civil strife extremist movements on the right and left promoted. Whatever the faults of Washington (and no one should doubt them), the case of Chile is a particularly clear-cut example of how a people of great promise for democratization in terms of their historic profile nonetheless proved unable to rally to the undertaking until the cold war had become a thing of the past.[25]

Nor did President Jimmy Carter's "human rights campaign" have terribly much success. His failure to see that human rights of the sort he spoke about implied radical political change in authoritarian countries once close to Washington—and that it would anger the Soviets and the Chinese as well—suggested a striking liberal naïveté on his part. Ultimately, the failure of the Carter administration to handle the fall either of the Shah in Iran or of Anastasio Somoza in Nicaragua (both occurring in 1979) underscored not simply the fragility of authoritarian regimes but the limited appeal of democratizing reforms in many countries around the world and the futility (if not the blindness) of invoking them in situations such as these two countries faced in 1978 and 1979. Once again, as with the fate of the Alliance for Progress, a traditional Wilsonian might have been disappointed, but not surprised, at the eventual defeat of Carter's well-intentioned ambitions. Realists, of course, expected these failures from the start.

Washington had more success with societies that were better primed to make a democratic transition. Thus in the aftermath of the cold war, Poland, Slovenia, the Baltic states, and the Czech Republic moved (in different ways, to be sure) in the direction of liberal reforms, just as South Korea made a transition. So too the expansion of the European Union to include Spain, Portugal, and Greece in the 1970s and to provide for membership in the EU for peoples of southeastern and Eastern Europe was a critical boost to liberal democratic fortunes in these areas. Two decades later, however, similar efforts in countries like Romania and Bulgaria met with far more obstacles.

So we return to the argument that however critical American (or EU) support for democratization may have been, equally, if not more important, decisive factors lay in the character of the peoples entering upon such a transition from authoritarianism. Put simply, the Spanish and Portuguese, like the

Czechs and the Slovenes, had a better pedigree for a transition to democracy than did the Bulgarians or the Romanians. As a reading of Wilson the academic would suggest, here was the heart of the matter—it was not only the intentions of Washington that counted for success (necessary though they be) but even more so the character of the peoples themselves when it came to confronting the dramatic change to liberal democracy that the EU and the United States proposed to foster.

To conclude: As this account reveals, the impact of American hegemony must surely often be respected as an active agent in the democratization process. Yet just as well it may be ineffective or rouse a degree of anarchy or resentment and brutality that actually is self-defeating. President Wilson's reluctance to involve himself in the domestic politics of Mexico, the Soviet Union, and Germany reflected this prudent calculation. Confident talk about the future of Vietnam being democracy by John Kennedy shortly before he was elected president most certainly did not:

> Vietnam represents a proving ground for democracy in Asia. . . . Vietnam represents the alternative to communist dictatorship. If this democratic experience fails . . . then weakness, not strength, will characterize the meaning of democracy in the minds of still more Asians. The United States is directly responsible for this experiment—it is playing an important role in the laboratory where it is being conducted. We cannot afford to permit that experiment to fail.[26]

Surely as president, Kennedy was more on the mark sounding like a traditional Wilson liberal realist when he learned of Rafael Trujillo's assassination in the Dominican Republic in June 1961: "There are three possibilities in descending order of preference: a decent democratic regime, a continuation of the Trujillo regime, or a Castro regime. We ought to aim at the first, but we really can't renounce the second until we are sure that we can avoid the third."[27]

CONTAINMENT AND LIBERALISM IN THE ACADEMIC WORLD, 1950–1980

It should come as no surprise that debates in the academic world over the relative merits of supporting authoritarian regimes or promoting a liberal agenda followed much the same terms as in the policy world in Washington. Some doubted that the high cost of defeating communism in Indochina or parts of Latin America could possibly be justified by the small stakes developments in these parts of the world represented. Others countered that the effect of any communist victory would possess a contagion effect like a "falling domino" or a "rotten apple" such that the United States must stand prepared to block communism wherever it appeared.

But the problem for those who would act to stop communist advances was how to conceptualize the nation- and state-building requirements that any such effort would need. It was painfully clear that few of the countries of Africa and Asia (Latin America was often looked at differently) had the kinds of preconditions for such government that Germany and Japan had possessed in 1945. Could a successful strategy be formulated that would block what was widely seen as the relative advantages enjoyed by Leninism—especially when complemented by Mao Zedong's model of peasant and working-class insurgency or Fidel Castro's "foco" concept of guerrilla warfare, all augmented by a neo-Marxist argument called "dependency theory" that had appeared in full flower by the late 1960s, uniting nationalism to world-class conflict with anti-Americanism as the focus of its wrath?[28]

During the 1950s and early 1960s, the most influential writing came from theorists of development who posited a linear set of "stages" from tradition to modernity, complete with personality types, social profiles, economic changes, and forms of political order whose understanding might be used to blunt the appeal of communism. Among the most influential writers of this period in economics were W. W. Rostow and Max Millikan; in social psychology Sidney Verba, Talcott Parsons, Daniel Lerner, and Lucian Pye; in politics Gabriel Almond, Seymour Martin Lipset, David Apter, and James. S. Coleman.[29]

The mix of those involved in these questions was extraordinarily varied. Area studies and distinct social science disciplines mixed with those who favored "macro," "micro," or "mid-level" forms of theory. If some writers came down on the side of supporting authoritarian governments against communist insurgencies in hopes that the former would eventually foster liberalization through economic development or political reforms, others settled for supporting authoritarians pure and simple. What was most striking was how few held out for democratic nation- and state-building aside from areas such as Latin America where it was obvious some indications of fertile ground existed.

Over time, emphasis changed; economic stages in modernization might be called dominant from the late 1950s to the early 1960s, after which political science moved firmly into control. The fields were so divided by area studies, academic disciplines, and theoretical grandstanding that we cannot do better than to agree with economist Albert Hirschman's contention in 1970 that "the compulsion to theorize . . . is often so strong as to induce mindlessness."[30]

What most surely should not be accepted is that liberal internationalist thinkers were particularly optimistic about democracy's chances in much of the late-industrializing world during the cold war. Consider, however, the widely read attack on the alleged thinking of liberals that appeared in 1973, when political science professor Robert A. Packenham published *Liberal America and the Third World*. Here Packenham criticized what he saw as the "liberal premises" of the "doctrines" guiding thinking in Washington as the cold war opened: that "change and development are easy"; that "all good things go together"; that "radicalism and revolution are bad"; and that "distributing power is more important than accumulating power." These are, he asserted, "the four main liberal assumptions" that "hang together in a coherent whole that explains and illuminates the doctrines even more than the simple sum of the parts."[31]

Who was thinking these thoughts and what made them "liberal"? Surely this model of thinking about the third world is nothing more than a straw man to set afire, for it is not at all an accurate representation of the overall field of political development during this period. Packenham is correct that some of the literature in the field was linear—there were prominent writers who posited a well-nigh universal course of economic or political development from the "traditional" to the "modern" through stages that bore resemblance to the path the West had taken in centuries past. Yet most students of the question would have wondered, with so many hurdles to jump in the form of stages with their preconditions, if a liberal end-goal could possibly be reached. Packenham's assertion that "change and development are easy" and that "all good things go together" are not naïve reassurances to be found at all often, and certainly not in liberals of Wilson's persuasion (whom Packenham never mentions, despite his invocation of apparently all of "liberal America").[32]

The idea that democratizing nation- and state-building efforts managed by the United States could bear fruit met with stiff resistance among many liberals for reasons that corresponded to concerns that Wilson might have expressed. For example, in 1969 Reinhold Niebuhr and Paul Sigmund wrote that what they clearly recognized as "the lack of success of democratic politics in the newly emerging nations" could be related to "three constant prerequisites" of democracy: "1) the unity and solidarity of the community, sufficiently strong to allow the free play of competitive interests without endangering the unity of the community itself; 2) a belief in the freedom of the individual and appreciation of his worth; and 3) a tolerable harmony and equilibrium of social and political and economic forces necessary to establish an approximation of social justice."[33]

It would be difficult to summarize Wilson's own thinking more succinctly than Niebuhr and Sigmund do, provided one adds the distinctly conservative emphasis he always placed on the role of established institutions in guiding the political life of a people. For social forces unable to coalesce their agendas through institutions giving rise to the rule of law quite obviously could be subject—as the French had been for over a hundred years, in Wilson's opinion—to anarchy and despotism, each in its turn. If anything, Wilson's thinking would have led to a deeper pessimism than Niebuhr and Sigmund professed so far as democracy promotion was concerned. Obviously, none of this had anything whatsoever to do with the misleading characterization ascribed to liberals by Robert Packenham.

Or take, as another example of the prudent reserve academics found with respect to American democracy promotion during the cold war, the analysis of Robert Dahl, a liberal Yale political scientist in *Polyarchy: Participation and Opposition,* published in 1971. Dahl's work was probably cited more frequently, over the two decades after which it appeared, than any other on the character of democracy as it is actually practiced. The book's opening line asks the critical question: "Given a regime in which opponents of the government cannot openly and legally organize into political parties to oppose the government in free and fair elections, what conditions favor or impede a transformation into a regime in which they can?" Dahl devotes a short chapter to "foreign control" in the birth of democratic regimes and acknowledges that in lands as different as Jamaica and Japan, American or British rule had made for important differences. Yet at the point where one might expect discussion of how these democratic grafts occurred, we find a warning that such efforts should be avoided. Dahl concludes his study arguing against efforts to promote democracy abroad:

> The whole burden of this book, I believe, argues against the rationality
> of such a policy. For the process of transformation is too complex and

too poorly understood to justify it. The failure of the American foreign aid program to produce any transformations of this kind over two decades gives additional weight to this negative conclusion.

Writing eighteen years later, in 1989, in *Democracy and Its Critics*, Dahl had not changed his position. He continued to caution (very much as Wilson might have put it) that "the capacity of democratic countries to bring democracy about in other countries will remain rather limited."[34]

Perhaps here is the reason that liberalism as a guide to policy in these parts of the world increasingly had to take a backseat to containment in the academy (exception made for the controversies noted with respect to military coups in Latin America and the war in Southeast Asia). Some theorists argued that an authoritarian stage was necessary on the path to democratization, for it could give rise both to economic growth favorable to the birth of a middle class and an increasingly liberal social contract.[35] Others were less inclined to be worried about the eventual outcome in the third world, provided the communist advance be stopped. Indeed, Samuel P. Huntington's enormously influential *Political Order in Changing Societies* (generally believed at the time to have been the single most important framework within which to understand the question of the logic of political development) made the embrace of authoritarianism even more explicit.[36] Still other leading scholars were agnostic in terms of predicting where development would lead over time, as Barrington Moore Jr. argued in *The Social Origins of Dictatorship and Democracy*.[37] In short, in most places we look, there was little faith that the spirit of democracy alone was likely to win out in the struggle with the appeal of communism.

By the early 1970s, it was becoming increasingly apparent that the widely diversified field of development studies had strikingly little cohesion to it. The unified, directive agenda for understanding and influencing political change that had given this field its mission since the 1950s was in disarray. But what contributed to its disintegration altogether was growing awareness of the inability of the United States to do more than bring misery to the peoples of Southeast Asia and Latin America. The collapse of the Alliance for Progress and the defeat in Vietnam—both evident by the early 1970s—contributed to an increased skepticism that the academic community had much to offer in the way of helping either thinking in Washington or conditions abroad. Instead, the suspicion arose that the academic world had failed in its mission to provide clarity as to the likely course of events—indeed, that in many ways it

had collaborated in the calamities befalling the regions they were profession-
ally trained to understand.

But history had a surprise in store. It came with the largely unanticipated
success of liberal movements in Portugal, Spain, and Greece in the mid- to
late 1970s, a development that appeared to embody precisely the changes
that an earlier generation of researchers had sought to understand so as to
promote but had failed to identify. Now history seemed to be moving in a
progressive direction on its own, without much help either from Washington
or the American intellectual community. A few years later, with the Reagan
presidency, optimism began to grow in policy-making circles that a liberal
future beckoned worldwide. More and more academics began to speculate on
developments in the same direction, but with different explanatory variables.
With the end of the cold war, a new day for liberal internationalism optimism
could be seen emerging from the shadow cast over it by the struggles of the
cold war.

It is to the character of this new phase of liberal developmentalist thought
that we now turn. With Woodrow Wilson liberal internationalism might be
said to have appeared in "classic" form. During the cold war, it had become
"hegemonic." By the time of the terrorist attack of September 11, 2001, neo-
Wilsonianism as a doctrine was in full flower and the tradition was set for its
"imperialist" stage.

CHAPTER SIX

The Rise of Neo-Wilsonian Theory

In politics nothing radically novel may safely be attempted. No result of value can ever be reached in politics except through slow and gradual development, the careful adaptations and nice modifications of growth. Nothing may be done by leaps. More than that, each people, each nation, must live upon the lines of its own experience. Nations are no more capable of borrowing experience than individuals are. The histories of other peoples may furnish us with light, but they cannot furnish us with conditions of action. Every nation must constantly keep in touch with its past; it cannot run towards its ends around sharp corners.

—*Woodrow Wilson, The State, 1911 ed.*

After we have already seen dictatorships toppled by democratic forces in such seemingly unlikely places as the Philippines, Indonesia, Chile, Nicaragua, Paraguay, Taiwan and South Korea, how utopian is it to imagine a change of regime in a place like Iraq? For that matter, how utopian is it to work for the fall of the Communist Party in China after a far more powerful and stable oligarchy fell in the Soviet Union? With democratic change sweeping the world at an unprecedented rate over the past decades, is it truly "realistic" to insist that we quit now? . . . The mission begins in Baghdad, but it does not end there. . . . America cannot escape its responsibility for maintaining a decent world order. The answer to this challenge is the America idea itself, and behind it the unparalleled military and economic strength of its custodian. Duly armed, the United States can act to secure its safety and to advance the cause of liberty—in Baghdad and beyond.

—*William Kristol and Robert Kagan, eds., Present Dangers: Crisis and Opportunity in America's Foreign and Defense Policy, 2000; repeated in Kristol and Lawrence Kaplan, The War over Iraq: Saddam's Tyranny and America's Mission, 2003*

The purpose of the preceding chapter was to establish that neither in Washington nor in the American academy was there much basis to believe that Wilson's hopes for the eventual expansion of democracy worldwide was likely to occur in the contest with international communism during the cold war. The principal reason lay in the obvious advantages communist movements enjoyed with respect to democratizing movements in so much of the world outside the liberal order of the European community (today the European Union); in countries around the Pacific periphery from Japan to Australia/New Zealand, where British rule had had liberal consequences, as also in India; or in countries held back from such development (such as the Czech Republic or Poland) by the boot of the Red Army, or in parts of Latin America (such as Chile) by Washington's concern to block communism at any price. In comparison, communist trumps elsewhere included Leninist organization in disciplined, hierarchical secret parties with tried and proven blueprints for action aimed at large masses of people who considered themselves exploited; appeals to nationalist and class consciousness stemming from a powerful Marxist ideology that combined a call for justice and freedom with one that promoted leftist nationalism and promised that world peace would follow world revolution; and the support local movements could receive from Moscow, later to be powerfully supplemented by assistance from Beijing (as early as 1950) and Havana (by the 1960s). In contrast, the promise of democracy—with its limited government and empowered citizenry, its message of ideological conciliation rather than militancy, and its base in what were almost invariably small middle classes and marginalized minorities—was a weak reed indeed for Washington to rely on.

In terms of the Wilsonian tradition of liberal internationalism, the difficulties that democratization faced in communism would not come as a surprise. Wilson had been clear, in his discussions of the origins, character, and challenges facing democracy, that such a government should not be expected to spread easily, quickly, or indeed in many places at all. In his reserve, Wilson differed markedly from Lenin, whose call for world revolution to bring about an end to war with social orders based on justice and freedom were exhortations for immediate action. By contrast, Wilson avoided intervening militarily in the domestic affairs of Mexico, the Soviet Union, and Germany during his presidency precisely because of the lessons he had learned from the French Revolution and the character of democracy in America. His greatest moment came with the creation of the League of Nations. But even here, Wilson was keenly aware of the fragility of that organization, seeing it more as a defensive than an aggressive force in world affairs.

Knowingly or not, liberal internationalists during the cold war demonstrated much the same reserve that Wilson had shown. Whatever their hopes to sponsor human rights and democracy abroad, they were cautious in their optimism, aware that authoritarian governments might be the only way to forestall communist takeovers. Liberal efforts would come to fruition most often when they could deepen, rather than broaden, the appeal of open markets, multilateral institutions, and governments based on human rights and democratic procedures under an American liberal hegemony during the cold war. Such a perspective meant strengthening the Atlantic Alliance, working with Japan and Australia/New Zealand, and cooperating with such other countries as could join the ranks of what by the 1990s were being called the "free market democracies."

The bottling up of liberal confidence within the confines of the world's market democracies was made all the more painful by developments in Southeast Asia and Latin America. By the early 1970s, the full scope of the American debacle in Vietnam, Laos, and Cambodia was impossible to deny, while the Alliance for Progress had nothing to show for its efforts, aside from support for oppressive military governments in the region. The sober reality seemed to be that democracy and authoritarianism had become bedfellows, while the prospects for détente with communism seemed like the best way to adjust to a world in which the appeal of democracy had been demonstrated to have little attraction outside the orbit of those peoples where the prerequisites for such a state and society were manifest.

Yet just as the curtain appeared to be coming down on liberal internationalism's prospects in Southeast Asia and Latin America, events in southern Europe breathed new life into the Wilsonian hope that indeed human rights and democratic government could find fertile fields in areas where hitherto the ground had not seemed receptive. By the mid-1970s, democracy movements had come to power in Portugal, Spain, and Greece. Between the late 1970s and the early 1980s, their hold on government was widely considered consolidated (in Portugal usually dating from the elections following the adoption of the Constitution of 1976; in Spain after the adoption of the Constitution of 1978—or for some the failure of an attempted coup against parliamentary government in 1981; and in Greece after the adoption of the Constitution of 1975).

While there is no reason to think these dramatic events elsewhere profoundly influenced American foreign policy, the presidency of Ronald Reagan (1981–1989) nonetheless fortuitously served as a bridge between the end of the cold war and the kind of changes in thinking among liberal international-ists that followed between the mid-1980s and 2001 (a period we might call the "long 1990s"). Reagan pursued a two-front offensive against Moscow, stressing the importance of winning in the arms race (as containment might recommend) but also pursuing a freedom agenda (as liberals might prefer).

With respect to containment, the president initially rejected the strategy of détente with the Soviet Union proposed by the administration of President Richard Nixon (1969–1974), not to speak of the policies of his predecessor, President Jimmy Carter, deemed "soft on communism." Instead, early on Reagan declared his commitment to a strategy of military superiority, as his positions on intermediate-range nuclear weapons in Europe and a new gen-eration of arms in space indicate, as well as his work to reverse communist gains in Central America (with his focus with the "contras" attacking the Sandinista government in Nicaragua), in Eastern Europe (working with Pope John Paul II to reduce communist power in Poland), and in Afghanistan (supporting the mujahideen, Islamic opponents to Soviet control of their country).

Yet at the same time, Reagan pursued "a freedom agenda" aimed at fight-ing communism through what he called "a crusade for freedom," confident that there was a worldwide "democratic revolution" that would eventually triumph if only people were given the opportunity. True to his convictions, and despite the advice of many of his advisers, President Reagan was eventu-ally open to the overtures of Soviet General Secretary Mikhail Gorbachev, initiatives that brought the cold war to an end on terms that sounded liberal, given the extent to which both *glasnost* (political opening) and *perestroika* (economic opening)—the essence of Gorbachev's "new thinking"—were fundamentally liberal reforms.[1]

Reagan's bold mixture of military preparedness dictated by containment, combined with liberal policy calling for the expansion of democracy and open markets, was to be an inspiration to the neoconservatives especially, many of whom served in his administration and that of his successor George H. W. Bush (1989–1993, where their role was especially evident in the Department of Defense under Secretary Dick Cheney), before going on to play more prominent roles in Washington under George W. Bush (2001–2009). In the process, Reagan became the patron saint of an assertive foreign policy after he left office in 1989.[2]

So far as democracy promotion was concerned, President Reagan's position was unequivocally combative. His most famous foreign policy address was delivered to the British Parliament on June 8, 1982, its themes echoing down through the decades that followed, its resonance apparent in speech after speech given not only by President George W. Bush, but by President Barack Obama as well. Focusing on totalitarianism in general, but in particular on Soviet control over Eastern Europe, Reagan concluded that "democracy is proving itself to be a not-at-all-fragile flower":

> We must be staunch in our conviction that freedom is not the sole prerogative of a lucky few, but the inalienable and universal right of all human beings. The objective I propose is quite simple to state: to foster the infrastructure of democracy, the system of a free press, unions, political parties, universities, which allow a people to choose their own way to develop their own culture, to reconcile their own differences through peaceful means. This is not cultural imperialism. It is providing the means for genuine self-determination and protection for diversity. Democracy already flourishes in countries with very different cultures and historical experiences.
>
> It would be cultural condescension, or worse, to say that any people prefers dictatorship to democracy. Who would voluntarily choose not to have the right to vote, decide to purchase government propaganda handouts instead of independent newspapers, prefer government to worker-controlled unions, opt for land to be owned by the state instead of those who till it, want government repression of religious liberty, a single political party instead of a free choice, a rigid cultural orthodoxy instead of democratic tolerance and diversity?[3]

The Reagan years thus served as an incubator for the ideas that in far more complex form were to become dominant among neoliberals (usually Democrats) and neoconservatives (typically Republicans) during the 1990s. President Reagan's emphasis on economic reform—giving the market domestically and internationally more leeway to expand, and thereby to reinforce democracy by removing state controls—could obviously be seen as one way to be liberal. In his arguments, the president was greatly aided by Secretary of State George Shultz (from July 1982 to 1989), a former economics professor at M.I.T. and Chicago, dean of the Chicago Graduate School of Business, and at other points secretary of labor and secretary of the treasury.

Sometimes called "the Washington Consensus," the administration's thinking called for privatization, deregulation, and opening of economic forces domestically and internationally. Its vision of a virtuous circle of inter-action—freeing the market nationally and internationally—would allegedly serve to prompt democratization by liberating social forces from the hand of government control, which in turn would prompt still more economic change. If Reagan rejected the constraints of many multilateral organizations over American foreign policy, so for Woodrow Wilson as well, such agencies, when not dominated by democratic peoples, were always liable to being held hostage by authoritarian obstructionism and so had no special legitimacy in liberal thinking so far as united action in world affairs was concerned. Even if Reagan, who always thought of himself as a "conservative," objected to al-most anything that was "liberal," when a president makes American leader-ship of a world community of democratic nations following free-market prac-tices the core features of his foreign policy, then whatever he may call himself, he is most certainly in the Wilsonian tradition.

Rhetorically, Presidents George H. W. Bush and Bill Clinton both echoed the Wilsonian spirit of Reagan's Farewell Address.[4] Democracy, open mar-kets, multilateralism, and American leadership (what might be called the tra-ditional Wilsonian "virtuous diamond" of liberal internationalist concepts set out in the introduction to this book) were the best guarantee of world peace—and with the victory over Soviet communism, this agenda might now be pushed more vigorously. Nevertheless, although the administration of Bush senior (1989–1993) could speak of "a new world order" following the victory over Iraq early in 1991, in the operation code-named Operation Des-ert Storm, and the implosion as well of the Soviet Union at the end of that year, his administration limited its initiatives to promoting democratic transi-tions in Eastern Europe (under the able leadership of Secretary of State James Baker) and pushing for broader integration of the world economic order.[5]

Significant as these actions were, Bush did not have, as he put it, "the vi-sion thing," nor would he "dance on the Berlin Wall," so marking his dis-tance from his predecessor Ronald Reagan by a determined show of restraint. Washington refused to march on Baghdad in 1991, following the victory of Operation Desert Storm, and the president reassured Beijing that it would not exploit the Tiananmen Square upheaval of June 1989. The conviction of his son President George W. Bush fourteen years later to democratize not just Iraq, but what his administration termed "the Broader Middle East," under what was code-named Operation Iraqi Freedom, was most certainly not an ambition of the Republican White House between 1989 and 1993.

President Clinton (1993–2001) was similarly reserved in terms of promoting a liberal internationalist agenda. Although in February 1994, he published the first of three annual National Security Strategies entitled "Engagement and Enlargement," with its commitment to promoting "free market democracies," and later in the decade he oversaw the expansion of NATO, Clinton resisted calls to directly take on Saddam Hussein in Iraq. At the same time, after the reversals America suffered in Somalia in 1993 (the famous "Blackhawk Down" event), he deliberately limited the scope of the military actions he undertook in Haiti and the former Yugoslavia (both successfully achieving their immediate objective). Similarly, after having campaigned in 1992 on a platform of hostility toward China for its human rights abuses, President Clinton softened with time, finally allowing that country into the World Trade Organization, justifying his position by saying membership might contribute to the eventual democratization of the People's Republic.[6]

THE ACADEMY AND LIBERAL INTERNATIONALISM AFTER THE COLD WAR

Yet outside Washington, in the great universities of the country, potentially more aggressive ideas were being mooted. The restraints on liberal thinking lifted by the end of communism (and thus the end of the predominance of policies based on containment) ushered in what seemed like the possibilities of a golden era for Wilsonianism. By the late 1980s, what might be called the "food chain of ideas"—going from prestigious universities with their "scholar-activists," thence to the "public intellectuals" in think tanks and pundits advising political leaders, after which they moved quickly enough to the policy-makers themselves—worked with unusual efficiency in Washington.[7]

The drive to mint new concepts that came of age in 2001 and 2002 should come as no surprise. The collapse of the Soviet Union was by any historical measure destined to have an enormous impact on world affairs. The liberation of tens of millions of people from Moscow's imperial hold; the peaceful way in which the collapse occurred; the end of the immediate threat of nuclear war; the disappearance of communism as a political doctrine that could be taken seriously; the unquestioned predominance of the United States in world affairs and the apparent supremacy of its arguments calling for a world order based on democracy, open markets, multilateralism, and peace—all this meant that policy-makers were looking for new ways to articulate a purpose for the unprecedented power America now possessed. Accordingly, American liberal internationalist intellectuals set themselves to the task of formulating new concepts to underpin fresh policies.

A series of questions dominated academic discussion. Granted that the Realism expressed in containment, with its commitment to American military superiority and diplomatic resolve, in the confrontation with Moscow had been an important part of the victory over the Soviet Union, it was equally clear that the Wilsonian agenda—with its support for democracy, open markets, and multilateral solidarity—had been essential, perhaps even more critical, as well. Thus what, rather exactly, were the virtues of democracy and free-market capitalism that had made the peaceful end of the cold war possible? To what extent had activism under President Reagan mattered relative to the long-term natural working of world capitalism and democratic culture and alliance politics since the early 1940s? Or again, how, rather explicitly, might the free world now protect, indeed expand, its perimeter of action so as to advance its security by laying the foundations for an enduring peace?

A new concept of power at the service of purpose was called for. Primed by the growth of think tanks, nongovernmental organizations (NGOs), and the appeals of high officials in Washington to be "policy relevant," shocked by the murderous outbreaks taking place in the Balkans and Central Africa, believing as liberals do that progress was possible (especially at historical watersheds such as the 1990s seemed to represent), the time was ripe for an examination of the century that was ending with a thought to controlling events in the century soon to open.

For the scholars of a liberal bent active in the long decade of the 1990s, three concepts, especially when working in unison, were to become of decisive importance: democratic peace theory (DPT), democratic transition theory (DTT), and a new "just war" doctrine eventually labeled "the responsibility to protect" (R2P). Taken one by one, each of them claimed legitimate liberal credentials, and given the emphasis they put on democracy, all could easily enough appear, on the face of it, to be orthodox products of the Wilsonian tradition.

The powerful synthesis that was to emerge when these ideas were conjoined nevertheless might not be evident. The most striking aspect of these three concepts was that only when they combined did they become a new form of high-octane liberal internationalism representing a sea change in the character of Wilsonianism. Thus, if the world might enjoy a stable peace thanks to the spread of democracy, this finding did not mean that such an expansion was likely to occur. Or if indeed a global democracy movement were to take place, this development by itself did not mean that a liberal peace would follow.

If, however, these two arguments were meshed into one, then they fed each other in a catalytic interaction that made them potentially aggressive. A more democratic world that would make for a more peaceful planet (DPT) and firmness in the conviction that a democratic transition from authoritarianism was no longer so difficult to imagine (DTT)—these two concepts, when joined, could be interpreted to justify determined action for the sake of freedom and peace. With the invention of a new doctrine of "just war" (R2P) formulated to legitimize the overthrow of governments that were guilty of serious and systematic human rights violations and to replace them with democratic states, the door was now open for liberals to engage in acts of progressive imperialism that in theoretical terms made anything Woodrow Wilson had ever contemplated pale in comparison.

In strictly intellectual terms, the argument was extraordinary. The new doctrine—the synergy of these ideas explaining its volatile appeal—became the new collective conscience of most of those who thought of themselves as liberal internationalists. With its new preeminence, the United States could actually offer the freedom and peace to the world that had been the country's age-old ambition. Reagan's appeal in 1982 thus expanded its impact. A country of seemingly indisputable imperial capability militarily now possessed a doctrine indisputably able to justify its bid for world supremacy.

America's claim to being "exceptional" was now recast. Whereas during its classic phase with Wilson and during the hegemonic stage of the cold war, America would define its national security interest as the defense of the "democratic" (under Wilson) or (during the hegemonic years) "free" world, now, in its imperialist mode, "world order" meant that virtually everywhere the promotion of "free market democracy" became America's mission. In other words, by a change in emphasis that went unnoticed by many, an essentially defensive posture had mutated into one that had become frankly aggressive.

The result by 2001 was an inventory of concepts created for the most part by neoliberals associated with the Democratic Party, although it was best purveyed to official Washington and the public at large by neoconservatives, most of whom were part of the Republican Party.[8] With the presidency of George W. Bush beginning in January 2001, and the terrorist attack of that September 11, what Reinhold Niebuhr had labeled the "fortunate vagueness" of American liberal internationalism (which was evident in the relative lack of clarity with respect to the terms of "Wilsonianism" that Woodrow Wilson himself had left as his legacy to his successors) was now giving way to a new concreteness of thought, one that articulated a forward policy in world affairs. A new stage of liberal internationalism was at hand. After the "classic" phase under Wilson and a stage of American liberalism that was "hegemonic" during the cold war, liberal "imperialism" had finally come of age thanks to the pieces of the argument that were falling into place with a conviction that came to dominate American foreign policy thinking—an integrated set of convictions whose novelty and coherence merits declaring them "neo-Wilsonianism."

DEMOCRATIC PEACE THEORY (DPT)

The jewel in the crown of neoliberal internationalism, as it emerged from the seminar rooms of some of the greatest American universities, became known as "democracy peace theory." Stated simply as "Democracies have never gone to war with one another," the theory contends that the democratic regime type breeds a peace among such states based on their domestic practices of nonviolent negotiated compromise adhering to the rule of law; on the prosperity and political commitment of an expanding middle class; on their increasingly integrated market economics; and on their participation in international organizations to adjudicate conflicts among themselves as well as to protect themselves from their enemies without, in a way that is destined to keep the peace. The striking success of European union during the seven decades that followed the announcement of the Marshall Plan in 1947, combined with the strong relations between Europe and the United States and other liberal democracies, such as Canada and Japan (to which should be added Australia and New Zealand), seems to be conclusive proof that global peace could expand should other countries join in what democratic peace theory dubbed "the pacific union," "the zone of democratic peace."

The extent to which DPT galvanized the liberal academic community by the 1990s was impressive. Political scientist Michael Doyle was among the first, and surely the most influential, to present the evidence for DPT.[9] Soon a flood of studies appeared to corroborate his argument. Empirically minded political scientists demonstrated conclusively to their satisfaction that "regime type matters," that it is in the nature of democracies to keep the peace together. A mass of statistical data going back well over a century seemed to them to leave little doubt. Democracies indeed do not fight one another. Theoretically inclined political scientists talked instead in logical terms, explaining how the various aspects of free market democratic peoples made an unprecedented difference in world affairs. To crown the argument, no less than the most prominent of liberal political philosophers (some say in all of American history), John Rawls, invoked Immanuel Kant and claimed that a way had been found out from Hobbes' state of nature by ending the anarchy of international relations through the spread of democratic ways to such a point that some now dared to speak of "post-history" or "the end of history" should the effort be successful.[10]

There is no reason to doubt that DPT was a powerful reassertion of Woodrow Wilson's single most important belief: that democracy created morally, and not only practically, a new kind of individual, society, and state. The possibility of reasoned discussion based on a moral commitment to the common good, as validated by popular consent that operates at the national level, might be transferred to the international level in a way that promotes a sense of general interest pursued through multilateral organizations whose collective action could give rise to a body of international law that would give birth to what at first would be a rudimentary form of constitutionalism at a transnational level. A common commitment to the peaceful negotiation of differences among democratic peoples could be combined with a security agreement to protect their way of life from external threat by military means if necessary. Here is what the neoconservative Francis Fukuyama hailed as "the end of history" should the convergence he expected of all peoples on the principles and institutions of liberal democracy come to pass.

> What we may be witnessing is not just the end of the cold war, or the passing of a particular period of post-war history, but the end of history as such: that is, the end point of mankind's ideological evolution and the universalization of Western liberal democracy as the final form of government.[11]

An extraordinary statement by arguably the most influential of the empirically based democratic peace theorists, political scientists Bruce Russett and John Oneal, illustrates the intellectual confidence a powerful new theory can provide. Choosing to invoke Kant rather than Wilson, they declared in 2001, "We have tested Kant's theses using social scientific methods, something that only recently became possible. . . . It is now possible, 205 years after Kant published *Perpetual Peace*, to evaluate his theory scientifically."

History, specifically the years 1885–1992, can be used as a laboratory to assess the peacefulness of democratic, interdependent states linked by IGOs [international governmental organizations]. Our research is also made possible because voluminous information about this historical period has become available in a form necessary for statistical analysis. In addition, the statistical procedure, software, and computing capacity necessary for analyzing this massive amount of information have been developed. Our data would be useless were it not for the technological revolution that has made computers so prodigious and so cheap.

After evaluating Kant's argument "scientifically," these authors make bold to conclude, "our findings and their implications for the future should encourage us to do what we can today to ensure that the Kantian peace is strengthened where it now operates and spread to areas gripped by realpolitik. . . . Kant would say it is a moral imperative."[12]

In short, what Wilson had left in the form of sketches in his writings and policies now acquired through DPT a clarity of argument in the 1990s that most decidedly confirmed the concepts that he had begun to propagate as early as the 1880s and the plans he ultimately set forth for a Pan-American Treaty and the League of Nations between 1915 and 1919. Wilson's primary article of faith—in the potential for democratic peoples and ways to change history by mitigating the threat of war through action favoring a common peace—had found resounding confirmation in the research of these neoliberals, his intellectual great-grandchildren.

Given this perspective, how could Wilson have been other than satisfied with the outcome of the American occupations of Germany and Japan, indeed with the leading part played by the United States in the construction of a united Europe, beginning with the Marshall Plan in 1947 and moving on through the establishment of NATO two years later? One could argue that here was the greatest success in the history of American foreign policy, leading as it did not only to the demilitarizing, democratizing, and free-market opening of these two great countries, but also to the dynamic that over time would ultimately convince a critical set of the leaders in the Soviet Union itself of the virtues of a liberal world order. The Wilsonian belief seemed especially convincingly vindicated by the story of Western Europe: democratic peoples, united in open economies, working through multilateral organizations, initially under American leadership, could lead hundreds of millions of people to freedom, prosperity, and the promise of an enduring peace among themselves despite a singularly bloody past. Centuries of fratricidal bloodshed had seemingly come to an abrupt end.

One might, of course, conclude that Wilsonianism had now run its course. Having consolidated democracy in Europe east and west, having seen free-market democracies take root in the western Pacific in a great arc from South Korea through Japan into Australia and New Zealand, having recognized the appeal of democracy in parts of Latin America and Africa, might American liberal internationalism not now "return to normalcy" and so solidify its gains by strengthening itself internally, perfecting its democracy and working on the pooling of compatible sovereignties?

Settling to consolidate the considerable gains they had made, liberals might show a prudent restraint about pressing further. In the Muslim world, China, Russia, and sub-Saharan Africa, liberal ways would presumably have less appeal and encounter more resistance. So Wilson had recognized with both his academic work and policies as president (even if his reasoning was implicit, for he did not consider these parts of the globe in his own work), and so had many American intellectuals and leaders concluded during the cold war. Considered on its own terms alone, then, DPT did not appear as the harbinger of neo-Wilsonian imperialism. Indeed, Michael Doyle had argued against using it to encourage "quixotic crusades." Yet the temptation was understandably there to use the window of opportunity provided by America's uncontested position in world affairs after 1991 to push ahead to expand the "pacific union" of the world's democracies. In due course, the temptation was embraced.

Nevertheless, rising to the temptation did not necessarily come easily. For to subscribe to DPT did *not* formally urge liberal internationalists on to seek other "converts" to the democratic capitalist way of life. Indeed, the effort to do so might unleash a "clash of civilizations." The action-oriented feature of DPT was that it promised an expansion of regional to perhaps global peace should other nations democratize, the ultimate ambition of the Wilsonian vision.

How could a window of opportunity, such as victory in the cold war after 1991, not beckon liberals to push the boundaries of their system further afield, producing such developments as the expansion of both NATO and the EU in the 1990s? Did the success of democratic movements in the mid-1970s in southern Europe, then after the fall of the Berlin Wall the coming of democratic transitions as well in Central Europe, not bid Washington to move into action? Could the pledge of "Never Again" now be given more than rhetorical significance? Was it possible that the age-long state of nature in which humanity had lived would finally be brought into a new form of existence?

As the Soviet flag was lowered for the last time over the Kremlin on December 25, 1991, American academics and policy-makers could speculate on whether a new, and better, world order could begin to be established as the world's bloodiest century finally drew to a close. Theoretically speaking, it was an intoxicating moment. Stanford political science professor Larry Diamond expressed well the DPT reason to welcome a new era, in which the march toward democracy was accelerating, in an essay published in 1994 and provocatively titled "The Global Imperative: Building a Democratic World Order":

> Democratic countries do not go to war with one another. Democracies do not sponsor terrorism against one another. They do not build weapons of mass destruction to use on one another or threaten each other with. Democratic countries are more reliable, open, and enduring trading partners. . . . They are more environmentally responsible. . . . They are better bets to honor international treaties. . . . Precisely because they respect within their own borders competition, civil liberties, property rights, and the rule of law, democracies are the only reliable foundation on which a new world order of international security and prosperity can be built.[13]

What nonetheless needed to be specified was how to proceed with this self-important "global imperative" of building a democratic world order— what we have seen Russett and Oneal calling a Kantian "moral imperative." Democratic peace theory dealt strictly with international relations. It did not have as part of its approach to world affairs an answer to the question of how actually to make the transition from authoritarian to democratic ways. It could only assert that should these transitions take place, the region, or globe, would have an increased capacity for a stable peace. The great question, obviously, was whether the transition from authoritarian to democratic order could be seen as a less daunting process than Wilson and liberals of the cold war era had believed.

For Wilson himself, the expansion of the boundaries of the liberal world would necessarily be slow and involve the cooperation of the people so to be integrated. He would act with progressive intent on the margins of countries like Mexico, but as with Germany and the Soviet Union, he would leave internal matters to decide events, with some reason to think the results would be positive, but not in blind confidence that democratization was inevitable. After World War II, liberal internationalist Washington had moved further afield, their great successes being in Japan and Germany, leading ultimately to victory in the cold war. Yet this generation too had seen limits to what they could expect in the way of democratic transitions at the moment containment became the dominating framework for American thinking about Latin America, Africa, and Asia. The key problem for those who would promote the "global imperative" of spreading the democratic peace in the 1990s and the two decades that followed was to find whether in fact its appeal could be carried to the four corners of the earth.

DEMOCRATIC TRANSITION THEORY (DTT)

The answer to the question of whether democratic societies and governments could take root worldwide was not long in coming. Given the tremendous forward momentum of democracy and open markets as the Soviet Union collapsed and the strength of liberal internationalism became apparent, where would the wave of change stop? Better yet, would it stop? Whereas both Wilson and most comparativists of the cold war period had believed that the transition of peoples under long-standing authoritarian regimes into democratic societies and governments might well be problematic, a group that could be called Wilson's intellectual great-grandchildren of the 1990s in quick order came to see things differently.

In its "classic" period with Wilson, and again in its "hegemonic" phase from the 1940s through the 1980s, the liberal tradition had had a healthy reserve to it, a restraint that was fast to change with the end of the cold war. By the 1990s, in contrast, the United States enjoyed a relative power position undreamed of in Wilson's time or during the cold war.

More, the passage of time seemingly revealed a blueprint for democracy far more clearly defined than it ever had been before. The Iberian Peninsula and Greece democratized in the 1970s. Later, world leaders of the quality of Vaclav Havel, John Paul II, Kim Dae Jung, Oscar Arias, and Nelson Mandela (a list that might be headed by none other than Mikhail Gorbachev), men who were not representative of nations (Czechoslovakia and Costa Rica aside) known in Wilson's time for their democratic proclivities, were determined to move the prospects for a better world forward in conjunction with liberal internationalist hopes. Should more of an assist be called for, Washington could act through its multiple agencies (for example, the Agency for International Development and the National Endowment for Democracy) to push democracy forward, just as a range of nongovernmental organizations might do (including Human Rights Watch, Amnesty International, Freedom House, Transparency International, and the Open Society Institute), their efforts joined by other countries, the Germans and the Scandinavians especially.

With this new sense of the appeal of liberal democratic ways, causes aplenty presented themselves for a solution: murderous civil wars in the Balkans and Central Africa; poverty and disease in regions of South and Southeast Asia and most parts of Africa; anti-American authoritarian governments in some countries of Latin America; simmering unrest in the Muslim world based on its perceived victimization at the hands of Washington as it supported corrupt and inefficient dictatorships throughout the Middle East (including North Africa and Iran in the past) and pledged to defend Israel's security (even when this included increased Jewish settlements in the occupied territories); and perhaps, above all, the question of where Russia and China would stand in the twenty-first century, as they were the most likely candidates to play dominant regional, if not world, roles as the new century opened.

Given these issues, why should the United States not press what might well be only a momentary advantage, and so promote a pacifying way of life globally at the moment its relative power position presented it with an unprecedented ability to act progressively? As neoconservative leaders Robert Kagan and William Kristol forcefully put it, how could this country afford to take "a holiday from history" when the opportunities for pushing forward successfully were everywhere at hand, while the dangers that could manifest themselves if the occasion was not seized were palpable?[14]

Enter democratic transition theory (DTT), the notion that establishing a democratic way of life after the collapse of the Soviet Union, and with the United States positioned as the world's sole superpower, would not be as difficult an undertaking as earlier generations of comparativists, or even most liberal internationalists, had supposed. The new thinking emerged from the academic domain of what in the United States is called the study of comparative politics (although it traditionally includes as well economics and sociology, with a historical perspective), a field of investigation that looks at the dynamics of political life in terms of specific countries or regions, but that can also look at more general waves of change that involve the entire international system. Here was precisely the field of study where Woodrow Wilson had made his greatest contributions as a political scientist, even if his work in this domain remained neglected by those in the same field nearly a century after he had left it.[15]

During the cold war, the mainstream argument trying to open a path for democracy had favored either waiting for economic development to produce a middle class favorable to democracy or instead hoping that authoritarian governments would reformulate their social contracts and internal workings in such a way that eventually democracy might emerge. Given the threat of communism, to push too quickly was dangerous. With its list of "preconditions," "sequences," "stages," and the like, what were then called "development" or "modernization" studies through the 1970s seemed pessimistic that the democratization of large parts of the world should be anticipated in any short- or medium-term span of time. By contrast, intent on making their reputations in a more positive and progressive manner, and in any case drinking deeply of the mood of the times, social scientists of the post–cold war period insisted that a new way forward could be found, one that promised quicker results in terms of the expansion of the democratic world.

At the risk of simplification, let me distinguish three stages in the process of discarding reservations as to the obstacles facing a democratic transition as the danger of communism receded. Stage one concentrated almost solely on political forces—leaving other "preconditions," which an early generation of comparativists had studied, such as those that were socioeconomic, cultural, or historical, largely out of the equation. If certain political variables were correctly aligned, democratization might proceed apace.

Stage two dramatically slimmed down further the requirements, looking to such matters as public opinion polls and "mobile ideas" in foreign cultures to assess whether a nation had democratic potential. It was the democratic spirit with a modern blueprint that as an ideology might triumph abroad. Here was the origin of the notion we find during the presidencies of George W. Bush and Barack Obama that democracy had "universal appeal" that, combined with an "arc" or "wind" of history, might sweep all before it.

Finally, stage three arrived at the conclusion that with the decapitation of the old order, democratic nation- and state-building might proceed apace thanks to the assurances of the first two stages, but combined now with what might be called "American militarized humanitarianism," tied as it was to "the responsibility to protect."

STAGE ONE IN RETHINKING THE DEMOCRATIC TRANSITION: THE SIMPLIFICATION OF THE PROCESS TO A SET OF POLITICAL VARIABLES

A milestone that signaled a fresh breath of hope that the pace of liberal change might be accelerated past pessimistic cold war social science thinking was political scientist Dankwart Rustow's widely read publication in 1970 of an article entitled "Transitions to Democracy: Toward a Dynamic Model."[16] His breakthrough was to simplify what had hitherto been a morass of conditions necessary for democratization to a process that now was slimmed down by explaining it through a series of essentially political developments occurring within specific peoples in terms of a particular historical context. Rustow's claim to being original in looking for the "generic" origins of democracy may have been misplaced (many others had taken on this challenge), and his emphasis on what he saw as essentially political variables alone to explain the emergence of democracy may have been simplistic, given the range of cases to be considered and the component social elements of what constituted the realm of the political. But the sense that he was on to something important quickly found confirmation in the dramatic changes that occurred on the Iberian Peninsula and Greece in the mid-1970s. Here political thought and movements under visionary leadership combined with sharply politicized historical moments in ways that opened the door to democratic solutions. The result was the emergence of what came to be called the field of "transitology," with Rustow seen as the person who had first singled out the clear predominance of political factors at critical historical moments, so giving new hope to finding a progressive way forward.

Although Rustow never mentioned Woodrow Wilson in his essay, which canvassed virtually all the major American thinkers of his day on the question of a democratic transition, in fact his conclusions were in important respects similar to Wilson's. His essential premises for change were political, as were Wilson's. For example, Rustow's emphasis on "national unity" as a precondition for democratization was very much like Wilson's emphasis on "organic unity" and "homogenization" that he had brought forward as early as 1885 (his construction of "patriotism" came later). Both thus had some notion of an effective social contract, or the capacity to engender one, that would keep the various forces that made up society effectively at peace with one another. So too Rustow's emphasis on the ability of determined leaders (not only from established governmental circles but from popular origins) to found institutions capable of establishing and enforcing a version of the rule of law that could be ratified by the citizenry was quite in line with the way Wilson conceived of the origins of democracy in America and the requirements for its appearance elsewhere.

Nevertheless, there were differences. Wilson considered more factors operating in the emergence of democracy than did Rustow. Two factors that Rustow ignored (or perhaps assumed, but left in the background so as to keep his variables limited) were the importance of a middle class that is independent of the state (that is, that did not depend on governmental protection and subsidies), and of a civic culture based on a sense of the common interest and the responsibility of the public to see that government rests on its informed consent. The existence of the middle class presupposed for Wilson a certain level of prosperity and education, as well as the values, interests, and abilities that make the bourgeoisie want a government of laws, not of men. "No bourgeoisie, no democracy" is Barrington Moore's famous summation.[17]

A second ingredient was necessary for Wilson for self-government to emerge as well: a civic culture. For Wilson, mainstream Protestant churches such as his own Presbyterianism, provided an example, promoting an engaged citizenry with a sense of common purpose, expressed in a covenanted or constitutional arrangement so as to maintain popular interaction with political leaders in such a fashion that government rested on the consent of the governed.

From this perspective, Wilson's approach, with its mix of economic and social ingredients basic for democratization to occur, had more in common with comparativists of the cold war period than with Rustow. That said, their mutual agreement on the leading importance of political forces at critical historical moments made for more convergence than divergence in their approaches.

In the aftermath of the events of the mid-1970s, comparative politics grew increasingly friendly toward what might be called this "slimmed down," or simplified, version of the democratization process in which the dominant explanation was political. Thus, in an important four-volume series (also published as a single, combined tome in 1986) entitled *Transitions from Authoritarian Rule: Prospects for Democracy*, noted social scientists Guillermo O'Donnell, Philippe Schmitter, Laurence Whitehead, and Adam Przeworski concluded that earlier writers who had invoked such issues as levels of economic development, the character of ethnic divisions, and cultural and historical legacies might have exaggerated their drag on democratization. By focusing more sharply instead on "political strategies" and introducing "indeterminacy" and "uncertainty" into the process of political change, democracy might indeed become a conceivable outcome of change. There was as well the welcome notion that different societies might have unique ways of making the transition. For example, in theory, "corporatism" in Latin America, which had allowed authoritarian regimes a reach into many sectors of civic life, might be turned against such a form of state and instead become an aspect of "pacted" (that is, controlled by agreements between governments and social forces as to the rules of the game) transitions to democracy involving large segments of the population. Once again, theory anticipated history when shortly thereafter the cold war ended and democracy spread quickly forward in places as different as Latin America and Central Europe, once again on the basis of factors that could be seen as essentially political.[18]

Consider as an example of the altered perception the work of a man most American academics in the field at the time would agree to have been from the mid-1960s to the late 1990s the most distinguished social scientist working in the area of political change, Harvard government professor Samuel Huntington. In 1968, Huntington had published an enormously influential book, *Political Order in Changing Societies*, one of whose major messages was that the "order" necessary in the political realm of countries emerging into "modernity" might have to be military so as to forestall the advent of communism (the counter-communism of the book was not explicit, but most certainly implicit). However, in 1991, Huntington published another widely read book, *The Third Wave: Democratization in the Late Twentieth Century*, in which the critical role of a democratizing elite now emerged as the single most important variable in any democratic transition, and this without undue concern over the social and economic variables the comparative field had previously covered so extensively. What Huntington labeled a "third wave" of democracy was gathering strength, not only in Central Europe (Poland and the Czech Republic, for example) but also in countries as different as South Korea, South Africa, and Chile. Over a period of twenty-three years, Huntington's ideas had obviously changed in league with his times.[19]

Others had already pushed the frontiers of this thinking a bit earlier than Huntington. In 1990, Giuseppe Di Palma had published a well-received book, *To Craft Democracies: An Essay on Democratic Transitions*, whose opening paragraph spoke for the hope of neoliberals everywhere:

Far be it from me to advocate a new social science orthodoxy. Yet there is a rekindled public and scholarly interest in the prospects for democracy where democracy does not now exist. That attention and the renewed theoretical optimism among a number of scholars deserve a fair hearing. [I am writing] in defense of that optimism.

Chapter titles for Di Palma's work instructively include "How Democracy Can Grow in Many Soils"; "Why Transferring Loyalties to Democracy May Be Less Difficult than We Think"; "On How to Sell One's Craft"; and, more ominously, "Democracy by Diffusion, Democracy by Trespassing."[20]

Reviewing the book in 1991 in an essay entitled, instructively, "Shortcuts to Liberty," Princeton University politics professor (today at Oxford) Nancy Bermeo saluted Di Palma for being in the vanguard of a growing "consensus on the importance of leadership. . . . Dozens of scholars in the United States are preparing manuscripts which argue that elite choices were critical to the transformation or consolidation of particular regimes. Arguments that underline the importance of choice are intrinsically hopeful and they seem to be multiplying." Bermeo then went on to praise such upbeat one-liners from Di Palma as his suggestions for how to "beat the odds against democracy" and "make the improbable possible." Crafting can be decisive anywhere, Bermeo remarked as she agreed with Di Palma that democracy imagined as "marketing" or a "game" opened fresh ways of thinking as opposed to the naysayers of an earlier generation with their list of "absolute obstacles to liberalization." Now Bermeo would embrace the new spirit of the post–cold war era and argue in favor of what she labeled "possibilism."[21]

STAGE TWO IN RETHINKING THE DEMOCRATIC TRANSITION: THE ROLE OF POLITICAL IDEAS AND IDEALS

The emphasis, in what I call stage one of the rethinking of the democratic transition, which insisted on the dominant position of committed leadership of social forces in the democratic transition, necessarily involved turning to the notion of political ideas and ideals as well. For if democracy were possessed of a blueprint, its attraction lay in its promise of individual and social freedom and justice in a state and world that was nonviolent. In a word, democracy as ideology came to the fore with the demise of the appeal of communism and the growth of the appeal of liberal constitutionalism.

The core message of stage two was that ideas alone might control future political developments. Democracy had by the 1990s a well-articulated conceptual plan for social and political order, one that could be adopted by virtually any people interested in assuring their interests in a stable and peaceful government.

For example, the widely read edited works of Larry Diamond, Juan Linz, and Seymour Martin Lipset, published collaboratively between 1989 and 1995, reflected this new optimism, which discounted factors traditionally considered important, such as socioeconomic or political preconditions, to insist instead on the role of ideas and ideology as fundamental elements in progressive change. In the 1995 version of their work, they saluted "the global advance of democracy," attributing it in part to "the demise of its historic ideological rivals . . . [so that] Democracy became—partly by choice and political learning and partly by default—the only model of government in the world with any broad ideological legitimacy and appeal."[22] Although these men acknowledged resistance to liberal ideas, they called for an ideological offensive—what by 2002 and thereafter would be called "a war of ideas"—to carry the argument forward against all opponents, be they Muslim fundamentalists, Confucian communists, or those who favored the return to authoritarian rule in places like Russia.

A concern with the advancement of human rights (and the power of ideas in general) appeared increasingly to overshadow the dominance of political factors in the liberal blueprint for a democratic transition. Consider as indicative of the new convictions a book published to general acclaim in 1999 by three social scientists, Thomas Risse, Stephen C. Ropp, and Kathryn Sikkink, *The Power of Human Rights: International Norms and Domestic Change*. True to the optimism of the time (and the painful jargon of the social sciences), the authors elaborated a "five phase" "spiral model" working on "four levels" passing through "world time" so as to demonstrate how human rights nongovernmental organizations, international institutions, and Western powers could act on the state and society of nondemocratic peoples so as to motivate them toward progressive change.[23]

The number of books and articles heralding a new age of successful democratic transitions from authoritarianism, based on the notion of human rights, defies counting. A few of the better-known titles convey their flavor: John Boli and George M. Thomas's edited volume *Constructing World Culture: International Nongovernmental Organizations Since 1875*; a second edition of Jack Donnelly's *Universal Human Rights in Theory and Practice*; Elizabeth

Borgwardt's *A New Deal for the World: America's Vision for Human Rights*. By 2001, even a person generally considered a Realist, like political scientist Michael Mandelbaum, would publish a long study called *The Ideas That Conquered the World: Peace, Democracy, and Free Markets in the Twenty-first Century* (its first chapter is entitled "Wilson Victorious").

Samuel Huntington was virtually alone among the prominent social scientists of the late 1990s to sense that all this optimism was getting more than a bit out of hand. In his *The Clash of Civilizations and the Remaking of World Order*, published in 1996, he looked at the way new lines of cleavages were appearing in world politics, with ominous prospects for the future. True to his arguments six years earlier in *The Third Wave*, that "reverse waves" might be expected following the American victory in the cold war, Huntington now called for a prudent realism to combat the excessive enthusiasm of liberal internationalism growing around him on every side toward the end of the century.

In Huntington's perspective, the characteristics of the world order coming into place with the end of the cold war deserved attention, not only because his view was in contrast with the mood of his times but especially because today it seems so prescient. In *The Clash of Civilizations*, he includes a chapter titled "A Universal Civilization? Modernization and Westernization," in which he doubts that the universalization of a single set of values and institutions on Western, much less American, terms is at all likely. Even though other chapter sub-sections of the book amplify this argument ("The Asian Affirmation" and "The Islamic Resurgence"), Huntington has special concern about "Western Universalism," expressing his doubts about "The Renewal of the West?" which is under assault from within by its own contradictions and from without by the rise of rival national and international creeds based on different codes of social contract and governmental legitimacy.[24]

If Huntington's 1996 book was widely debated (for the most part negatively), the liberal flood tide nonetheless continued unabated. Perhaps the leading theorist of the "possibilism" of the universal spread of democracy was the political scientist Larry Diamond, who by the 1990s had published (often with others) an impressive number of studies analyzing these trends. What also made Diamond singular was that he recognized the enormous obstacles to the establishment of democratic institutions (and thus showed his roots in what might be called "the old school"), yet affirmed his optimism that meaningful change was almost everywhere possible toward a progressive liberal outcome if one looked at the human desire for freedom.

Thus, by 2001, Diamond was complementing his faith in democratic peace theory (which limited itself to affirming the virtues of democracy in world affairs without specifying how such a system would emerge) with an emphasis on the ability of democratization to take place virtually anywhere. Building on his counsel of 1994 that there was a "Global Imperative: Building a Democratic World Order," he repeated his advice for policy-makers in Washington that for "an overarching mission and purpose there is no more appealing and compelling goal than the promotion of liberal democracy." Sounding as if he were in a warm-up for what soon would be called the Bush Doctrine, Diamond declared:

> In short, never in world history has there been a more fertile and propitious moment for wedding the founding principles of America to its global strategy and power. *It is now possible to imagine a world in which all the major component states will be liberal democracies.* It is now time to declare this our goal as a country, and to turn our resources, our energy, our imagination, and our moral and political leadership in the world to that end.[25]

Given his stature as surely the most important academic expert and scholar-activist or public intellectual working on democratization of his generation, Diamond's declaration is well worth noting. For in his confidence that there soon might be "a world in which all the major component states will be liberal democracies," Diamond (unlike Rustow) was breaking entirely with Wilson and the classical and hegemonic stages of American liberal internationalism, with their far more cautious analyses of the possibility of democratic transitions in countries without certain cultural and historical prerequisites.

The result was that on the eve of the invasion of Iraq in March 2003, Diamond gave a published lecture entitled "Can the Whole World Become Democratic?"—a question he answered without hesitation in the affirmative. He presented his empirical evidence based on a review of ideas and ideals that "even in countries lacking virtually all of the supposed 'conditions for democracy' . . . the understanding and valuing of democracy is widely shared across cultures."

Whereas Wilson in the classical phase and liberal internationalists in the hegemonic phase had limited their confidence in the expansion of democratic ways, Diamond saw only blue sky. As a man who had worked with the National Endowment for Democracy and the Agency for International Development, who became director of Stanford's Center on Democracy, Development, and the Rule of Law, who was coeditor of the democracy-promoting *Journal of Democracy*, and who went to Iraq to participate in writing a constitution for that country, Diamond has always championed a forward policy for the United States in pushing a democracy agenda for its own national security reasons. But over time he had reached a new level of confidence.

Diamond's assurance was based on empirical evidence showing that democracy was on the march for the important reason that "the understanding and valuing of democracy is widely shared across cultures." Relying on "barometers of public opinion," he concluded:

> Two-thirds of Africans surveyed associate democracy with civil liberties, popular sovereignty, or electoral choice . . . [and] also say democracy is "always preferable" to authoritarian rule. The same proportion rejects one-party rule and four in five reject military or one-man rule. . . . Latin Americans . . . are more ambivalent. But overall 57 percent still believe democracy is always preferable and only about 15 percent might prefer an authoritarian regime. In East Asia, only a quarter in Taiwan and Korea, about a fifth in Hong Kong and the Philippines, but less than a tenth in Thailand believe that democracy is not really suitable for their country. In all five of these systems, consistently strong majorities (usually upwards of two-thirds) reject authoritarian alternatives to democracy.

Diamond did note Arab exceptionalism: "Only in the Middle East is democracy virtually absent. In fact, among the sixteen Arab countries, there is not a single democracy, and with the exception of Lebanon, there never has been." Nevertheless, he was quick to reassure his readers: "Arab thinkers, scholars, and civil society activists are themselves challenging the democracy and freedom deficit that pervades the Arab world." Nor did he find that the stronger the commitment to Islam, the weaker the commitment to democracy.[26]

That all of these confident assertions could be based exclusively on polling questions called "barometers of public opinion" only demonstrates the extent to which the field of transitology had declined intellectually in the years since it was first introduced in the 1970s. To be sure, transitology itself could be revealed as a relatively shallow form of explanation. But compared to the simplistic use of polling data that now replaced political variables, transitology must be credited with having had at least some serious explanatory value. However, Diamond's work heralded the mood that pervaded Washington after the attack of September 11, 2001—that democracy had achieved the status of a "universal value" with a "universal appeal," as both Presidents George W. Bush (2001–2009) and Barack Obama (2009–2017) tirelessly affirmed in the years that followed. All that seemingly mattered was ideas and ideology, which alone might sweep all else before them.

Diamond's upbeat reflections on the question of democracy as a universal value did not end despite the evidence of events in Iraq and Afghanistan after 2003. In 2005, he published a book on the American invasion of Iraq entitled *Squandered Victory: The American Occupation and the Bungled Effort to Bring Democracy to Iraq*. In the January 2005 *Journal of Democracy* (which he coedited), Diamond published, as a companion article to his book, an essay he entitled "Lessons from Iraq." His list of recommendations ran: "1. Prepare for a major commitment . . . 2. Commit enough troops . . . 3. Mobilize international legitimacy and cooperation." Diamond's obvious point was that it was not so much that Iraq was infertile ground for democracy, but that America had bungled a job that with just a bit more social science Washington might have pulled off. As I pointed out at the time, Diamond was encouraging the United States to pursue nothing less than a fool's errand.[27]

Time did not stay Diamond's optimism. In 2008, he published *The Spirit of Democracy: The Struggle to Build Free Societies Throughout the World*, boldly entitling its first chapter, on the democratic spirit, "The Universal Value." Here he marshaled once again the evidence of "regional barometers" and "the World Values Survey" to conclude that the appeal of democracy remained robust, a conclusion he confirmed yet again in 2011.[28]

Yet perhaps the most surprising part of Diamond's 2008 book lay toward its conclusion. After examining in a thoughtful chapter the myriad difficulties those seeking to institutionalize democratic government may face in areas where such institutions, values, and habits are quite foreign, just as one might conclude that "the spirit of democracy" had defined cultural limits to its likely expansion easily or quickly, in the following chapter Diamond has the cavalry riding around the corner to save the day *in the form of international intervention* designed to overcome the obstacles to democracy's triumph.[29]

The notion that various international organizations or governments have the capacity to bring democratic society and government to a people without the substantial prerequisites for such a transformation reveals as clearly as any conviction can the danger into which neo-Wilsonian convictions led American foreign policy. No list of conditions for the extension of foreign aid so as to promote democratic government is likely to have much effect in many circumstances, even when backed by the threat of force. Nothing is easier for an authoritarian host government to do, if it is so inclined, than to wave away a list of "conditions" that are supposed to tie its hands and promote human rights and democratic government when they receive money from a foreign benefactor.[30]

Wilson's attitude toward Diamond's approach and his conclusions, like those of the earlier generation of comparativists who wrote on the likelihood that democracy might be easily adopted by peoples with authoritarian backgrounds, would surely have been dismissive. For Wilson, the question was not who wants freedom and good government—for words such as these obviously have large, if not "universal" appeal, as does the word "democracy" if attached to them. But that is not the issue; who does not approve of motherhood and apple pie? The nub of the problem—which cannot be measured by "barometers" or "values surveys"—is the enormous difficulty of embedding these desires in institutions that will formulate and enforce the rule of law for the sake of the common good and win the support of the bulk of the citizenry.[31]

Not all peoples have the capacity to generate such institutions, and a great many do not want them in any case. Their social cleavages may run too deep; their inheritance historically of institutions may be too limited; their culture may reveal itself to be too intolerant, fearful, or proud; they may lack leaders who are capable of envisioning the institutions and articulating the values upon which democracy rests but who are able instead to articulate ideas that legitimate an authoritarian political order. Or again, many peoples are apparently comfortable under authoritarian rule, provided it be efficient and justified in terms of local cultural values and practices, for it may assure social unity, national strength, and a citizenry that knows itself to profit in many ways from an enforced tranquillity. Sharia as a form of religious law has an unquestioned appeal for many millions of people. So too, "Asian values," as opposed to those that are Western but styled "universal," is an argument to be attended to, not rejected out of hand.[32] Yet another consideration is the way outside actors working under the guise of democracy promotion in effect develop social forces and political institutions that they can manage as Washington likes, whatever the objection of local political movements. An imperialist flavor to conditionality is difficult to avoid.

At bottom, a nationalist spirit based on a sense of ethnic, religious, or national identity may very well repel efforts by outsiders to micromanage change not only at the political and economic levels but also with respect to social, cultural, indeed even family matters (as the American insistence on women's rights in the Muslim world suggests—going so far in 2003 as insisting that a democratic Iraq have equal parliamentary representation by women). "Our Culture Is Our Resistance" is a battle cry often saluted by liberals in the United States when it is a matter of indigenous peoples under outside assault, but rejected by these same liberals when entire civilizations respond defensively to the universalist claims of the West. The insistence that democracy is a "universal value" supported by an "arc of history" that justifies Western powers invading peoples who do not have liberal social and political contracts under the just-war guise of "the responsibility to protect," is an exercise in neo-Wilsonian thinking that has little in common with earlier American liberal internationalist conceptions.

But the widespread neoliberal insistence on the universal appeal of democracy was not to be stayed. Consider as a final example of what could be a multitude of such exuberant expressions of confidence the faith shown by Harvard law professor Noah Feldman in what he called "mobile ideas." In his thinking, "Democracy and Islam are both what might be called mobile ideas—the kind that spread across the world, appealing to many people living in far-flung, strikingly different countries . . . [they] tend to be very flexible and therefore capable of coming together to produce unanticipated new configurations. Islamic democracy is not a contradiction. . . . Islam and democracy are starting to find means of mutual accommodation."[33]

As a poster boy for mobile ideas, Feldman published a large number of promotional editorials in the *New York Times* and the *Wall Street Journal*: "Democracy, Closer Every Day"; "A New Democracy, Enshrined in Faith"; "Political Islam: Global Warming"; "Muslim Democrats? Why Not!"; and "Operation Iraqi Democracy."[34]

STAGE THREE IN RETHINKING THE DEMOCRATIC TRANSITION: THE ABOLITION ALTOGETHER OF PREREQUISITES FOR DEMOCRATIZATION SO LONG AS AMERICA AND ITS ALLIES WERE COMMITTED TO THE PROCESS

Whereas the first stage of democratic transition theory had at least focused on a complex set of political factors precedent to democratization, and the second had insisted on the role that ideas might play in history (including as agents of change foreign peoples themselves), the third and final stage of democratic transition theory explicitly abandoned altogether the notions of "preconditions," "sequences," and "stages" as necessary aspects of the democratization process, just as it passed over without comment the political suggestions of stage one DTT or the ideological component of stage two. Instead, during the third stage, emphasis shifted to focus almost exclusively on what Americans could do once they had conquered forces that were defending whatever authoritarian governments were in place so as to prepare for a transition to democratic government. Nor were those in the third stage who plotted ways to further democratization through nation- and state-building scenarios they put forward concerned by "mobile ideas" or "barometers of public opinion." For them, as even Larry Diamond seemed to have concluded by 2008, little mattered besides the determination of the United States and its allies to bring about democracy for others, presumably because of its worldwide resonance combined with America's determined commitment to a certain definition of its "exceptionalism," which appeared to dictate a moral "responsibility to protect."

Here the widely influential works on democracy promotion by James Dobbins and David Petraeus make the point that American occupation forces may bring about democratic transitions without any regard for local circumstances with dramatic clarity. The directors of these ambitious volumes intended them to be blueprints of democratic nation- and state-building, works to be read by the tens of thousands of American practitioners of their assignment to accomplish such a mission as they went out to attend to their duties—what Secretary of State Hillary Clinton lauded as "the civilian surge."[35] Yet anyone familiar with the analogous literature that appeared in the 1960s during the Vietnam War, designed to lay out how the United States might "win the hearts and minds" (WHAM) of the Indochinese peoples, would suspect how thin these thousands of pages of recommendations in fact were.

As the head of a RAND team, James Dobbins published as early as 2003 *America's Role in Nation-Building from Germany to Iraq*. The study looked for lessons for success not only in Japan and Germany but also in Somalia, Haiti, Bosnia, Kosovo, and Afghanistan. Four other studies followed between 2007 and 2009, with such upbeat titles as *The Beginner's Guide to Nation-Building* and *After the Taliban: Nation-Building in Afghanistan*.[36] Whereas Dobbins and his associates look at problems on a country-by-country basis, General David Petraeus and his team, in the widely disseminated *Counterinsurgency Field Manual* (2006), looked instead at historical examples of insurgency and counterinsurgency (including Napoleon in Spain, the United States in the Philippines, the French in Vietnam, and Mao Zedong in China).

The ambition of these lengthy studies with so broad a scope was obviously to have a political impact in Washington and a practical effect on the ground in the countries the United States was occupying militarily. And they did.[37]

The Petraeus study is more specific than the Dobbins volumes in identifying distinct phases of nation- and state-building, but in terms of their approach through stages, these studies are quite similar. (Dobbins's *A Beginner's Guide* does lay out an approach that might be seen as incremental even if it were not as specific as Petraeus's.) In his *Counterinsurgency Field Manual*, Petraeus proposes a three-part sequence for counterinsurgency (COIN) labeled "control, hold, and build." To simplify, "control" is largely military and involves "warriors"; "hold" requires the conquerors to engage in economic development and social stabilization that builds a public arena, allowing for political change; and "build" denotes the process by which the local political forces agree to the terms establishing a legitimate government, which in turn heralds the success of an American intervention, which we might now call Mission Accomplished.

Dobbins, by contrast, is more interested in quantitative measures that show the occupier's efforts as measured in treasure and troops expended per capita and over periods of time in order to see in these terms what effect is achieved. His work tends to be more quantitative (all his variables can be measured), whereas Petraeus's volume is more qualitative (it argues by historical analogy).

But the Dobbins and Petraeus volumes aim at the same end: an understanding of the forces that make nation- and state-building possible so that the transition from authoritarian to democratic culture and rule may be achieved. (In later publications in this series, as reality finally sets in a bit, "peace" is identified as the goal to be reached, but eventually this goal is associated with democracy, as it must so as to be properly liberal.)

It is worth noting that all of these volumes are accompanied in their release by positive statements from leading presses and/or distinguished personalities. *A Beginner's Guide to Nation-Building*, for example, receives commendation on its cover from no less than former UN General Secretary Kofi Annan, Joschka Fisher (former German foreign minister and vice-chancellor), Carl Bildt (former Swedish prime minister, foreign minister, and high representative of the UN in Bosnia-Herzegovina), and Larry Diamond. Moreover, they were made available free of charge on the Internet, with literally millions of copies downloaded by a public anxious to win the global war on terrorism by fostering democracy abroad, especially in the Muslim world.

Yet the most striking thing about these studies is that they failed altogether to analyze the first thing either Wilson or the comparativist community of the cold war would have expected: the cultural, social, economic, historical, or political profile of the people under occupation. Apparently a military occupation, followed by policing, economic stability, and social quiet, would in due course, of itself, breed a political outcome that might actually be democratic. The German experience, say, was to be laid aside that of Haiti or Iraq not with respect to an understanding of the peoples concerned and their disposition for democracy—their profiles in terms of class and ethno-religious structures (from cleavages to a social contract); their experience with institutions restricting centralized power or resting on popular consent; the existence of a robust middle class or a moderate labor union; the presence of democratizing leaders with popular status—but rather in terms of stages of change or indices of effort, all focused on the quality of the American occupation. Freed of the onerous task of considering the complexity of local conditions under American military rule, Dobbins and his group would compare Germans to Haitians, considering only the character of the American intervention.[38]

As a consequence, there is no analysis in these lengthy volumes of what was now the well-nigh complete disregard for a host of local preconditions basic to the likelihood that a people can create a stable—much less democratic—national state structure. At the risk of sounding hopelessly old-fashioned, let me say that basic considerations should necessarily have included—as Woodrow Wilson and the social-science intellectuals of the cold war period would have insisted—such basic matters in these occupied lands as:

> —the history and politics of their ethnic and religious cleavages, and the terms of an already existing social contract that provided a sense of national unity and so nationalism as a political force (if any);
> —the history of class formation, cooperation, and conflict, including a review of the extent of national economic development, leading to the rise of an organized labor movement and, more importantly, a self-aware, educated middle class (if of any significance);
> —institutional arrangements or values that rested on popular consent (if any);
> —a discussion of culturally established limitations on the power of the central government as they had existed internally or externally to the state (if any);

—forms of state power that had an ethic of honor and civic duty enshrined in law and binding on the elite that could serve leaders and bureaucratic institutions of a transitional order;
—an account of the sources of revenues the new state might collect and the character of a likely bureaucracy to expend such funds;
—a review of the competence of other leading bureaucracies staffed by the local population, especially those of the judiciary, the military, and the interior;
—an account of the character of democratizing leaders (a Mahatma Gandhi or a Nelson Mandela, for instance) or movement (such as Solidarity in Poland) capable of forming a national party (if any);
—a profile of the likely behavior of powerful forces, from military to religious establishments, that might *oppose* a democratic transition;
—a review of forces outside the country in question in terms of their likelihood to foster or to oppose efforts at democratization.

Yet on such critical issues, these lengthy and influential publications written under the auspices of Dobbins (and RAND) and Petraeus (and the U.S. military) had nothing whatsoever to say. Let us be clear: the inattention to the character of local populations was no oversight; *it was a deliberate methodological choice.*

So the RAND group explicitly dismissed "Western culture, economic development, cultural homogeneity" as factors that might determine the success of an America occupation. Instead, Dobbins and his colleagues favored analyzing almost solely "the level of effort the United States and the international community put into their democratic transformations."

An example of their reasoning: "The United States and its allies have put 25 times more money and 50 times more troops, on a per capita basis, into post-conflict Kosovo than into post-conflict Afghanistan. This higher level of input accounts in significant measure for the higher level of output measured in the development of democratic institutions and economic growth." When the RAND authors arrived at a list of eight conclusions indicating success, seven had to do with actions of the occupier. The single variable concerning the character of populations subject to American control was trivial: "accountability for past injustices" of incumbents of the deposed regime (which the RAND team saw as a particularly difficult task to tackle). The last two lines of the book combine realism with optimism in a startling way given the pretensions of the study to insight: "There is no quick route to nation-building. Five years seems the minimum required to enforce an enduring transition to democracy."[39]

The *Counterinsurgency Field Manual* is equally disappointing on these critical matters. "The primary objective of any COIN operation is to foster development of effective governance by a legitimate government," the study that got so much attention states. But just how the political variables are to be identified and worked with is not a subject that is even mentioned, aside from calling for "sensitivity to local cultural factors." Yet in a country divided by profound ethnic, tribal, religious, and geographical differences that could engender fear, hatred, or a sense of superiority; lacking altogether a tradition of effective central government with a reach to the periphery; existing without an organized labor or self-conscious middle-class movement; and absent a democratizing political elite, just how far is "cultural sensitivity" going to get us toward democracy promotion or indeed any form of stable government? Closer study might indeed have persuaded us to give up such an unrealistic ambition instead of expending the trillions of dollars that brought about enormous loss of life and mass migrations on a scale unprecedented since the end of World War II.

Petraeus subsequently received a great deal of commendation for leading the "surge" in Iraq that momentarily helped the country find stability and allowed the Americans to withdraw with some rhetorical show of victory. His later promotions in Afghanistan and thence to sensitive positions in Washington were evidence of the high regard for his alleged accomplishments.

But, in fact, his stage model never arrived at anything close to its third phase. It accomplished only its two primary phases and then appeared successful for reasons that were fortuitous—a momentary split in Sunni ranks. The period of hope was unfortunately not enduring as the Shi'a government in Baghdad murderously asserted an authority that excluded both Sunni and Kurdish leadership from important offices. The result was that Petraeus's achievements were sand castles (built at huge expense in terms of lives lost and treasure squandered) quickly washed away by the tide of conflict that soon reappeared as the Americans withdrew. What then appeared was not *democracy*, but rather authoritarian control exercised from Baghdad by the Shi'a majority, confronted in due course by the emergence by the spring of 2014 of fundamentalist Sunni forces attempting to establish "the Islamic State" (ISIS), which, like the Taliban in Afghanistan (as well as in Pakistan), had its own notions on nation- and state-building centered on the creation of a caliphate.

Dobbins and his RAND colleagues eventually came to sense that leaving the local actors out had been something of an oversight. In 2013, they published a volume entitled *Overcoming Obstacles to Peace: Local Factors in Nation-Building*. After recognizing that their previous works had dealt exclusively with the actions of outsider interventionists, the Dobbins group reviewed six settings (expanded toward the end of the volume to a total of twenty) in terms of how the peoples forced into change had reacted themselves. Even if it were just a bit late to be engaging in such questions—a decade after the invasion of Iraq, we finally see some attention to the internal realities of the peoples invaded by the American military—what is nonetheless striking is that the study presents no general set of factors to be examined in terms of a composite sense of movement toward a democratic peace, but instead proposes a few rubrics for analysis that are intellectually impoverished if compared to the enormous literature that had appeared between 1950 and 1980 on the subject. Moreover, in no case do they suggest that one might leave bad enough alone and abandon their democratizing mission. Afghanistan and Iraq get relatively good grades, while Libya goes unstudied. The result is that this volume, like the others, continues to cheer such projects on.

Its chief shortcoming is that by losing themselves in the morass of individual country-level studies, the 2013 RAND study misses the forest for the trees as it presents no general theory of transition. In addition, unlike the earlier literature on the prospects for democratic transitions from the cold war years, which for the most part was distinctly pessimistic about how easily democratization might occur in some parts of the world, the RAND team remains quite positive about the progress that had been made and, reverting to type, credits not local actors but outside interventionists for the success they claim to have found (on the basis of statistical data that reveals far less than the study claims).

Thus, with respect to a section they label "Democracy," RAND insisted in the 2013 study that "nation-building interventions" had on balance produced positive results (including in Afghanistan and Iraq, with Bosnia deemed a more difficult case). The quantitative language the study adopts is the perfect mask to conceal its baffling conclusions:

> Table 9.2 shows levels of anticipatable difficulty alongside progress in democratization. The fourth, fifth, and sixth columns show each society's Freedom Index at intervention, after five years, and after ten years, or, if ten years have not passed, in 2011, the last year for which figures

were available. The seventh column shows the net change in Freedom Index scores over ten years. (As noted earlier, we have inverted and converted Freedom House's seven-point Freedom Index to a ten-point index, with 10 being the best possible score.) With the exceptions of Sudan and Côte d'Ivoire, every one of these 20 societies, even those that remained in conflict, registered advances in democratization over ten years and, in some cases, quite significantly so. On a scale of 1 to 10, these 10 societies experienced an average (mean) improvement of 2.15 points, or 21.5 percentage points. If we remove Sudan and Eastern Slavonia from the sample, there is a positive significant correlation between the probability of war and peak international military presence per capita at the 1-percent level (the correlation is 0.74, with a p-value of 0.0005); the correlation is also positive but not significant for peak international civilian police presence.

If these figures are difficult (perhaps impossible) to decipher, the "Conclusion" clarifies matters in a way that positively reinforces the United Nations' mission (and presumably RAND's eligibility to conduct further research under its well-paid auspices).

As the statistical analysis . . . shows, the great majority of post-conflict missions in the past two decades have resulted in improved security, progress in democratization, significant economic growth, and improvements in human development, and most have done so with a modest commitment of international military and civilian manpower and economic assistance.[40]

I invite readers to go online themselves to view the reasoning of these prominent publications. Almost all of them have been purposely released for general distribution by their authors and can be downloaded without charge. If the many hundreds of pages of information seem daunting to digest, be aware that they are vital texts to tens of thousands of practitioners in the field, whose language conveys better than any commentary such as mine the thinking behind the perilous course the United States (or NATO or the United Nations) has engaged in when it takes upon itself to engage in democratic (or "pacifying") nation- and state- building. To reflect on the influence these publications have had on the Americans charged to bring "freedom" to others, without at the same time placing efforts such as this one within the context of related facts showing these efforts have involved the death or displacement of millions of people, and trillions of dollars expended, all in the name of creating a better world, should be a sobering exercise. To claim, as the 2013 study does, significant if modest success, and to be aware of the distribution of this false confidence to policy-makers and those on the ground charged with pushing nation- and state-building forward, suggest the depths into which American social science had fallen since the 1990s.

JUST WAR: THE RESPONSIBILITY TO PROTECT (R2P)

Of all the theories that provided for the coming of age of American liberal imperialism in the 1990s, the thinnest in terms of its argument, but the most influential in terms of its impact, was surely the redefinition of the rights of sovereignty and the terms of "just war" provided by the responsibility to protect (R2P). The theory was thin for a simple reason: if democratic transition theory was mistaken—as I have tried to demonstrate was self-evidently the case—then R2P had no role in practical policy for the obvious reason that without the conditions for democracy to flower, no moral responsibility to encourage it could be persuasive. Why spend time worrying about it? But it was influential because it grew from a liberal discourse that promised peace (DPT) and an ease of transition (DTT) and thus legitimized a universal American mission to redeem humanity from the scourge of tyranny. What was nevertheless still required was a legal sanction that could justify imperialism in morally uplifting terms.

Enter the liberal jurists. In their hands, in an argument that in modern form went back to the late 1980s, a "right to intervene" against states or in situations where gross and systematic human rights were being violated, or weapons of mass destruction accumulated," became a "duty to intervene" in the name of what by 2001 was called a state's "responsibility to protect." The jurists hereby transformed the Westphalian meaning of "sovereignty," which was to be extended to a state by virtue of its control over a specific territory and its population, by giving to the democracies the right to intervene at will against any authoritarian state they deemed oppressive or dangerous by virtue of possessing weapons of mass destruction.[41]

To repeat: if DTT were correct, the outcome of decapitating the authoritarian state would be the relatively easy democratization of the people liberated in the operation. If DPT were correct, the spread of democracy was equivalent to the stabilization of world order. Thanks to the jurists, it only remained to find the organization that could act as judge in the matter. The International Commission on Intervention and State Sovereignty (ICISS), called for by UN General Secretary Kofi Annan in 1999 and convened by Canada, with a distinguished Algerian and a respected Australian as chairpersons, deliberated on the matter in 2000 and 2001 and before the attack of 9/11 and came to an answer.[42]

The Commission's decision was to go first to the United Nations to seek Security Council support for action. However, if this failed, any other multilateral institution, especially one controlled by democracies, might act on its own behalf. As the United Nations had states like China and Russia with a veto power to obstruct, why not breathe new life into a Community of Democracies, as Madeleine Albright had proposed in 1998? What might be dubbed "militarized humanitarianism" thanks to "muscular multilateralism" was now seen as eminently justifiable.

With it a new theory of the sovereignty of the state came into being, one that no longer affirmed, as had been the case since the Treaty of Westphalia of 1648, that states considered sovereign were immune from intervention in terms of the way they conducted their rule internally; instead states were now subject to oversight from a watchdog group in the international community that could revoke their sovereignty and invade at will a state failing in its responsibilities to protect its own population.

In a word, liberal imperialism now had juridical sanction. The basis of this right (indeed, obligation) to intervene had converted a liberalism that had once been defensive of democracies into a cohort of states that could go on the offensive. The ICISS took for its argument one first made by law professor Thomas M. Franck, that any state which signs the UN Charter "accepts the responsibilities of membership flowing from that signature. There is no transfer or dilution of state sovereignty. But there is a necessary re-characterization involved: from sovereignty as control to sovereignty as responsibility, in both internal functions and external duties. . . . The emerging principle in question is that intervention for human protection purposes, including military intervention in extreme cases, is supportable when major harm to civilians is occurring or imminently apprehended, and the state in question is unable or unwilling to end the harm, or is itself the perpetrator."[43]

Once a liberal invasion had taken place, the ICISS declared that it was now the task of the conquerors to exercise what was deemed their "responsibility to rebuild." For the Commission, "this might involve democratic institution and capacity building; constitutional power sharing; power alternating and redistribution arrangements; confidence building measures between different communities or groups; support for press freedom and the rule of law; the promotion of civil society; and other types of similar initiatives that broadly fit within the human security framework." With these words, liberal jurisprudence confirmed the "mission possible" of the democratic transition theorists, by moving the responsibility for democratization from the local community itself to the guardians of the emerging liberal world order headed by the United States.

WOODROW WILSON VERSUS NEO-WILSONIANISM

The problem with the neo-Wilsonians was that they had taken on a universal mission that knew no boundaries. Lacking restraint, their self-righteous imperialism had launched a clash of civilizations, whose eventual intensity they then attributed not to their own actions but to the character of their adversaries, whose opposition to liberal values and institutions only served to strengthen their conviction that pushing the liberal agenda was the only way to move forward. The irony—or better, the tragedy—should be apparent. Having unleashed catastrophic forces, the liberals pushed forward, digging themselves ever more deeply into the mayhem they had created. The Wilsonian tradition of anti-imperialism, using international organizations to protect, and if possible promote, constitutional democracy was now converted into an imperialist venture depending on military power.

Yet despite the change, there was certainly continuity as well—enough that neo-Wilsonianism may confidently be placed within the American liberal tradition. There is no reason to suppose that Woodrow Wilson's confidence in democracy and the findings of democratic peace theory are at serious odds with each other. Wilson's accounts are not as sharply formulated as that of the proponents of DPT, but political science had changed a great deal between 1910, when he became active politically, and the 1980s, when DPT was first argued. Similarly, his definition of American exceptionalism can be seen as reflected in the arguments supporting the responsibility to protect. The contribution of Wilson's faith in the spirit of democracy to engender freedom and peace was that it infused the imperialism of his intellectual great-grandchildren with a moral assurance in the cause they pursued, aggravated all the more by the patriotism that flowed from a widespread belief in the country's "exceptional" historical vocation.

By contrast, the fateful deviation from the Wilsonian tradition is strikingly apparent with democratic transition theory as it was formulated by the 1990s and pushed even further after 2002, along with its companion arguments laying out the extraordinary new terms of a "just war" that flowed out of the arguments surrounding the responsibility to protect. The mutation of liberalism into imperialism necessarily presupposed a blindness to local conditions, a monumental and murderous intellectual mistake that Woodrow Wilson and the liberal social-science community of the cold war era never would have made for a simple reason: their intellectual presuppositions would have laughed the idea out of the seminar or the policy-making room.[44]

The fundamental opposition between classical and hegemonic American liberal internationalism and neo-Wilsonianism centers, then, on the question of how difficult a democratic transition can be anticipated to be. Wilson limited his exercises in progressive imperialism to only a few countries, all of which were small and had populations typified by authoritarian states that had little public sense of a civic (or "organic") consensus on political values and interests. All of them mounted a nationalist resistance to American intervention, to be sure, but whether it was Emilio Aguinaldo in the Philippines or Augusto Sandino in Nicaragua, Washington met no serious obstacle to controlling events in Manila or Managua so long as it was determined to stay. That all of these interventions ultimately failed in their ambition to found democratic institutions in Central America and the Caribbean illustrates once again the decisive importance of local conditions. Moreover, compared to the kinds of efforts the Europeans were making to secure imperial possessions in Africa and Asia, Washington's bid for influence, from President William McKinley's day until Wilson's, was quite restrained.

When President Wilson encountered larger countries with established civilizations and civil debates turning in nationalist and revolutionary directions, his background as a historian and a political scientist with a focus on domestic culture combined with his understanding of the historical origins of democracy to keep the United States aloof from all but indirect intervention. True, his remedy to the chaos of the world was to work for the expansion of democratic ways. Yet he was careful to keep American ambitions in line with the character of peoples and events abroad. The notion that democracy would have a universal applicability that might be brought at the point of bayonets is something his deep appreciation of the force of nationalism (gained from his own experience as the first president born and reared in what had once been the Confederacy, and confirmed by his encounter with Mexico between 1913 and 1917) would have made him distrust instinctively. In sum, if countries had the likely capacity to become democracies, so much the better, and the United States would aid where it could—for example, by offering them the benefits of membership in the League. But if they did not, Washington would respect their sovereignty and hope for the best.

So, too, Wilson would presumably have understood that the assertion that the neo-Wilsonian mantra "our values and interests are one"—repeated time and again by both Presidents Bush and Obama (even if less so toward the end of the latter's presidency)—made no sense at all in a world where in many instances one's values had no likely hope of being realized but one's interests most certainly were at stake. In short, despite all the claims we hear today about the intrinsically "imperialist" nature of liberal thinking, the charge is ill-founded when applied to Wilson or cold war liberal internationalism even if it is quite appropriate as a label for the thinking that emerged during the 1990s and consolidated its hold on much of elite thinking about world affairs after 2002.

The split between the liberal internationalist tradition such as it existed until about 1990 and the neo-Wilsonian argument can be simply put: the former predicated the likelihood of a democratic transition on the character of the people under consideration; the latter made success a matter of Washington's determination. Herein lies the bad name that liberal internationalism has today deservedly acquired: that it has come to assume a universalism to its values that is a mistaken presumption, leading to the very imperialism it claims to oppose in the process of imposing values and institutions in places to which they are not suited, such that it unleashes a clash of civilizations.

Surely the most important lesson that Wilson brought with him into high office, so far as his ambitions for America's role in international relations was concerned, was that his hopes to promote democracy for others had to be pursued with caution, restraint, and prudence; that we should expect resistance to outside interference in other peoples' internal debates and conflicts; and that the eventual emergence of democratic ways was by no means to be thought inevitable for many of the great civilizations outside the peoples of the North Atlantic and Anglophone world, who were already predisposed to its acceptance. For this reason, Wilson worked on the margins—encouraging the Mexicans and the Germans in a progressive direction, but only to a point and then with no assurance of success. So too the multilateral coalition of democracies that Wilson hoped for through the League of Nations was far more a protective coat thrown over them through measures of collective security than it was an instrument of liberal expansion. Whatever the confidence

Wilson at times had shown for "progressive imperialism," the basic thrust of his policies was anti-imperialist. His reward was the Mexican Constitution of 1917 and the Weimar Constitution of 1919. If we would understand correctly his often-debated pronouncement of April 1917 that "the world must be made safe for democracy," we must value it for its restraint, not for its aggressive ambition.

SOME EXAMPLES OF TRADITIONAL WILSONIANISM VERSUS NEO-WILSONIANISM

Let me insist at this point that I am not trying to make the case that American influence can never matter. Certainly there are circumstances where United States foreign policy has made a tremendous difference so far as its liberal internationalist ambitions are concerned. This influence may continue to matter today as examples from Latin America to Central Europe passing by a country like Tunisia can attest. Let us look at some clear-cut examples of where Washington's policies succeeded brilliantly and contrast them to others where the failures were abysmal.

Consider the most obvious successes. In Germany and Japan, there was the human material that could indeed be remolded out of its authoritarian, militarist, protectionist ways and made into willing participants with other "free market democracies" in the creation of a liberal world order. The same had been true of Czechoslovakia after 1918, where outside troops never entered. A similar argument holds as well regarding the countries such as Poland, the Czech Republic, and Slovenia, which with relative ease became democratic without outside intervention after the fall of the Soviet Union between 1989 and 1991. Other cases from Chile to South Korea tell the same story: the evolution of internal political forces based on deep-set cultural, social, political, and historical predispositions allowed the emergence of democratic governments in these lands. Such a development is very much what Woodrow Wilson would surely have expected, as too the mainstream community of comparativist scholars during the cold war might have anticipated.

By contrast, the effort of outsiders to bring about the same results more recently in Pakistan, Afghanistan, or Iraq (to which list one could add many countries in the Muslim world, as well as other important peoples with an ancient civilization and a strong nationalist identity, such as the Chinese and the Russians) was from the start a fool's errand. The sharp break introduced by neo-Wilsonianism is apparent in its confidence about the suitability of democratic ways to all the world. The way this optimism went virtually unquestioned within the liberal internationalist establishment itself was an intellectual failing of the first order.

For Wilson the question was not so much whether a people wanted "freedom" but whether they knew how to build organizations capable of generating the rule of law and have them rest on the consent of the governed. Here was Wilson's conservative insight, one that drew him to Edmund Burke as the thinker who had most influenced his own beliefs. We should recall Wilson's preferred example: the French Revolution, with its enthusiasm for the promise of "the Rights of Man," but the difficulty the French had found in achieving stable government to give legal protection and thus meaning to these lofty "rights." As Wilson phrased it in 1908:

> No doubt a great deal of nonsense has been talked about the inalienable rights of the individual and a great deal that was mere vague sentiment and pleasing speculation has been put forward as fundamental principle. The Rights of Man [proclaimed by the French Revolution of 1789] are easy to discourse of, may be very pleasingly magnified in the sentences of such constitutions as it used to satisfy the revolutionary ardor of French leaders to draw up and affect to put into operation; but they are infinitely hard to translate into practice. . . . Only that is "law" which can be executed, and the abstract rights of man are singularly difficult of execution.[45]

In fact, as early as 1885, Wilson had asked the hard question he was to spend his life working to answer:

> Why has democracy been a cordial and a tonic to little Switzerland and big America, while it has been as yet only a quick intoxicant or a slow poison to France and Spain, a mere maddening draught to the South American states?

Here was an apt expression of the analytic position of classical and hegemonic phases of American liberal internationalism with respect to democracy promotion. A people that would make the transition to democracy with outside help must nonetheless play a decisive role itself. Instead, by reducing the challenges to democratization through the results of opinion polling or an appeal to something as vacuous as "mobile ideas," or even worse by assuming that a three-stage operation called COIN (or counterinsurgency) held the key to democratization, neo-Wilsonianism was obviously formulating a new vision of democratic change that was quite unique unto itself—one with disastrous results for American foreign policy, not to speak of the populations on which these "altruistic" gifts were to be bestowed.

To make this point clearly—that democratization is possible in some circumstances but almost surely impossible in others—let us consider what such an old-fashioned analysis as those current from 1950 to 1990 might well have suggested by comparing Iraq and Afghanistan to Germany and Japan (as President Bush as well as his national security adviser and later Secretary of State Condoleezza Rice were forever doing). An equally sobering comparison might be made between President Obama and his advisers thinking about intervention in Libya in 2011 or in prolonging American involvement in Afghanistan after yet another "democratic" election in 2014, or to the pious pronouncements that human rights and democracy could save the day in Iraq and Syria that started in 2011 and continued throughout early 2015.

First, unlike Iraq or Afghanistan—to which we might add Pakistan and Libya or areas of the Middle East such as Syria—Germany and Japan each had an integrated industrial economy that before their occupation had had predictable, accountable governmental supervision to perform responsibly and that counted on an already educated middle class for its development to proceed. With its rule of law, democracy was thus a form of government that corresponded to the stage of economic development, class relations, and state functions of these two countries in 1945. Nothing of the same could be said of any of the aforementioned countries, to which list a host of other countries might be added, where the United States is involved in a seemingly endless effort to promote "good governance" in democratic terms, with no indication whatsoever of success.

Second, domestic conflicts in Japan and Germany after World War II were more along class than ethnic or religious lines in a way that never threatened to undermine a firm sense of national identity. Long before 1945, nationalism had become firmly entrenched in both countries, and ways of resolving class conflict through organized political means had emerged. Social divisions most certainly existed in both countries, but they were greatly exceeded by the depth of the splits we see in the five countries cited above—splits that are in different measure religious, linguistic, and territorial but lodged as well in fearful historical memories of domestic adversaries that had had murderous conclusions.

Third, Japan and, to a greater extent, Germany had traditions of parlia-

mentary government that could make their democratization seem a legitimate development out of past internal circumstances. Both also had inherited
from their imperial governments entrenched elite values of honor and civic
duty that made for bureaucratic effectiveness so far as all the major services
housed in the government were concerned. Even when Germany was not a
democracy, it worked to be a *Rechtsstaat*—that is, a government that recognized and enforced certain civil rights. None of the countries in contention
today enjoy any such legacies whatsoever.

Fourth, Japan and again, to a greater extent, Germany enjoyed leaders and
popular movements that preferred democracy to authoritarian government
and understood what this meant in terms of institutional innovations and a
change in cultural norms. To think of Hamid Karzai or any Iraqi leader (including the neoconservative favorite Ahmed Chalabi, but more importantly
Nuri al-Maliki) or any leader with hopes of gaining power in Pakistan, Libya,
or Syria as an equivalent to the Japanese and German leaders under American
occupation is to have a gallows sense of humor.

Fifth, strong majorities of nationalists in Japan and Germany could see
clearly enough that, in terms of the international forces surrounding them,
their choice was between accepting the terms of American occupying forces
or facing alone the rising tide of world communism. The Soviets were en-
camped in East Germany, and Mao had come to power in Beijing in 1949.
What was occurring in much of the Muslim world by 2013 at the latest was
a vast civil conflict that compared to no other region in recent history, although political scientist John M. Owen has made an insightful comparison
with the wars of religion that raged in Europe among Christians centuries ago
with those happening now.[46]

THE DEMOCRATIZATION OF
CZECHOSLOVAKIA AFTER 1918

The direct use of American power is not a necessary prerequisite for democracy to take root. Consider, for example, the striking case of the transition to
democratic government in Czechoslovakia after World War I, a development
that demonstrates once again the importance of understanding the people
who are to undergo a transition from authoritarianism to democracy, and to
privilege this understanding over the role outside forces can play. Here is the
one place Woodrow Wilson himself did have a major success promoting democracy, but this without aiming a gun. In Czechoslovakia after 1918, a

democratic nation was born that still today, a century later, gives ample credit to Woodrow Wilson as one of its founders. What we see in this country's historic change confirms the argument made above: it was not simply the lift Wilson gave to this country's desire for independence and democracy that mattered, but the critical significance of the Czechoslovaks themselves.

The most important domestic factor explaining the emergence of democracy in that country during the interwar period is that there was no traditional right in power and so no obvious social base for an authoritarian reaction. The country was born from a fragment of empire with no native monarchy—the Slovaks having been under Hungarian rule, the Czechs under Austrian. Nor was there a Czech or Slovak landed elite with which the new republic had to contend. Instead, most of the large landowners were Germans or Magyars. By 1920, a reform bill had provided for the redistribution of these lands to small farmers, who became enthusiastic supporters of the new republican government and whose Agrarian party combined elements of both the Czech and Slovak populations—as well as some Magyars and Ruthenians.

By historical coincidence, then, Czechoslovakia came into being as a "bourgeois republic." A Social Democratic movement was solidly republican, and in due course even the communists decided to cooperate with the new order. It helped that the country was rich—in 1937, the Czech regions enjoyed a per-capital income higher than that of France. A solid middle class had the skills to administer the government ably, under the leadership of outstanding democrats such as Thomas Masaryk and Eduard Benes. When the farmers rallied to the republic, the democratic consensus was firmly established. In addition, the country was balanced economically between agrarian and industrial activities, which helped to mitigate the interwar economic tensions that beset the area.

Tensions between the country's ethnic groups did seem at times to threaten political stability. Of its population of 14 million, more than 3 million were German, 700,000 were Hungarians, and 300,000 were Ruthenians. These minorities did not reconcile themselves easily to Czechoslovakian sovereignty and could complain that the Paris settlements had deprived them of the right to national self-determination afforded to others.

Nor were the relations between the dominant Czechs and Slovaks smooth, as their eventual separation in 1992 into two countries was to attest. Historically, they had lived separate political lives; their first joint association was in the state founded in 1918. Moreover, the relative economic backwardness of the Slovaks and their cultural particularities meant that they resented the more prosperous and secular Czechs and their leading role in the affairs of the new regime.

It is nevertheless possible to speculate that these very tensions helped the democratic transition in Czechoslovakia. A single dominant group could have proved more hostile to minorities. By having to bid constantly for Slovak support, the Czechs had to ensure the viability of a system of mutual understanding and compromise.

This ethnic compromise was worked out within a political system borrowed in part from the French Third Republic. The president was elected by the legislature, which also selected a cabinet. Thanks to proportional representation, the country had a multiparty system—cabinets typically counted the participation of five parties. In other Eastern European countries after the war, and in France, such a party system made governing coalitions difficult to sustain. In Prague, cooperation between Czechs and Slovaks proved crucial. Though there were fourteen different cabinets in power between 1920 and 1938, the multiparty democracy survived. When the country fell to Nazi Germany, it was a moral loss of the first order to the West and to the prospects for liberal internationalism in general.

As statements by the republic's foreign minister and later president Eduard Benes demonstrate, Wilson's League of Nations was indeed the kind of international guarantee a vulnerable democracy such as that housed in Prague needed. These salutes were repeated when Vaclav Havel, the first president of democratic Czechoslovakia, addressed a joint session of Congress on February 21, 1990, mentioning Woodrow Wilson before all other Americans of importance to his country.

The Czechoslovak example thus illustrates once again the decisive importance of a people's political character in nation- and state-building undertakings. Other peoples allowed to self-determine after 1918 were not so fortunate. The conclusion is obvious. Great civilizations, deep-set cultural forces, or simply anarchy itself may oppose democratization. If Spain and Portugal successfully democratized in the 1970s, it was thanks in part to the European community but as critically to their own internal evolution as a people. The same is true of South Korea in the 1990s, which obviously depended on Washington's support for its transition but even more on its own internal evolution since 1945.

In the case of Latin America, where Washington's interference under Republican presidents (Eisenhower, Nixon, and Reagan) to the detriment of local liberal forces was recurrent, it is even more true that these peoples them-

228 – CHAPTER SIX

selves made their transition to democracy. Ask liberal Chileans or Brazilians or Argentines today if their democracy is thanks to the United States, and see their reaction. In this region, the United States was of little help, and indeed on balance was a clear impediment, to such a political evolution.

The fatal mistakes of the neo-Wilsonians was to betray the restraint of their predecessors, to argue with an intellectual hubris unmatched in the annals of the American social sciences on world affairs the justification for policies that have brought death and destruction upon territories inhabited by tens of millions of people, to erode seriously the international standing of the United States, and to bring the liberal internationalist tradition itself to the brink of extinction.[47]

LENINISM AND NEO-WILSONIANISM: A STRIKING SIMILARITY

One can recall with profit, in regard to this account of the optimism with which neo-Wilsonians viewed the transition from authoritarianism to democracy during the presidencies of George W. Bush and Barack Obama, an event that occurred involving Karl Marx in 1882. Writing to Engels after traveling to Paris and hearing the plans of a group of French anarchists who called themselves "Marxists," under the leadership of his son-in-law Paul Lafargue, Marx declared: "One thing is certain, I am not a Marxist." Marx pointed out that material conditions had to be ripe for capitalism to collapse and a proper communist "dictatorship of the proletariat" to come into being. Political action was no substitute for the power of social reality. Marx opposed his "materialistic" understanding of change in history prompted by the coming of communism with the understanding of history he found in Lafargue's "voluntarism."[48] Would Woodrow Wilson say any less of many of those today who continue to talk of the ease of democratization, who promote ends Wilson might have endorsed but whose practice nearly a century after he left the presidency he would surely denounce for its lack of understanding of the material conditions basic to the creation of a democratic society and state?

Some thirty-odd years later, as debate broke out among Russian Marxists as to whether they should launch a revolution against the czarist regime caught in the grip of World War I, much the same debate pitted Lenin and the Bolsheviks against the Menshevik Marxists, who opposed direct action to bring about communism in Russia and thereafter throughout the world. Lenin had good arguments to make to defend his credentials as an orthodox

Marxist. Like Marx, he was struggling for the working class to come to power through a party organized to tie workers together nationally and internationally. His idea was to strike when the czarist government was weakened through war and the Russian masses desperately wanted out of the conflict with Germany. To justify himself as a Marxist given the kind of secret, hierarchical party he was forming, he could point to the relative backwardness of the "class consciousness" of the workers and to the need to rouse the peasantry to revolutionary action as well in order to justify his political expediency, the extent of which had no foundation in Marxist theory. The result was Marxism-Leninism, or communism, whose "dictatorship of the proletariat" (essentially a dictatorship of the party) was distinct from Marxists who rejected Leninism and called themselves Social Democratic.

The difference between Woodrow Wilson and the liberal interventionists and market enthusiasts of the early twentieth-first century can in this fashion be fruitfully compared to the opposition of Marxists in the early twentieth century to Lenin. In each case a "Bolshevik" voluntarist push to "hasten history"—that is, to override considerations of culture and history for the sake of betting on a near-term golden age—was at the center of the debate, even if there is a certain irony in pointing out the analogy between communist and neo-Wilsonian theorists.

Yet just as a link between Marx and Lenin is undeniable, so too is the link between traditional Wilsonians and neo-Wilsonians today. The tie in the case of American liberal internationalist thinking is democratic peace theory, whose origins lie in Wilson's thinking (or better, in liberal internationalism in general). Like the neo-Wilsonians, Wilson was an idealist whose sense of history led him to work for progressive change. But unlike his intellectual great-grandchildren, he was a realist as well, for he had learned from history, and his own efforts to influence it, of the difficulties inherent in democratic nation- and state-building.

TO CONCLUDE

In closing, let us consider the statement by Robert Kagan, the leading American neoconservative intellectual cheering on the invasion of Iraq in his book *Of Paradise and Power*, one of the most influential publications justifying the war to appear in 2003. In the concluding section of his book, which with characteristic bravado he entitles "Adjusting to Hegemony," Kagan affirms that:

America did not change on September 11. It only became more itself. Nor should there be any mystery about the course America is on, and has been on, not only over the past year or over the past decade, but for the better part of the past six decades, and, one might even say, for the better part of the past four centuries. . . . When the Bush administration released its new National Security Strategy in September [usually called the Bush Doctrine, NSS-2002] . . . the new strategy was seen as a response to September 11. . . . But the striking thing about that document is that aside from a few references to the idea of "pre-emption," which itself was hardly a novel concept, the Bush administration's "new" strategy was little more than a restatement of American policies, many going back a half century . . . viewed from the perspective of the grand sweep of American history, a history marked by the nation's steady expansion and a seemingly ineluctable rise from perilous weakness to the present global hegemony, this latest expansion of America's strategic role may be less than shocking.[49]

"Shocking," however, this statement most certainly is—with respect to its insistence that the Bush Doctrine "was hardly a novel concept." Here is the nub, precisely in these words of the leading neoconservative theoretician, of the betrayal of the traditional Wilsonian position with all the travails that would follow from changing theory to practice with the enactment of this doctrine.

Kagan's assertion that America did not change on 9/11, that it was in perfect continuity with its history of the past decade, in fact if not over the past six decades, indeed perhaps over the past four centuries, is breathtaking in its effort to cover what was surely the greatest mistake in the history of United States foreign policy with the mantle of a patriotism centuries old. As a boldly, unapologetically, brutally imperialist country, the United States did indeed change thanks to the manipulations of the Bush Doctrine, which in 2002 managed to turn this country in a way that had in many respects no continuity with "the past six decades," much less almost "the past four centuries" (which would have taken us back to the days of the Mayflower Compact). In Kagan's words, we have a perfect example of what should be called the "9/11 Industry," an effort to turn this tragedy into an argument calling for an imperialist foreign policy without precedent in the nation's history. And this legitimized in the name of freedom, democracy, and peace—the essential building blocks of the liberal internationalist agenda. The tragedy of American liberal internationalism by late 2011 was that a framework for policy that had done so much to establish America's preeminence in world affairs between 1945 and 2001 should have contributed so significantly to its decline thereafter.

As the years passed, Kagan was not to change his essential argument: that America had a liberal world order to defend, that to do so required leadership with respect to every significant development on the planet, and that the flag that should fly over this noble enterprise was nothing less than liberal internationalism. Eleven years after he had first announced that the United States "did not change on September 11. It only became more itself," he bemoaned the fact that the country had indeed begun to change in significant ways, that it had become not simply "war-weary" but instead that it had become "world-weary." Regrettably, the question of American decline was not based on a realistic assessment of this land's relative capacities measured against the impossible ends it had set out to achieve, but instead reflected "an intellectual problem, a question of identity and purpose."[50] That the change Kagan laments may have been due to the catastrophic failure of a Middle East policy that he had enthusiastically endorsed but from which he had learned no salutary lesson was not a matter to which he gave the slightest thought (just as neoconservatives had earlier reproached those who would learn "lessons from Vietnam" that implied a scaled-back involvement in world affairs to be suffering a regrettable condition they labeled "the Vietnam syndrome").

In order to see the dramatic change from Wilsonianism to neo-Wilsonianism, consult the epigraphs at the opening of this chapter. There is Woodrow Wilson cautioning restraint for the sake of making the world safe for democracy, and below it one finds William Kristol and Robert Kagan in one of their many imperialist exhortations ostensibly directed to the same end of democracy promotion, but one their efforts would badly undermine. No contrast could show in a more glaring light the prudence of the president and the recklessness of the neoconservatives and their neoliberal allies.

For those who believe that ideas have little consequence in world affairs, considering the results of neo-Wilsonian arguments may be an encouragement to think again. For no more dramatic demonstration can be made of the role of ideas in dictating policy than a consideration of the role played in the highest circles in Washington than those reviewed here. The idea that Woodrow Wilson would have subscribed to General Petraeus's COIN strategy for state-building—or to James Dobbins's lessons in *A Beginner's Guide to Nation-Building* or to Larry Diamond's "barometers of public opinion" to forecast the possibilities of a transition from authoritarian to democratic government—beggars the imagination. Similarly he would surely have strongly doubted "the universal right of democracy" and that our "interests and values are one," as Presidents George W. Bush and Barack Obama ceaselessly asserted, or that we had a "responsibility to protect" in situations where intervention could make a bad situation much worse given the lack of material with which to construct a democratic future. While others goaded him on to march on Mexico City in 1914 or Moscow and Berlin in 1918, Wilson wisely declined, working only on the margins for a constitutional outcome in these circumstances but not contributing a major deployment of American force to his hopes. But the terms of the Bush Doctrine overwhelmed traditional liberal internationalist reserve with a braggadocio of deadly consequence that still today exercises a tantalizing appeal on many in the liberal internationalist community, people like those Lenin supposedly called "useful idiots" for their inability to see the awful reality pious thinking could condone.[51]

In the introduction, I cited Reinhold Niebuhr's congratulation to liberals for their "fortunate vagueness"—that is, their inability to formulate in an ideologically watertight fashion their goal for the world and the way to achieve it. The problem with neo-Wilsonianism is that it replaced the relatively amorphous thinking of liberal internationalism with a much "harder" ideology, one that gave its adherents a moral commitment to a more militant foreign policy based on social-science reasoning that represented a new argument in American liberal internationalism. The irony is that just as communism was collapsing as an ideology that claimed to understand the logic of history and the role of Marxism-Leninism in the struggle for a better tomorrow, liberal internationalism was becoming intoxicated by much the same convictions for its way of understanding the world.

In its transformation from a hegemonic to an imperialist ideology during the 1990s, liberal internationalism became a danger to the very values it professed to champion. Whatever progressive features it undeniably possessed needed henceforth to be weighed against the damage it might plausibly inflict, which in the Middle East and Southwest Asia was enormous. Democratic peace theory, democratic transition theory, and the responsibility to protect in combination were a heady brew, one with murderous consequences for the people of the region as well as for American pretensions to hegemony in world politics. American liberal internationalism is in crisis in good measure because its terms of engagement were used to legitimize the invasion of Iraq and the policies that were subsequently pursued in the Muslim world, from North Africa to Afghanistan. Neither human rights nor democratic government abroad was served by these imperialist adventures, nor was the national security of the United States in any way enhanced. Instead disaster followed disaster as American policy sowed the whirlwind. The idea that policies such as the responsibility to protect should continue to be promoted in a blanket manner was to expose liberalism to the charge that moralistic folly was intrinsic to its character. In instance after instance, r2p seemed the perfect embodiment of the saying "the road to hell is paved with good intentions."

In 1951, in *The Origins of Totalitarianism*, Hannah Arendt had warned against precisely the dangers of tightly constructed ideological political arguments that promised a golden age if only decisive action were taken today. Only months before Niebuhr completed *The Irony of American History*, wherein he had developed his appreciation of "fortunate vagueness," Arendt had pointed out that the structures of modern fundamentalist political systems:

> are known for their scientific character; they combine the scientific approach with results of philosophical relevance and pretend to be scientific philosophy. . . . Ideologies pretend to know the mysteries of the whole historical process—the secrets of the past, the intricacies of the present, the uncertainties of the future—because of the logic inherent in their respective ideas . . . they pretend to have found a way to establish the rule of justice on earth. . . . All laws have become laws of movement. . . .
>
> Ideologies are always oriented toward history. . . . The claim to total explanation promises to explain all historical happenings . . . hence ideological thinking becomes emancipated from the reality that we perceive with our five senses, and insists on a "truer" reality concealed behind all perceptible things, dominating them from this place of concealment and requiring a sixth sense that enables us to become aware of it. . . . Once it has established its premise, its point of departure, experiences no longer interfere with ideological thinking, nor can it be taught by reality.[52]

Arendt was talking about fascism and communism, of course, but the pseudo-scientific certitude of neo-Wilsonianism could fit this profile as well.

Hannah Arendt's concerns now might be applied to those whom she surely never would have imagined they could involve, the liberal internationalist imperialists whose traditions of an earlier time had sheltered her, as well she understood, from the dangers intrinsic to both fascism and communism but that now had mutated into a danger to the basic values she defended.[53]

CHAPTER SEVEN

From Theory to Practice: Neo-Wilsonianism in the White House, 2001–2017

Once you begin a great movement, there's no telling where it will end. We meant to change a nation, and instead, we changed a world. Countries across the globe are turning to free markets and free speech and turning away from the ideologies of the past. For them, the great rediscovery of the 1980s has been that, lo and behold, the moral way of government is the practical way of government: democracy, the profoundly good, is also the profoundly productive.

—*Ronald Reagan, "Farewell Address," January 1989*

History's lesson is clear. When a war-weary America withdrew from the international stage following World War I, the world spawned militarism, fascism and aggression unchecked. . . . But in answering the call to lead after World War II, we built from the principles of democracy and the rule of law a new community of free nations, a community whose strength, perseverance, patience and unity of purpose contained Soviet totalitarianism and kept the peace.

No society, no continent should be disqualified from sharing the ideals of human liberty. The community of democratic nations is more robust than ever and it will gain strength as it grows . . . abandonment of the worldwide democratic revolution would be disastrous for American security. History is summoning us once again to lead.

—*George H. W. Bush, December 12, 1992*

In the new era of peril and opportunity, our overriding purpose must be to expand and strengthen the world's community of market-based democracies. During the Cold War, we fought to contain a threat to the survival of free institutions. Now we seek to enlarge the circle of nations that live under those free institutions, for our dream is that of

a day when the opinions and energies of every person in the world
will be given full expression in a world of thriving democracies that
cooperate with each other and live in peace.
—*Bill Clinton, September 27, 1993*

The origin of the mutation of classical and hegemonic Wilsonianism into
an imperialist phase that I call "neo-Wilsonianism" emerged as the constraints of American foreign policy existing under the exigencies of containment were lifted. Although a wave of change had begun to gather within the
liberal tradition during the Reagan presidency, the flood tide came in the
1990s following the demise of the Soviet Union. During the administrations
of both George H. W. Bush (1989–1993) and Bill Clinton (1993–2001), a
sense of self-confidence in the expansion of the free-market democratic world
was understandably anticipated—as the citations above by three successive
presidents at the close of the cold war testify. But just how would this take
place?

With containment dead, official Washington was hungry for new ideas,
and in short order got them. As the example of the leading neoconservative
intellectual Robert Kagan showed at the end of the previous chapter, there
were those who denied that radical change was being infused into the American political outlook over the decade that preceded the election of George W.
Bush to the White House. "America did not change on September 11. It only
became more itself," Kagan wrote in 2003, saluting the invasion of Iraq yet
again, in one of the most influentially misleading and mistaken statements of
the times.

Kagan is misleading because he camouflages the greatest break in the history of the Wilsonian tradition with the invasion of Iraq as nothing other than
a continuation of business as usual, calling the Bush Doctrine "hardly a novel
concept." And he is mistaken because an analysis of the Bush Doctrine (often
referred to as the National Security Strategy of the United States, September
2002, or NSS-2002) shows that this statement of American purpose heralded
an unprecedented act of liberal imperialism quite outside the boundaries of
this tradition as it had existed since the time of Woodrow Wilson, or—in the
liberal internationalist perspective—during the cold war; indeed it stands
alone in the annals of the history of American foreign policy since the Republic's founding for its daring act of imperialist aggression.

The evidence that theory became policy is clearly at hand. For what NSS-2002 embodied was the transition from neo-Wilsonian theory to imperialist practice. Here is the document to examine, as the neoconservative movement proudly asserted when its leading voices claimed authorship of the program.[1]

THE BUSH DOCTRINE AND THE NEOCONSERVATIVE/NEO-WILSONIAN ASCENDENCY

I proposed in the introduction that since Wilson's time, American liberal internationalism has held that the United States can best promote world peace (the long-term primary goal of the tradition), and thus this country's security, by committing itself to four separate, but interrelated, elements that constitute its essence: (1) cooperation among democratic governments, (2) linked in economic openness, (3) that negotiate their differences and common interests through well-structured multilateral institutions that foster a robust sense of the importance of economic integration, international law, and a commitment to mutual defense, (4) under an America that willingly assumes the responsibilities of leadership of a community of nations pledged to peace through collective security, even if this means going to war to preserve it.

In terms of their rhetoric, President George W. Bush's words in NSS-2002 were seemingly quite in line with the liberal tradition for the obvious reason that each of these four points and their relationship to world peace was strongly affirmed. Thus, with respect to fostering peace, the patina of Wilsonianism is apparent from the first two pages of the National Security Strategy, where President Bush mentions America's dedication to promote peace seven times, democracy four times, and freedom thirteen times; he uses the word "free" several times as well to speak of the international market conditions that should prevail, in combination also with the term "freedom-loving." In addition, several sections of the document itself are dedicated to "global economic growth through free markets and free trade." Despite the later criticism of the invasion of Iraq as a unilateral operation, the doctrine as published gives repeated lip service to the importance of American exceptionalism engaging through multilateral institutions in the defense of the world's freedom.

Not even Wilson at his most fulsome could compete with the rhetoric of the Bush Doctrine, for nothing he had ever written or said was as explicitly "Wilsonian" as NSS-2002. If liberal internationalism had proved difficult to articulate as a conceptually coherent framework for policy in Wilson's own time, in President Bush's hands it now had a comprehensive integration of its synergist parts such that we can finally confidently call it a "grand strategy."

However, the continuity with past assertions in Washington should not mask the fundamental difference that NSS-2002 marked from earlier thinking. For beneath the Bush Doctrine's highly polished surface veneer of traditional Wilsonian values lay not the defensive posture that we can associate with Wilson and his concept of the League of Nations, or the rather pessimistic view of promoting democracy in many parts of the world that marked liberalism during the cold war, but instead an offensive intention altogether remarkable in the Republic's history. The opening lines of the Bush Doctrine mark the sea change in history:

> The great struggles of the twentieth century between liberty and totalitarianism ended with a decisive victory for the forces of freedom—and a single sustainable model for national success: freedom, democracy, and free enterprise. In the twenty-first century, only nations that share a commitment to protecting basic human rights and guaranteeing political and economic freedom will be able to unleash the potential of their people and assure their future prosperity.
>
> People everywhere want to be able to speak freely; choose who will govern them; worship as they please; educate their children—male and female; own property; and enjoy the benefits of their labor. These values of freedom are right and true for every person, in every society— and the duty of protecting these values against their enemies is the common calling of freedom-loving people across the globe and across the ages. . . .
>
> The United States will use this moment of opportunity to extend the benefits of freedom across the globe. We will actively work to bring the hope of democracy, development, free markets, and free trade to every corner of the world. . . . Freedom is the non-negotiable demand of human dignity; the birthright of every person—in every civilization. Throughout history, freedom has been threatened by war and terror; it has been challenged by the clashing wills of powerful states and the evil designs of tyrants; and it has been tested by widespread poverty and disease. Today, humanity holds in its hands the opportunity to further freedom's triumph over all these foes. The United States welcomes our responsibility to lead in this great mission.[2]

Accordingly, NSS-2002 makes it plain in two of its nine parts that it is confident that democratic government could spread to parts of the world it has not yet penetrated, bucked up in four parts when it concedes that it might be necessary to use force preemptively or "preventively" to achieve this access. So in its opening section, it puts forth an aggressive design with an assurance that Woodrow Wilson never possessed—for he never had the confidence, born in the 1990s, of democratic transition theory (DTT) holding democracy (or "freedom") as a "universal right" with "universal appeal." Thus, with respect to democracy, free markets, and America's responsibility to promote these rights, the Bush Doctrine insists in an opening chapter, in tones reminiscent of Reagan, but foreign to Wilson's thought:

> In pursuit of our goals, our first imperative is to clarify what we stand for: the United States must defend liberty and justice because these principles are right and true for all people everywhere. No nation owns these aspirations, and no nation is exempt from them. . . . America must stand firmly for the nonnegotiable demands of human dignity: the rule of law; limits on the absolute power of the state; free speech; freedom of worship; equal justice; respect for women; religious and ethnic tolerance; and respect for private property . . . the national security of the United States must start from these core beliefs and look outward for possibilities to expand liberty.[3]

Moreover, the Bush Doctrine asserts that multilateral institutions should collaborate in the American-led effort, but affirms that if America has to act unilaterally, or with a "coalition of the willing," its exceptional character will show the United States capable alone of providing an order of peace, prosperity, and freedom that the world so badly needs and wants. Sounding every bit the reincarnation of Ronald Reagan, President Bush could declare American leadership proceeding from a "position of unparalleled military strength and great economic and political influence," which would guarantee "building the infrastructure of democracy" with efforts such as what later would come to be baptized "Operation Iraqi Freedom."

Where did this sense of the ease of the democratic transition come from? The contrast between traditional liberalism and NSS-2002 arose from the character of DTT, by whose lights in the 1990s (and for years thereafter) the relative speed of the transition from authoritarian to democratic government emerged as the distinctive mark of neo-Wilsonianism. Woodrow Wilson's guarded hopes for liberal internationalism had stood in stark contrast to the appeal of proletarian internationalism heralded by Lenin and Trotsky and embodied in the revolutionary intentions of the Third International, founded in 1919 (with terms of engagement specified over the next two years). Like Marxism-Leninism, the Bush Doctrine's progressive imperialist agenda was central to its ambitions. That Wilsonianism had in 2002 become "voluntarist," much as Leninism had once been, should not escape notice for anyone with a sense of irony (or tragedy).

In the formulation of expanded objectives for fostering change abroad, neoliberals in the Democratic Party could readily be convinced to participate in the ambitions of the Bush Doctrine (after all, most of the new concepts had been formulated by intellectuals of the center-left), even if the animating center for action lay with the neoconservatives within the Republican Party, themselves the product of the Reagan years. What this thinking and the triumphal attitude it bred in reaction to the attack of September 11, 2001, signaled was a change with the past that preserved the appearance of continuity in certain respects by endorsing the traditional features of a Wilsonian foreign policy while simultaneously introducing under these familiar points what in fact were radical innovations into the way Washington understood its role in world affairs.

For those who doubt the profound impact that well-formulated ideas may have on public policy at critical historical junctures, the story of the impact of neo-Wilsonian thinking in Washington, D.C., should be a corrective.

Change, Not Continuity, as the Mark of the Bush Doctrine

The stage was now set for a reversal of fortune in liberal internationalist objectives. Whereas in the 1940s, policies appeared that constituted a strengthening of democracy both nationally and internationally within the compass of countries that fell under American hegemony, with the new, imperialist agenda of 2002, efforts were undertaken that were fated to meet with disaster—even more for the people abroad subject to these purposes than to the United States itself.

Put in a few words, despite the claims of the Bush administration:

—Afghanistan and Iraq were not Germany and Japan;
—The European Recovery (or Marshall) Plan of 1947 had little to do with Bush's 2002 Millennium Challenge Account (which was to increase foreign aid to promote good government, health and educa-

tion, and economic freedom in the poorest countries by $5 billion annually by 2006, a group manifestly different in terms of their capacity to democratize from those to be aided in Europe in the 1940s);

—The Washington Consensus (economic privatization, deregulation, and national opening) turned out in practice to betray the spirit of Bretton Woods;

—The integrity of the collective security through NATO of democratic nations was badly threatened by Washington's insistent call on its members to join "out of area"—that is, outside the defense perimeter established during the cold war—in the occupation of Iraq and Afghanistan, as well as by the invitation to the "New Europe" liberated from Soviet communism to break with the "Old Europe," our traditional transatlantic allies;

—The invocation of American exceptionalism moved from a defensive posture with respect to the free world democracies—one that typified both Wilson's League of Nations in 1919 as well as NATO at its creation in 1949—to one that was boldly offensive;

—The Arab Spring of 2011 was not the equivalent of the fall of the Berlin Wall, even if it occurred on President Obama's watch but was initially claimed by the Republican conquerors of Iraq as an offshoot of their bold move in 2002.

As these contrasts indicate, change, not continuity, between the decade of the 1940s and NSS-2002, itself the product of the 1990s, is thus what we need to appreciate.

I do not know exactly how neo-Wilsonian thinking moved to the highest levels of the American government. One place to start is with policies proposed by the Reagan administration and seemingly verified by the collapse of the Soviet empire and the Soviet Union itself between 1989 and 1991. Another focal point can be located during the administration of President George H. W. Bush (1989–1993), within Secretary Dick Cheney's Defense Department with its cadre of neoconservative thinkers, of whom the best known was Paul Wolfowitz, then an undersecretary of defense. Yet a third source lay with intellectuals within the Democratic Party, through the Progressive Policy Institute (PPI), individuals who, despite differences in party labels, were typically on much the same page with respect to foreign policy as the Republican neoconservatives in the Project for a New American Century (PNAC).

Then there is the character of those who were closest to President Bush after the attack of 9/11. For example, the president was exposed on a personal level to the idea that a democratic transition from authoritarianism was an easy transformation to imagine by Natan Sharansky, when in 2002 he met that Israeli politician, a man often described as charismatic. The president subsequently gave a copy of Sharansky's book—published in 2004 and instructively entitled *The Case for Democracy: The Power of Freedom to Overcome Tyranny and Terror*—to high officials in his administration and visitors to his office. As the president remarked, "If you want to understand my political DNA, read this book."[4]

A sample line from the book shows Sharansky's adhesion to democratic transition theory. As we might expect from the exposition of democratic transition theory analyzed in the preceding chapter, it maintains how simple progressive nation- and state-building could be, without the slightest cultural, social, political, or historical preconditions for democratization being of any importance whatsoever:

> I believe that all people are capable of building a free society. . . . I am convinced that all people desire to be free . . . the free world can transform any society on earth, including those that dominate the current landscape of the Middle East. In doing so, tyranny can become, like slavery, an evil without a future.[5]

However, the dominant influence on President George W. Bush's thinking unquestionably came from his cadre of neoconservative contacts and advisers. Long before the Bush Doctrine, well before 9/11, indeed as early as 1996, neoconservative leaders Robert Kagan and William Kristol had converted the optimism about the ease of a democratic transition away from authoritarian government from its status as a theory to a call for practice. So, in an essay published in *Foreign Affairs* in the summer of 1996 instructively titled "Toward a Neo-Reaganite Foreign Policy," Kagan and Kristol called for "a full-scale ideological confrontation and massive increase in defense spending" in order to engender "an elevated patriotism" capable of "preparing and inspiring the nation to embrace the role of global leadership. . . . The re-moralization of America at home ultimately requires the re-moralization of American foreign policy."

> Because America has the capacity to contain or destroy many of the world's monsters, most of whom can be found without much search-

ing, and because the responsibility for the peace and security of the international order rests so heavily on America's shoulders, a policy of sitting atop a hill and leading by example becomes in practice a policy of cowardice and dishonor.[6]

Before the election of 2000, the same authors made their vision even more dramatically explicit:

[W]hen it comes to dealing with tyrannical regimes, especially those with the power to do us or our allies harm, the United States should not seek coexistence but transformation . . . how utopian is it to imagine a change of regime in a place like Iraq? How utopian is it to work for the fall of the Communist Party oligarchy in China. . . . With democratic change sweeping the world at an unprecedented rate over these past thirty years, is it "realistic" to insist that no future victories can be won?[7]

It should be apparent that the terms of this thinking, articulated before the election victory of George W. Bush in 2000, were preludes to what would be the Bush Doctrine only a bit later in time. Indeed we have none other than the neoconservatives themselves to claim the title. So, in 1995, Robert Kagan and William Kristol (with the support of Rupert Murdoch, Fred Barnes, and John Podhoretz) started the neoconservative flagship publication *The Weekly Standard*. In 1997, Kristol and Kagan founded the Project for a New American Center (PNAC). A year later, the group articulated a framework for what these two men in 1996 had called the "benign hegemony" of a *Pax Americana*, after which most of them came to the support in 2000 of George W. Bush for president.[8]

The stage was now set. Three weeks after the attack of September 11, 2001, *The Weekly Standard* claimed that their supporters were everywhere to be found in the Bush administration. Although some prominent voices articulating the neoconservative view who had been close to these circles for nearly a decade, such as Vice President Dick Cheney, Jeb Bush, Lewis "Scooter" Libby, and Richard Perle, were not mentioned in the piece, despite having signed certain of its declarations, the list presented was nonetheless impressive.

[They] are today a Who's Who of senior ranking officials in this administration. Secretary of Defense Donald Rumsfeld, U.S. Trade Representative Robert Zoellick, Deputy Secretary of State Richard Armitage, Deputy Secretary of Defense Paul Wolfowitz, Undersecretary of State

John Bolton, Undersecretary of State Paula Dobrinsky, Assistant Secretary of Defense Peter Rodman and National Security Council officials Elliott Abrams and Zalmay Khalilzad.[9]

As this list of "who's who" suggests, the link between neoconservatism and the Bush Doctrine could now be proudly affirmed. So the neoconservative proponent of Iraq's invasion Max Boot called the NSS-2002 "a quintessentially neoconservative document." Two days before the invasion of Iraq began, William Kristol declared that "Our policy specified in 1997 is now official. It has become the policy of the U.S. government, . . . History and reality are about to weigh in, and we are inclined simply to let them render their verdicts." For his part, Charles Krauthammer proudly insisted that in effect everyone was now a neoconservative. "The remarkable fact that the Bush Doctrine is, essentially, a synonym for neoconservative foreign policy marks neoconservatism's own transition from a position of dissidence . . . to governance."

> What neoconservatives have long been advocating is now being articulated and practiced at the highest levels of government by a war cabinet composed of individuals . . . [whose] differences have, if anything, narrowed . . . it is the maturation of a governing ideology whose time has come.[10]

Now, as Kristol and Lawrence Kaplan explained, the neoconservatives could applaud the fact the "holiday from history" was over. The invasion of Iraq, they declared in 2003 on the opening page of their book welcoming the attack on Baghdad, "is so clearly about more than Iraq. It is about even more than the future of the Middle East and the war on terror. It is about what sort of role the United States intends to play in the world in the 21st century." The very last lines of their book dramatically convey their intent:

> The mission begins in Baghdad, but it does not end there. . . . America cannot escape its responsibility for maintaining a decent world order. The answer to this challenge is the American idea itself, and behind it the unparalleled military and economic strength of its custodian. Duly armed, the United States can act to secure its safety and to advance the cause of liberty—in Baghdad and beyond.[11]

To be sure, the neoconservatives were not alone in their enthusiasm for NSS-2002, even if they alone claimed its authorship. Consider, for example, the appeal the doctrine could elicit from the senior Yale historian of American foreign policy John Lewis Gaddis, a founder of the well-known Grand Strategy Seminar at that university. Calling NSS-2002 the "grand strategy" that Washington had long needed, Gaddis declared that "the United States must now finish the job that Woodrow Wilson started. The world, quite literally, is to be made safe for democracy, even those parts of it, like the Muslim Middle East, that have so far resisted that tendency . . . [so generating the] frustrations growing out of the absence of representative institutions within their own societies, so that the only outlet for dissent was religious fanaticism. . . . Bush's solution to this complex problem is breathtakingly simple: it is to spread democracy everywhere."

So Gaddis continued confidently:

> We could set in motion a process that could undermine and ultimately remove reactionary regimes elsewhere in the Middle East, thereby eliminating the principal breeding ground for terrorism . . . this was, then, in every sense a *grand* strategy . . . a plan for transforming the entire Muslim Middle East: for bringing it, once and for all, into the modern world. There'd been nothing like this in boldness, sweep, and vision since Americans took it upon themselves, more than half a century ago, to democratize Germany and Japan, thus setting in motion processes that stopped short of only a few places on earth, one of which was the Muslim Middle East.[12]

By undertaking this mission, Gaddis asserted, the United States was expressing once again a spirit supposedly "embedded in our national consciousness . . . that for the United States safety comes from enlarging, rather than from contracting, its sphere of responsibility."

A year later, Gaddis repeated his conviction in terms not of Middle Eastern but of world History (with a capital H): "Democratization has indeed been delayed in the Arab world. . . . To conclude that it can never take hold there, however, is to neglect the direction in which the historical winds have been blowing."[13] "Never," of course, is a long time. But well over a decade after these brave words first appeared in favor of the Bush Doctrine, the scale of destruction has been such that one can doubt whether the end sought might ever justify the means used given the Pandora's Box of "grand tragedy," rather than grand strategy, which the implementation of NSS-2002 so tragically opened.

Many others who were not neoconservatives agreed with Gaddis. Consider the remarks of a noted commentator on the United States in world affairs, Walter Russell Mead, on NSS-2002, which he called "Revival Wilsonianism" and "Wilsonianism on steroids." In an argument without any reference to Wilson's academic thinking or presidential policy, Mead nonetheless found that "the general tendency of Wilsonian foreign policy . . . is for an active, interventionist United States. A sense of moral duty drives Wilsonians to seek out monsters to destroy."[14] From this, Mead concluded that President George W. Bush's decision to invade Iraq was not simply a "grand strategy" but in fact "a choice that was right and inevitable." He, like Gaddis and Kagan, related Bush's decision to Wilson directly but also back to further antecedents in American history; as such, these three commentators are examples of how apologists for neo-Wilsonianism avoided recognizing the degree to which the strategy elaborated after 9/11 was in fact a new form of Wilsonianism in world affairs, whose roots reached back only to the 1990s.

The list of such opinions could be extended indefinitely, but take, finally, the words of a well-known liberal writer and Canadian politician, Michael Ignatieff. Recognizing that America was creating an empire—"if America takes on Iraq, it takes on the reordering of the whole region"—Ignatieff endorsed Herman Melville's words that Americans "bear the ark of the liberties of the world." "Just remember how much America itself needed the assistance of France to free itself of the British. . . . Who else is available to sponsor liberty in the Middle East but America? . . . Multilateral solutions to the world's problems are all very well, but they have no teeth unless America bares its fangs."[15]

George W. Bush and the Bush Doctrine

Whatever reservations about the exultant mood of his influential neoconservative supporters and others President Bush may have had, he most certainly never expressed them. To the contrary, his confidence in invading the Middle East under the flag of democratic transformation was unwavering.

As the president phrased it at a gathering at the American Enterprise Institute, a headquarters for neoconservative thinkers, on February 26, 2003, scarcely two weeks before the invasion of Iraq:

There was a time when many said that the cultures of Japan and Germany were incapable of sustaining democratic values. Well, they were wrong. Some say the same of Iraq today. They are mistaken. The nation of Iraq—with its proud heritage, abundant resources and skilled and educated people—is fully capable of moving toward democracy and living in freedom . . . there are hopeful signs for freedom in the Middle East . . . from Morocco to Bahrain and beyond, nations are taking genuine steps toward political reform. A new regime in Iraq would serve as a dramatic and inspiring example of freedom for other nations in the region.[16]

Some nine months later, when an enormous amount of information had accumulated as to the problems encountered by the American invasion of Iraq, Bush's attitude, if anything, sounded sunnier still. Speaking to the National Endowment for Democracy on November 6, 2003, the president evoked President Reagan's legacy beginning more than two decades earlier, then offered the observation that while there were only some forty democracies around the world in the early 1970s, thirty years later there were perhaps 120, "and I can assure you more are on the way. Ronald Reagan would be pleased, and he would not be surprised." Speaking of his "forward strategy of freedom in the Middle East," Bush continued, in the spirit of Reagan's self-assurance, in phrases that deserve close attention:

We have witnessed, in a little over a generation, the swiftest advance of freedom in the 2,500 year story of democracy. . . . It is no accident that the rise of so many democracies took place in a time when the world's most influential nation was itself a democracy. . . .

Because we and our allies were steadfast, Germany and Japan are democratic nations that no longer threaten the world. A global nuclear standoff with the Soviet Union ended peacefully—as did the Soviet Union . . . And now we must apply that lesson in our own time. We've reached another great turning point—and the resolve we show will shape the next stage of the world democratic movement. . . .

Are the peoples of the Middle East somehow beyond the reach of liberty? . . . I for one do not believe it. I believe every person has the ability and the right to be free. . . . Many Middle Eastern governments now understand that military dictatorship and theocratic rule are a straight, smooth highway to nowhere. . . . These vital principles are being applied in the nations of Afghanistan and Iraq. With the steady leadership of President Karzai, the people of Afghanistan are building a modern and peaceful government . . . a free and stable democracy.

In Iraq, the Coalition Provisional Authority and the Iraqi Governing

Council are also working together to build a democracy. . . . Iraqi democracy will succeed—and that success will send forth the news, from Damascus to Teheran—that freedom can be the future of every nation. The establishment of a free Iraq at the heart of the Middle East will be a watershed event in the global democratic revolution.

In his Second Inaugural Address of January 20, 2005, President Bush put his conviction in its most oft-cited fashion:

We are led by events and common sense to one conclusion: The survival of liberty in our land increasingly depends on the success of liberty in other lands. The best hope for peace in our world is the expansion of freedom in all the world . . . So it is the policy of the United States to seek and support the growth of democratic movements and institutions in every nation and culture, with the ultimate goal of ending tyranny in our world.

Three years after the invasion of Iraq, on March 16, 2006, in an update of the Bush Doctrine in that year's National Security Strategy, the president reasserted his mission:

It is the policy of the United States to seek and support democratic movements and institutions in every nation and culture, with the ultimate goal of ending tyranny in our world. In the world today, the fundamental character of regimes matters as much as the distribution of power among them. The goal of our statecraft is to help create a world of democratic, well-governed states that can meet the needs of their citizens and conduct themselves responsibly in the international system. This is the best way to provide enduring security for the American people.

In the course of his presidency, Bush stayed consistently on message. Thus, he invoked repeatedly what had become two mantras of his neo-Wilsonian conviction: that democracy had "a universal appeal" and that "our vital interests and our values are one." The former obviously derived directly from democratic transition theory; the latter from democratic peace theory. Together, and in combination with the invocation of American "exceptionalism," they constituted his commitment to the doctrine of "just war" that we have seen as the third underlying concept of neo-Wilsonianism, the responsibility to protect. That the end result was to be peace was seemingly to make legitimate the liberal international credentials of the Bush administration's war-fighting agenda.

To conclude this amazing genealogy of ideas, we must emphasize that the intellectual gamesmanship practiced here was of a very high order. An assemblage of scholars, newsmakers, and policy-makers had camouflaged change as continuity in American practice, war as peace, a bid for world supremacy as a continuation of American exceptionalism exercised for the common good— all legitimized under a novel juridical doctrine that overthrew the Westphalian definition of sovereignty in terms that allowed democracies to invade authoritarian countries at will in the name of a new "just war" doctrine.

In the annals of American foreign policy there had never been anything even remotely like NSS-2002, its façade of Wilsonianism covering a far more aggressive imperialist claim for American exceptionalism than Woodrow Wilson had ever espoused, which in due course threatened to destroy altogether the credentials of good stewardship for world affairs that American liberal internationalism had enjoyed from the 1940s through the 1980s.

As neo-Wilsonian theory was to the Bush Doctrine, so this doctrine was to political action. One month after NSS-2002 appeared, in early October 2002, the Iraq Resolution (or the Iraq War Resolution, formally entitled the Authorization for Use of Military Force against Iraq Resolution) passed Congress with strong majorities in both chambers. The House of Representatives voted in favor 297–113 (with 96 percent of Republicans and 39 percent of Democrats approving it), while the Senate endorsed the Resolution by a vote of 77–23 (98 percent of Republicans and 58 percent of Democrats voting in favor).

Neo-Wilsonianism, born in theory during the 1990s, entered into practice five months after this historic vote, with the invasion of Iraq, code-named Operation Iraqi Freedom and starting with an attack of "shock and awe" that began on March 20, 2003.

THE OBAMA PRESIDENCY

The extent to which the Obama presidency followed in the traces of the Bush Doctrine is self-evident through at least the first administration, 2009–2013. Whatever the efforts of some to discern an "Obama Doctrine," the parallels between these two presidencies so far as world politics is concerned greatly outweigh the differences during this period. Allowance nonetheless must be made for changes that set in during Obama's second term in office as he came to recognize the bankruptcy of some measures he had been following in the Muslim world, the most important of which was the belief that somehow America could oversee nation- and state-building there.

The First Obama Administration, 2009–2013

Let us recall the three primary markers: democratic peace theory (DPT), defining the trustworthy partners of the United States (usually phrased as "our closest friends and allies are other democratic peoples"); democratic transition theory (DTT), laying out an American ability to transform other peoples into democracies (habitually put in terms of "the universal appeal of democracy"); and the theory of just war, named the responsibility to protect (R2P), which legitimized military intervention to this end (defended with the observation that "our interests and our values are one" and thus America's "exceptional" calling).

To these three might be added a fourth, which flowed out of the other three: a redefinition of American "exceptionalism." For Wilson, America was exceptional by the fact that it would defensively protect democratic order wherever it existed for the sake of our country's national security and regional, if not world, peace. By contrast, in neo-Wilsonian hands exceptionalism mutated into an offensive doctrine whereby the entire world had to be made liberal for democracy to be safe in America—a mission for the sake of a liberal hegemony that by its very nature was expansionist and hence imperialist. This distinction is basic, for, as we have seen, the redefinition achieved by such neoconservatives as Robert Kagan—for whom virtually no event in the world is without an impact on America's leadership role and hence on the viability of liberalism everywhere—is a telling illustration of the way a subtle remaking of definition implies an enormous change in the American liberal internationalist doctrine prior to the 1990s, from one that is essentially defensive to one that is necessarily offensive and frankly imperialist.[17]

In this grouping of this set of concepts, the only ones that are easily recognizable as traditional Wilsonianism are democratic peace theory and the claim of national "exceptionalism." It is DPT that allows neo-Wilsonianism to be identified as a variant of the liberal internationalist mind-set. So too does the invocation of American exceptionalism—the belief that America sees its self-interest as world peace, so that its policies are at the service of a greater good rather than deriving from a narrow definition of national security, even if the limits of this definition are open to debate. By contrast, simply waving the flag of democracy promotion regardless of the lay of the land, as democratic transition theory does, contradicts the fundamental postulates of traditional Wilsonianism. By the same logic, assertions of the "responsibility to protect" as a justification of imperialism and the redefinition of exceptionalism to be without limit are not Wilsonian but rather neo-Wilsonian.

These neo-Wilsonian refrains of liberalism were evident by the time Obama declared he was running for the presidency early in 2007. Later that year, he published one important article on world politics and gave two notable speeches, one before the Chicago Council on Global Affairs, the other at the Woodrow Wilson Center. The themes were the same, forcefully put. Not for a second did he entertain idea of a "post-American world" or anything that might be seen as "declinist." "The American moment is not over, but it must be seized anew," he proclaimed in one of the several formulas he used to express his convictions. The place it would be renewed, he affirmed with special vigor at the Woodrow Wilson Center, would be by a return to Afghanistan, which by the end of 2009 (and still until his departure from office in 2017) would rightly come to be called "Obama's War."[18]

The prime evidence of Obama's neo-Wilsonianism take on world affairs would come, as we have seen, from his commitment to democratic transition theory—that is, to the idea that democracy was a "universal value" with "universal appeal," that its spread worldwide would serve not simply American national security interests but also regional (or global) peace, and that as "our interests and values are one," then the essential framework for American foreign policy would be to promote democracy abroad, along with its associated liberal aspects of economic openness and participation in multilateral agencies, where American leadership would prove indispensable. If in his first term as president Obama made these assertions fewer times than his Republican predecessor in office had done, I would be surprised.

A leading characteristic of democratic transition theory was its confidence that under American auspices, liberal constitutional nation- and state-building could be fostered for the sake of peace virtually everywhere. So in Chicago in April 2007, in considering the task of "renewing American leadership," Obama found that Washington's task would be "to lead the world in battling the immediate evils and promoting the ultimate good. . . . America's larger purpose in the world is to promote the spread of freedom—that is the yearning of all who live in the shadow of tyranny and despair." To achieve this end, he proposed increasing nation-building aid by $50 billion *annually* so as to promote "accountable institutions," funds that would be an investment "in our common humanity," for they would permit the creation of the pillars of sustainable democracy—a strong legislature, an independent judiciary, the rule of law, a vibrant civil society, a free press, and an honest police force. It requires building the capacity of the world's weakest states and providing them what they need to reduce poverty, build healthy and educated communities, develop markets, and generate wealth.

As we would know from the democratic transition literature of the times reviewed in the preceding chapter, funds for nation- and state-building would alone be far from enough to achieve the desired objective. Accordingly, Obama would expand the Army and Marine Corps by 92,000 in order to have "a 21st century military to stay on the offense from Djibouti to Kandahar. . . . Now it's our moment to lead—our generation's time to tell another great American story."[19] Obama's confidence that these blueprints would work stood as representative of the influence of neoliberals on the young and inexperienced president's thinking.

However, in due course, an important and unique variation appeared in President Obama's conviction that democracy might come in good time to peoples without it. What made his perspective singular was that he recognized that deep ethnic, racial, and religious divides might impede a nation's democratization. That is, the transition from authoritarian rule required much more than cutting off the head of the snake, as had seemed to be all that was called for in the years of the Bush presidency from 2001 to 2009. Instead, it meant healing the deep and multiple divisions that foreign peoples might confront internally, something presumably far more difficult to handle than simply removing a tyrant from the throne.

Given the enormity of the challenges, one might well conclude that Obama's insights as to their magnitude might have turned him away from an optimistic belief in a democratic transition from authoritarianism. Indeed, as we shall see in the next section, it was exactly this conviction that became apparent as he contemplated the series of setbacks his policies had encountered from Afghanistan to the Arab Spring. Yet at an earlier point, he instead restated for world affairs the spirit of "the politics of hope," which had been one of his leading slogans in his election to the presidency in 2008. The mood of this spirit is evident in all of his addresses to the United Nations General Assembly (delivered annually, in September), where he delivered without fail the balm for all problems, a magic wand to fix whatever our troubles might be: democracy.[20]

In this vein, in the broadly covered address to university students in Cairo that the new head of state gave on June 4, 2009, President Obama's refrain had to do with the elevated moral values of the democratic world, the solutions they promised to those in need of solving problems of civil disorder and political oppression, and the fraternity that existed between the United States and its closest allies, the other democratic peoples. Although Obama was to repeat this theme innumerable times in the years to come, its full and clear exposition in a speech that he expected to have wide circulation marked early on his commitment to a traditional hallmark of Wilsonianism, democratic peace theory, a belief anchored in both domestic and international relations.

The neo-Wilsonian aspects of President Obama's approach to the Muslim world came with an expression of his confidence that there was a "universal appeal" and "universal right" to democracy. So, sounding as if he had cribbed his position from Ronald Reagan at Westminster in June 1982, or from President Bush before the National Endowment for Democracy in November 2003, Obama declared in Cairo:

> I do have an unyielding belief that all people yearn for certain things: the ability to speak your mind and have a say in how you are governed; confidence in the rule of law and the equal administration of justice; government that is transparent and doesn't steal from the people; the freedom to live as you choose. These are not just American ideas; they are human rights. And that is why we will support them everywhere. . . . So no matter where it takes hold, government of the people and by the people sets a single standard for all who hold power.

Yet should the spirit of democracy not prevail of itself, military means might be the necessary solution to finding a way forward. Thus, in his Nobel Peace Prize acceptance address of December 10, 2009, President Obama laid out a concept of "just war" (a term he explicitly endorsed) that had played its part years before in the invasion of Iraq:

> Make no mistake: evil does exist in the world. I believe that force can be justified on humanitarian grounds. . . . Inaction tears at our conscience and can lead to more costly intervention later. That is why all responsible nations must embrace the role that militaries with a clear mandate can play to keep the peace.

This address was also notable because in keeping with the more extreme versions of democratic peace theory, authoritarian states were especially stigmatized as oppressive at home and predatory abroad (unlike democratic states, to be sure). Hence, "only a just peace based upon the inherent rights and dignity of every individual can be truly lasting. . . . If human rights are not protected, peace is a hollow promise." Were this not enough, Obama stressed a major point of democratic transition theory: that democracy is a "universal value" that trumps all others:

> In some countries the failure to uphold human rights is excused by the false suggestion that these are Western principles, foreign to local cultures or stages of a nation's development. . . . I believe that peace is unstable where citizens are denied the right to speak freely or worship as they please, choose their own leaders or assemble without fear. Pent-up grievances fester, and the suppression of tribal and religious identity can lead to violence. . . . Only when Europe became free did it finally find peace. America has never gone to war against a democracy, and our closest friends are governments that protect the rights of their citizens. . . . So even as we respect the unique culture and traditions of different countries, America will always be the voice for those aspirations that are universal.

Such talk was not to end after 2009. Indeed, new shades of rhetoric were added. If we are to believe his words on June 22, 2011, President Obama seemed to have thought that the surge in Afghanistan he had insisted upon in 2009 had succeeded. He forecast that American forces should be withdrawn in increments, the last departing in 2014, with the Afghan army of well over 100,000 soldiers and 30,000 police trained and in place to play their role in a mission "responsibly ended."[21] Strengthened by what he mistakenly assumed were the advances American forces had made, the president could turn with some confidence to playing a democratizing role with the Arab Spring:

> In all that we do, we must remember that what sets America apart is not solely our power—it is the principles upon which our union was founded. We're a nation that brings our enemies to justice while adhering to the rule of law, and respecting the rights of all our citizens. We protect our own freedom and prosperity by extending it to others. We stand not for empire, but for self-determination. That is why we have a stake in the democratic aspirations that are now washing across the Arab world. We will support those revolutions with fidelity to our ide-

als, with the power of our example, and with an unwavering belief that all human beings deserve to live with freedom and dignity.

As Obama had already put it with respect to Egypt on February 11, 2011:

There are very few moments in our lives where we have the privilege to witness history taking place. This is one of those moments. The people of Egypt have spoken, their voices have been heard, and Egypt will never be the same. . . . For Egyptians have made it clear that nothing less than genuine democracy will carry the day. . . . And I know that a democratic Egypt can advance its role of responsible leadership not only in the region but around the world. Egypt has played a pivotal role in human history for over 6,000 years.

But over the last few weeks, the wheel of history turned at a blinding pace as the Egyptian people demanded their universal rights . . . while the sights and sounds that we heard were entirely Egyptian, we can't help but hear the echoes of history—echoes from Germans tearing down a wall, Indonesian students taking to the streets, Gandhi leading his people down the path of justice.

Again, on February 23, 2011, Obama asserted that the United States "strongly supports the universal rights of the Libyan people. That includes the rights of peaceful assembly, free speech, and the ability of the Libyan people to determine their own destiny. These are human rights. They are not negotiable. They must be respected in every country. And they cannot be denied through violence or suppression." Consequently, the United States will "not stop asserting principles that are consistent with our ideals . . . we will reject the notion that these principles are simply Western exports, incompatible with Islam or the Arab World." The president added his full commitment to "effectively support the peaceful transition to democracy in both Tunisia and in Egypt . . . throughout this time of transition, the United States will continue to stand up for freedom, stand up for justice, and stand up for the dignity of all people."

At times, as in his Cairo address of June 2009, President Obama appeared to distance himself from using force to further a democratic transition. Yet, as on March 28, 2011, he explained his decision to join France and Great Britain in launching air and missile strikes on Libya so as to oust strongman Muammar Qaddafi from power in "just war" terms related to the neo-Wilsonian assertion of a responsibility to protect:

[If not for our intervention] the democratic impulses that are dawning across the region would be eclipsed as oppressive leaders concluded that violence is the best strategy to cling to power. . . . So while I will never minimize the costs involved in military action, I am confident that a failure to act in Libya would have carried a far greater price for America. . . .

To brush aside America's responsibility as a leader and—more profoundly—our responsibilities to our fellow human beings under such circumstances would have been a betrayal of who we are. Some nations may be able to turn a blind eye to atrocities in other countries. The United States of America is different.

In accord with these statements, on October 20, 2011, the president announced the death of Muammar Qaddafi, saying, "This is a momentous day in the history of Libya. The dark shadow of tyranny has been lifted . . . the Libyan people now have a great responsibility—to build an inclusive and tolerant and democratic Libya that stands as the ultimate rebuke to Qaddafi's dictatorship. . . . For the region, today's events prove once more that the rule of an iron fist inevitably comes to an end. Across the Arab world, citizens have stood up to claim their rights. Youth are delivering a powerful rebuke to dictatorship. And those leaders who try to deny their human dignity will not succeed." The next day, speaking to CBS News, Secretary of State Hillary Clinton summed up her reaction: "We came, we saw, he died."[22]

The apparent weakness of Qaddafi, under these pressures, raised hopes that Bashar al-Assad might be removed in Syria and democracy take root there. In tandem with the president, Secretary Clinton, on June 19, 2011, insisted that, in the face of "long-denied universal rights," Syria must have "a real transition to democracy and a government that honors [its citizens'] universal rights and aspirations." Foreseeing a "democratic, peaceful, and tolerant Syria," the secretary closed her remarks saying that Syrians "deserve a nation that is unified, democratic, and a force for stability and progress. That would be good for Syria, good for the region, and good for the world."[23] On July 11, 2011, Clinton repeated her conviction that "President Assad is not indispensable, and we have absolutely nothing invested in him remaining in power. Our goal is to see that the will of the Syrian people for a democratic transformation occurs." America would also "help a free Libya emerge from the dictator's shadow"; at the same time, Clinton evoked America's "commitment to support the democratic transitions underway in Egypt and Tunisia" to which Americans had committed themselves and aid in the "hard work of building sustainable democracies rooted in guaranteed human rights, accountable institutions, and the rule of law."

Obama's emotional decision to threaten the Syrian dictator over his use of chemical weapons in a civil conflict illustrates yet again his faithfulness to the neo-Wilsonian pledge to enforce a responsibility to protect. Heinous as Assad's actions against his own people unquestionably were, given the likelihood that in the event of his overthrow at least as many atrocities would be committed by the victors, without any prospect of either the area's democratization or the national security interests of the United States being served, could Obama stay the course? Indeed he could. So the president moved ahead, apparently fully prepared to authorize military strikes, very much in the spirit of R2P, yet apparently completely oblivious to the serious negative consequences that could result for everyone concerned should he put his emotions into practice. As he put it on September 10, 2013, some two and a half years after he had sanctioned intervention in Libya and the disasters this had contributed to had become abundantly clear:

> When dictators commit atrocities, they depend upon the world to look the other way until those horrifying pictures fade from memory. But these things happened. The facts cannot be denied. The question now is what the United States of America, and the international community, is prepared to do about it. Because what happened to those people—to those children—is not only a violation of international law, it's also a danger to our security.
>
> This is not a world we should accept. This is what's at stake. And that is why, after careful deliberation, I determined that it is in the national security interests of the United States to respond to the Assad regime's use of chemical weapons through a targeted military strike. The purpose of this strike would be to deter Assad from using chemical weapons, to degrade his regime's ability to use them, and to make clear to the world that we will not tolerate their use.[24]

In all the instances concerning the Arab Spring, the Obama administration's position corresponded to its allegiance to just war doctrine as formulated by the terms of the responsibility to protect. But did the president understand just how obligated a country was that intervened in the name of R2P? As defined by the International Commission of Intervention and State Sovereignty of 2001 (sponsored by the United Nations and the Canadian government), in all cases of military intervention the invading powers were required to leave behind a duly constructed democratic state—not leaving it to the liberated peoples alone to create such a government. Obviously, then, R2P could not be justified unless democratic transition theory were correct practically. Logically, therefore, if DTT were a mistaken conceptualization of a country's ability to make the transition from authoritarianism to democracy, then the arguments behind R2P evaporated completely and instantly.[25] Here, then, lay Obama's problem. The United States intervened in Libya in 2011, and threatened to do so as well in Syria in 2013, but without any apparent idea as to how the use of military force there would lead to a democratic to-morrow, so compounding the confusions that surrounded the Iraq invasion of 2003 and the decision for a surge in Afghanistan in 2009.

Rather than facing head-on the dilemma of democratic nation- and state-building in societies without the slightest preconditions for such a development, Obama maintained his insistence that this would come to pass seemingly on its own. So, on May 19, 2011, he could insist, speaking of the Arab Spring, "The status quo is not sustainable. Societies held together by fear and repression may offer the illusion of stability for a time, but they are built upon fault lines that will eventually tear asunder."

> The United States supports a set of universal rights. And these rights include free speech, the freedom of peaceful assembly, the freedom of religion, equality for men and women under the rule of law, and the right to choose your own leaders—whether you live in Baghdad or Damascus, Sanaa, or Tehran. Our support must also extend to nations [including Tunisia and Egypt] where transitions have yet to take place.

Evoking respect for human rights and individual freedom as "the beacon that guided us through our fight against fascism and our twilight struggle against communism," the president put all three of the neo-Wilson arguments into a single speech when addressing the British Parliament on May 25, 2011:

> And today, that idea is being put to the test in the Middle East and North Africa. In country after country, people are mobilizing to free themselves from the grip of an iron fist. And while these movements for change are just six months old, we have seen them play out before—from Eastern Europe to the Americas, from South Africa to Southeast Asia. . . .

We must show that we will back up these words with deeds. But we must also insist that we reject as false the choice between our interest and our ideals; between stability and democracy. For our idealism is rooted in the realities of history—that repression offers only the false promise of stability, that societies are more successful when their citizens are free, and that democracies are the closest allies we have . . . the longing for freedom and human dignity is not English or American or Western—it is universal, and it beats in every heart.

Disillusioned by Iraq (a "dumb and rash war," as he had called it in 2002 and again in 2007), Obama had returned in 2009 to Afghanistan. Mistakenly believing success was around the corner in Afghanistan by June 2011, he moved on to the Arab Spring, playing a decisive role in removing Muammar Qaddafi from power, which in turn generated an anarchy without precedent in North Africa and beyond to Syria, where many of the recruits to the Islamic State that materialized in the spring of 2014 had come from Libya. Next on his agenda was Syria, where he expressed his confidence that "moderate" and "free" Syrians would rid the country of Assad, only to admit by the fall of 2015 that no such force could conceivably be assembled.[26]

In a seemingly endless series of talks, then, the president sounded the familiar refrain. But it gained special prominence in certain addresses intended for wide circulation. Thus, in his Commencement Address at West Point on May 28, 2014, Obama cited Somalia, Yemen, and Libya as places the American military might have to be deployed, and Jordan, Lebanon, and Iraq as needing additional assistance. And he noted that "the upheaval of the Arab world reflects the rejection of an authoritarian order that was anything but stable, and now offers the long-term prospect of more responsive and effective governance." The all-too-overused tropes of neo-Wilsonian had not in the least faded: "I believe that a world of greater freedom and tolerance is not only a moral imperative; it also helps keep us safe." "I believe in American exceptionalism with every fiber of my being." "Here's my bottom line: America must always lead on the world stage."[27] The ultimate goal?

America's support for democracy and human rights goes beyond idealism; it is a matter of national security. Democracies are our closest friends and are far less likely to go to war. Economies based on free and open markets perform better and become markets for our goods. Respect for human rights is an antidote to instability and the grievances that fuel violence and terror.

What must be underscored here is that Obama was speaking not in the limited, largely defensive meaning of Woodrow Wilson, which made the United States the defender of the democratic and democratizing world alone. Instead, we find him using the nation's exceptionalism in the broader sense, as the promotion of liberal constitutionalism around the globe—the "world order" sense of America's mission, one far wider than Wilson had imagined, but much more as the neoconservative leader Robert Kagan did an effective job of redefining it.

In 2012, Kagan published *The World America Made*, intending it to be material for the Republican Party in that year's presidential election.[28] He was a leading figure on Mitt Romney's team of foreign policy advisers. In this book, Kagan warned against "premature superpower suicide" should the United States not understand that a liberal order needed military force to prevent power vacuums from arising into which enemies of America would quickly move, in the process provoking a collapse of the world liberal order. Decline was thus a matter of "choice," not of "necessity."

President Obama publicly declared his appreciation of Kagan's book, saying he had found it useful for his own thinking on world affairs.[29] Two years later, Kagan restated his argument:

> What gives the United States the right to act on behalf of a liberal world order? In truth, nothing does; nothing beyond the conviction that the liberal world order is the most just. . . . A liberal world order, like any world order, is something that is imposed, and as much we in the West might wish it to be imposed by superior virtue, it is generally imposed by superior power.[30]

Here lie the ideological underpinnings of President Obama's repeated liberal mantras—as, for example, that which came as he ended a trip to Beijing. On November 12, 2014, in what many observers took as a gratuitous slap at Chinese President Xi Jinping at a joint press conference, the president concluded his remarks:

> I reiterated to President Xi, as I have before, that America's unwavering support for fundamental human rights of all people will continue to be an important element of our relationship with China, just as it is with all the countries that we interact with around the world. And we had a very healthy exchange around these issues. President Xi gave me his sense of how China is moving forward. I described to him why it is so

important for us to speak out for the freedoms that we believe are universal, rights that we believe are the birthright of all men and women, wherever they live, whether it is in New York or Paris or Hong Kong.

We think history shows that nations that uphold these rights—including for ethnic and religious minorities—are ultimately more prosperous, more successful, and more able to achieve the dreams of their people. In that context, I did note that we recognize Tibet as part of the People's Republic of China. We are not in favor of independence. But we did encourage Chinese authorities to take steps to preserve the unique cultural, religious and linguistic identity of the Tibetan people.

Despite the obvious disasters that by 2014 were evident in good part thanks to American policies in Iraq, Syria, and Libya, President Obama was unable to do anything more than pronounce what to many in other countries were now increasingly recognized to be the platitudes of neo-Wilsonianism. So in his speech to the United Nations General Assembly on September 28, 2015, the president evoked problems confronting the world community by Russian actions in Ukraine, China's expansion into the South China Sea, the question of nuclear weapons for Iran, and, most pressing, the ongoing war in Syria. Yet he had recourse to no proposition for action other than to blame it all on the "erosion of the democratic principles and human rights that are fundamental" to the United Nations, to insist that "I believe in my core that repression cannot forge the social cohesion for nations to succeed," and to say yet again that "internal repression and foreign aggression are both symptoms of the failure to provide this foundation." In the matter at the forefront of the General Assembly's deliberations, he could do no better than to affirm that "Lasting stability can only take hold when the people of Syria forge an agreement to live together peacefully."

Explaining Barack Obama's Dedication to Neo-Wilsonian Thinking

Many more examples of President Obama's neo-Wilsonian convictions could be cited, but the more interesting question at this point concerns how it came to be that he echoed so many of the major themes of the Bush presidency. Two sources are evident: the one his experience before coming to Washington, the other his contacts as he arrived there in January 2005.

The experiential basis of President Obama's commitment to liberal internationalism came to him, we may presume, as a community organizer and defender of civil rights at home, through his training in systematic reasoning as a law professor trained at Harvard, then by his teaching constitutional law over twelve years at the University of Chicago. There were also his spiritual mentors, particularly Martin Luther King Jr., Mahatma Gandhi, and Nelson Mandela. Most importantly of all, perhaps—as he frequently pointed out— Barack Obama would not have become the forty-fourth president of the United States without this country being a constitutional democracy whose progress on race relations, the most salient internal divide in our history, having in important measure been bridged.

Accordingly, when he spoke of democracy as a way of bringing together other peoples in faraway ethnically, racially, and especially religiously divided lands, Obama sometimes sounded almost as if he believed he could be a Martin Luther King Jr. to the world. Whether it was with respect to the Arab Spring in general beginning in 2011 or to specific countries such as Libya and Syria, he repeatedly appealed to what he had called at the Democratic National Convention in 2004 "the politics of hope" in a way that summoned up to those familiar with the spirit of an earlier times the aspirations of "I Have a Dream," the magnificent address given by King before the Lincoln Memorial in August 1963. In Obama's words:

> There's not a liberal America and a conservative America—there's the United States of America. There's not a black America and white America and Latino America and Asian America; there's the United States of America. The pundits like to slice-and-dice our country into Red States and Blue States; Red States for Republicans, Blue States for Democrats. But I've got news for them, too. We worship an awesome God in the Blue States, and we don't like federal agents poking around our libraries in the Red States. We coach Little League in the Blue States and have gay friends in the Red States. There are patriots who opposed the war in Iraq and patriots who supported it. We are one people, all of us pledging allegiance to the stars and stripes, all of us defending the United States of America.[31]

Yet even if it were true that Obama was a Wilsonian in world affairs, indeed a neo-Wilsonian, without quite knowing it, how did it come to be that his phrasing was so exact, his terminology so consistent, the meaning given to his phrases so familiar? The answer I propose is that we go back to his arrival in Washington in early 2005. At this point, Barack Obama was only forty-three years old. As a terrifically ambitious young man with no experience in foreign affairs (his references to time he had spent in Kenya and Indonesia in his youth impressed few), and with a need to gain allies for what within but two short years would be his announcement of his candidacy for president of the United States, Obama presumably looked for ideas and for support.

We can only speculate as to the gauntlet of advice-givers he encountered. Since the 1990s the Democratic liberal internationalist establishment, to which Obama would naturally have gravitated given his ambitions and lack of background, was every bit as much a center of neo-Wilsonian thinking as the Republicans enjoyed with the neoconservatives. There were differences, of course, which centered in the Democrats insisting on multilateral support for Washington's policies and expressing a new confidence in nation- and state-building strategies.

But in fact it was the neoliberals, more than the neoconservatives, who had formulated the terms of neo-Wilsonianism. As noted earlier, the neoconservative contribution was to militarize and to popularize them, but not to have been original in their formulation. That was largely the work of those who identified themselves as Democrats. In short, after his arrival in the nation's capital, the combination of then-Senator Obama's inexperience and need for allies to advance his ambitious personal goals would have naturally led him into neoliberal circles.[32]

Thus, whether from direct contact, or from some kind of osmotic process, the ideas from a group like the Progressive Policy Institute (PPI) must quickly have reached Senator Obama in 2005. The PPI was believed to be the most important single voice within the Democratic Party by 2005, having been founded by Bill Clinton and Al Gore in 1989, and often being thought of as the think tank of the Democratic Leadership Council. There was one critical difference between Obama and the PPI: they favored the war in Iraq—criticizing the Bush administration for how poorly it was run, but not that it had been begun in the first place. Yet here were the ideas that Iraq could have been won had there been multilateral support for the American invasion combined with a strategy of nation- and state-building in that country after its conquest. Obama might well have repudiated the invasion of Iraq but nonetheless appropriated these ideas for use in another setting: Afghanistan.

The various statements issued by the PPI during these years were efforts at one-upmanship with respect to the Bush Doctrine. To cite but one of their many efforts, consider the volume PPI's president Will Marshall edited in 2006 called *With All Our Might: A Progressive Strategy for Defeating Ji-*

hadism and Defending Liberty. A cavalcade of neoliberal intellectuals contributed in terms such as Marshall and his associate Jeremy Rosner put it in their introduction to the volume: "Progressives and Democrats must not give up the promotion of democracy and human rights abroad just because President Bush has paid it lip service. Advancing democracy—in practice, not just in rhetoric—is fundamentally the Democrats' legacy, the Democrats' cause, and the Democrats' responsibility." Supporting comments were penned by Kenneth Pollack, Anne-Marie Slaughter, Larry Diamond, and Michael McFaul.[33]

An indication that Obama was close to this group comes from the number of liberal hawks who became public signatories of PPI position papers on world affairs and whom Obama invited to join his administration or whom he worked with later. Other circles of neo-Wilsonian Democrats existed as well, and it was likely there that Senator Obama met the likes of Susan Rice, Samantha Power, and Peter Beinart or their associates—from whom he could easily have picked up the basic concepts of the new liberal internationalist vernacular. Later, some of them went on to become part of his White House team.

A partial list of neoliberal Democrats who surely met Obama in these circles shows the new president's contacts. These included his chief of staff, Rahm Emmanuel; his secretary of state, Hillary Clinton (and in his second administration, John Kerry); Anne-Marie Slaughter as head of policy planning at the State Department; Michael McFaul (author of *Advancing Democracy Abroad: Why We Should, How We Can*), first in the National Security Council (NSC), then as ambassador to Russia; Susan Rice, ambassador to the United Nations, then national security adviser; Ivo Daalder, ambassador to NATO; Ronald Asmus, assistant secretary of state for European affairs; Samantha Power, special assistant to the president and at the NSC working on human rights before becoming ambassador to the United Nations.

Obama well may have met with articulate neoconservative Republicans as well. The PPI was in close contact with the Project for a New American Center (PNAC), as reflected in the favorable review the editor of the neoconservative paper *The Weekly Standard* gave to the PPI volume edited by its president Will Marshall, president of this organization since 1989.[34]

Important as the PPI presumably was to Obama's thinking after his arrival in Washington, a far more unified and ambitious agenda-setting effort taken by liberal internationalists with regard to the way American leadership should be expressed prior to Obama winning the presidency came late in 2006 with the publication of the "Princeton Project on National Security." Codirected by professors G. John Ikenberry and Anne-Marie Slaughter (both of whom were declared Wilsonians and Democrats), the report, three years in the making and described as a "bipartisan initiative . . . to write a collective 'X' article," had as honorary cochairs former Democratic National Security Adviser Anthony Lake and former Republican Secretary of State George Shultz. In its formulation, the project convened and published the findings of seven working groups, held nine conferences in the United States and abroad, commissioned seventeen working papers, and consulted some 400 "leading thinkers on national security from government, academe, business, and the non-profit sector to analyze key issues and develop innovative responses to a range of national security threats."[35]

What was striking about the report was not that it repudiated the Bush Doctrine—although it implicitly criticized the conduct of the Iraq War for its unilateralism and its failure to consider strategies of nation- and state-building—but that it looked to keep American hegemony intact by multilateralizing a grand strategy whose terms were remarkably similar to those heard in the nation's capital since 2002. Here, all the recurrent neo-Wilsonian tropes were to be found—democratic peace theory, democratic transition theory, and just war arguments.

Sections of the project thus included "A Revived NATO," "A New United Nations" (which would require "U.S. leadership and determination"), and as an "alternative body" to the UN, "a global Concert of Democracies [to] institutionalize and ratify the 'democratic peace.' If the United Nations cannot be reformed, the concert would provide an alternative forum for liberal democracies to authorize collection action."

Washington's leadership was obviously critical for such a concert to be effective: "The United States should work to sustain the military predominance of liberal democracies and encourage the development of military capacities by like-minded democracies in a way that is consistent with their security interests." World peace itself hung in the balance: "The predominance of liberal democracies is necessary to prevent a return to great power security competition between the United States and our allies, on one side, and an autocracy or combination of autocracies on the other—the sort of competition that led to two World Wars and one Cold War." Here was the updating of democratic peace theory asserting both the natural compatibility of the interests and abilities of the democracies as contrasted with an inherent opposition to autocracy.

In such a perspective, the report endorsed "the preventive use of force" since "some states simply cannot be trusted with nuclear or biological weapons capable of creating mass destruction." Democratic transition theory combined with just war theory now came into play, for the Concert of Democracies could exercise "the preventive use of force" to restructure rogue autocratic states by "Bringing Governments Up to PAR," which the authors defined as "Popular, Accountable, and Rights-Regarding." Although the project downplayed the fostering of "democracy" in favor of taking measures to consolidate a government that was "liberal" (one based on a system of legal rights that constrain the state subject to intervention), such an undertaking obviously meant that nation- and state-building should be an integral part of an agenda that in the American tradition can only be called neo-Wilsonian.

The intellectual result was dramatic. A single clearer and more forceful statement of neo-Wilsonianism than the Princeton Report has not yet appeared, nor should one be thought likely given its exhaustive coverage of such a framework for American foreign policy. In the sharpness of its concepts for multilateralism and nation- and state-building, the report far surpassed the Bush Doctrine in the clarity of its blueprint for action. That the report was drawn up at Woodrow Wilson's home institution, Princeton University, and should be understood as reflecting his spirit, is underscored by its subtitle, which was perhaps meant as an indirect homage to him, for it well expressed his wishes for the League of Nations: "Forging a World of Liberty under Law."

At the same time that the bipartisan Princeton Report was being drawn up and circulated, the work on nation- and state-building (discussed in the preceding chapter) that flooded official Washington was available for then-senator Obama's consultation. We can surmise from the talk he gave in August 2007 at the Woodrow Wilson Center that Obama was directly borrowing ideas on the subject from General Petraeus's *Counterinsurgency Field Manual*, and presumably from the team under James Dobbins (who had strong bipartisan credentials at a high level in Washington) at RAND as well.

The leitmotif of these studies was that for outsiders to accomplish their goals of nation- and state-building, a good amount of resources, time, and, above all, Washington's determination were indispensable. These studies did not say, but left it understood, that here was the kind of careful planning that the Bush White House, with Donald Rumsfeld at the Pentagon, had spurned. But success could yet be achieved. Indeed success was imperative. What the

Bush administration (by implication) had failed to address with any serious-ness after 2001 were the terms of this complicated issue, with the result that although there had been a quick military victory over Saddam Hussein in 2003, America had failed to win such peace as followed. Thanks to the kind of analysis that General David Petraeus especially had later provided, the "surge" of 2007 had (allegedly) saved the day. Required reading was there-fore Petraeus's manual *Counterinsurgency*, published in 2006 before it ap-peared for distribution in a more convenient form, with a somewhat differ-ent title, by the University of Chicago Press in 2007. By 2007, the manual had been downloaded without payment (as intended) by some 2 million readers.[36]

All these forces taken together suggest that Obama found himself in Wash-ington in 2005 with little experience in foreign affairs and with goals that made conforming to this consensus mandatory to his acceptance in its ranks. As someone who always called for bipartisan agreement on matters of na-tional significance, Obama found it on every side with respect to the impor-tance and possibility of democracy promotion in lands where it was virtually completely unknown before he declared his bid for the presidency. The neo-liberal PPI Democrats and the neoconservative PNAC Republicans were es-sentially on the same page in endorsing the neo-Wilsonian agenda. At the same time, bipartisan voices such as those in the Princeton Report, or non-partisan studies issued by RAND or the American military, saw the invasions of Iraq and Afghanistan as winnable, *and this in liberal terms*. The point is only underscored by Obama's glowing references during the 2012 presiden-tial campaign to the writings of Robert Kagan, the leading theoretician of the neoconservative movement since the mid-1990s.

That Barack Obama would be a liberal internationalist in the Wilsonian tradition was surely preordained by his personality and the circumstances of his life until his arrival in Washington early in 2005. That he would become a neo-Wilsonian is surely better explained by the contacts he made when he arrived in the nation's capital—liberal internationalist themselves, who de-spite the setbacks in Iraq visible within months after the invasion nonetheless stayed hepped up on the toxic cocktail of democratic peace theory (the prom-ise of a golden age), democratic transition theory (the passageway to such an age), and R2P (which had enormous emotional appeal). That the normaliza-tion of American relations with Cuban and the Iran nuclear accord that were concluded in the summer of 2015 marked a break with this neo-Wilsonian predisposition on Obama's part (for he was negotiating with authoritarian

governments without demanding the regime change that the Bush administration had always called for) is to be saluted. That it took years in office for
him to come to this recognition is nonetheless to be noted, for the legacy of
his policies toward Afghanistan in 2009 and Libya in 2011 should not for a
moment be overlooked.

The Second Term: Does Obama Begin to Chart a New Course?

If, in many respects, Barack Obama's first term in office was strikingly neo-
Wilsonianism in thought and deed as it confronted world affairs, the argument can be taken too far. For instance, President George W. Bush had identified an "axis of evil" in his State of the Union Address of January 29, 2002,
including Iraq, Iran, and North Korea. Such states were said to be helping
terrorism or amassing weapons of mass destruction, a list to which Undersecretary of State (later ambassador to the United Nations) John Bolton added
Syria, Cuba, and Libya on May 6, 2002. Washington would not deal with
such governments until regime change had been initiated. By contrast, in his
Inaugural Address of January 20, 2009, President Obama did not ask for
regime change in Iran before there could be a working out of differences,
instead, addressing the leadership in Tehran, offering "to extend a hand, if
you are willing to unclench your fist." Six months later, although he was not
"silent" after the Iranian government repressed the Green Movement in June
2009 following disputed elections there (twice that month the United States
registered protests), his reaction was much more measured than his Republican critics would have preferred.

Moreover, before arriving in Washington, Obama had won plaudits for his
realistic sense of the threat Saddam Hussein represented. In the views that
had first made Obama nationally well known on October 2, 2002, speaking
to an anti-war rally in Chicago, he put forward a far less aggressive stance
toward the world's dictators than the Bush Doctrine heralded.

> Now let me be clear. I suffer no illusions about Saddam Hussein. He is
> a brutal man. A ruthless man. A man who butchers his own people to
> secure his own power. . . . The world and the Iraqi people would be
> better off without him. But I also know that Saddam poses no immi-
> nent and direct threat to the United States or to his neighbors . . . and
> that in concert with the international community he can be contained
> until, in the way of all petty dictators, he falls away into the dustbin of
> history. I know that even a successful war against Iraq will require a

U.S. occupation of undetermined length, at undetermined cost, with undetermined consequences. I know that an invasion of Iraq without a clear rationale and without strong international support will only fan the flames of the Middle East and encourage the worst, rather than best, impulses of the Arab world, and strengthen the recruitment arm of al-Qaeda. I am not opposed to all wars. I'm opposed to dumb wars.[37]

Nevertheless, President Obama's subsequent policies with respect to Afghanistan and the Arab Spring had been confident with respect to America's ability to bring about nation- and state-building of a democratic sort in parts of the world where this form of government had never existed. Could it be that his exposure to neo-Wilsonian thinking during his stay in Washington since January 2005 had amounted to brainwashing? As we have seen, the evidence suggests that Obama had effectively signed on to the Bush Doctrine when he announced his decision to return in force to Afghanistan late in December 2009. The same month, he justified this commitment in his Nobel Peace Prize acceptance speech by laying out a support for "just wars" in the name of what could be understood as "the responsibility to protect." Again, nearly two years later, the president expressed neo-Wilsonian convictions in his support for the Arab Spring in 2011, including his decision to abandon Hosni Mubarak in Egypt, as well as to intervene in Libya to depose Muammar Qaddafi—both in the name of promoting democratic governments in these lands. Indeed, well into 2013, the president appeared to back the use of military force to bring to power in Damascus "the moderate Syrians"—a largely fictitious group if one discounts the Kurdish opposition, as Obama himself eventually recognized—once again affirming a neo-Wilsonian regime-change policy.

Only at long last, at the end of August 2013, did President Obama arrive at the point of discarding core aspects of the neo-Wilsonian agenda on the American role in bringing democracy—or even stable government—to the Middle East. Here the moment came with his unexpected decision not to attack the chemical weapons holdings of the Syrian government of Bashar al-Assad despite having staked his credibility to a red line drawn against the use of these materials.

As journalist Jeffrey Goldberg has documented, Obama's change of heart was a surprise, opposed by virtually his entire top advisory staff as well as by a wide range of America's allied leaders.[38] The president may have been aided in his decision by a recent vote in the British Parliament not to back an

American attack, as well as by a report from the CIA that there was reason to doubt that all Syrian weapons could be destroyed, and that the attacks would not threaten civilian lives. It certainly helped to alter his thinking, when he decided to go to the Congress for authorization for a strike, that he was warned he was quite likely to be denied. He later worked out with Russian President Vladimir Putin an arrangement whereby Syrian chemicals would be removed by the Russians. Nevertheless, as the president reflected in extended interviews with Goldberg early in 2016 on his decision not to launch an attack, he saw the position he had taken as a watershed event. Whatever trepidations he may have had at the moment, the events that had followed had confirmed his belief that this difficult decision had been correct.

In deciding not to attack the Assad government with American air or ground forces, Obama was rejecting what Goldberg reports he called "the Washington playbook." Goldberg interpreted the comment to mean that the president was resisting pressure to think of the power of the American armed forces as the best solution to any problem that presented itself, a policy that had been pushed on him first by General Stanley McChrystal and his neoconservative advisers in August 2009 as the president concluded his deliberations on whether to increase American troop strength in Afghanistan.

But as we have seen, the "playbook" had far more chapters in it for policy than military action alone. It contained as well scenarios of nation- and state-building that could move with progressive intent from creating a stable, pro-American regime in a foreign capital to one that had the trappings of constitutional democracy. Winning the peace might be more difficult than winning the war, the playbook recognized, but that did not mean that victory was unattainable. Was Obama consciously jettisoning these designs as well?

Perhaps the most extravagant claim of the playbook lay in its justification for the supposedly necessary global reach of American "exceptionalism." By this account, not simply was the United States the "indispensable nation" (that is, one that would be involved in all the world's major undertakings), but more grandly, it was a country endowed with the responsibility to create an overarching world order based on liberal hegemony centered in Washington but stretching along the "northeast corridor" and so also containing Boston and New York. Would these ideas now be reformulated more modestly but so as to avoid making the Democrats appear to be "declinists"?

To throw overboard the "Washington playbook" was implicitly to rein in a series of key elements of the neo-Wilsonian agenda as embodied in the mind-set of what Obama was criticizing as the "think tank complex." The

president well might remain a liberal internationalist of the traditional Wilsonian sort, extolling the virtues of democratic government at home and abroad
for the sake of national security and a better world, yet when asked by Goldberg to choose a label to identify himself, Obama rejected not only "realist"
and "isolationist" but also "liberal interventionist" in favor of seeing himself
an "internationalist," plain and simple—in the image, he reported, of none
other than George H. W. Bush and Brent Scowcroft!

Only one thing seemed certain: Washington's role in bringing progressive
political reform, by the use of military force, to the Muslim world was at an
abrupt end. Air attacks against ISIS would continue, and advisers would be
on the ground to aid groups America deemed friendly. But in remarks widely
circulated, Philip Gordon, a principal adviser to the president on the Middle
East from 2013 to 2015, put the lesson succinctly:

> In Iraq, the U.S. intervened and occupied, and the result was a costly
> disaster. In Libya, the U.S. intervened and did not occupy, and the re-
> sult was a costly disaster. In Syria, the U.S. neither intervened nor oc-
> cupied, and the result is a costly disaster.[39]

Gordon's summary of a decade of nation- and state-building efforts in the
Middle East amounted to a declaration of Washington's bankruptcy on this
score. As the president had put it to David Remnick in 2014, referring to the
much-touted "modern Syrian opposition," "When I hear people suggesting
that somehow if we had just financed and armed the opposition earlier, that
somehow Assad would be gone and we'd have a peaceful transition, it's magical thinking."[40]

Needless to say, Obama's policy reversal with respect to Syria did not come
to him overnight. He reported to Goldberg both his doubts that a moderate
Islam might easily emerge out of struggles in the Middle East and, just as
importantly, his long-standing conviction that "tribalism" based on ethno-
religious cleavages, and not just dictatorship, explained the difficulties of regime change in many parts of the world.[41] Both of these insights contributed
to a pessimism that American intervention in this region could successfully
occur if its aim were a "moderate" pro-American government whose rule
could be legitimized in liberal terms.

We need more studies of the time to know exactly how his thinking
changed. Surely a part of it was his recognition by 2012 that the decision to
return with a surge to Afghanistan late in 2009 had been a terrible mistake,
one that he had been far too slow to perceive as such but that he subsequently

blamed on the military's influence over him in the first year of his administration. Sometime early in 2012, he presumably had also come to realize that his embrace of the Arab Spring in 2011, and especially his contribution to the overthrow of Muammar Qaddafi during the course of that year, had been badly ill-advised. A "shit show," as he called it, according to Goldberg in 2016, as the collapse of a governing authority in Libya led to civil war there followed by the spread of the armaments and militias there to other parts of northern Africa, then on to Iraq and Syria.

Nor had other White House initiatives in the Middle East ended favorably. In Egypt, the fall of Mubarak, whose ouster was supported by the Obama administration, spelled more serious problems. Efforts to end Jewish settlements in the occupied territories and to create a Palestinian state had gone nowhere, while Israeli Prime Minister Benjamin Netanyahu's continued rebuffs of American policy had been humiliating. Here was the origin of what was presumably a rift between the president and his team of neo-Wilsonian enthusiasts, including most notably National Security Council official Samantha Power (from 2013, ambassador to the United Nations) and Secretary of State Hillary Clinton. Apparently Secretary of State John Kerry's enthusiasm for an aggressive policy in the Middle East, and so his disappointment with Obama's decision of August 2013, put distance between him and the president as well.[42] When in the spring of 2014, the president asked a group of reporters aboard Air Force One on a flight home from Asia to repeat what had been his mantra that day, when he might have been reflecting on the Middle East, regretting that he could not deal more with dynamic Asia, they called out in unison (following his lead): "Don't do stupid shit."[43]

Harvard government professor Stephen Walt was quite right to point out that Obama's new insights on world affairs (including those concerning apparent realism toward Russia) were in many respects too little, too late. And Walt was surely correct to say that the president's new take on world affairs lacked anything like "an overarching vision" to guide American foreign policy, and that only with great difficulty could he be defined as much of a "realist."[44] The question for our purposes, however, is what kind of liberal internationalist President Obama remained after his momentous decision not to attack militarily the Assad regime in Syria.

As Walt finds limits to Obama's realism, so we may conclude with respect to the president's liberalism—he had no such "overarching vision." For example, just how much did he break with his own "magical thinking" about nation- and state-building? In an interview with Chris Wallace reported by the BBC (British Broadcasting Corporation) on April 11, 2016, the president concluded that policy toward Libya was "the 'worst mistake' of his presidency." Yet he then went on to blame not the intervention itself but the failure to plan for what to do after Qadaffi's fall—adding to this his criticism of the British and French for their failure to draw up such plans as well.[45] We can conclude from his words that a better-orchestrated attack on Libya might well have been a success, a confidence more than a bit reminiscent of American beliefs about the invasions of Iraq and Afghanistan earlier—failures because of mission shortcomings, not as the result of their inherent impossibility.

Moreover, as the epigraphs earlier in this chapter indicate, and as the reading of any of his annual addresses in September to the United Nations General Assembly attests, the president continued to sound many of the liberal internationalist mantras well after his difficult decision to call off military strikes against Assad. Thus, in July 2015, the president traveled to East Africa to buck up democratic breakthroughs by championing entrepreneurship and strong institutions in the region. Or again, as relations were normalized with Cuba and a "nuclear deal" reached with Iran that same year, he could also suggest that the reduction of tensions with the outside world would favor the emergence of liberal forces in these two countries.[46]

Obama's recasting—but certainly not outright rejection—of other neo-Wilsonian concepts was also evident. Given the association of efforts to foster a transition to democracy implicit in the "responsibility to protect" with imperialism, he simply said to Goldberg, "We've got to be hardheaded at the same time as we're bighearted. . . . There are going to be times where our security interests conflict with our concerns about human rights. There are going to be times where we can do something about innocent people being killed, but there are going to be times where we can't."[47]

So too, how greatly had Obama reformulated the meaning of American exceptionalism? In his May 24, 2014, West Point Commencement Address, it seemed he was as dedicated to taking on responsibility for global order as ever the Bush Doctrine had been. Is this what it took "to make the world safe for democracy"—establishing a liberal hegemony to the four corners of the earth?

Hence, much as Obama was disappointing in the extent to which he was a realist in the sense Walt defines the term, so too the sense in which he was a liberal internationalist remained in doubt, whatever his well-founded pessimism with respect to armed intervention in the Muslim world. For example, the president had little to say involving questions of international or domestic economic reform, although these were of basic importance for the sake of the democratic community's economic vigor, the strength of its middle class, and the robustness of constitutional government. The golden opportunity— which he deliberately avoided—of debating these matters publicly with respect to the Trans-Pacific Partnership signed in February 2016 (to be ratified by 2018) or the Trans-Atlantic Trade and Investment Partnership, which may not be completed until 2020 and whose terms are kept secret, are cases in point. Nor did he seem overly concerned in terribly precise terms with the future of NATO and European unity, multilateral issues that would be priorities for a liberal internationalist to consider, despite his ringing endorsements of the American commitment to the military alliance on the twenty-fifth anniversary of the fall of the Berlin Wall—in Warsaw on June 4, 2015, and in Estonia on September 3, 2015, confirmed by his speech in Hanover, Germany, on April 25, 2016.

The contrast with Republicans in the last two years of his eight years in office nonetheless shows them to be far more militant about how Washington should conduct relations with authoritarian regimes than Obama was prepared to be. So Republicans found Obama's unwillingness to give offensive weapons to Ukraine unacceptable in the summer of 2015. Moreover, neither the normalization of relations with Cuba that was concluded that same summer nor the terms of an agreement with Iran at about the same time (the so-called "Nuclear Deal," or the Joint Comprehensive Plan of Action between that country, the European Union, and five permanent members of the United Nations Security Council plus Germany) fit at all well within precedents set by the Republican Party in the White House between 2001 and 2009. Regime change prior to negotiation remained their conviction, one that the president had long since abandoned.

The differences were vividly illustrated by the outspoken attacks on the administration by the Republican candidates for president as reported in July 2015. In a field packed with hopefuls—at one point a total of seventeen—all but Rand Paul denounced the reestablishment of diplomatic relations with Havana, and all but John Kasich attacked the Iran nuclear agreement.[48] Clearly President Obama—with the support of all the Democratic candidates for his office in 2017—had broken with the Republican elite. But Obama's policies here can be seen more in terms of realism than liberalism. Moreover, his continuing admonitions that democracy was the answer to all the world's ills, whether domestic, regional, or global, became increasingly platitudinous, hollow in their exhortation. In short, too many key subjects were treated summarily, and virtually nothing appeared that resembled a coherent liberal internationalist overview informed by a healthy dose of realism.

Obama ended his presidency neither as a clear-cut traditional liberal nor as a realist nor as a hybrid of the two. He had broken with the more extreme terms of neo-Wilsonianism and had returned to some degree to a liberalism that was somewhat reminiscent of the cold war or Wilson himself. But much remained missing. What the country was left with, then, was a work in progress. President Obama left no "doctrine" behind him, nor even a clear indication of the direction liberal internationalism might take to renew itself. Still, by breaking with the more radical terms of the neo-Wilsonian playbook, he opened the door in a way that invited his successors to address for the nation what a progressive framework for American foreign policy could mean.

CONCLUSION

Reviving Liberal Internationalism

And don't let anybody make you think that God chose America as his divine, messianic force to be a sort of policeman of the whole world. God has a way of standing before the nations with judgment, and it seems that I can hear God saying to America, "You're too arrogant! And if you don't change your ways, I will rise up and break the back-bone of your power. . . . Be still and know that I am God."
—*Martin Luther King Jr., "Speech against
the Vietnam War" (April 1967)*

Pride goeth before destruction, and an haughty spirit before a fall.
—*Proverbs 16:18*

For they have sown the wind, and they shall reap the whirlwind.
—*Proverbs 22:8*

A major purpose I had in writing *Why Wilson Matters* was to redeem as best I might the American tradition of human rights and democracy promotion in world affairs from the crisis it faces today. Invading Iraq in 2003 under the banner of sponsoring a democratic transition of that country, with thoughts of doing the same for "the Broader Middle East" thereafter—all in the name of winning "the global war on terrorism"—was a betrayal of the character of the American liberal internationalist tradition as it had been handed down from Woodrow Wilson to leadership in Washington, D.C., after World War II. In that betrayal lay the seeds of the destruction of the tradition itself—its victims' lives numbering in the many millions, its expenditure of treasure measured in the many trillions. That President Obama through most of 2013 should have followed this example by invoking human rights and democracy promotion as a task of American "exceptionalism" while he engaged the American military from Afghanistan to Libya and Syria only compounded the crisis facing liberal arguments, which presided over policy during four presidential terms, Republican and Democratic alike. That all this damage to American democracy and the national interest has been deeply aggravated by the political deregulation of the domestic and international capital markets only augments the extent to which this tradition is in self-inflicted peril.[1] Who, acquainted with the signal successes of liberal internationalism in the decade of the 1940s and the half century thereafter, could view this collapse of the promises and accomplishments of Wilsonianism without alarm?

In the introduction, I presented a graph suggesting that Wilsonianism could be conceived as a "synergistic diamond" wherein democratic government, open and integrated markets, multilateralism, and American leadership could lead to increasing prosperity, freedom, and peace for those people who were part of these processes. But by 2016, a "vicious diamond" was instead at work, in which flaws in democratic governance in the common interest, questions about international economic integration and collective security, and debates over the role of American leadership in world affairs were increasingly interacting in a way that synergistically led to a downward spiral in them all.

It remains unclear through all this whether America is in decline; the rise of a national security state with an imperial presidency based on populist support as the middle class weakens perhaps might endow this country with the continued status of being the world's sole superpower. Yet as President Wilson made clear on more than one stop on his Western Tour in September 1919 to bolster public support for the League of Nations, militarism and imperialism, combined with the overweening demands of business influence (what President Eisenhower labeled in his Farewell Address of January 1961 the "military-industrial complex"), could sound the death knell of American democracy.[2] Whatever the fate of America as the world's sole superpower, what is patently clear today is that liberal internationalism as a framework for political action at home and abroad is at risk of becoming nothing more than vain rhetoric.

BACK TO THE FUTURE

The key that this book suggests for an understanding of the basic dynamic of the liberal internationalist tradition in American foreign policy, and for a means to save it from self-destruction, stems from renewed attention to Woodrow Wilson's legacy in terms of our country's conduct in world affairs. Going "back to the future" would involve a policy of deepening, rather than broadening, democracy and so serve as the corrective we need.

The conclusion to this book is not the place to spell out in any detail what such a program would look like. But certain of its features seem to be obvious. For example, given the centrality of democratic government to Wilson's conception of America domestically and in world affairs, deepening democracy would require renewed attention to the strength of what Secretary of State Madeleine Albright called the Community of Democracies.

Thus, a good case can be made that the North Atlantic Treaty Organization should be renovated by reforms that include a strengthening of what since the 1960s has been called "the European pillar." That is, the members of the European Union need to work more closely together so as to increase their power potential both alongside and independently of the United States. This responsibility means more defense spending on the part of our allies, combined with the harmonization of their respective abilities. What such an approach does not mean is any retreat on America's part from participation in NATO's governance. Solving the contradiction between these two requirements has never been easy, given the American penchant to make decisions alone while the Europeans demonstrate a preference for a free ride. But a meeting of the minds can, and should, be achieved.[3]

In addition to the question of the structure of collective security, the United States should work with the European Union and other democratic, capitalist powers such as Japan, South Korea, Chile, Canada, Australia, and New Zealand to improve the international regulations supervising world banking, investment, and technology practices. The aim should be to encourage the growth of labor unions and to strengthen the position of the middle class within this grouping of peoples, while discouraging practices that transfer capital, technology, and jobs to countries like China that make no pretense of being democratic (and thus transparent and accountable to rules decided by groups such as the World Trade Organization) but rather give every indication of being our rivals. It also means a reining in of the tax loopholes that have allowed corporations to evade taxes, and individuals to hide trillions of dollars of undeclared income, in complex transactions that only sometimes have legal sanction, and even then illustrate the power of money to control the legal systems of state after state, including especially the United States of America. Countries where the government plays a more directive mode—

those in Scandinavia, Canada, and Germany, among others—have not only avoided the most serious disruptions of the past decade, but their economies have prospered relative to the rest of the capitalist democratic world and contributed, again in comparison to the rest of us, to the general welfare, in terms of preserving the middle class and moderating mass poverty.

Economic reform is called for at home as well. As works by Joseph Stiglitz, Elizabeth Warren, Emmanuel Saez, Thomas Piketty, Robert Reich, and others cited earlier in this book have argued (with no effective rebuttal in the literature that I have seen so that their conclusions can be accepted as being as accurate as they are astonishing), the growth of the economic power of the top 1 percent in the United States (or the top 20 percent, if one prefers) has reduced not simply the relative, but in fact the absolute, income level of the middle and working classes over the past three decades; has raised dangers for American democracy as the money of the economically powerful has bought election after election in Congress; and has put in question our relative power position as leading industries and know-how are transferred abroad. The release of a mass of information on tax havens for sheltering funds by world leaders, as well as others, in the "Panama Papers," published in the spring of 2016, added to the anger of many citizens. The large numbers of voters who supported Bernie Sanders and Donald Trump in the 2016 Democratic and Republican primaries underscored the public anger at these long-standing practices.[4]

As Wilson warned time and again, from 1889 through his presidency, capitalism might reinforce democracy in America and abroad if properly regulated; but it would surely undermine our system of government if left to its own devices. Measures as politically apparent (provided the will were there) as sharply raising income taxes on the top 20 percent, forcing the repatriation of personally held capital stashed abroad, and removing corporate tax privileges through a tightening of international rules of investment and taxation lack feasibility because of the political obstacles in their way raised by the economically powerful. But in a genuine democracy, the rules of the game can, and in these instances should, be changed.

To engage in defensive and economic reforms of this magnitude means imposing stricter rules for membership in the Community of Democracies than has hitherto been the practice. Reforming the EU or NATO does not need to mean enlarging them. Indeed, among the changes to be considered should be the right to exclude members from its ranks (or, more narrowly, from the eurozone) who fail to live up to legitimate expectations of the group, whether it be in terms of economic, military, or political conduct. A good argument can be made that both NATO and the European Union expanded too quickly in the 1990s, inviting problems into the interior of their institutions dedicated to the preservation of constitutional democracies, invitations that weakened, rather than strengthened, the fabric of the democratic zone of peoples.

But the necessity of setting and enforcing strict norms of membership in the Community does not mean we should fail to be alert to signs of liberal democratic life in other countries where prospects for a transition from authoritarian rule are real. As an example, liberals saluted the Nobel Prize Committee's decision to grant the Tunisian National Quartet its Peace Prize in 2015 "for its decisive contribution to the building of a pluralistic democracy in Tunisia in the wake of the Jasmine Revolution of 2011."

The reason for the applause is apparent when we look at the chances for progress in that country. Tunisia has the profile to make a successful transition to democracy: a relatively large, well-educated, liberal middle class; a well-organized national labor movement; a leading Muslim political organization, Ennahada, held by most to be moderate; a well-structured legal and human rights community; some outstanding national political leaders (especially the grand old man Beji Caid Essebsi); a sense of national unity that comes from a common dialect of Arabic and the lack of marked geographical divisions; the absence of oil revenues or a strategic position that might attract outside predators; and a relatively weak military establishment.[5]

To be sure, no transition to democracy is without its serious obstacles. In the Tunisian case, these include a weak economy lacking promising jobs for the young, a conflict in the Middle East that has called thousands of young men into the ranks of the Islamic State, and the pressures of jihadists, or troublemakers in general, crossing from neighboring Libya, a country in seemingly unending anarchy that has spread far beyond its borders. The world's democratic community has an interest in helping Tunisia meet these challenges.

Tunisia is far from alone. Myanmar, Nicaragua, and Cuba are among the many countries whose movement toward liberal democracy should be welcomed, and there is good reason to think that the Iranians may in due course follow suit. Indeed, large parts of Latin America need to be considered, as does much of Eastern Europe, as appropriate venues for human rights and democracy promotion by the Community of Democracies. Human Rights Watch, Amnesty International, the Open Society Institute, and Transparency

International—all independent of government financing—may act in the private sphere on behalf of liberal causes. The same may be said for the multiplicity of organizations such as Doctors Without Borders, the Argentine Forensic Anthropological Team, or responsible micro-funding initiatives that have done so much to improve the quality of life (politically as well socially) in large parts of the world. Speaking in more general terms, the empowerment of women worldwide is generally agreed to be at the top of the liberal agenda.

Such an approach to world affairs would be neither imperialist nor isolationist—the binary opposition that neoconservatives and neoliberals alike too often say are our only choices. Instead, the much-vaunted American exceptionalism would satisfy itself not by taking all the world's problems on its shoulders with liberal solutions, but more modestly contenting itself, first and foremost, with putting its own house in order. It would stress liberalism for those to whom this tradition has appeal, yet look to cooperate with what the liberal American philosopher John Rawls called "relatively decent hierarchical regimes" while acting aggressively only toward "outlaw states" still living in the state of nature.[6] Its primary mission would be nation- and state-building exercises at home and within the democratic community of states without the illusion that all the world would be part of the undertaking, thanks to the fictions made current of "a universal appeal of democracy" involving "non-negotiable human rights," and in the name of a just war doctrine that has caused such harm, the responsibility to protect. Finally, it would understand that the endless invocation of an American "exceptional" responsibility to improve the human condition worldwide sounds to many abroad like pure hypocrisy given the enormous amount of suffering this country has caused others in the name of high-flown principles—from Latin America and Southeast Asia during the cold war to those who have experienced the murderous consequence of United States military interventions in Iraq, Afghanistan, and Libya since 2003.

Without trying to make an exhaustive list of matters that liberals could attend to, other issues sometimes overlooked merit attention. First, how can the United States fail to assist the millions of refugees from North Africa to Afghanistan who are victims of our armed interventions there? Or again, in 2014 and 2015, nearly 60,000 unaccompanied children arrived in the United States from Mexico and Central America. They were largely victims of drug wars in their own countries related to narcotics consumption in the United States (estimates are that 10,000 Mexicans die annually of drug-related violence) or to American interventions in Guatemala in the mid-1950s and our counterinsurgency efforts that began in Nicaragua in the early 1980s, creating waves of violence in El Salvador and Guatemala thereafter, leading to hundreds of thousands of deaths and the forced migration of many hundreds of thousands more. For all the talk of a "responsibility to protect," many in this country fail to see our connection to the plight of these refugees.

In fiscal 2013 (ending in September that year), the United States naturalized some 780,000 immigrants as citizens and gave permanent resident status to over 1 million more. Over 1 million of our citizens are today descendants of our involvement in Iran, and 2 million more of our incursions into Indochina (Vietnam, Laos, and Cambodia). These newcomers have for the most part been integrated with very good effect. Why not invite in many of those fleeing problems of our making from the Middle East, Afghanistan, Mexico, and Central America in expectation of their positive integration over a generation?

One source of the grievous damage we have done in several parts of the world is drug addiction in the United States, which needs attention by liberals as well. The proliferation of failed states in Central America and the Caribbean, as well as the pressure put on other governments, such as those of Colombia and Peru, shows that our "war on drugs" met with defeat long ago. It is time to legalize the consumption of a wide variety of these substances, in controlled conditions, in the United States. To say this is not to encourage their consumption, nor is it to argue that the consumption of poisonous substances made out of opiates or synthetically manufactured should be tolerated. It is to point out simply the need to free both these foreign countries and segments of the American society from the social and political disasters that follow from failing to admit defeat on prohibition of these substances, one of whose most obvious consequences is the unwarranted incarceration of vast numbers of young Americans, usually from black or Hispanic backgrounds, for nonviolent drug offenses. Prison reform is thus another issue for liberals to address seriously in terms of improving life in the United States.

WILSON AND THE UNITED STATES
A CENTURY LATER

These rather obvious suggestions arise of themselves from going back to the spirit of the liberal internationalist tradition. In a review of Wilson's writings and speeches from 1885 through 1908 (the dates of his first and last major academic publications) lies the story of a patriot who had dedicated his life to the protection and promotion of democracy in America. As a leading student of his era of comparative politics, as a man whose work focused almost exclusively on questions concerning the origin, character, promise, and challenges to democratic life, he had an ambition as president to safeguard democracy at home through economic reform and to expand the horizon of democracy's power to bring peace to world affairs through multilateral institutions under the leadership of the United States. His cause was that of freedom under law—that is, of liberty bestowed on a citizenry through institutions capable of generating a code of legal conduct contributing to the public welfare and resting on the consent of the governed.

In due course, seeing the moral and practical benefits of such a society and government domestically for the United States and other democratic peoples, Wilson turned his attention to promoting a regional, and later a global, environment conducive to freedom through international institutions devoted to keeping the peace by generating rules of behavior fostering cooperation and mitigating conflict somewhat as they had done at home. His expectation was that such organizations might serve to bind the world's democracies into a system of collective security based on international law, against what were likely to be the challenges originating with autocratic peoples and states that saw their self-interest in protectionism, militarism, and conquest through war. He envisioned as his crowning achievement American leadership of the League of Nations, which through collective security and economic integration could conceivably "make the world safe for democracy."

In generating a framework for American foreign policy, Wilson was indeed, as sometimes disparagingly charged, a "moralist" and an "idealist." He saw the cause he pursued as morally justified (and in this he had the entire Enlightenment behind him, as leavened by his Presbyterian faith—the marriage of reason with conscience), yet he recognized that his goals were idealistic in the sense that they would never be free of challenge. Democracy itself would always have its internal contradictions so that political life would be ceaselessly undergoing change.

However (as it is often alleged), Wilson was neither a "utopian" nor an "imperialist." Instead, he was a realist and an anti-imperialist, cognizant of the problems facing even "advanced" democratic peoples in the preservation of their heritage and dedicated to the fostering of a world order that might eventually find its way to a peace based on "self-government," a form of political organization that, exceptional cases aside, imperialism was by the nature of freedom incapable of bestowing. His hope was that such a process could be encouraged by the example of other democracies at home and by the cooperation they might provide to one another through a dense network of multilateral organizations, the most important of which was the League of Nations.

Wilson was not a utopian for a simple, basic reason. His studies of history and the mechanics of political life in the United States especially made him well aware that the prerequisites for a democratic life require a mix of characteristics in the citizenry, the institutions, and the leadership of such an order that "eternal vigilance" was ever called for. He counted on the practical, and especially moral, qualities of democratic life to make those people who could become, and remain, constitutional democrats capable both internationally and domestically of providing for themselves a stable political order. The result could be peace through freedom, the ambition of liberalism as a historical tradition dating back to the late eighteenth century, but expressed with particular force by Wilson as an academic, and then with genuine historical importance once he became president of the United States.

Such an achievement would not come easily, nor could it be assured once and for all. Wilson feared, above all, the strength of corporate capitalism as a threat to American democracy (and so oversaw by far the most substantial reform of the power of money in American life until his day with his Progressive agenda, and so set the stage to inspire both Franklin Roosevelt's New Deal and Lyndon Johnson's Great Society). As a man born shortly before the Civil War and reared in Virginia and Georgia, he was quite aware as well of the fractious nature of internal American politics based on geography, historical memory, and ethno-religious division. Nor was he himself above criticism. He was slow to support women's equality, and as president he reintroduced a color line in Washington, the greatest shame of his presidency.

That racism was part of those presidential administrations that preceded and followed his does not exonerate him from this failing. Yet, neither should the fact of his racism blind us to his administration's extraordinary achievements. Just as we may condemn the racism of George Washington and Thomas Jefferson before him—both of whom owned hundreds of slaves and in Jefferson's case had children by them—I suggest we measure this failing against his many accomplishments in economic reform at home and political institution-building abroad, measures that in due course could be used by others to mitigate the force of racism.

Indeed, we might conclude from the spirit of Wilson's writings and policies that the greatest dangers to democracy today in America—the inequality of economic wealth, the control of the political system by the richest quintile of the population as a result of our campaign financing laws, and a growing populism based on insecurity but blind to the class realities of the country today—would be at the top of his causes calling for reform. That he might today see these measures as working for the sake of African Americans, Hispanics, and women—citizens whose interests he had ignored in his own time—would be quite in keeping with the spirit of Wilson's own arguments as to the meaning of democracy in America. In charity to the past, and remembering Wilson's many admonishments that democracy constantly needs renewal and improvement, we might agree with Martin Luther King Jr. that for the United States, at least, "The arc of the moral universe is long, but it bends toward justice."[7]

In foreign affairs, because he was not a utopian, Wilson was not an imperialist either. While he came to believe that democracy regionally (and perhaps one distant day globally) could provide the same benefits of peace and freedom that it did domestically (and so was a precursor of what came to be called by the 1990s "democratic peace theory"), he did not think one country should suppose it could engender democratic life for another. To be sure, from an early age, he did maintain that the heritage of the United States under English kings and colonial institutions had allowed our country to become almost effortlessly democratic. Still, he was skeptical that other great cultures or civilizations with their own historical experiences would tend easily, if at all, to democratic ways unless they possessed internally the requisite elements for change provided by their own history and culture.

Nor did he have a "color line" in world affairs as he did in domestic matters. His conviction that the Philippines should be recognized as an independent, democratic country in the 1920s (when its population was Malay, not white) and that it was of great moral importance to do what Washington could to foster democracy in Mexico (which calls itself a mestizo nation) should be evidence enough of this. His regrettable veto of the Japanese request for a "racial equality clause" in the Covenant of the League can perhaps be understood, at least in part, as a matter he felt would be determined by future deliberations within the League (given especially strong British and Australian objections to the Japanese proposal), as a reflection of his fear of southern congressmen at home when the country's admission into the League was being considered, and as the consequence of a general understanding that what Japan wanted was not "racial equality," which has never been a calling card of that country, but instead the recognition of its great power status pure and simple.[8]

With peoples who had little sense of national unity (Hispaniola or the mandates of the League of Nations), he held out hope that governments capable of generating the rule of law resting on the consent of the governed could be formed with the help of democratic outsiders. But faced with the Mexican and Soviet Revolutions alongside the political situation in Germany after the end of war in November 1918, Wilson displayed a prudent reluctance to do more than to work through the spirit of self-determination on the margins, and so to support the eventual emergence of constitutional government for these countries stemming from the hopes and values of these people themselves. It is impossible to understand how Woodrow Wilson would ever have seen the transition from authoritarian to democratic government as an easy process (if possible at all) for peoples for whom the ingredients for such a way of life and government were not in evidence. His distance from the neo-Wilsonianism of the 1990s—notwithstanding democratic peace theory, which echoed Wilson as it called for the unity of like-minded liberal governments—should be strikingly evident.[9]

Wilson's approach to progressive change found expression in a form of gradualism that operated through multilateral institutions, with the League of Nations his greatest legacy. His drafts of a Pan-American Treaty (which by 1916 was stillborn) prepared him to think about postwar reconstruction in Europe and to be the major author of the League's Covenant. Here was the mechanism that might eventually serve to institutionalize his ambition to defend the world, as best conceivable, from another war such as that which had just ended.

The League's primary mission was to protect and to help reform those countries that could be called democratic (even the British could come under suspicion for their established church, their monarchy, their empire, and their practiced ways in balance-of-power calculations) through the creation of a "society of nations" (as the French called it), generating a body of international law capable of guiding a series of multilateral institutions that would provide for more open markets and collective security against what were sure to be eventual enemies. The outcome, however, was not assured, and if successful would not have come easily. As he put it, he "was playing for a hundred years hence."

Because the outcome was in doubt, we should remember that his system of collective security also contained a balance-of-power mechanism, with Article 17 of the Covenant protecting members of the League from aggression on the part of autocracies. So, too, during the cold war, liberalism could embrace some of the tenets of containment, given liberalism's opposition to communism. The idea that for even a second Wilson would have failed to see Hitler (or Stalin or Muslim extremism today) as the menaces they were to his hopes for a world of peace based on freedom is difficult to imagine.

There was, of course, a democracy promotion project for the League as well. Imperialism was not on the agenda (including with respect to the mandates such as Wilson envisioned them in his drafts of the Covenant early in 1919, not as they were finally promulgated later that spring, when imperialist they most certainly were). Still, self-determination would allow peoples to be free of imperialist meddling in their internal affairs, while the growth of a middle class based on increasing prosperity, combined with the possibility of joining the League and sharing in its benefits, might in due course extend the zone of democratic peace that this organization was intended to establish. (Whatever the obvious shortcomings of the agreement with Germany, Berlin's entry into the League had to be at the top of his hopes for the League's effectiveness, assuming that the United States was the leading member.) Wilson thus reaffirmed the basic tenets of the Peace of Westphalia, which had dominated international law since the end of the Thirty Years War in 1648, by asserting the obligation to respect noninterference in the internal affairs of states recognized as sovereign by the world community.[10]

The fruit of Wilson's insights were to become manifest a generation after his death. For I believe it was liberalism, even more than containment, that can be said to have won the cold war. The groundwork set up in the 1940s for what was properly called "the free world" was indispensable to the eventual victory over the Soviet Union between 1989 and 1991. During these later years, it was every bit as much Mikhail Gorbachev as it was Ronald Reagan who deserved recognition—yet without the decade of the 1940s how could such an outcome to the deadly contest on the terms that came to end the rivalry between these superpowers have been at all assured? That Gorbachev himself had in many respects "converted" to liberalism seems to me a compelling interpretation of this great historical development.

In this respect, the crowning achievements of the Wilsonian decade deserve to be recalled: the Bretton Woods system, the United Nations, the North Atlantic Treaty Organization, and, above all, the internal reforms promoted by Washington in Japan and, even more importantly, Germany (opening the way to the creation of what we today call the European Union). The fact that this decade could not be called by the name "Wilsonian" attests to criticism such as that by George Kennan (to whom we could add Hans Morgenthau, Walter Lippmann, and Henry Kissinger), who only later in his life came to recognize that he had badly overstated his criticisms of America's twenty-eighth president.[11]

Yet from early 2002 until today, American foreign policy has been premised on convictions that are both utopian and imperialist in a fashion quite foreign to the liberal internationalist tradition as it existed prior to 1990s. With its confidence in the ease of a transition from authoritarian to democratic order, its insistence on a "just war" doctrine that overthrew the Westphalian system of states by legitimizing the armed intervention of democracies against autocratic states, and its redefinition of American "exceptionalism" from a defense of the democratic world to a world-order project that knew no limits, neo-Wilsonianism sabotaged the very tradition from which it had emerged.

The question, then, is whether the liberal internationalist tradition can be resuscitated in such a way that it contributes positively to world affairs. Other than very indirectly, this book cannot serve as a guide to the answer of complex contemporary questions. Its ambition instead is to try to provide background to these pressing matters of today by looking back in time for some insight into what has transpired in the past three decades.

I therefore encourage those confronted with these issues today—the young and those in policy-making or implementing positions, and others for whom human rights and democracy promotion at home and abroad are of importance—to learn what they can from the past. The Wilsonian tradition is in crisis—first, because it does not have a clear sense of its history and hence of its identity; and second, because its appropriation by neo-Wilsonians has understandably given it a bad name. For those who consider themselves liberal internationalists—who believe in protecting, and where possible promoting, human rights and democratic government, who encourage regulated market intercourse among nations, who endorse participation in multilateral organizations capable of producing a body of international law that can provide a sense of unity through justice—there is need of rejuvenation. Yet standing in the way is a lack of historical self-awareness combined for many with the enduring appeal of neo-Wilsonianism as a panacea for all that ails us.

In trying to gain the perspective on today such as the historical record provides, we might well recall the words of Woodrow Wilson's famous address at Princeton in the fall of 1896:

> The world's memory must be kept alive, or we shall never see an end to its old mistakes. We are in danger to lose our identity and become infantile in every generation. . . .
>
> I need not tell you that I believe in full, explicit instruction in history and in politics, in the experiences of peoples and the fortunes of governments, in the whole story of what men have attempted and what they have accomplished through all the changes both of form and purpose in their organization of their common life . . . It is plain that it is the duty of an institution of learning set in the midst of a free population and amidst signs of social change, not merely to implant a sense of duty, but to illuminate duty by every lesson that can be drawn from the past . . .
>
> You do not know the world until you know the men who have possessed it and tried its ways before ever you were given your brief run upon it. And there is no sanity comparable with that which is schooled in the thoughts that will keep. . . .
>
> Do you wonder, then, that I ask for the old drill, the old memory of times gone by, the old schooling in precedent and tradition, the old keeping of faith with the past as a preparation for leadership in the days of social change?[12]

Acknowledgments

I am thankful for the generous support—material and moral—I have received in writing this book. Historians John Milton Cooper Jr. and Tom Knock were of enormous help in sharing their knowledge of Woodrow Wilson's life and work with me. Chuck Myers, director of the University of Kansas Press, has long been an editor I have appreciated, particularly through our discussion of the impact on American democracy of reformed Calvinism of the sort that Woodrow Wilson—the son and grandson of Presbyterian ministers and the president of Princeton, the greatest of the Presbyterian schools—would have taken in as his mother's milk. Professors Toni Chayes, Mick Cox, Art Goldhammer, Patrice Higonnet, Bob Jervis, Miles Kahler, Michael Lind, John Owen, Inderjeet Parmar, Dick Samuels, Mary Elise Sarotte, Jim Scott, Ibrahim Sundiata, John A. Thompson, and Isabelle Vagnoux offered critical counsel over the years this book was in gestation. Professors Ronald Steel, Jeff Taliaferro, and David Fromkin—Realist thinkers all and unending critics of everything they believed Wilson stood for—pushed me to rethink my conclusions time and again. Another Realist theorist, Professor Mike Desch, read an earlier version of the text and commented in such a way that I could appreciate even more his notions of the "illiberalism of liberal international relations theory," an argument highly relevant to the dangerous metamorphosis this approach to world affairs has taken since the mid-1990s.

German historian Klaus Schwabe laid out for me in Boston and Aachen the complexities of Wilson's approach to the problem of democratizing Germany after 1918. French jurist Mario Bettati and Professor Justin Vaisse talked to me at length about their understanding of the liberal internationalist tradition from their national perspective. French historian Diana Pinto and political theorist Dominique Moisi were founts of information on events in the Middle East following the American invasion of Iraq in 2003. Their concern for the future of democratic government at home as well as abroad meshed closely with mine as well in a way that made us partners in a common endeavor.

Robert Azencott, Bonnie Cronin, Sylve Desmeuzes-Balland, Alex Gladstein, Barbara Kellerman, Jan Krc, Barbara Leaver, Gerry Peck, Freia Schierenberg, Ann Tucker, and Catherine Widgery—with their strong interest in political theory and practice—were never-failing discussants on American foreign policy as the book progressed. The Battle family—Byron, Margarita, Lars, and the memory of Eric—have long been an inspiration for their lifelong dedication to a better world, which it is a pleasure here to acknowledge. The same may be said for French jurist Léa Réus, Guatemalans Claudia Escobar and Miguel Zamora, Swedish doctor Stephen Goldin, and Tunisian professor Taoufik Djebali—human rights and pro-democracy activists all.

The Woodrow Wilson International Center for Scholars at the Smithsonian Institution and Tufts University were generous in providing me the office space and financial backing to bring the work to completion. Special thanks, at the Wilson Center, to Rob Litwak, its director of studies, as well as to Lindsay Collins and Arlin Charles for their organizational support and good humor.

At Tufts, I benefited from the outstanding political theory section of our department, where Rob Devigne, Yannis Evrigenis, Dennis Rasmussen, and Vickie Sullivan discussed with me the originality of the place Wilson's theory of democracy enjoyed within the liberal political tradition dating back to the Enlightenment. Consuelo Cruz was equally helpful in reviewing with me the character of comparative political theory during the cold war. Will Freeman wrote an insightful seminar paper with respect to President Wilson's thinking on self-determination as it emerged in his response to the Mexican Revolution. Menglu Wang wrote an original study of Wilson's decision to award Shantung to Japan at the Paris Peace Conference in 1919. Sophia Goldberg effectively demonstrated the parallels between the contemporary writings of the Nobel Prize economist Joseph Stiglitz and Woodrow Wilson, writing a century earlier.

I am pleased that Princeton University Press is bringing out this book. With Eric Crahan as senior social science editor, this press carries an imprimatur on subjects such as mine that is second to none. My study carries forth the analysis this press launched in 1994 when it published the first edition of *America's Mission: The United States and the Worldwide Struggle for Democracy* (with an expanded edition in 2012). Ellen Foos, Ben Pokross, and especially Patricia Fogarty were critical to the final appearance of this book.

At Princeton, I also had the good fortune of being invited by politics Professor John Ikenberry to talk on this book. He then introduced me to Professors Daniel Deudney and David Hendrickson, whose vigorous exchanges on the American liberal tradition and U.S. imperialism are evident in parts of this book.

In the course of writing this study, I have often had occasion to reflect on the thinking of three distinguished American political theorists—once my professors, later my friends, and sadly no longer with us: Barrington Moore Jr. (1913–2005), Samuel P. Huntington (1928–2008), and Stanley Hoffmann (1928–2015), respectively a radical, a conservative, and a man for all seasons. What ties these men to my book was that with their feet firmly grounded in comparative politics, all three were interested as well in world affairs. While they saluted the fortunes of democracy at home and abroad, all three were well aware of the possibility that no certain future for democratic government should be counted on. Indeed, the United States itself might contribute to the decline of the liberal internationalist tradition by a foolhardy self-confidence that did not respect the realities of international politics and foreign cultures distant from our own, or by its own decay from within.

In this respect, Moore, Huntington, and Hoffmann were much like Wilson—liberals in their hopes, realists in their expectations. All strongly opposed the American invasion of Iraq in 2003, and none had truck with the neo-Wilsonian arguments (especially with those concerning "the universal appeal of democracy" and the alleged "winds and arcs of history") that became the conventional wisdom in so many liberal circles after the mid-1990s. With Wilson, these three academics understood that unless thinking about international relations were to be combined with a steady grip on the domestic realities of those peoples and states engaged in the world arena, nothing positive could be accomplished. They also grasped the danger to democracy itself in the United States should mindless imperialism come to rule the day.

Let me end on the customary note that none of these friends and colleagues is necessarily in agreement with the conclusions I reached here. In many cases, rather the contrary is true, although I hope that my argument, now spelled out in detail, persuades them of the originality and strength of Wilson's worldview, as well as the distance between what I call "classical" international liberalism (with Wilson) and its "hegemonic" stage (during the cold war), contrasted with the renegade "neo-Wilsonians" who emerged in the 1990s and whose utopian-imperialist practices put their thinking and policies in direct contradiction to the mainstream of the liberal tradition from Wilson's time to the 1980s.

Most of all, I appreciate the support of my husband, José-David Ovalle-Diaz. His patience came in good part thanks to the distractions of his grand-children, Aurelia and Allen, his nephews, Samuel and Daniel, as well as his nieces, Andrea and Alejandra. It is a pleasure to dedicate another work to him, *de todo corazon*, as an expression of my appreciation for our many happy years together.

Notes

PREFACE

1. For this fact, plus other measurements of the ignorance of the American public on basic affairs of state, see Michael J. Glennon, *National Security and Double Government*, Oxford: Oxford University Press, 2015, 8f.
2. The most influential attacks on Wilson from these early years include Edward Hallett Carr, *The Twenty Years' Crisis, 1919–1939: An Introduction to the Study of International Relations*, first published in 1939, then rewritten by Carr, but best studied in the edition edited by Michael Cox, New York, Palgrave, 2001; Walter Lippmann, *U.S. War Aims*, Boston: Little Brown, 1944; George F. Kennan, *American Diplomacy*, Chicago: University of Chicago Press, 1951; Hans J. Morgenthau, *In Defense of the National Interest: A Critical Examination of American Foreign Policy*, New York: Knopf, 1951.
3. John Milton Cooper Jr. and Thomas Knock, eds., *Jefferson, Lincoln, and Wilson: The American Dilemma of Race and Democracy*, Charlottesville: University of Virginia Press, 2010; Editorial Board, "The Case Against Woodrow Wilson at Princeton," *New York Times*, November 24, 2015.
4. Naoko Shimazu, *Japan, Race, and Equality: The Racial Equality Proposal of 1919*, New York: Routledge, 1998, 7, 161f; Margaret Macmillan, *Paris 1919: Six Months That Changed the World*, New York: Random House, 2002, 316ff, with remarks on China, 336ff, and on African Americans, 319; Erez Manela, *The Wilsonian Moment: Self-Determination and the International Origins of Anticolonial Nationalism*, New York: Oxford University Press, 2007.
5. My comments can be found in the 1994 edition of *America's Mission: The United States and the Worldwide Struggle for Democracy*, Princeton, NJ: Princeton University Press, 1994, republished in an expanded version in 2012, 11–12, 338–45.
6. See, among other comparative studies, Tony Smith, "Requiem or New Agenda for Third World Studies?" *World Politics*, July 1985, reprinted several times, including in a collection of leading articles that appeared in *World Politics* by Samuel Huntington, Robert Putnam, Gabriel Almond, David Easton, and Ted Gurr, edited by Ikuo Kabashima and Lynn T. White III, and titled *Political System and Change*, Princeton, NJ: Princeton University Press, 1986. See also Smith, "The Underdevelopment of Development Literature: The Case of Dependency Theory," *World Politics*, January 1979; "A Comparative Study of French and British Decolonization," *Comparative Studies in Society and History*, Winter 1977.

INTRODUCTION. KNOW THYSELF: WHAT IS "WILSONIANISM"?

1. Reinhold Niebuhr, *The Irony of American History*, Chicago: University of Chicago Press, 1952, chap. 4.

2. Ibid.
3. See, for example, Barry R. Posen, *Restraint: A New Foundation for U.S. Grand Strategy*, Ithaca, NY: Cornell University Press, 2014; Christopher Layne, *The Peace of Illusions: American Grand Strategy from 1940 to the Present*, Ithaca, NY: Cornell University Press, 2006.
4. John A. Thompson, "Wilsonianism: The Dynamics of a Conflicted Concept," *International Affairs* 86, no. 1, 2010; Stephen Wertheim, "The Wilsonian Chimera: Why Debating Wilson's Vision Hasn't Saved American Foreign Relations," *White House Studies* 10, no. 4, 2011; Thomas Knock, "Playing for a Hundred Years Hence," in G. John Ikenberry, Anne-Marie Slaughter, Thomas Knock, and Tony Smith, *The Crisis of American Foreign Policy: Wilsonianism in the Twenty-first Century*, Princeton, NJ: Princeton University Press, 2009.
5. Ikenberry et al., *The Crisis of American Foreign Policy*, Princeton, NJ: Princeton University Press, 2009.
6. Citation from *New York Times*, "At Site of 'Iron Curtain' Speech, Gorbachev Buries the Cold War," May 7, 1992. For an extended discussion, see Tony Smith, "American Liberalism and Soviet 'New Thinking'," in Pierre Melandri and Serge Ricard, eds., *Les Etats-Unis et la fin de la guerre froide*, Paris: Harmattan, 2005.
7. Henry Kissinger, *World Order*, New York: Penguin, 2014, 262ff. See, for later examples of explicit statements endorsing American exceptionalism in these terms, President Barack Obama at the West Point commencement on May 28, 2014, and in Warsaw, Poland, on July 9, 2014. For citations throughout this book from speeches or talks given by American presidents, the preferred place for follow-up reading today is the *Public Papers of the Presidents* published by the Federal Register, National Archives and Records Administration, http://www.archives.gov/federal-register/publications/presidential-papers.html. An alternative, related site is the American Presidency Project, http://www.presidency.ucsb.edu/. Presidential statements are exhaustive, authoritative, and arranged for easy access by name and exact date.
8. "Defensive Realism" is a theoretical approach that tries to take account of regime type, yet it is not a dominant theme in Realism but represents something of an intellectual heresy to Realist purists.
9. The work most often cited on Constructivism is Alexander Wendt, *Social Theory of International Politics*, New York: Cambridge University Press, 1999.
10. Other presidents were more selectively liberal, such as John F. Kennedy with the Alliance for Progress, Jimmy Carter with his human rights crusade, and George H. W. Bush in his policies toward the former Soviet empire and Soviet Union after 1991. Occupation policies toward Japan and Germany after 1945 are obviously the most successful examples of liberal internationalist practice. For a more lengthy discussion, see chapter five.
11. Tony Smith, *America's Mission: The United States and the Worldwide Struggle for Democracy*, Princeton, NJ: Princeton University Press, exp. ed., 2012, chap. 13.
12. By the beginning of 1912, Wilson was linking his recognition that the United States must leave isolation to a greater appreciation of the country's need for an increase in international commerce. See Harley Notter, *The Origins of the Foreign Policy of Woodrow Wilson*, Baltimore, MD: Johns Hopkins University Press, 1927, 182ff, 230ff, 267f.
13. See, for example, Robert O. Keohane and Joseph S. Nye, *Power and Interdependence*, 4th ed., Boston: Longman, 2011 (1st ed., 1977); and John Gerard Ruggie, ed., *Multilateralism Matters: The Theory and Praxis of an Institutional Form*, New York: Columbia University Press, 1993.
14. See, Anne-Marie Slaughter, "Wilsonianism in the Twenty-first Century," and

Thomas Knock, "Playing for a Hundred Years Hence," in Ikenberry et al., *The Crisis of American Foreign Policy.*

15. This is suggested by Samuel P. Huntington, *The Clash of Civilizations and the Remaking of World Order*, New York: Simon and Schuster, 1996.

16. A particularly strong assertion of this claim is Robert Kagan, *The World America Made*, New York: Knopf, 2012.

17. Woodrow Wilson, *The State: Elements of Historical and Practical Politics*, Boston: D. C. Heath, 1889, 659, and the revised edition of 1911, 632f.

18. Arthur Link et al., eds., *The Papers of Woodrow Wilson [PWW]*, 69 vols., Princeton, NJ: Princeton University Press, 1966–1994, 22, 12/27/1910, 268, 270. Also Woodrow Wilson, *Constitutional Government in the United States*, New York: Columbia University Press, 1908, chap. 3; citations throughout this book are from the 1921 edition with an interesting preface by Walter Lippmann, 268ff. The book is reprinted in *PWW*, 18, 3/24/1908, 69ff.

19. *PWW*, 28, 10/27/1913, emphasis added.

20. *PWW*, 30, 6/1914, 231ff. See also Arthur S. Link, *Wilson: The New Freedom*, Princeton, NJ: Princeton University Press, 1959, 337f.

21. Ibid.

22. *PWW*, 68, 7/1923, 394f.

23. Princeton Report, "Forging a World of Liberty Under Law," Princeton Project on National Security, September 27, 2006; John McCain, "An Enduring Peace Built on Freedom," *Foreign Affairs*, November-December, 2007.

24. Walter McDougall, *Promised Land, Crusader State: The American Encounter with the World Since 1776*, Boston: Houghton Mifflin, 1997, chap. 6, tellingly entitled "Wilsonianism, or Liberal Internationalism (so called)." That his argument is virtually absent of any analysis of Wilson's own writings is typical of a vast literature that asserts without evidence an important criticism without foundation. The list of writers who charge Wilson with being "messianic" defies counting. For recent examples, see Perry Anderson, *American Foreign Policy and Its Thinkers*, London: Verso, 2015, 8f, who has Wilson at the origins of an American "messianic pitch," and Michael Ignatieff, who agrees, although calling himself a "dyed-in-the-wool liberal," in "Messianic America," *New York Review of Books*, November 19, 2015. In contrast, see John Milton Cooper Jr., "Wilson Revisited: Making a Case for Wilson," in Cooper, ed., *Reconsidering Woodrow Wilson: Progressivism, Internationalism, War and Peace*, Washington, DC: Woodrow Wilson Center Press, 2008.

25. Wilson, "Leaders of Men," *PWW*, 6, 6/1890, 646ff; see John Milton Cooper Jr., *Woodrow Wilson: A Biography*, New York: Knopf, 2009, who repeatedly emphasizes Wilson's avoidance of abstract theory. See also Wilson's comments on Edmund Burke, whose "generalizations are never derived from abstract premises. The reasoning is upon familiar matter of today. . . . He is not constructing systems of thought but simply stripping thought of its accidental features. He is even deeply impatient of abstractions in political reasoning, so passionately is he devoted to what is practicable and fit for wise men to do. . . . [Yet he had a broad philosophy of politics but not a] system of political philosophy. He was afraid of abstract system in political thought, for he perceived that questions of government are moral questions, and that questions of morals cannot always be squared with the rules of logic, but run through as many ranges of variety as the circumstances of life itself. . . . And yet Burke unquestionably had a very definite and determinable system of thought, which was none the less a system for being based upon concrete, and not upon abstract premises." In a word, what both Wilson and Burke despised was "utopian thought." *PWW*, 8, 9/1893, 328.

298 – NOTES TO CHAPTER 1

26. *PWW*, 5, 12/1/1885, 55, emphasis added.
27. Woodrow Wilson, "Princeton in the Nation's Service," *PWW*, 10, 10/1896.
28. *PWW*, 5, 58. See, in a similar judgment, Niels Aage Thorsen, *The Political Thought of Woodrow Wilson, 1875–1910*, Princeton, NJ: Princeton University Press, 1988.
29. There are exceptions, such as John A. Thompson, *Woodrow Wilson*, New York: Longman, 2002.
30. Woodrow Wilson, "Abraham Lincoln," in *Atlantic Monthly*, *PWW*, 8, 10/1893, 295. Nearly a century later, Henry Kissinger made much the same observation: "It is an illusion to believe that leaders gain in profundity while they gain experience. The convictions that leaders have formed before reaching high office are the intellectual capital they will consume as long as they continue in office. There is little time for leaders to reflect. They are locked in an endless battle in which the urgent constantly gains on the important. The public life of every political figure is a continual struggle to rescue an element of choice from the pressure of circumstance." Henry Kissinger, *White House Years*, Boston: Little, Brown, 1979, 54.

CHAPTER 1. WOODROW WILSON
ON DEMOCRACY PROMOTION IN AMERICA

1. Arthur Link et al., eds., *The Papers of Woodrow Wilson [PWW]*, 69 vols., Princeton, NJ: Princeton University Press, 1966–1994, 12, "The Real Idea of Democracy," 8/1901, 176–78. For a discussion of the tensions and the evolution of Wilson's thinking with respect to society and the state, see John M. Mulder, *Woodrow Wilson: The Years of Preparation*, Princeton, NJ: Princeton University Press, 1978, chap. 5.
2. On Marxist thought, see Tony Smith, *Thinking Like a Communist: State and Legitimacy in the Soviet Union, China, and Cuba*, New York: W. W. Norton, 1987, introduction and chap. 1.
3. *PWW*, 5, 12/1/1885, 70, emphasis added.
4. *PWW*, 7, "A Lecture on Democracy," 12/1891.
5. *PWW*, 5, "The Modern Democratic State," 1885. In his study *Woodrow Wilson: A Biography*, New York: Knopf, 2009, 81, 385, John Milton Cooper Jr. repeatedly describes Wilson's ambitious personality, writing of his "incorrigibly activist temperament. Presented with alternatives he almost always chose the path of boldness"; and Cooper notes Wilson's "penchant for bold action; in situations where he had a choice, he nearly always picked the grander, riskier course."
6. *PWW*, 10, "Princeton in the Nation's Service," 10/1896. On Witherspoon, see also A. Scott Berg, *Wilson*, New York: G. P. Putnam's Sons, 2013, 53ff.
7. *PWW*, 5, 1885, 65, and *PWW*, 63, 9/9/1919, 147.
8. Woodrow Wilson, *Congressional Government: A Study in American Politics*, Boston: Houghton Mifflin, 1885; Wilson, *The State: Elements of Historical and Practical Politics*, Boston: D. C. Heath, 1889; *A History of the American People* (5 vols.), New York: Harper and Brothers, 1902; Wilson, *Constitutional Government in the United States*, New York: Columbia University Press, 1908; "The Study of Administration, " *Political Science Quarterly* 2, no. 2, 1897; and a series of articles of which the most important for our purposes are those on democracy: "The Modern Democratic State" (unpublished, *PWW*, 5, 1/12/1885); "A Lecture on Democracy" (*PWW*, 7, 12/1891); "Democracy and Efficiency" (*PWW*, 12, 10/1900); "The Real Idea of Democracy" (*PWW*, 12, 8/1901); "The Ideals of America" (*PWW*, 12, 12/1901); and "On Edmund Burke," *PWW*, 8, 9/1893, as well as, especially, two speeches, "On Leaders of Men" (*PWW*, 6, 6/1890) and "Princeton in the Nation's Service" (*PWW*, 10, 10/1896).

9. For the background of his ambition, see Woodrow Wilson, *The New Freedom: A Call for the Emancipation of the Generous Energies of a People*, New York: Double-day, Page, 1913.
10. John Milton Cooper Jr., in "Wilson Revisited: Making a Case for Wilson," in Cooper, ed., *Reconsidering Woodrow Wilson: Progressivism, Internationalism, War and Peace*, Baltimore, MD: Johns Hopkins University Press, 2009, 13.
11. Woodrow Wilson, *The State: Elements of Historical and Practical Politics*, Boston: D. C. Heath, publisher of every edition from 1889 through 1911. The 1918 edition was extensively revised with work added by Wilson's brother-in-law.
12. Jack Scott, ed., *An Annotated Edition of Lectures on Moral Philosophy*, Dover: University of Delaware Press, 1982. For parallels with Wilson, see *Constitutional Government*; the recommended edition, with a useful preface by Walter Lippmann, is New York: Columbia University Press, 1921, 18f, 23. The book is also reprinted in *PWW*, 18, 3/24/1908.
13. *PWW*, 12, "Democracy and Efficiency," 10/1900, 388, printed in *Atlantic Monthly*, March 1901.
14. *PWW*, 7, "A Lecture on Democracy," 12/1891, 358.
15. *Constitutional Government*, chap. 3, 1908, in the cited edition with an introduction by Walter Lippmann, 1921. Or find in *PWW*, 18, 3/24/1908, 69ff. For interesting reading on debates about elitist leadership in the United States in the late eighteenth century, see Eric Nelson, *The Royalist Revolution: Monarchy and the American Founding*, Cambridge, MA: Harvard University Press, 2015.
16. *The State*, 1911; *Constitutional Government*, 1921 edition, 18ff, or find in *PWW*, 18, 3/24/1908.
17. *PWW*, 22, "The Law and the Facts," 12/27/1910, 263. On law, see also Wilson in *The State*, 1889 and 1911, chap. 14.
18. *PWW*, 7, "Lecture on Democracy," 12/1891, 363f.
19. *PWW*, 5, "The Modern Democratic State," 1885, emphasis added.
20. *Constitutional Government*, 1921 edition, 8f. or find in *PWW*, 18, 3/24/1908.
21. Ibid., 357 (emphasis in original). See also John A. Thompson, "Woodrow Wilson and a World Governed by Evolving Law," *Journal of Political History*, 20, 1, 2008.
22. *Constitutional Government*, 45. Or, as Wilson saluted Daniel Webster for his efforts a full generation later (1782–1852), "He called the nation into being. What he said had the immortal quality of words which almost create the thoughts they speak. The nation lay as it were unconscious of its unity and purpose and he called it into full consciousness. It could never again be anything less than what he had said it was. It is at such moments and in the mouths of such interpreters that nations spring from age to age in their development." Ibid., 33.
23. Ibid., 3. Wilson offers a shorthand version of his conception of the stages of history and the role of the organic spirit of the population therein. "A first stage in which the government was master, the people veritable subjects; a second in which the government, ceasing to be master by virtue of sheer force and unquestioned authority, remained master by virtue of its insight and sagacity, its readiness and fitness to lead; a third in which both sorts of mastery failed it and it found itself face to face with leaders of the people who were bent upon controlling it, a period of deep agitation and full of the signs of change; and a fourth in which the leaders of the people themselves became the government, and the development was complete."
24. *PWW*, 5, "The Modern Democratic State," 74f, emphasis added.
25. On patriotism, see *PWW*, 12, 1901, 475, 35, 321.
26. *Constitutional Government*, 1921 edition, 25, or find in *PWW*, 18, 3/24/1908.

27. Wilson, "The Real Idea of Democracy," *PWW*, 12, 8/1901, 176–78. Also, Mulder, *Woodrow Wilson*, chap. 5.
28. *The State*, chap. 14.
29. All citations from *PWW*, 6, "Leaders of Men," 6/1890. In a similar manner, Wilson wrote in the *The State*, 1911, chap. xiv: "there is always a social basis to rule that constricts the elite." Thus, "No 'law-maker' may force upon a people Law which has not in some sense been suggested to him by the circumstances or opinions of the nation for whom he acts." For example, Roman law was the will of the Roman people and thus a fundamental aspect of Roman rule even if the land were not democratic. For an insightful account of Burke's thinking, see David Bromwich, *The Intellectual Life of Edmund Burke: From the Sublime and Beautiful to American Independence*, Cambridge, MA: Belknap Press of Harvard University Press, 2014.
30. *Constitutional Government*, 1921 edition, 4f.
31. *PWW*, 12, "Democracy and Efficiency," 10/1900, 16.
32. *Constitutional Government*, 1921 edition, 4; see also *The State*, 69.
33. *PWW*, 5, "The Modern Democratic State," 69.
34. *Constitutional Government*, 1921 edition, 51–57.
35. The Presbyterian Church publishes a *Book of Order* at regular intervals. But it is instructive to consult one that Wilson himself might well have used, published in Richmond, VA, in 1876, available online thanks to Google.
36. Richard Niebuhr, "The Idea of Covenant and American Democracy," *Church History* 23, no. 2, June 1954.
37. *Constitutional Government*, 1921 edition, 4f, 22f. Classic writings on Calvinist thought and covenanting remain those by Perry Miller (d. 1963)—for example, *Errand Into the Wilderness*, Cambridge, MA: Harvard University Press, 1956. See as well the interesting work by John Witte, *The Reformation of Rights: Law, Religion, and Human Rights in Early Modern Calvinism*, New York: Cambridge University Press, 2007.
38. Among the many references by Wilson to the political importance of his faith, see his Address in Denver on the Bible (to which 12,000 came), *PWW*, 23, 5/7/1911; his Campaign Address in Jersey City, *PWW*, 24, 5/25/1912; and his Remarks to the Gridiron Club, *PWW*, 35, 12/11/1915, 35. See also Mulder, *Woodrow Wilson*, especially 97ff; Malcolm D. Magee, *What the World Should Be: Woodrow Wilson and the Crafting of a Faith-Based Foreign Policy*, Waco, TX: Baylor University Press, 2008, and Milan Babik, *Statecraft and Salvation: Wilsonian Liberal Internationalism as Secularized Eschatology*, Waco, TX: Baylor University Press, 2013.
39. *PWW*, 63, 9/6/ 1919, 75. A fruitful area for future research would surely be the way in which mainstream Protestant missionary movements from the mid-19th century promoted not so much Christianity as constitutionalism in their important educational institutions abroad, including the American University in Cairo and in Beirut, as well as significant establishments in Iran and Turkey. An example of one useful study is Betty S. Anderson, *The American University of Beirut: Arab Nationalism and Liberal Education*, Austin: University of Texas Press, 2011.
40. *PWW*, 1, 9/1879, 515ff.
41. *PWW*, 5, "The Modern Democratic State," 67.
42. Ibid., 67.
43. *PWW*, 10, "Princeton in the Nation's Service," 10/1896.
44. *PWW*, 5, "Modern Democratic Government," 11/1885.
45. *PWW*, 12, "The Ideals of America," 12/1901.

46. *Constitutional Government*, 1921 edition, 25, 51; also *PWW*, 8, 316.
47. *PWW*, 8, "Edmund Burke: The Man and His Times," 9/1893, 318ff.
48. *PWW*, 68, "Plans and Notes for a Book," 5/1922. For a pertinent update on Wilson's charges (with no mention of him), see Mark Lilla, "The Strangely Conservative French," in a review of Sudhir Hazareesingh, *How the French Think: An Affectionate Portrait of an Intellectual People*, in *New York Review of Books*, October 22, 2015. Both writers date the eventual emergence of Anglo-American thinking in France to the 1980s, under the influence of writers like Raymond Aron and Francois Furet.
49. *PWW*, 5, "The Modern Democratic State," 63.
50. *Constitutional Government*, 1921 edition, 25f, or find in *PWW*, 18, 3/24/1908.
51. *The State*, section 1160 of the 1889 edition; section 1393 of the 1911 edition.
52. *The State*, 1911, 555.
53. Ibid., 639. The same statement is present in *The State* in the 1889 edition.

CHAPTER 2. DEMOCRACY PROMOTION THROUGH PROGRESSIVE IMPERIALISM

1. Adam Quinn, "Theodore Roosevelt," in Michael Cox et al., *US Foreign Policy and Democracy Promotion: From Theodore Roosevelt to Barack Obama*, New York: Routledge, Taylor & Francis, 2013.
2. See, especially, Philip Gleason, "American Identity and Americanization," in Stephan Thernstrom, ed., *Harvard Encyclopedia of America Ethnic Groups*, Cambridge, MA: Harvard University Press, 1980, 31ff. For accounts I find less persuasive because of their insistence on race or religion as being of overriding importance in American foreign policy, see Reginald Horsman, *Race and Manifest Destiny: The Origins of American Racial Anglo-Saxonism*, Cambridge, MA: Harvard University Press, 1981; Matthew Frye Jacobson, *Barbarian Virtues: The United States Encounters Foreign Peoples at Home and Abroad, 1876–1917*, New York: Hill and Wang, 2000; Michael H. Hunt, *Ideology and U.S. Foreign Policy*, New Haven, CT: Yale University Press, 1987.
3. Arthur Link et al., eds., *The Papers of Woodrow Wilson [PWW]*, 69 vols., Princeton, NJ: Princeton University Press, 1966–1994, 15, 11/1895, 53.
4. And Wilson continues: "The force of modern governments is not often the force of minorities. The sanction of every rule not founded on sheer military despotism is the consent of thinking peoples. Military despotisms are now seen to be necessarily ephemeral. . . . Monarchies exist only by democratic consent . . . the result has been to give to society a new integration. . . . Society is not the unity it once was—its members are given freer play, fuller opportunity for origination. . . . It is the Whole which has emerged from the disintegration of feudalism and the specialization of absolute monarchy. The Whole, too, has become self-conscious and by becoming self-directive has set out upon a new course of development." *The State: Elements of Historical and Practical Politics*; in both the 1889 and 1911 editions these statements appear with only a slight change in the wording. In both editions, see chap. 13, "The Nature and Forms of Government."
5. *PWW*, 7, "Lecture on Democracy," 12/ 1891, 348ff.
6. *PWW*, 5, "The Modern Democratic State," 1/12/1885, 90.
7. *PWW*, 12, "Democracy and Efficiency," 10/1900.
8. John Milton Cooper Jr. recounts Wilson's enthusiasm as early as when conflict opened in 1898, in *Woodrow Wilson: A Biography*, New York: Knopf, 2009, 74ff.
9. *PWW*, 12, "Democracy and Efficiency," 10/1900.
10. Ibid.

11. Ibid.
12. *PWW*, 12, "The Ideals of America," 12/26/1901.
13. Ibid.
14. Wilson, as recorded by Ray Stannard Baker, October 13, 1910, cited in Harley Notter, *The Origins of the Foreign Policy of Woodrow Wilson*, Baltimore, MD: Johns Hopkins University Press, 1937, 171; also found in *PWW*, 21, 317.
15. Cooper, *Woodrow Wilson: A Biography*, 76.
16. *PWW*, 12, "The Ideals of America," 12/26/1901.
17. *PWW*, 29, 12/1913, 8f.
18. *PWW*, 66, 12/1920, 490.
19. Enrique Krauze, *Mexico: Biography of Power. A History of Modern Mexico, 1810–1996*, New York: HarperCollins, 1997, 246–47, 264.
20. Buchanan, cited in Howard F. Cline, *The United States and Mexico*, Cambridge, MA: Harvard University Press, rev. ed., 1963, 141.
21. I thank John Milton Cooper for his comments on the British practice of diplomatic recognition.
22. Arthur Link, *Wilson: The New Freedom*, Princeton, NJ: Princeton University Press, 1959, 379.
23. *PWW*, 28, 10/1913, 481.
24. Link, *Wilson: The New Freedom*, chaps. 11–12, 386f. Link did not reprint the Circular Note, dated November 24, 1913, in his collection of presidential papers. The terms correspond closely, however, to drafts of such a note and to President Wilson's words addressing the Congress.
25. *PWW*, 29, 12/1913, 4.
26. E. Victor Niemeyer, *Revolution at Queretaro: The Mexican Constitutional Convention, 1916–1917*, Austin: University of Texas Press, 1974; and *The Political Constitution of the Mexican United States*, translated by Carlos Perez Vasquez, Mexico City: Universidad Autonoma de Mexico, 2003.
27. I thank Will Freeman, a student of the Mexican Revolution, for his insistence on this point. See also Lucas N. Frank, "Playing with Fire: Woodrow Wilson, Self-Determination, Democracy and Revolution in Mexico," *The Historian*, 76, 1, 2014.
28. Citation in Ray Stannard Baker and William E. Dodd, *The New Democracy: Presidential Messages, Addresses and Other Papers, 1913–1917*, New York: Harper and Brothers, 1926, reprinted in Krauze, *Mexico*, 111f. See also *PWW*, 29, 516ff; Link dates the interview as April 27, 1914.
29. Memo of Ray Stannard Baker, "A Talk with the President," *PWW*, 37, May 12, 1916, 36. See also Arthur Link, *Wilson: Campaigns for Progressivism and Peace, 1916–1917*, Princeton, NJ: Princeton University Press, 1965, 336ff.
30. On planning, *PWW*, 28, 10/1913, 476ff and 585f; Wilson's note is in *PWW*, 30, 8/1914, 362.
31. John Reed in *PWW*, 30, 6/1914, 231ff.
32. Arthur S. Link, *Wilson: The Struggle for Neutrality, 1914–1915*, Princeton, NJ: Princeton University Press, 1960, 459.
33. For a more extended discussion, see Tony Smith, *America's Mission: The United States and the Worldwide Struggle for Democracy*, Princeton, NJ: Princeton University Press, expanded ed., 2012, chap. 2.
34. Howard F. Cline, *The United States and Mexico*, Cambridge, MA: Harvard University Press, 1953, 141. On Wilson in Mexico, see also Arthur S. Link, *Woodrow Wilson and the World of Today*, Philadelphia: University of Pennsylvania Press, 1957, chaps. 10–12.
35. Smith, *America's Mission*, n. 33, 71ff, 76ff. Bruce Calder, *The Impact of Interven-*

tion: The Dominican Republic During the U.S. Occupation of 1916–1924, Austin: University of Texas Press, 1984.

36. Link, *Wilson: The Struggle for Neutrality*, 501, but see all of chap. 15.
37. Ibid., 512.
38. Ibid., 513f; on a similar *pronunciamientio* to Haitian leaders, see 535ff.
39. *PWW*, 53, 685f.
40. *PWW*, 54, 457.
41. David Hunter Miller, *The Drafting of the Covenant*, 2 vols., New York: G. P. Putnam's Sons, 1928, vol. 2, documents 7 and 14, 151ff.
42. David Fromkin, *A Peace to End All Peace: The Fall of the Ottoman Empire and the Creation of the Modern Middle East*, New York: Henry Holt, 1989. For a close study of the League and the mandates, see Susan Pedersen, *The Guardians: The League of Nations and the Crisis of Empire*, New York: Oxford University Press, 2015.
43. 66th Congress 2nd Session, House of Representatives, Document 791. The San Remo Conference, held in April 1920, determined the authority of the Allied powers in those domains now freed from Turkish rule under the terms of the peace settlement arrived at in Paris a year earlier. The United States was not present at this meeting. See also Lloyd Ambrosius, "Wilsonian Diplomacy and Armenia: The Limits of Power and Ideology," in Jay M. Winter, ed., *The American Response to the Armenian Genocide*, New York: Cambridge University Press, 2003.
44. For the context of these deliberations, see Thomas Knock, *To End All Wars: Woodrow Wilson and the Quest for a New World Order*, New York: Oxford University Press, 1992, 39ff, 81ff; also Ross Kennedy, *The Will to Believe: Woodrow Wilson, World War I, and America's Strategy for Peace and Security*, Ohio: Kent State University Press, 2009, chap. 3. For Wilson's important address in Mobile of October 1913, consider especially his words, "It is a spiritual union which we seek. . . . I mean the development of constitutional liberty in the world. Human rights, national integrity and opportunity as against material interest. What is at the heart of all our national problems? It is that we have seen the hand of material interest sometimes about to close upon our dearest rights and possessions. We have seen material interests threaten constitutional freedom in the United States." *PWW*, 10/27/1913.
45. *PWW*, 37, 6/18/1916, Edward Mandell House, 265.
46. *PWW*, 35, 10/26/1915, 111f.
47. Ibid., 11/11/1915, 188; *PWW*, 37, 6/17/1916, 241ff.
48. Knock, *To End All Wars*, 39ff.

CHAPTER 3. DEMOCRACY PROMOTION
THROUGH MULTILATERALISM

1. David C. Hendrickson, *Union, Nation, or Empire: The American Debate over International Relations, 1769–1941*, Lawrence: University of Kansas Press, 2009, chaps. 37–39, especially 306ff; John A. Thompson, *A Sense of Power: The Roots of America's Global Role*, Ithaca, NY: Cornell University Press, 2015, chap. 2.
2. Lloyd C. Gardner, *Safe for Democracy: The Anglo-American Response to Revolution, 1913–1923*, New York: Oxford University Press, 1984, 104ff.
3. The idea of something like the League long predated Wilson's interest, to be sure, and its actual creation represented the thinking of many men besides him. John Milton Cooper Jr. notes that Theodore Roosevelt suggested a League of Peace as early as May 1910 in *Breaking the Heart of the World: Woodrow Wilson*

and the Fight for the League of Nations, New York: Cambridge University Press, 2001, 11 and chap. 1.

4. Arthur S. Link et al., eds., *The Papers of Woodrow Wilson [PWW]*, 69 vols., Princeton, NJ: Princeton University Press, 1966–1994, 55, 2/14/1919, 175.

5. See the discussion by John Milton Cooper Jr., "Wilson Revisited: Making a Case for Wilson," in Cooper, ed., *Reconsidering Woodrow Wilson: Progressivism, Internationalism, War and Peace*, Washington, DC: Woodrow Wilson Center Press, 2008; also John A. Thompson, "Woodrow Wilson," in Michael Cox et al., eds., *U.S. Foreign Policy and Democracy Promotion: From Theodore Roosevelt to Barack Obama*, New York: Routledge, Taylor & Francis, 2013.

6. On Wilson's sense of disagreement with France and the United Kingdom, see, for example, *PWW*, 43, 7/21/1917, 237f.

7. Michael Desch writes that Wilson might well have become acquainted with Kantian thought through his contacts with the philosophy department at Harvard University. I have been able to confirm through members of this department today that it was fully under the control of Kantians during the time Wilson made visits there, so it is indeed possible that even if he had not read Kant, he was familiar with his ideas. See Michael C. Desch, "America's Liberal Illiberalism: The Ideological Origins of Overreaction in U.S. Foreign Policy," *International Security* 32, no. 3, Winter 2007/08, 12, n. 19. In a message to me on May 2015, however, John Milton Cooper Jr. doubted this influence given Wilson's typical practice of noting the record of the thinking of others on his own and his silence on Kant.

8. *PWW*, 63, 9/1919, 132f.

9. *PWW*, 63, 9/9/19, 145. Wilson's distinction among autocracies is similar to that made by John Rawls, *The Law of Peoples*, Cambridge, MA: Harvard University Press, 1999, chap. 5. See also Wilson's reflections on the minor role Germany's allies played in the war. Thus, "Austria-Hungary is for the time being not her own mistress, but simply the vassal of the German Government." He also depicted Turkey and Bulgaria as "tools of Germany." *PWW*, 45, 12/4/1917; *PWW*, 63, 1919, 200.

10. Article 17 as finally adopted reads: "In the event of a dispute between a Member of the League and a State which is not a Member of the League, or between States not Members of the League, the State or States not Members of the League shall be invited to accept the obligations of membership in the League for the purposes of such dispute, upon such conditions as the Council may deem just. If such invitation is accepted, the provisions of Articles 12 to 16 inclusive shall be applied with such modifications as may be deemed necessary by the Council.

    Upon such invitation being given the Council shall immediately institute an inquiry into the circumstances of the dispute and recommend such action as may seem best and most effectual in the circumstances.

    If a State so invited shall refuse to accept the obligations of membership in the League for the purposes of such dispute, and shall resort to war against a Member of the League, the provisions of Article 16 shall be applicable as against the State taking such action." Article 16 lists the measures to be taken, including warfare.

11. *PWW*, 47, 4/6/1918, 267ff.

12. *PWW*, 63, 9/8/1919, 11.

13. *PWW*, 63, 7/4/1918, 516f, emphasis added.

14. *PWW*, 55, 2/1919, 135f.

15. *PWW*, 63, 9/9/1919, 134.

16. Ibid., 9/8/1919, 108.

17. Ibid., St. Louis, 46f, a point of view he repeated in Sioux Falls, 112, and St. Paul,

144. For an elaboration of this point and a cogent, composite review of the Western Tour, see Thomas J. Knock, *To End All Wars: Woodrow Wilson and the Quest for a New World Order*, New York: Oxford University Press, 1992, 261. See also Michael Lind, *The American Way of Strategy*, New York: Oxford University Press, 206, 94.

18. Ibid., *PWW*, 9, 6/1919, 76; for Wilson on the oppressive imperialism of the Austro-Hungarian empire, see 9/4/1919, 9f.

19. *PWW*, Address to the Senate, 61, 7/10/1919, 429f.

20. Ibid., 9/1919, 372. As Wilson put it in July 1919, the League "meant that new nations were to be created—Poland, Czechoslovakia, Hungary itself." To these he added Bohemia and the Slavs under Austrian control. Under imperial rule "these were all arrangements of power, not arrangements of natural union or association. It was the imperative task of those who would make peace . . . to establish a new order which would rest upon the free choice of peoples rather than upon the arbitrary authority of Hapsburgs or Hohenzollerns." So too the Turkish Empire "had never had any real unity. It had been held together only by pitiless, inhuman force. Its people cried aloud for release, for succor from unspeakable distress, for all that the new day of hope seemed at last to bring within its dawn. Peoples hitherto in utter darkness were to be led out into the same light and given at last a helping hand. . . . And out of the execution of these great enterprises of liberty sprang . . . an opportunity to throw safeguards about the rights of racial, national and religious minorities by solemn international covenant . . . [for which] a league of free nations had become a practical necessity." See also Derek Benjamin Heater, *National Self-Determination: Woodrow Wilson and His Legacy*, New York: St. Martin's Press, 1994, especially chaps. 3 and 4.

21. *PWW*, 9/10/1919, 154. Or again in Columbus, OH, "Revolutions don't spring up overnight. Revolutions gather through the ages; revolutions come from the long suppression of the human spirit. Revolutions come because people know that they have rights and that they are disregarded. [A chief effort of the League is] to remove that anger from the heart of great peoples. . . . And the makers of the treaty knew that if these wrongs were not removed, there could be no peace in the world, because, after all, my fellow citizens, war comes from the seed of wrong and not from the seed of right. This treaty is an attempt to right the history of Europe." *PWW*, 63, 9/4/ 1919.

22. *PWW*, 45, 11/12/1917. Or, as he phrased it in September 1919: "Is there any man here or any woman, let me say is there any child here, who does not know that the seed for war in the modern world is industrial and commercial rivalry? The real reason that the war we have just finished took place was that Germany was afraid that her commercial rivals were going to get the better of her. . . . The seed of the jealousy, the seed of deep-seated hatred was hot, successful commercial and industrial rivalry." *PWW*, 63, 9/4/1919.

23. *PWW*, 40, 1/22/1917, 535ff.

24. *PWW*, 37, 5/27/1916, 114f.

25. In his speech in Pueblo, Colorado, on September 25, 1919, Wilson reminded his audience in his closing words of this speech to the Congress in April 1917, which concluded: "It is a fearful thing to lead this great peaceful people into war, into the most terrible and disastrous of all wars, civilization itself seeming to be in the balance. But the right is more precious than peace and we shall fight for the things which we have always carried nearest our hearts—for democracy, for the right of those who submit to authority to have a voice in their own governments, for the rights and liberties of small nations, for a universal dominion of right by such a

concert of free peoples as shall bring peace and safety to all nations and make the world itself at last free." *PWW*, 63, 9/25/1919.

26. Allowance should be made for inconsistency in Wilson's use of the term, nonetheless. For example, on September 4, 1919, he stated flatly, "Germany was self-governed" (*PWW*, 63, 9/4/1919, 8). The trouble was that power was concentrated and the people deceived. As already cited in chapter one, however, and more consistent with his thinking, Wilson found that the United States "is a country not merely constitutionally governed, but also self-governed. Self-government is the last, the consummate stage of constitutional development. . . . Self-government is not a mere form of institutions. . . . It is a form of character. . . . [Hence democracy falls] under the theory of organic life. It is accountable to Darwin, not to Newton. . . . There can be no successful government without leadership or without the intimate, almost instinctive, coordination of the organs of life and action. . . . Living political constitutions must be Darwinian in structure and in practice . . . modified by [their] environment, necessitated by their tasks, shaped to their functions by the sheer pressure of life." Cited from Woodrow Wilson, *Constitutional Government in the United States*, New York: Columbia University Press, 1908, 1921 ed., 51–57, or *PWW*, 18, 3/24/1908, 69ff.
27. *PWW*, 53, 1919, 678. The reference is to dates set by Arthur Link, which may at times vary from those given by David Hunter Miller, *The Drafting of the Covenant*, 2 vols., New York: G. P. Putnam's Sons, 1928, vol. 2, document 7, 65ff.
28. *PWW*, 54, 1/18/1919, 138f.
29. *PWW*, 54/1919, 489ff, but see discussion in Miller, *The Drafting of the Covenant*, vol. 1, 164ff.
30. Ibid., 165.
31. Ibid., 166f, emphasis added.
32. Miller, *The Drafting of the Covenant*, vol. 2, document 19, February 13, 1919, 303; *PWW*, 55, 135f.
33. For the larger setting of deliberations at the League, see Knock, *To End All Wars*, chaps. 11 and 12; John Milton Cooper Jr., *Woodrow Wilson: A Biography*, New York: Knopf, 2009, chaps. 20 and 21; and Margaret Macmillan, *Paris 1919: Six Months That Changed the World*, New York: Random House, 2002.
34. *PWW*, 63, 9/9/ 1919, 134f.
35. Ibid.
36. Cited in Thompson, *A Sense of Power*, 93, from *The Collected Writings of John Maynard Keynes*, vol. 2, *The Economic Consequences of the Peace*; H. G. Wells, *The Shape of Things to Come: The Ultimate Revolution*.
37. *PWW*, 51, 10/14/1918, 222.
38. *PWW*, 40, 1/22/1917, 538f. And see Harley Notter, *The Origins of the Foreign Policy of Woodrow Wilson*, Baltimore, MD: Johns Hopkins University Press, 1927, 268f, who dates to 1913 Wilson's increased belief that popular consciousness in favor of democracy in many parts of the world was growing.
39. *PWW*, 40, 2/14/1919, 173f, 177.
40. In *Woodrow Wilson, The State: Elements of Historical and Practical Politics*, Boston: D. C. Heath (1889), 1911 ed., 604f, Wilson had saluted the idea of creating a body of international law but admitted that without the backing of power such efforts were limited in their ability to control events. International law "is simply the body of rules, developed out of the common moral judgments of the race, which ought to govern nations in their dealings with one another," but clearly, at the time he was writing, it lacked an organic basis as well as an authority to use force on its behalf. See also John A. Thompson, "Woodrow Wilson and a World Governed by Evolving Law," *The Journal of Policy History* 20, no. 1, 2008.

41. *PWW*, 41, 3/5/1917, 332ff.
42. For Wilson's concern about Jews in postwar Poland and Romania, see Arthur Link and Manfred F. Boemeke, eds., Paul Mantoux, *The Deliberations of the Council of Four (March 24–June 28, 1919)*, vol. 1, May 1 and May 3, 439f, 472. Also *PWW*, 59, 5/1919, 629f, 645f.
43. For a more extended discussion of democracy in Czechoslovakia, see chapter six.
44. See Wilson's comments reported in Mantoux, *The Deliberations*, vol. 1, May 9, 10, 20, 24, 1919, especially his comment of May 20 that the situation was so fluid and the liberal forces so weak that staying out entirely was the best policy to pursue.
45. Lawrence A. Gelfand, *The Inquiry: American Preparations for Peace, 1917–1919*, New Haven, CT: Yale University Press, 1963, on Russia 212f.
46. *PWW*, 51, 10/16/1918, 347ff.
47. *PWW*, 53, 11/21/ 1918, 152ff.
48. Arno J. Mayer, *Politics and Diplomacy of Peacemaking: Containment and Counterrevolution at Versailles 1918–1919*, New York: Knopf, 1967. By contrast, see Betty Miller Unterberger, "Woodrow Wilson and the Russian Revolution," in Arthur S. Link, *Woodrow Wilson and a Revolutionary World, 1913–1921*, Chapel Hill: University of North Carolina Press, 1982, and Unterberger, *The United States Revolutionary Russia and the Rise of Czechoslovakia*, Chapel Hill: University of North Carolina Press, 1989, chaps. 14 and 15, especially 259ff; Lawrence Gelfand, *The Inquiry*, 213f; Daniel Lerner on the Soviet Union in "Abandoning Democracy: Woodrow Wilson and Promoting German Democracy, 1918–1919," *Diplomatic History* 37, no. 3, 2013, 477, 483ff.
49. Cited in Arthur S. Link, *Woodrow Wilson: Revolution, War, and Peace*, Arlington Heights, IL: Harlan Davidson, 1979, 96.
50. *PWW*, 51, 1918, 350f.
51. Klaus Schwabe, *Woodrow Wilson, Revolutionary Germany and Peacemaking, 1918–1919*, Chapel Hill: University of North Carolina Press, 1985. See also Schwabe's later account in "President Wilson and the War Aims of the United States," in Holger Afflerbach, ed., *Der Sinn des Krieges* ("The Purpose of the First World War"), Oldenbourg: De Gruyter, 2015.
52. Mantoux, *The Deliberations*, vol. 1, 31.
53. *PWW*, 44, 8/27/1917, 57ff.
54. *PWW*, 45, 12/1917, 196.
55. *PWW*, 51, 340ff, 10/15/1918. Colonel House wrote that in a discussion with the president, Wilson had referred to his July 4 speech as still the basis of his viewpoint.
56. *PWW*, 51, 419.
57. *PWW*, 51, 10/30/ 1918, 518f.
58. Ibid., 10/1918, 518ff, dated in Wilson's papers as 10/30 but sent 10/27/1918 via Switzerland.
59. Schwabe, *Woodrow Wilson, Revolutionary Germany and Peacemaking, 1918–1919*, chap. 3.
60. Ibid., chap. 2. I thank Klaus Schwabe for his discussions with me on this subject in July 2014.
61. *PWW*, 47, 4/8/1918, 288. But see American reservations on recognizing the new government of Mexico late in April 1917 to show this country's displeasure at measures restricting and confiscating American property there, *PWW*, 42, 4/25/1917, 130ff.
62. *PWW*, 35, 12/8/1915, 314f.
63. Klaus Schwabe, "World War I and the Rise of Hitler," *Diplomatic History* 38, no.

4, 2014. See also Schwabe, "President Wilson and the War Aims of the United States."

64. Cited in John Milton Cooper Jr., *Woodrow Wilson: A Biography*, New York: Random House, 2009, 495. On this matter at more length, see the authoritative account in Cooper, chap. 21. See also the declaration by Count von Brockdorff-Rantzau, the leader of the German Peace delegation to Paris, in May 1919, after a review of the "Diktat" imposed on Germany by the Allies and the United States. Also Ross Kennedy, *The Will to Believe: Woodrow Wilson, World War I, and America's Strategy for Peace and Security*, Kent, OH: Kent State University Press, 2009, especially chap. 9.

65. John B. Judis, *The Folly of Empire: What George W. Bush Could Learn from Theodore Roosevelt and Woodrow Wilson*, New York: Scribner, 2004, 111.

66. *PWW*, 51, 10/14/1918, 339.

67. For an extended discussion, see Cooper, *Breaking the Heart of the World*.

68. *PWW*, 63, 9/5/1919, 51.

69. Ibid., 9/8/1919, 113, 115.

70. The same day, Wilson sounded a similar message in Minneapolis: Americans must "see how the affairs of America are linked with the affairs of men everywhere, see how the whole world turns with outstretched hands to this blessed country of ours and says, 'If you lead, we will follow.' God helping us, my fellow countrymen, we will lead when they follow. The march is still long and toilsome to those heights upon which there rests nothing but the pure light of the justice of God, but the whole incline of affairs is toward those distant heights. And this great nation, in serried ranks, millions strong—presently hundreds of millions strong—will march at the fore of the great procession, breasting those heights with its eyes always lifted to the eternal goal." Ibid., 9/9/1919, 138, 148, emphasis added.

71. *PWW*, 63, 9/15/1919, 283.

72. *PWW*, 63, 9/9/1919, 145.

73. *PWW*, 66, 12/7/1920, 485.

74. *PWW*, 63, 9/5/1919, 43.

CHAPTER 4. WILSON'S WILSONIANISM

1. Arthur Link et al., eds., *The Papers of Woodrow Wilson [PWW]*, 69 vols., Princeton, NJ: Princeton University Press, 1966–1994, 68, 5/1/1922, 39ff.

2. Wilson, "The Significance of American History," in *Harper's Encyclopaedia of United States History*, 1902, reprinted in Mario R. DiNunzio, *Woodrow Wilson: Essential Writings and Speeches of the Scholar-President*, New York: New York University Press, 2006, 216f.

3. *PWW*, 6, 1889.

CHAPTER 5. WILSONIANISM: THE CONSTRUCTION OF AN AMERICAN VERNACULAR

1. For an interesting discussion of the term, see Hal Brands, *What Good Is Grand Strategy? Power and Purpose in American Statecraft from Harry S. Truman to George W. Bush*, Ithaca, NY: Cornell University Press, 2014.

2. Many authors could be cited, but a particularly egregious example that is recent and by a noted social scientist is Perry Anderson, *American Foreign Policy and Its Thinkers*, London: Verso, 2015.

3. Robert A. Divine, *Second Chance: The Triumph of Internationalism in America*

during World War II, New York: Athenaeum, 1967. For a provocative study of the evolution of this thinking in U.S. foreign policy, see Lloyd C. Gardner, *A Covenant with Power: America and World Order from Wilson to Reagan*, New York: Oxford University Press, 1984. On the importance of FDR in the resurgence of Wilsonianism (and on the influence of Theodore Roosevelt as well), see John Milton Cooper Jr., *The Warrior and the Priest: Woodrow Wilson and Theodore Roosevelt*, Cambridge, MA: Belknap Press of Harvard University Press, 1983, chap. 21.

4. For remarks on the links between Wilson and FDR and his associates, see, among others, Emily S. Rosenberg, "Progressive Internationalism and Reformed Capitalism: New Freedom to New Deal," in John Milton Cooper Jr., ed., *Reconsidering Woodrow Wilson: Progressivism, Internationalism, War, and Peace*, Baltimore, MD: Johns Hopkins University Press, 2008; Elizabeth Borgwardt, *A New Deal for the World: America's Vision for Human Rights*, Cambridge, MA: Harvard University Press, 2005; John B. Judis, *The Folly of Empire: What George W. Bush Could Learn from Theodore Roosevelt and Woodrow Wilson*, New York: Scribner 2004; Tony McCulloch, "Franklin D. Roosevelt," in Michael Cox et al., *U.S. Foreign Policy and Democracy Promotion: From Theodore Roosevelt to Barack Obama*, New York: Routledge, Taylor & Francis, 2013. On Truman, see Anne Rice Pierce, *Woodrow Wilson and Harry Truman: Mission and Power in American Foreign Policy*, Westport, CT: Praeger, 2003, chaps. 7 and 10; and Martin H. Folly, "Harry Truman," in Michael Cox et al., *U.S. Foreign Policy and Democracy Promotion*.

5. Cordell Hull, *The Memoirs of Cordell Hull*, New York: Macmillan, 1948, 364ff. See also Richard Gardner, *Sterling-Dollar Diplomacy in Current Perspective: The Origins and Prospects of Our International Economic Order*, New York: Columbia University Press, 2nd ed., 1980, chap. 1.

6. Henry Kissinger, *World Order*, New York: Penguin, 2014, 269. For an argument that even were the United States to enter into decline in the world system, the liberal order it established in the more than sixty years since World War II would likely survive, see G. John Ikenberry, *Liberal Leviathan: The Origins, Crisis, and Transformation of the American World Order*, Princeton, NJ: Princeton University Press, 2011. See also Michael Mandelbaum, *The Ideas That Conquered the World*, New York: Public Affairs, 2002, with its opening chapter, "Wilson Victorious."

7. Preamble to the Charter of the United Nations, http://www.un.org/en/sections/un-charter/preamble/.

8. The North Atlantic Treaty, http://nato.int/cps/en/natohq/official_texts_17120.htm.

9. Yale University Library, The Avalon Project, "The Atlantic Charter," August 14, 1941.

10. Yale University Library, The Avalon Project, Proceedings of Crimea Conference, "Declaration on Liberated Europe," February 1945.

11. Tony Smith, *America's Mission: The United States and the Worldwide Struggle for Democracy*, Princeton, NJ: Princeton University Press, expanded ed., 2012, 146 and chap. 6.

12. For the sake of brevity, I will concentrate here on Germany, but on Japan, see the insightful studies of John W. Dower, *Empire and Aftermath: Yoshida Shigeru and the Japanese Experience, 1878–1854*, Cambridge, MA: Harvard University Press, 1979; Chalmers Johnson, *MITI and the Japanese Miracle*, Stanford, CA: Stanford University Press, 2982; Richard Samuels, *Machiavelli's Children: Leaders and Their Legacies in Italy and Japan*, Ithaca, NY: Cornell University Press, 2003; and

Yoshida Shigeru, *The Yoshida Memoirs: The Story of Japan in Crisis*, Boston: Houghton Mifflin, 1962. The story of Japan is every bit as important as that of Germany, and it also demonstrates the critical role played by local cultures and leaders in a democratic transition. I thank Richard Samuels for his discussions with me on this subject.

13. For an extended discussion, see Smith, *America's Mission*, 155ff, and the information contained in the United States Department of State, *Foreign Relations of the United States* (FRUS) 1945 (various volumes) and *Documents on Germany, 1945–1985*, Washington, DC: Government Printing Office, 1985.

14. University of California, Santa Barbara, *The American Presidency Project, Papers of Harry S. Truman*, listed by date, http://www.presidency.ucsb.edu/harry_s _truman.php.

15. "A Report to the National Security Council—NSC 68," April 1, 1950, Truman Library, University of Missouri.

16. Tony Smith, "New Bottles for New Wine: A Pericentric Framework for the Study of the Cold War," *Diplomatic History*, Fall 2000; Smith, "The Spirit of the Sierra Maestra: Five Observations on Writing on Cuban Foreign Policy," *World Politics*, October 1988.

17. I discuss this at more length in Tony Smith, *Thinking Like a Communist: State and Legitimacy in the Soviet Union, China, and Cuba*, New York: W. W. Norton, 1987, chap. 3.

18. See the discussion in chapter one and the reference to the recommended edition with a useful preface by Walter Lippmann, New York: Columbia University Press, 1921, but *Constitutional Government in the United States* is more easily available in Arthur Link et al., eds., *The Papers of Woodrow Wilson [PWW]*, 69 vols., Princeton, NJ: Princeton University Press, 1966–1994, 18, 3/24/1908.

19. The Czechoslovakian case receives more attention in chapter six of this book.

20. Lansing, Memorandum of October 26, 1918, cited in Lawrence A. Gelfand, *The Inquiry: American Preparations for Peace, 1917–1919*, New Haven, CT: Yale University Press, 1963, 212f.

21. *PWW*, 63, Kansas City on September 6, 1919, 70. Such remarks were frequent during the Western tour, as in Billings, Montana, on September 11, 1919, 174.

22. Ibid.

23. Arno J. Mayer, *Politics and Diplomacy of Peacemaking: Containment and Counterrevolution at Versailles 1918–1919*, New York: Knopf, 1967.

24. Woodrow Wilson, *Constitutional Government in the United States*, New York: Columbia University Press, 1908, 1921 edition, 33.

25. Smith, *America's Mission*, chap. 9.

26. Ibid., 202.

27. Arthur Schlesinger, *A Thousand Days: John F. Kennedy in the White House*, New York: Fawcett, 1965, 769.

28. Tony Smith, *Thinking Like a Communist*, chaps. 3 and 4; Smith, "The Underdevelopment of Development Literature: The Case of Dependency Theory," *World Politics*, January 1979.

29. Max F. Millikan, W. W. Rostow, et al., *A Proposal: Key to an Effective Foreign Policy*, New York: Harper, 1957; Rostow, *The Stages of Economic Growth: A Noncommunist Manifesto*, London: Cambridge University Press, 1964; Gabriel A. Almond, James. S. Coleman, et al., *The Politics of Developing Areas*, Princeton, NJ: Princeton University Press, 1960; Seymour Martin Lipset, *Political Man: The Social Bases of Politics*, New York: Doubleday, 1960, and *The First New Nation: The United States in Historical and Comparative Perspective*, New York: Basic Books, 1963; Talcott Parsons and Edward A. Shils, eds., *Toward a General Theory*

of Action, New York: Harper and Row, 1962 (c. 1951); Daniel Lerner, *The Passing of Traditional Society: Modernizing the Middle East*, Glencoe, IL: The Free Press, 1958; Sidney Verba and Gabriel Almond, *The Civic Culture: Political Attitudes and Democracy in Five Nations*, Boston: Little, Brown, 1965; David E. Apter, *The Politics of Modernization*, Chicago: University of Chicago Press, 1965. For the coming together of these social scientists, see Donald L. M. Blackmer, *The MIT Center for International Studies: The Founding Years, 1951–1969*, Cambridge, MA: MIT Center for International Studies, 2002.

30. Tony Smith, "Requiem or New Agenda for Third World Studies?" *World Politics*, July 1985, reprinted several times, including in Ikuo Kabashima and Lynn T. White III, eds., *Political System and Change*, Princeton, NJ: Princeton University Press, 1986, a collection of leading articles appearing in *World Politics* by Samuel Huntington, Robert Putnam, Gabriel Almond, David Easton, and Ted Gurr; Albert Hirschman, "The Search for Paradigms as a Hindrance to Understanding," *World Politics* 22, April 1970, 329, and Albert Hirschman, *Essays in Trespassing: Economics to Politics and Beyond*, New York: Cambridge University Press, 1981.

31. Robert A. Packenham, *Liberal America and the Third World: Political Development Ideas in Foreign Aid and Social Science*, Princeton, NJ: Princeton University Press, 1973, chap. 3. Much the same argument is made by Michael E. Latham, *The Right Kind of Revolution: Modernization, Development, and U.S. Foreign Policy from the Cold War to the Present*, Ithaca, NY: Cornell University Press, 2011, introduction, although he does not cite Packenham. What Latham does do, however, is to take the liberal argument back through Wilson to Thomas Paine and indeed to the American Enlightenment—so reading the present into the past in a way that is totally unjustified.

32. Packenham's major source for the ideas that constitute "liberal America" are drawn from Louis Hartz, *The Liberal Tradition in American: An Interpretation of American Political Thought Since the Revolution*, New York: Harcourt, Brace, 1955. Even as a student of Hartz in the 1960s, I found his rendition of liberalism curious.

33. Reinhold Niebuhr and Paul E. Sigmund, *The Democratic Experience: Past and Prospects*, New York: Praeger, 1969, opening page and 73. For a later discussion, couched in much the same terms, of the characteristics of a people capable of democratic government, see Charles Tilly, *Democracy*, New York: Cambridge University Press, 2007.

34. Robert Dahl, *Polyarchy: Participation and Opposition*, New Haven, CT: Yale University Press, 1971, 203, 214; Dahl, *Democracy and Its Critics*, New Haven, CT: Yale University Press, 1989, 317.

35. For example, Robert Heilbroner, *The Great Ascent: The Struggle for Economic Development in Our Time*, New York: Harper & Row, 1963.

36. Samuel P. Huntington, *Political Order in Changing Societies*, New Haven, CT: Yale University Press, 1968.

37. Barrington Moore Jr., *The Social Origins of Dictatorship and Democracy: Lord and Peasant in the Making of the Modern World*, Boston: Beacon Press, 1966.

CHAPTER 6. THE RISE OF NEO-WILSONIAN THEORY

1. Tony Smith, "American Liberalism and Soviet 'New Thinking'," in Pierre Melandri and Serge Melandri, eds., *Les Etats-Unis et la fin de la guerre froide*, Paris: Harmattan, 2005.

2. In my opinion, Reagan's speech of June 1982 was not only the most important of his presidency on world affairs, but arguably the most important in this respect

of any presidential address from 1950 until today. It stands out by its mix of themes, its clarity and coherence, its boldness and originality, and its influence on the rhetoric and thinking of subsequent presidents, especially George W. Bush and Barack Obama.

3. *The Public Papers of President Ronald W. Reagan*, Ronald Reagan Presidential Library, reaganlibrary.archives.gov/archives/speeches/1982.

4. Ronald Reagan, Farewell Address, January 1989: "Once you begin a great movement, there's no telling where it will end. We meant to change a nation, and instead, we changed a world. Countries across the globe are turning to free markets and free speech and turning away from the ideologies of the past. For them, the great rediscovery of the 1980s has been that, lo and behold, the moral way of government is the practical way of government: democracy, the profoundly good, is also the profoundly productive."

5. Mary Elise Sarotte, *1989: The Struggle to Create Post–Cold War Europe*, Princeton, NJ: Princeton University Press, 2014; Robert S. Litwak, *Rogue States and U.S. Foreign Policy: Containment after the Cold War*, Washington, DC: Woodrow Wilson Center Press and Johns Hopkins University Press, 2000, chap. 1, covering the administrations of Presidents George H. W. Bush and Bill Clinton.

6. Bill Clinton, "U.S. Trade with China Opens a Door for Freedom," *New York Times*, September 25, 2000.

7. Indeerjet Parmar, *Foundations of the American Century: The Ford, Carnegie and Rockefeller Foundations in the Rise of American Power*, New York: Columbia University Press, 2012. See too James McGann, Think Tanks and Civil Societies Program, Lauder Institute, University of Pennsylvania, which is a center devoted to the analysis and ranking of some 6,600 think tanks.

8. See Justin Vaisse, *Neoconservatism: The Biography of a Movement*, translated by Arthur Goldhammer, Cambridge, MA: Harvard University Press, 2010. This study includes an online list of basic documents separately from the book.

9. Michael Doyle, "Kant, Liberal Legacies and Foreign Affairs," *Philosophy and Public Affairs* 12, Summer and Fall 1983; Doyle, *Ways of War and Peace: Realism, Liberalism, and Socialist*, New York: W. W. Norton, 1997, part 2; and "An International Liberal Community," in Graham Allison and Gregory F. Treverton, eds., *Rethinking America's Security: Beyond the Cold War to New World Order*, New York: W. W. Norton, 1991. See also John M. Owen, IV, *Liberal Peace, Liberal War: International Politics and American Security*, Ithaca, NY: Cornell University Press, 1997.

10. Perhaps the most serious studies championing the new liberalism were, empirically speaking, Bruce Russett and John Oneal, *Triangulating Peace: Democracy, Interdependence, and International Organizations*, New Haven, CT: Yale University Press, 2001; methodologically speaking, Andrew Moravschik, "Taking Preferences Seriously: A Liberal Theory of International Politics," *International Organization* 51, no. 4, 1997; and philosophically speaking, John Rawls, *The Law of Peoples*, Cambridge, MA: Harvard University Press, 1999. For a fuller discussion of DPT, see Tony Smith, *A Pact with the Devil: Washington's Bid for World Supremacy and the Betrayal of the American Promise*, New York: Routledge, Taylor & Francis, 2007, chap. 4.

11. Francis Fukuyama, "The End of History?" *The National Interest*, Summer 1989. Fukuyama later expanded his argument in *The End of History and the Last Man*, Toronto: The Free Press, 1992.

12. Russett and Oneal, 272; for more on Kant, 273ff, 78; on Wilson and Kant, 30.

13. Larry Diamond, "The Global Imperative: Building a Democratic World Order," *Current History* 93, no. 579, January 1994. In fact, Diamond had introduced his

main theme three years earlier in "An American Foreign Policy for Democracy," Washington, DC: Progressive Policy Institute, July 1991.

14. Robert Kagan and William Kristol, "Toward a Neo-Reaganite Foreign Policy," *Foreign Affairs* 75, no. 4, 1996; and Kagan and Kristol, eds., *Present Dangers: Crisis and Opportunity in American Foreign and Defense Policy*, San Francisco: Encounter Books, 2000.

15. Interesting discussions are to be found in Christopher Hobson and Milja Jurki, eds., *The Conceptual Politics of Democracy Promotion*, London: Routledge, Taylor & Francis, 2013.

16. Dankwart Rustow, "Transitions to Democracy: Toward a Dynamic Model," *Comparative Politics* 2, no. 3, 1970, 361ff.

17. Barrington Moore Jr., *Social Origins of Dictatorship and Democracy: Lord and Peasant in the Making of the Modern World*, Boston: Beacon Press, 1967.

18. Guillermo O'Donnell et al., *Transitions from Authoritarian Rule: Tentative Conclusions about Uncertain Democracies*, Baltimore, MD: Johns Hopkins University Press, 1986.

19. Samuel P. Huntington, *Political Order in Changing Societies*, New Haven, CT: Yale University Press, 1968; Huntington, *The Third Wave: Democratization in the Late Twentieth Century*, Norman: University of Oklahoma Press, 1991.

20. Guissepe Di Palma, *To Craft Democracies: An Essay on Democratic Transitions*, Berkeley and Los Angeles: University of California Press, 1990, 1.

21. Nancy Bermeo, "Shortcuts to Liberty," *The Journal of Democracy* 2, no. 2, Spring 1991.

22. The scope and depth of the series deserves commendation and appears as Larry Diamond et al., eds., *Democracy in Developing Countries*, Boulder, CO: Rienner, 1989.

23. Thomas Risse, Stephen C. Ropp, and Kathryn Sikkink, eds., *The Power of Human Rights: International Norms and Domestic Change*, New York: Cambridge University Press, 1999, opening and concluding chapters.

24. Samuel P. Huntington, *The Clash of Civilizations and the Remaking of World Order*, New York: Simon and Schuster, 1996, chaps. 3, 5, 8, and 12.

25. Larry Diamond, "Building a World of Liberal Democracies," in Thomas H. Henriksen, ed., *Foreign Policy for America in the Twenty-first Century*, Stanford, CA: Hoover Institution Press, 2001, 50, 73, emphasis added. His optimism continued through 2014 in "The Next Democratic Century," *Current History* 113, no. 759, January 2014.

26. Larry Diamond, "Can the Whole World Become Democratic? Democracy, Development and International Policies," University of California, Irvine: Center for the Study of Democracy, March 2003.

27. Tony Smith and Larry Diamond, "Was Iraq a Fool's Errand?" *Foreign Affairs*, November-December 2004. See also Larry Diamond, "Iraq and Democracy: The Lessons Learned," *Current History*, January 2006.

28. Larry Diamond, "Democracy's Third Wave Today," *Current History*, November 2011.

29. Larry Diamond, *The Spirit of Democracy: The Struggle to Build Free Societies Throughout the World*, New York: Holt/Times Books, 2008, chaps. 13 and 14.

30. For an extended discussion of foreign aid conditioned on democracy promotion, see Diamond, *The Spirit of Democracy*, chap. 14, especially 321ff.

31. Diamond reasserts the importance of public opinion in *The Spirit of Democracy*, 28ff.

32. An interesting literature includes Fareed Zakaria, "A Conversation with Lee Kuan Yew," *Foreign Affairs*, March-April 1994; Jack Donnelly, *Universal Human*

Rights in Theory and Practice, Ithaca, NY: Cornell University Press, 2013; Uyen P. Le, "A Culture of Human Rights in East Asia: Deconstructing 'Asian Values' Claims," *Journal of International Law and Policy* 18, no. 2, 2012.

33. Noah Feldman, *After Jihad: America and the Struggle for Islamic Democracy*, New York: Farrar, Straus and Giroux, 2003, 11f.

34. Noah Feldman, "Democracy, Closer Every Day," *New York Times*, September 24, 2003; Feldman, "A New Democracy, Enshrined in Faith," *New York Times*, November 13, 2003; Feldman, "Political Islam: Global Warming," *New York Times*, February 8, 2005; Feldman, "Muslim Democrats? Why Not!" *Wall Street Journal*, April 8, 2003; Feldman, "Operation Iraqi Democracy," *Wall Street Journal*, July 15, 2003.

35. Hillary Clinton, "Leading Through Civilian Power," *Foreign Affairs*, November-December 2010.

36. All publications were brought out by the RAND Corporation, Santa Monica, CA. Other titles in the series include *After the War: Nation-Building from FDR to George W. Bush* (2008), *Europe's Role in Nation-Building: From the Balkans to the Congo* (2008), and *The UN's Role in Nation Building: From the Congo to Iraq* (2005). Yet a seventh volume appeared in 2013 and is discussed below: *Overcoming Obstacles to Peace: Local Factors in Nation-Building*.

37. David H. Petraeus and James Amos, *The U.S. Army/Marine Corps Counterinsurgency Field Manual*. U.S. Army field manual 3-24: Marine Corps warfighting publication 3-33.5. A "final draft" appeared in June 2006 with its eventual publication that December, when it was available on-line to be downloaded by whoever was interested. The Manual was reprinted in book form by the University of Chicago Press (Chicago), 2007. Earlier copies of the Manual on-line have apparently been replaced by a shorter version *Insurgencies and Countering Insurgencies*, Department of the Army FM 3-24; MCWP3-33.5, May 2014.

38. See also the discussion in Michael MacDonald, *Overreach: Delusions of Regime Change in Iraq*, Cambridge, MA: Harvard University Press, 2014, 227ff.

39. James Dobbins et al., *America's Role in Nation-Building: From Germany to Iraq*, Santa Monica, CA: RAND Corporation, xixff, 166.

40. James Dobbins et al., *Overcoming Obstacles to Peace: Local Factors in Nation-Building*, Santa Monica, CA: RAND, 2013, 214–21.

41. The argument started in France in the late 1980s with the ideas of Bernard Kouchner (a founder of Doctors Without Borders, later French foreign minister) and the jurist Mario Bettati. See Bettati, *Le Droit d'ingérence: mutation de l'ordre international*, Paris: Odile Jacob, 1996. See also Kofi A. Annan, *Global Values: The United Nations and the Rule of Law in the 21st Century*, Singapore: Institute of Southeast Asian Studies, 2000; Annan, *We the Peoples: The Role of the United Nations in the 21st Century*, New York: United Nations, 2000; Annan, *Facing the Humanitarian Challenge: Towards a Culture of Prevention*, New York: United Nations Department of Public Information, 1999; Annan, *The Question of Intervention*, New York: United Nations Department of Public Information, 1999; Gareth Evans, *The Responsibility to Protect: Ending Mass Atrocities Once and For All*, Washington, DC: Brookings Institution Press, 2008.

42. The International Commission on Intervention and State Sovereignty, *The Responsibility to Protect*, Ottawa, Ontario: International Development Research Center, 2001.

43. In the United States, the most influential thinker was professor Thomas M. Franck in a series of articles in the *American Journal of International Law*, the most important of which are "The Emerging Right to Democratic Governance" 86, no. 1, 1992, and "Is Personal Freedom a Western Value?" 91, no. 4, 1997. Franck's

influence is apparent in this citation from the International Commission on Intervention and State Sovereignty, "The Responsibility to Protect," Ottawa, Ontario: International Development Research Centre, 2001, sections 2.11–2.29.

44. Exception should perhaps be made for the Vietnam War, which many observers would maintain had an important degree of liberal support.

45. Woodrow Wilson, *Constitutional Government in the United States*, New York: Columbia University Press, 1908, 1921 edition, 16–17; more easily found in *PWW*, 18, 3/24/1908, 69ff.

46. John M. Owen, *Confronting Political Islam: Six Lessons from the West's Past*, Princeton, NJ: Princeton University Press, 2015.

47. As early as 1994, I had warned my fellow liberal internationalists against exactly such a miscalculation. My comments can be found in the 1994 edition of my *America's Mission: The United States and the Worldwide Struggle for Democracy*, republished in an expanded version in 2012 by Princeton University Press, 11, 12, 338–45.

48. "*Ce qu'il y a de certain, c'est que moi, je ne suis pas Marxiste.*" See also Tony Smith, *Thinking Like a Communist: State and Legitimacy in the Soviet Union, China and Cuba*, New York: W. W. Norton, 1987, chaps. 1–2.

49. Robert Kagan, *Of Paradise and Power: America and Europe in the New World Order*, New York: Knopf, 2003, 85f, 93, 96. In his article of 1996, authored with William Kristol, "Toward a Neo-Reaganite Foreign Policy," *Foreign Affairs* 75, no. 4, July–August 1996, a section heading calls it "Benevolent Hegemony." I doubt, however, that the Realist strain apparent in Kagan's work would have led him to endorse R2P.

50. Robert Kagan, "Superpowers Don't Get to Retire: What Our Tired Country Still Owes the World," *The New Republic*, May 26, 2014.

51. A parallel is evident between the thinking, at once idealistic and realistic, of Wilson and the work of the Polish dissident Adam Michnik, complete with lessons both men draw from the failures of the French Revolution. See Adam Michnik, *The Trouble with History: Morality, Revolution, and Counterrevolution*, New Haven, CT: Yale University Press, 2014.

52. Hannah Arendt, *The Origins of Totalitarianism*, New York: Harcourt, new edition, 1966, 486.

53. What is striking is the extent to which Wilson made something of the same point, even if from a different background, in October 1896, in "Princeton in the Nation's Service" (*PWW*, 10, 10/1896), saying, "Science is a child of the 19th century. It has transformed the world and owes little debt of obligation to any past. It has driven mystery out of the universe . . . worst of all, we believe in the present and in the future more than in the past, and deem the newest theory of society the likeliest. . . . I should tremble to see social reform led by men who had breathed [the spirit of science]; I should fear nothing better than utter destruction from a revolution conceived and led in the scientific spirit. Science has not changed the laws of social growth or betterment. [Whatever its accomplishments, science] has not purged us of passion or disposed us to virtue. It has not made us less covetous or less ambitious or less self-indulgent."

CHAPTER 7. FROM THEORY TO PRACTICE: NEO-WILSONIANISM IN THE WHITE HOUSE, 2001–2017

1. For a criticism by President George H. W. Bush of leading officials in his son's administration, see John Meacham, *Destiny and Power: The American Odyssey of George H. W. Bush*, New York: Random House, 2015, 585ff.

2. National Security Strategy of the United States, September 2002, available online (e.g., at http://www.state.gov/documents/organization/63562.pdf), with citations selected from various sections of the document, except those identified as in the introductory section.

3. *The National Security Strategy of the United States of America*, The White House, September 2002, 3, http://www.state.gov/documents/organization/63562 .pdf.

4. Cited by several sources, including jewishagency.org/executive-members/natan -sharansky-o (downloaded November 2015) and Clare Murphy, "Bush's New Book for a New Term," *BBC News*, 1/21/2005.

5. Natan Sharansky (his name sometimes transcribed as Anatoly Shcharansky) with Ron Dermer (later the Likud government's ambassador to the United States), *The Case for Democracy: The Power of Freedom to Overcome Tyranny and Terror*, New York: Public Affairs, 2004, 88.

6. William Kristol and Robert Kagan, "Toward a Neo-Reaganite Foreign Policy," *Foreign Affairs*, 75, no. 4, July-August 1996.

7. Robert Kagan and William Kristol, eds., *Present Dangers: Crisis and Opportunity in American Foreign and Defense Policy*, introduction, San Francisco: Encounter Books, 2000, 20.

8. Kristol and Kagan, "Toward a Neo-Reaganite Foreign Policy."

9. *The Weekly Standard*, October 1, 2001; Stefan Halper and Jonathan Clarke, *America Alone: The Neoconservatives and Global Order*, New York: Cambridge University Press, 2004, 64ff; and Gory Dorrien, *Imperial Designs: Neoconservatism and the New Pax Americana*, New York: Routledge, 2004, 143.

10. Max Boot, "Myths about Neoconservatism," *Foreign Policy*, 2004, reprinted in Irwin Stelzer, *The Neocon Reader*, New York: Grove Press, 2004, 46; Charles Krauthammer, "The Neoconservative Convergence," *Commentary*, July-August 2005. See also Joshua Muravchik, "The Neoconservative Cabal," *Commentary*, September 2003, reprinted in Stelzer, *The Neocon Reader*, 256.

11. Lawrence F. Kaplan and William Kristol, *The War Over Iraq: Saddam's Tyranny and America's Mission*, San Francisco: Encounter Books, 2003.

12. John Lewis Gaddis, *Surprise, Security and the American Experience*, Cambridge, MA: Harvard University Press, 2004, citations from chap. 4, 80ff, emphasis in original.

13. Gaddis, "Grand Strategy in the Second Term," *Foreign Affairs* 84, no. 1, January-February 2005.

14. Walter Russell Mead, *Power, Terror, Peace and War: America's Grand Strategy in a World at Risk*, New York: Knopf, 2004, see chap. 6, 89, 91ff, and his own support for the invasion of Iraq in chap. 8.

15. Citations from Michael Ignatieff, "The Burden," *New York Times*, January 5, 2003, and Ignatieff, "Who Are Americans That Think That Freedom Is Theirs to Spread?" *New York Times*, June 6, 2005.

16. For citations throughout this book from speeches or talks given by American presidents, the preferred place for follow-up reading today is the *Public Papers of the Presidents* published by the Federal Register, National Archives and Records Administration, http://www.archives.gov/federal-register/publications /presidential-papers.html. An alternative, related site is the American Presidency Project, http://www.presidency.ucsb.edu/. Presidential statements are exhaustive, authoritative, and arranged for easy access by name and exact date. Citations in this book of President George W. Bush may be found here.

17. Robert Kagan, *The World America Made*, New York: Knopf, 2012, and Kagan,

"Superpowers Don't Get to Retire: What Our Tired Country Still Owes the World," *The New Republic*, May 26, 2014.

18. Barack Obama, "The American Moment," Chicago Council on Global Affairs, April 22, 2007; Obama, "The War We Need to Win," Woodrow Wilson Center, August 2007; Obama, "Renewing American Leadership," *Foreign Affairs*, July-August, 2007. That Afghanistan was not a "war of choice" but one of "necessity" is expressed in these statements from 2007.

19. While Obama first made these assertions publicly in Chicago, they were repeated, almost exactly, in his *Foreign Affairs* article of July-August 2007. He added new features in his speech at the Wilson Center that August, including direct reference to the counterinsurgency manual of General Petraeus, discussed in the preceding chapter: a call for "Mobile Development Teams that bring together personnel from the State Department, the Pentagon, and USAID . . . to work with civil society and local governments and to make an immediate impact in peoples' lives, and to turn the tide against extremism." At the same time, Obama saluted efforts at "operations to win hearts and minds" (WHAM), a program that had proved such an empty ambition in Vietnam but had been resurrected by the literature from Petraeus and Dobbins. For those who do not think that ideas matter, here is an example to be considered under a microscope.

20. *Public Papers of the Presidents*, cited above, has all of President Obama's speeches, remarks, and addresses online by exact date. Major libraries carry copies of the *Public Papers of the Presidents* in book form, appearing about a year after the texts appear.

21. An alternative interpretation of Obama's remarks is that he was well aware of the setbacks in Afghanistan and was disguising the American retreat as a victory. In 2015, the president extended the time American troops would be in Afghanistan until 2017, thus leaving the question of America's military presence there to his successor in office.

22. See Alan J. Kuperman, "Obama's Libya Debacle: How a Well-Meaning Intervention Ended in Failure," *Foreign Affairs*, March-April 2015.

23. Secretary Clinton's remarks may be located by date, 2009–2013, at state.gov/ secretary/20092013clinton/; downloaded from the U.S. Department of State website, April 2016.

24. As he said on September 24, 2011, before the United Nations General Assembly, the United States will always choose "hope over fear. We see the future not as something out of our control but as something we can shape for the better through concerted and collective effort." Only the politics of hope could bring him to say, "The only lasting solution to Syria's civil war is political—an inclusive political transition that responds to the legitimate aspirations of all Syrian citizens, regardless of ethnicity, regardless of creed."

25. Obama continued such assertions a year later, in his speech to the UN General Assembly on September 25, 2012. Reconfirming his policy toward Libya, extending it to Egypt and Yemen, and declaring that "the regime of Bashar al-Assad must come to an end," he saluted as well the "democratic spirit" that he saw in Malawi, Senegal, Somalia, and Burma. For a more extended discussion of R2P, see Tony Smith, *A Pact with the Devil: Washington's Bid for World Supremacy and the Betrayal of the American Promise*, New York: Routledge, Taylor & Francis, 2007, chap. 6.

26. Scarcely a speech on foreign affairs was made where Obama's articles of faith were not repeated. Among the many was his address to the United Nations General Assembly on September 25, 2012, holding not only that he also could sense a

"democratic spirit" in Malawi, Senegal, Burma, and Somalia, but that "We have taken these positions because we believe that freedom and self-determination are not unique to one culture. These are not simply American values or Western values—they are universal values. And even as there will be huge challenges that come with a transition to democracy, I am convinced that ultimately government of the people, by the people and for the people is more likely to bring about the stability, prosperity and individual opportunity that serve as a basis for peace in our world."

27. As Obama put it before the United Nations General Assembly in September 2013, "I believe America must remain engaged for our own security. But I also believe the world is better for it. . . . I believe America is exceptional . . . because we have shown a willingness through the sacrifice of blood and treasure to stand up . . . for the interests of all."
28. Robert Kagan, *The World America Made*, New York: Alfred A. Knopf, 2012.
29. Michiko Kakutani, "Historian Influences Both Obama and Romney," *New York Times*, February 13, 2012.
30. Robert Kagan, "Superpowers Don't Get to Retire: What Our Tired Country Still Owes the World," *The New Republic*, May 26, 2014, 24f.
31. See also Obama's speech on race relations in the United States of March 18, 2008.
32. Tony Smith, *"La promotion de la démocratie pendant le premier mandat du président Obama"* ("Democracy promotion during the first administration of President Barack Obama"), in Isabelle Vagnoux, ed., *Obama et le monde*, University of Aix-Marseille, 2014.
33. Will Marshall, ed., *With All Our Might: A Progressive Strategy for Defeating Jihadism and Defending Liberty*, Lanham, MD: Rowman & Littlefield, 2006, 5.
34. Tom Donnelly in *The Weekly Standard*, May 22, 2006.
35. Princeton Report, "Forging a World of Liberty Under Law," Princeton Project on National Security, September 27, 2006.
36. On General Petraeus and his "cult of personality," endowed with "myth making of a higher order," see Andrew J. Bacevich, *Washington Rules: America's Path to Permanent War*, New York: Metropolitan Press, 2010, chap. 5; also Bacevich, *America's War for the Greater Middle East*, New York: Random House, 2016. See also Michael MacDonald, *Overreach: Delusions of Regime Change in Iraq*, Cambridge, MA: Harvard University Press, 2014, 227ff; and Antonia Chayes, *Borderless Wars: Civil Military Disorder and Legal Uncertainity*, New York: Cambridge University Press, 2015, chaps. 3–5.
37. The text of the speech exists in many online sources, including National Public Radio (NPR), January 20, 2009; downloaded March 2016.
38. Jeffrey Goldberg, "The Obama Doctrine," *Atlantic*, April 2016.
39. Gordon cited in David Remnick, "Negotiating the Whirlwind," *New Yorker*, December 21 and 28, 2015, op. cit., and in Goldberg, op. cit. See also Philip Gordon, "The Middle East Is Falling Apart," *Politico*, June 4, 2015.
40. Remnick, "Negotiating the Whirlwind," referring back to an interview with the president in 2014.
41. Goldberg cites the president as tying his understanding of the power of tribalism to his encounter with it as a young man in Kenya. He cites the president: "It is literally in my DNA to be suspicious of tribalism. I understand the tribal impulse, and acknowledge the power of tribal division. I've been navigating tribal divisions my whole life. In the end, it's the source of a lot of destructive acts." See Barack Obama, *Dreams from My Father: A Story of Race and Inheritance*, New York: Three Rivers Press, 1995, 347ff.

42. See the detailed essays on Clinton with respect to Libya in Joe Becker and Scott Shane, "Hillary Clinton, 'Smart Power' and a Dictator's Fall" and "A New Libya with Very Little Time Left," *New York Times*, February 28, 2016. On Kerry, see both Goldberg, "The Obama Doctrine," and Remnick, "Negotiating the Whirlwind."

43. David Rothkopf, "Obama's 'Don't Do Stupid Shit' Foreign Policy," *Foreign Policy*, June 4, 2014.

44. Stephen M. Walt, "Obama Was Not a Realist President," *Foreign Policy*, April 7, 2016. Walt notes that "a genuinely 'realist' foreign policy would have left Afghanistan promptly in 2009, converted our 'special relationships' in the Middle East to normal ones, explicitly rejected further NATO expansion, eschewed 'regime change' and other forms of social engineering in foreign countries such as Libya or Syria, and returned to the broad strategy of restrained 'offshore balancing' that served the United States so well in the past."

45. "President Obama: Libya Aftermath 'Worst Mistake' of Presidency," BBC, April 11, 2016, bbc.com/world-us-canada-36013703.

46. For other efforts on democracy promotion in East Africa, after his August 30, 2013 decision, see the president's interview with John Sopel, BBC, July 24, 2015, bbc.com/world-us-canada-33646542. On Cuba, see BBC, "Barack Obama, 'Change is going to happen in Cuba,'" March 21, 2016, bbc.com/news/word-latin-america-35856126.

47. Goldberg, "The Obama Doctrine."

48. On the "Iranian Nuclear Deal," see "2016 Presidential Candidates on the Iran Nuclear Deal," Ballotpedia.org, July 15, 2015. On Cuba, see "Republicans Stand Against Cuba Change Despite Public Opinion," NPR, July 27, 2015. For the text of Obama's speeches on Eastern Europe during the summer of 2015, see *Public Papers of the Presidents*.

CONCLUSION. REVIVING LIBERAL INTERNATIONALISM

1. This book deals with democracy promotion, but an aspect of the theme unavoidably involves American calculations of the contribution of an increasingly open and interdependent world economy to the prospects for democracy at home and abroad. What occurred beginning in the Reagan years with the deregulation, privatization, and opening of the international market, the so-called "Washington consensus," is where the story begins. An abundant literature exists on this matter, including works by Elizabeth Warren, Thomas Piketty, Robert Reich, and Paul Krugman. An early contribution comes from Thomas Piketty and Emmanuel Saez, in their publication "Income Inequality in the United States, 1913–2002," November 2004, eml.berkeley.edu/~saez/piketty-saezOUP04US.pdf. For the problems associated with the liberal economic direction taken by the United States, see especially Nobel Prize winner in economics Joseph E. Stiglitz, *Globalization and Its Discontents*, New York: W. W. Norton, 2002; Stiglitz, *Freefall: America, Free Markets, and the Sinking of the World Economy*, New York: W. W. Norton, 2010; Stiglitz, *The Price of Inequality: How Today's Divided Society Endangers Our Future*, New York: W. W. Norton, 2012; and Stiglitz, *The Great Divide: Unequal Societies and What We Can Do About Them*, New York, W. W. Norton, 2015. See also the special section on global inequality in the January-February 2016 issue of *Foreign Affairs*.

2. David C. Hendrickson, *The Republic in Peril: American Empire and the Liberal Tradition*, manuscript copy.

3. See the arguments in Barry Posen, *Restraint: A New Foundation for U.S. Grand Strategy*, Ithaca, NY: Cornell University Press, 2014.

4. Gabriel Zucman, *The Hidden Wealth of Nations: The Scourge of Tax Havens*, Chicago: University of Chicago Press, 2015. Zucman estimates such wealth at some $7.6 trillion. Other experts maintain it is as high as $11.5 trillion, with one authority estimating it at $21–32 trillion. See John Christensen et al., "The Offshore Trillions," *New York Review of Books*, March 10, 2016. See also James Surowiecki, "Why the Rich Are So Much Richer," *New York Review of Books*, September 24, 2015.

5. I laid out this analysis as early as April 2011 in Tony Smith, "Democracy as a 'Deviation'," in Mounir Guirat and Mounir Triki, eds., *Deviations(s)*, Sfax, Tunisia: Imprimerie Reliure d'Art, for the Faculty of Arts and Humanities of Sfax, 2014.

6. For a powerful philosophical defense of dividing the world's states into at least three categories—and so avoiding the binary choice so many give us today—see the last work of John Rawls, *The Law of Peoples*, Cambridge, MA: Harvard University Press, 1999.

7. A cogent statement of Wilson's position on race relations in the United States is by Thomas Knock, in a letter he wrote for inclusion in the *Wilson Legacy Review* in January 2016. It can be accessed at http://wilsonlegacy.princeton.edu/sites/wilsonlegacy/files/media/wilsonlegacy_knock.pdf.

8. Naoko Shimazu, *Japan, Race, and Equality: The Racial Equality Proposal of 1919*, New York: Routledge, 1998.

9. For an interesting study of liberal imperialism that demonstrates there were various strands of anti-imperialism in Enlightenment thinking, and thus that the charge that liberalism somehow has an imperialist urge as part of its genetic code, see Sankar Muthu, *Enlightenment Against Empire*, Princeton, NJ: Princeton University Press, 2003.

10. I thank John Ikenberry and Daniel Deudney for stressing this point in an important, but as yet unpublished essay, "America's Impact: The End of Empire and the Globalization of the Westphalian System," presented at the American Political Science Association, September 2015, http://scholar.princeton.edu/sites/default/files/gji3/files/am-impact-dd-gji-final-1-august-2015.pdf.

11. An important exchange is in Thomas J. Knock, "Kennan versus Wilson," and George Kennan, "Comments on the Paper Entitled 'Kennan versus Wilson' by Professor Thomas J. Knock," in John Milton Cooper Jr. and Charles E. Neu, eds., *The Wilson Era: Essays in Honor of Arthur S. Link*, Arlington Heights, IL: Harlan Davidson, 1991. What might be called Kissinger's apologies can be found in his book *World Order*, New York: Penguin, 2014.

12. Wilson, "Princeton in the Nation's Service," Arthur Link et al., eds., *The Papers of Woodrow Wilson [PWW]*, 69 vols., Princeton, NJ: Princeton University Press, 1966–1994, 10, 10/1896.

Index

Other Publications by Tony Smith

America's Mission: The United States and the Worldwide Struggle for Democracy

A Pact with the Devil: Washington's Bid for World Supremacy and the Betrayal of the American Promise

Foreign Attachments: The Power of Ethnic Groups in the Making of American Foreign Policy

Thinking Like A Communist: State and Legitimacy in the Soviet Union, China, and Cuba

The Pattern of Imperialism: The United States, Great Britain, and the Late-Industrializing World Since 1815

The French Stake in Algeria, 1945–1962

The End of the European Empire: Decolonization After World War II

Co-authored, *The Crisis of American Foreign Policy: Wilsonianism in the Twenty-First Century*